The Global Economic Order

To Michael,
with love and
infinite gratitude
Ed

The Global Economic Order

The International Law and Politics of the Financial and Monetary System

Elli Louka

President, Law-in-Action, USA

Edward Elgar
PUBLISHING

Cheltenham, UK • Northampton, MA, USA

Published by
Edward Elgar Publishing Limited
The Lypiatts
15 Lansdown Road
Cheltenham
Glos GL50 2JA
UK

Edward Elgar Publishing, Inc.
William Pratt House
9 Dewey Court
Northampton
Massachusetts 01060
USA

A catalogue record for this book
is available from the British Library

Library of Congress Control Number: 2019956779

This book is available electronically in the **Elgar**online
Law subject collection
DOI 10.4337/9781839102684

Printed on elemental chlorine free (ECF)
recycled paper containing 30% Post-Consumer Waste

ISBN 978 1 83910 267 7 (cased)
ISBN 978 1 83910 268 4 (eBook)
ISBN 978 1 83910 309 4 (paperback)

Printed and bound in the USA

Contents

v

PART IV   GLOBAL BODIES, SOCIETIES AND GUILDS

Figures

Tables

Boxes

Abbreviations

ABS	asset-backed securities
AIG	American Insurance Group
AIIB	Asian Infrastructure Investment Bank
AML	anti-money laundering
ASEAN	Association of Southeast Asian Nations
BCBS	Basel Committee on Banking Supervision
BGE	Entscheidungen des Schweizerischen Bundesgerichts (Decisions of Swiss Federal Supreme Court)
BIS	Bank of International Settlements
BITs	bilateral investment treaties
BoG	Board of Governors
BOJ	Bank of Japan
BOP	balance of payments
BOT	balance of trade
CA	current account
CACs	collective action clauses
CB	Central Bank
CBCS	central bank currency swaps
CCPs	central counterparties
CDS	credit default swaps
CEPAL	Economic Commission for Latin America
CEPR	Center for Economic Policy Research
CFETS	China Foreign Exchange Trade System
CFR	Code of Federal Regulations
CFT	combating the financing of terrorism
CFTC	Commodity Futures Trading Commission
CGFS	Committee on the Global Financial System

CHIPS	Clearing House Interbank Payments System
CIA	Central Intelligence Agency
CIGI	Centre for International Governance Innovation
CIPS	Cross-Border Interbank Payment System
Cmd.	Command papers
CMIM	Chiang Mai Initiative Multilateralization
CPMI	Committee on Payments and Markets Infrastructure
CPSS	Committee on Payment and Settlement Systems
CRAs	credit rating agencies
CRS	Congressional Research Service
DEP	domestic economic policy
DJIA	Dow Jones Industrial Average
DoD	Department of Defense
DSB	Dispute Settlement Body
DTCC	Depository Trust & Clearing Corporation
DTCs	deposit-taking corporations
DW	Deutsche Welle
ECB	European Central Bank
ECGI	European Corporate Governance Institute
ECJ	European Court of Justice
ECR	European Court Reports
EFB	European Fiscal Board
EFSF	European Financial Stability Facility
EFSM	European Financial Stabilization Mechanism
EIR	Executive Intelligence Review
ELA	emergency liquidity assistance
EM	emerging market
EMU	Economic and Monetary Union
ER	exchange rate
ERR	exchange rate regime
ESF	Exchange Stabilization Fund
ESM	European Stability Mechanism
ESMA	European Securities and Markets Authority

ESMT	European School of Management and Technology
ETFs	exchange-traded funds
ETS	European Treaty Series
EU	European Union
F.2d	Federal Reporter 2d
F.3d	Federal Reporter 3d
F.Supp.	Federal Supplement
FA	fiscal authority
FAA	Fiscal Agency Agreement
FATF	Financial Action Task Force
FCA	Federal Court of Australia
FDI	foreign direct investment
FDIC	Federal Deposit Insurance Corporation
Fed.Cl.	Federal Claims Reporter
FEP	foreign economic policy
FFR	Federal Funds Rate
FinCEN	Financial Crimes Enforcement Network
FLAR	Latin American Reserve Fund
FOMC	Federal Open Market Committee
FRBNY	Federal Reserve Bank of New York
FRBs	Federal Reserve Banks
FRS	Federal Reserve System
FSB	Financial Stability Board
FSOC	Financial Stability Oversight Council
FT	Financial Times
FX	foreign exchange
FXC	Foreign Exchange Committee
GAB	General Arrangements to Borrow
GAO	Government Accountability Office
GATT	General Agreement on Tariffs and Trade
GDP	gross domestic product
GPIF	Government Pension Investment Fund
GRIPS	Graduate Institute for Policy Studies

GSA	General Services Administration
GSEs	government-sponsored enterprises
GSIBs	global systemically important banks
HIPC	heavily indebted poor countries
HQLA	high-quality liquid assets
HRADF	Hellenic Republic Asset Development Fund
ICE	intercontinental exchange
ICJ	International Court of Justice
ICSID	International Centre for Settlement of Investment Disputes
IDB	Inter-American Development Bank
IEO	Independent Evaluation Office (of IMF)
IFSWF	International Forum of Sovereign Wealth Funds
IIF	Institute of International Finance
IIMA	Institute for International Monetary Affairs
IISS	International Institute for Strategic Studies
ILDC	(Oxford Reports on) International Law in Domestic Courts
ILM	International Legal Materials
ILR	International Law Reports
IMF	International Monetary Fund
INSTEX	Instrument in Support of Trade Exchanges
IOSCO	International Organization of Securities Commissions
IOU	I owe you
IR	interest rate
IROR	interest rate on reserves
IRS	Internal Revenue Service
ISDA	International Swaps and Derivatives Association
ISIS	Islamic State of Iraq and Syria
ISMA	International Securities Markets Association
ITLOS	International Tribunal for the Law of the Sea
IZA	Forschungsinstitut zur Zukunft der Arbeit (Institute for the Study of Labor)
LAFB	Libyan Arab Foreign Bank
LBMA	London Bullion Market Association

LIBOR	London Interbank Offered Rate
LNTS	League of Nations Treaty Series
LSE	London Stock Exchange
MA	monetary authority
MAS	Monetary Authority of Singapore
MB	monetary base
MBS	mortgage-backed securities
MFM	Macroeconomics and Fiscal Management Global Practice (World Bank)
MMFs	money market funds
MMoU	multilateral memorandum of understanding
MOU	memorandum of understanding
MS	money supply
MTO	medium-term budgetary objective
NAB	new arrangements to borrow
NAFTA	North American Free Trade Agreement
NASA	National Aeronautics and Space Administration
NASDAQ	National Association of Securities Dealers Automated Quotations
NATO	North Atlantic Treaty Organization
NBER	National Bureau of Economic Research
NCB	National Central Bank
NGO	non-governmental organization
NIRP	negative interest rate policy
NRSROs	nationally recognized statistical rating organizations
NSIA	Nigeria Sovereign Investment Authority
NYT	New York Times
OMT	outright monetary transactions
OTC	over the counter
PBOC	People's Bank of China
PCIJ	Permanent Court of International Justice
PIIE	Peterson Institute for International Economics
PIIGS	Portugal, Ireland, Italy, Greece, Spain

PPP	public–private partnership
PSI	private sector involvement
QB	Queen's Bench
QE	quantitative easing
RIAA	Reports of International Arbitral Awards
RRR	required reserve ratio
RWAs	risk weighted assets
S.Ct.	Supreme Court Reporter
SBA	stand-by agreement
SDNY	Southern District of New York
SDRM	Sovereign Debt Restructuring Mechanism
SEC	Securities and Exchange Commission
SGE	Shanghai Gold Exchange
SIBOS	SWIFT International Bank Operations Seminar
SIFI	systemically important financial institution
SIFMU	systemically important financial market utility
SIPS	systemically important payment systems
SMP	Securities Market Program
SNB	Swiss National Bank
SOFR	secured overnight financing rate
SPV	special purpose vehicle
SWF	sovereign wealth fund
SWFI	Sovereign Wealth Fund Institute
SWIFT	Society for Worldwide Interbank Financial Telecommunications
TAF	term auction facility
TARP	Troubled Asset Relief Program
TEU	Treaty on European Union
TFEU	Treaty on the Functioning of the European Union
THPA	Thessaloniki Port Authority
TIAS	Treaties and other International Agreements
TSLF	term securities lending facility
U.S.	United States Reports

UKSC	UK Supreme Court
UNCITRAL	United Nations Commission on International Trade Law
UNCTAD	United Nations Conference on Trade and Development
UNTS	United Nations Treaties Series
USC	United States Code
UST	United States Treaties Series
WB	World Bank
WL	WestLaw
WSJ	Wall Street Journal
WTO	World Trade Organization
ZIRP	zero interest rate policy

Introduction

Chapter 1 examines the economic policy of a fictional world consisting of only one state. This fictional world allows us to examine how states make domestic economic policy (DEP) when they are free from foreign economic policy (FEP) constraints, and doubts regarding whether and how to control private capital. We analyze the basic tools of economic policy, such as the banking system and creation of money, interest rate, government bond market and the yield curve as the fundamental building blocks of financial infrastructure of states. We compare the monetary authority, the central bank (CB) and the fiscal authority (FA) in their role as makers of economic policy. We elucidate the policy options of states by building up a framework that exposes the trade-offs involved in each of them.

Chapter 2 uses a two-state world to examine an intractable trilemma or impossible trinity: when private capital is free to move from state to state, countries cannot pursue, simultaneously, DEP autonomy and a stable FEP. This chapter introduces concepts such as the balance of payments, and examines how states intervene in the market to gain a comparative advantage over other states. We explore how countries live with the impossible trinity by controlling capital and building foreign exchange reserves as a war chest.

Chapter 3 investigates how the United States, because of its position as the global economic sovereign, shapes and often dictates the policy options of other states. States, as this book elaborates, fall into a pyramid in terms of economic power. Their currency, a vehicle of economic dominance, determines whether they make it to the top or bottom of the pyramid. This chapter examines, in detail, the US economic system and policy and how this system has been used to address financial crises. The coordination, between the US Treasury and the Federal Reserve System (FRS) provides diverse insights into how economic policy works in practice.

Chapter 4 examines the policies of core and peripheral states and how these policies accommodate the economic stance of the sovereign. We probe into how China succeeded in making the yuan a global reserve currency and what it needs to accomplish next if it aspires to dethrone the dollar and establish its currency as the prime global reserve currency. We analyze the economic policies of open peripheral states and their dependence on the DEP of the United States, the global sovereign. The accumulation of large amounts of dollar-denominated debt and fixed exchange rates often lock these states into an irresolvable trilemma, as the cases of Nigeria and Argentina demonstrate. The case study of Japan helps us understand the phenomenon of prolonged deflation and psychological barriers that prevent countries from exiting that state. The eurozone case study is a demonstration of how the first monetary union has dealt with crises by adopting emergency measures and imposing fiscal austerity.

Part III chronicles the evolution of global economic institutions and provides real world examples of how states have conflicted with each other or worked together to coordinate their economic policies. We explore the roles of International Monetary Fund (IMF), Group of 7 states (G-7) and Group of 20 states (G-20) in managing the international financial system. Chapter 6 scrutinizes the period of first globalization, when the gold standard reigned, by exploring how states struggled to neutralize the havoc unleashed into their economies by the abrupt movements of gold. The interwar period, set forth in Chapter 7, is an instructive example of how uncoordinated national economic policies and haphazard tit-for-tat devaluations can breed an economic war that harms all states. The Bretton Woods system established after World War II, analyzed in Chapter 8, gives us the opportunity to delve into the foundations of the first international monetary institution, the IMF. We discuss the underpinnings of the Bretton Woods and negotiations that led to the establishment of the first formally agreed-upon economic order. We shed light on a conundrum that has driven most economic conflicts: how to distribute the burden of 'adjustment' among states that face external imbalances. The clashes between surplus states and deficit states, about who should bear the burden of changing their DEP to correct global imbalances, are a source of acrimony and resentment in the international community.

Chapter 9 analyzes the politics that led the United States to abolish the convertibility of the dollar into gold, a decision that triggered the Bretton Woods demise and boosted the role of dollar as the global reserve currency. Chapter 10 focuses on two agreements, the Plaza and Louvre accords, that helped states coordinate their economic policies in the 1980s. It further investigates the causes of Latin American debt crisis and measures adopted to address that crisis. Chapter 11 deals with the 1990s East Asian crisis and lessons learnt from it. Chapter 12 explores how the G-20 dealt with the 2008 global financial crisis, including the adoption of coordinated fiscal expansion and subsequent austerity during that period. Chapter 13 focuses on the structure of the IMF, and its policies of conditionality and surveillance and the backlash they have provoked in developing states. Part IV delves into the club-like makeup of international financial infrastructure and international regulatory organizations. Chapter 14 exposes the roots of transnational financial law-making and modalities through which it shapes the global financial order. Chapter 15 examines the global financial infrastructure. It explores how financial markets have tried to police themselves and why this may be insufficient, as demonstrated by the various financial scandals that shake the world and worsen crises. We analyze how global financial institutions have been harnessed to impose economic sanctions on states and how informal networks and alternative currencies have been used to bypass official systems.

Chapter 16 examines the global financial organizations, such as the Basel Committee on Banking Supervision and its contribution to the shaping of banking standards. Other institutions examined in this chapter include the Financial Stability Board and the Financial Action Task Force. We evaluate the effectiveness and legitimacy of these institutions, especially because they promulgate rules that impact states beyond their members. The Bank of International Settlements and its role as CB of CBs, and how successfully it has played that role, are examined in Chapter 17. We also explore a number of regional arrangements including the Chiang Mai Initiative, the Latin American Reserve Fund and the BRICS Contingent Reserve Arrangement. This chapter focuses on the institutions and tools used in the debt re-organization of states including the London and Paris clubs and the collective action clauses in government bonds. We analyze further the case law stemming from disagreements between debtor states and their creditors. The feasibility of developing a Sovereign Debt Restructuring Mechanism is discussed at length.

In Chapter 18, the case study of Greece elucidates the perpetual conflict between states and their creditors as it unfolded between 2009 and 2018 in the eurozone. This chapter investigates the causes of the Greek debt crisis. The travails of Greece and the frustration of its creditors provide numerous insights into the constraints placed on open democracies that are unable to print their own currency and cannot run a DEP that fits their needs. Part IV concludes that the global economic status quo is primed to endure well into the future. The political motivations of economic policy-makers propel them toward the zealous preservation of the current minimum order and against the pursuit of a maximum order, the development of a global safety net that could benefit all states. As long as a dose of economic instability, controlled by the few, remains necessary to safeguard their global dominance, a maximum world order – defined as the minimum conditions for a dignified human existence for all – will remain elusive.

PART I

Making economic policy

1. The one and only sovereign

1.1 ONE-STATE WORLD

Let us imagine a world with only one state. The state, Kyber, prints a paper currency called kobank (ƚ) that its citizens use to buy goods and services and to pay their taxes. The currency is used as a medium of exchange, unit of account and store of wealth.[1] Kyber is run by a government that has many branches, such as those that deal with education, transportation and security. The fiscal authority (FA) and the monetary authority (MA), the central bank (CB), are responsible for making economic policy. Economic policy includes both domestic economic policy (DEP) and foreign economic policy (FEP), the management of a state's currency in relation to other states' currencies. In our example, though, Kyber is the only state in the entire world. Therefore, it does not have to conduct FEP – establish a price, an exchange rate (ER) – between its currency and foreign currencies. Kyber is not concerned, furthermore, that its citizens may take their assets and money, their capital, out of its territory and move them to other states. Kyber is the true one and only sovereign since it does not have to deal with other states and can keep people's wealth trapped in it.

Kyber is a market economy. In a market economy decisions are based on supply and demand dynamics – the supply of goods and services by producers and demand for goods and services by consumers. On a basic level, the supply/demand forces work in the following way: *scarcity* in the supply of a good, that happens to be in *high* demand, drives its price up, motivating producers to ramp up production of that good. This increases its availability and, consequently, brings the price down. *Abundance* in the supply of a good, when combined with *tepid* demand, drives the price of that good down. This dispirits producers, which reduce production. The resulting scarcity brings the price of the good up, especially if demand has, in the meantime, rebounded.

A fundamental feature of this well-organized market economy are well-functioning securities markets – a stock market and a bond market. A stock market is a place where business sell and people buy *stocks*, shares,

---

[1] Charles Proctor, *Mann on the Legal Aspect of Money* 10 (2012).

that is units of ownership in a company. A bond market is a place where business and, as we will see below, the government, borrow. Bonds are 'I owe you' (IOU) instruments that acknowledge debt. Business issue bonds and stocks because they want to raise money from the public to create new products or improve the goods and services they offer. The government issues bonds, borrows from the public, to fix the public infrastructure or to pay for public schools and other public welfare projects. The general public is free to invest in the stock market and in the corporate and government bond markets.

The government makes its policy based on the conditions of the economy, but also on many other factors that are important for the maintenance of a peaceful polity. To simplify matters here we assume that the government is popular. However, there are minor insurgencies and terrorist acts that, from time to time, rattle the society. Major and minor natural disasters do occur. Because of the uncertain future condition of the world and, as we will see below, the structure of the financial system, the economy is vulnerable to crises. The world government tries to keep its economy strong. The gross domestic product (GDP) is a rough way to calculate the total economic activity of both the state and its people. The GDP is calculated annually and it reflects the total value of goods and services produced in the economy by the state and population. The government uses a simple formula to calculate the GDP: GDP = C + G + I (where C stands for private consumption, G for government spending and I for all investment in the economy – public and private). When GDP is up, it means that the economy is growing. When GDP is stagnant or decreasing, it means that the economy may be in trouble or even in recession. When a recession is prolonged and severe, the economy is in depression.

All through its life span, the state has faced a number of economic conditions: rapid growth, slow growth, recessions and depressions. Periods of rapid economic growth are usually characterized by price inflation while recessions are accentuated by deflation. This makes intuitive sense. High economic growth means high consumption and investment. If increasing consumption and investment are not matched by the increasing production of goods and services, the outcome will be inflation, an accelerating increase in prices. On the contrary, recessions are marked by low consumption and investment. If, during an economic downturn, producers continue to produce as many goods as they did before, the weak demand for those goods will cause deflation, a decrease in prices, and the economy will eventually enter into recession.

Inflation can be caused by many factors, such as a shortage of basic supplies, the resources that are needed to run the economy – a supply shock. For instance, an unexpected shortage in the supply of oil, owing to sabotage by a group of people, may trigger unexpected inflation. Given the oil shortage, oil companies will have to bid against each other for the limited oil output, triggering a spike in oil prices. As oil suppliers increase their prices, producers of other goods, whose production depends on oil, will have to increase their prices as well. If most economic production depends on oil, most businesses will resort to price increases. As the prices of products and services increase, employees, who are also consumers, will have to ask for higher wages. Unless the oil supply quickly bounces back to its prior level, expectations of continuing rising prices can trigger accelerating inflation and possibly hyperinflation.

Inflation can be caused also by the scarcity of human labor. When GDP is up and businesses are booming, they are prone to hire people to help them boost their production. When too many businesses bid for too few laborers, wages increase. Businesses, in turn, pass the higher labor costs to consumers by increasing the prices of goods they sell. Higher prices generate demands for higher wages – the vicious circle of inflation.

Accelerating inflation can have a corrosive effect on an economy. As people need more and more money to buy goods, services and assets, the currency gradually loses its value. Kyber does not want people to lose faith in the value of its currency. If people start to view the kobank as something no better than a piece of paper, they will be likely to discard it and establish another means of exchange (such as barter, gold or an underground crypto-currency). When a currency is not associated with something deemed to have lasting value (e.g. gold), its worth is measured by the confidence of the public in the state that issues the currency. Loss of faith in a currency means loss of trust in the state that prints that currency. In fact, there is no surer means of sabotaging a state than debauching its currency.[2]

Recessions are an anathema to states as much as uncontrollable inflation. Recessions are often caused by unpredictable events and catastrophes. During recessions many businesses lose money. As a result, they fire workers or stop hiring. People who are laid off are unlikely to find new jobs in a recessionary economy. Many may resolve to live in poverty or resort to petty crime. When recessionary conditions last long, it is hard to get the economy back on the growth path. As companies lay off workers, private consumption and investment decrease. This reduces further corporate profits and spurs more layoffs. An economic recession can, thus, turn quickly into depression. A chronic depression can create a fertile ground for revolt. Chronic depressions undermine the authority of the sovereign as they lay bare its inability to provide the conditions that would help people prosper.

---

[2]   Paraphrasing Keynes, *see* John Maynard Keynes, *The Economic Consequences of the Peace* 139 (1920, reprinted in 2013 by Keynes Press).

1.1.1 Basic Economic Functions

The FA, called also Finance Ministry or Treasury, decides how much to spend and to collect in taxes. By doing so, it determines how much money people have at their disposal. The more the taxes the FA collects, for instance, the less money people have. The more it spends – by paying government employees or companies that build the public infrastructure – the higher the money, the liquidity, in the economy. The FA may decide to deal with the distribution of money. It may tax the rich and direct the money it collects from them to the poor. In this book, we do not deal with the distributional aspects of fiscal policy. We focus, instead, on how decisions of a government to tax, spend and, as we will see below, borrow affect the total amount of money in the economy.

The government tries to keep the economy growing at a sustainable rate to avoid the adverse effects of uncontrollable inflation or deflation. The role of the MA is to figure out what that growth rate is and use its toolkit to keep the economy growing at that rate. We can think of the MA, the CB, as the economy's primary assessor and regulator. The CB has concluded, after repeated trials and errors, that a 2% yearly inflation is the magic number that keeps the economy growing at a *sustainable growth rate*. The CB has determined that when inflation fluctuates around 2%, *almost all* people (Box 1.1) who are capable and willing to work can find gainful employment. This eliminates the risk that shortages of labor will trigger wage increases and, in turn, price increases. The CB has the flexibility to change the inflation target of 2% upward or downward when it diagnoses that this is what is needed to ensure that the economy functions close to full employment with low risk of runaway inflation or deflation.

BOX 1.1 DEFINITION OF UNEMPLOYMENT

In market economies, some unemployment is considered necessary to prevent accelerating inflation. Therefore, the government's goal of elimination of unemployment is not equivalent to 100% employment – the employment of *all* the civilian labor force. The government counts as unemployed persons unemployed for 15 weeks or longer and people with temporary jobs who prefer permanent ones. *Discouraged* workers, those who were looking for a job for a long time but were unable to find employment, and, therefore, are inactive, are not considered *officially* unemployed.

Source: US Bureau of Labor Statistics.

The CB uses the interest rate to guide the economy to a sustainable growth rate – stable inflation and low unemployment.[3] Determining the sustainable growth rate and using the interest rate to ensure that the economy keeps growing at that rate is the art and science of central banking.

Figure 1.1 presents the economic functions of Kyber. We place Kyber on one of the corners of a triangle despite the fact that the other two corners are of no use – Kyber does not have to deal with the flows of private capital in and out of its borders and does not need to establish a price for its currency in terms of another currency. The shape of the triangle will be useful to us when we explain in Chapters 2–4 how the real multistate world copes with an intractable trilemma.

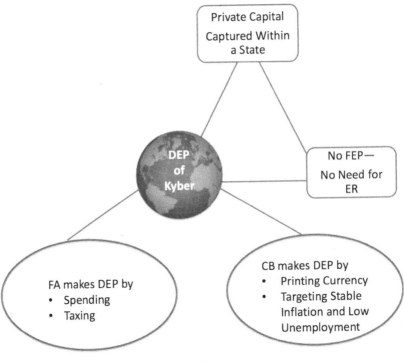

Figure 1.1   One-state economic policy

---

[3]   This is known as the Non-Accelerating Inflation Rate of Unemployment (NAIRU) – that is, low unemployment that does not produce more than the targeted inflation rate.

1.1.2   Calibrating the Economy: The Interest Rate

A tool that the CB has at its disposal to guide the economy to sustainable growth (stable inflation rate with low unemployment) is the interest rate (IR) – the cost of borrowing. The CB sets the *benchmark* IR in the economy, the rate that helps people decide how much interest to charge when they lend money to each other. If the economy is already growing at a sustainable rate, the CB will set an IR that is *neutral* – called also *natural* IR. This neutral IR keeps inflation stable, neither stimulating the economy nor slowing it down.

An inflation rate above 2% signals that the economy is overheating and the IR is below the natural rate. If the economy is overheating, inflation is above 2%, the CB will increase its benchmark IR to encourage people to save. A high IR should boost savings and reduce borrowing. Since people would prefer to save rather than consume, this should reduce inflation (Fig. 1.2).

An inflation rate below 2% signals that the IR is above its natural rate and that it is choking off growth. In that case, the CB will decrease the benchmark IR to dampen savings and encourage borrowing. Citizens who spend rather than save can create revenues for businesses. These businesses, in turn, will invest more, generating economic growth (Fig. 1.2).

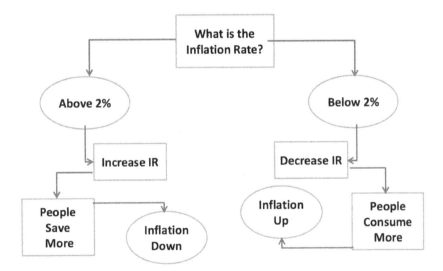

Figure 1.2   The IR as a tool of DEP

In other words, the cues provided by the inflation rate help the CB infer the neutral IR.[4] Sometimes, the CB will wait until there is clear evidence that the IR has diverged from the natural rate before changing it. Other times, it may decide to tweak the IR in a more preemptive way depending on the severity of risks that may threaten economic growth.

The CB sets the benchmark IR, but it does not dictate the market IRs. Borrowers and lenders bargain among themselves to set the IRs for individual loans. The various IRs set by this bargaining process take into account the benchmark IR set by the CB and add to it a *risk premium* that reflects the creditworthiness of various borrowers. People and business with bad credit, because they have defaulted on their loans in the past or have not paid back their lenders in time, tend to be charged higher IRs by the banks that lend money to them than people with good credit.

Furthermore, before making a decision whether to lend their money at all, creditors have to consider whether it is worth getting into the trouble of doing so. A high inflation rate can wipe out the returns that creditors receive when they lend their money. For example, if the benchmark IR set by the CB is 3%, a commercial bank may decide to charge an 8% IR for a loan to a business – adding a 5% risk premium to the benchmark 3% IR because of the bad credit of the borrower. If inflation runs at 8% per year, though, the bank may decide not to lend at all. This is because the interest it plans to collect from the borrower (8%) will be wiped out by inflation (8%). In other words, while the *nominal* IR is 8%, and it seems high, the *real* IR is zero.

1.1.3   The Banking System and Creation of Money

Private banks are the intermediaries between the CB and the people. Individuals and businesses deposit their money with banks to safeguard it and earn an interest. Depositors are the banks' creditors. They deposit their money in checking accounts with banks and can demand, at any moment, their money back – including the interest accrued. The money people deposit with banks as on-demand deposits is called M1. People also deposit money in savings accounts. Setting money aside as savings in time deposits,[5] that typically offer higher interest than regular deposits, helps people grow their nest egg for a rainy day. M2 is a measure of the money in the economy that includes these short-term time deposits that can be converted quickly into cash plus the

---

[4]   *See* Thomas Laubach and John C. Williams, *Measuring the Natural Rate of Interest Redux*, at 6, Federal Reserve Bank of San Francisco, Working Paper 2015–16, Oct. 2015.

[5]   A time deposit cannot be withdrawn before a specific date.

M1. M1 and M2 measure how much money circulates in the economy that can be quickly converted into cash. The M1 and M2, unlike other assets like real estate, are the most liquid, cash-type, assets in the economy.

The role of banks is to recycle these liquid assets by lending them to firms and households. The traditional business of banking consists of borrowing money from depositors and lending it, at higher rates and over longer periods, to borrowers. Banks borrow short term from depositors and lend long term to various borrowers. Banks make money by offering depositors lower IRs on the money they deposit with them than those they charge borrowers. This is not usury. Banks need to be compensated for doing the work necessary to ensure that borrowers are creditworthy and will pay them back. In addition, banks take on the risk of *maturity mismatch*[6] – they borrow short term but they usually lend long term to individuals, who may wish to buy a house, or to businesses that wish to invest in a new opportunity. This is a significant risk to undertake. During economic crises, depositors typically run to their banks en mass to collect their deposits and expect their money back on demand. However, the loans the banks have granted, by using these deposits, mature much later. Banks cannot ask borrowers to pay back loans that mature in years just because depositors are on their doorstep asking for their cash back.

Banking is a risky business and people are well aware of that. This is why they are unwilling to put their money in banks. To convince people that banks are safe, Kyber has introduced a deposit insurance scheme. Through this scheme it acts as the guarantor of the banking system. The government has figured out that ₭250 000 is the average amount that people keep in banks – the rest being invested in real estate and the stock and bond markets. It promises that, if banks fail, all people's deposits are guaranteed up to the amount of ₭250 000 per deposit account. Kyber is the only entity that can be trusted to keep this promise. Its CB, that prints the currency, is capable of churning out as many kobanks as needed to ensure the government's promise is not an empty one.

Kyber has also adopted prudential regulation to prevent banks from loaning out all of the money deposited with them. Banks are required, by law, to keep with the CB or in their vault a percentage of the money deposited with them. This is the *required reserved ratio* (RRR). Banks are required to keep 10% of the depositors' money as reserves – they can lend the remaining 90%. Because banks are required to keep only a fraction of the money deposited with them as reserves, the banking system is called *fractional reserve* banking system (as opposed to the 100% reserve banking system, *see* Box 1.2). As demonstrated

---

[6]   Charles Engel, *Macroprudential Policy in a World of High Capital Mobility: Policy Implications from an Academic Perspective*, at 4, Working Paper 20951, Feb. 2015.

in Figure 1.3, the fractional reserve banking system is the engine of money creation in the economy.

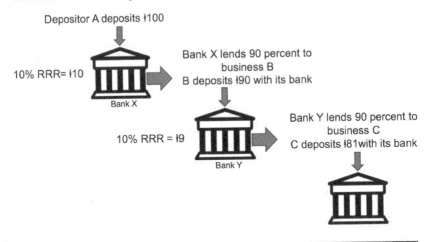

Depositor A deposits ₦100

10% RRR= ₦10 Bank X

Bank X lends 90 percent to business B
B deposits ₦90 with its bank

10% RRR = ₦9 Bank Y

Bank Y lends 90 percent to business C
C deposits ₦81 with its bank

Out of the ₦100 in initial deposits, banks are able to create ₦171 (₦90+₦81). Banks are required to keep only a fraction (10%) of the money deposited with them and lend the rest. This is factional banking.

Figure 1.3   *Money creation through fractional banking*

BOX 1.2   THE 100% RESERVE BANKING SYSTEM

The fractional reserve banking system adopted by Kyber is not the only possible banking system. The full (or 100%) reserve banking system requires that banks keep the full amount of each depositor's money in cash, ready for immediate withdrawal on demand. Under this system, banks do not have the capacity to create new money in the form of credit as they currently do. Instead, the CB of a state is solely responsible for the creation of all money, including money in the form of credit. A full reserve banking system makes it possible for a state to have precise control over the money supply.

Source: Jaromir Benes and Michael Kumhof, *The Chicago Plan Revisited,* IMF Working Paper, WP/12/202, August 2012; Ronnie J. Phillips, *The 'Chicago Plan' and the New Deal Banking Reform,* Working Paper No. 76, Jerome Levy Economics Institute of Bard College, June 1992.

In addition to required reserves, banks may keep *excess reserves*. This happens when banks are unable (because there are not enough borrowers)

Table 1.1   *Simplified balance sheet of a bank*

Assets (what they own)	Liabilities (what they owe)
Loans to firms and individuals	Deposits of clients
Reserves	Loans received from CB
Assets – liabilities = capital	

or choose not (because they fear borrowers may default) to lend some of the money deposited with them (Box 1.3).

BOX 1.3   RESERVES OF PRIVATE BANKS

Required Reserves* + Excess Reserves** = Total Reserves***

*10% of deposits (by law), **optional, ***deposited with CB or in vault

The loans banks make[7] and their reserves constitute their assets – what they own. Their depositors' money,[8] and the money they borrow from the CB, are banks' liabilities – what they owe. The difference between assets and liabilities makes up banks' capital (Table 1.1).

Banks' liabilities can exceed their assets. This happens when individuals and businesses who borrow from banks cannot pay back their loans. If those who borrow from a bank cannot pay it back, the bank will be unable to pay back the money it owes depositors. Rumors of the imminent insolvency of a bank can generate a 'bank run'. Depositors run to the bank expected to become insolvent to collect the money they have deposited there. Bank runs often lead to bank failures. The bank, because it has used 90% of depositors' money to make loans, will not have the cash in hand to pay all depositors at once. Fears about the failure of a bank are highly contagious. Those who have deposited money with other banks may also panic and run on their banks. At this stage, the CB usually steps in to guarantee bank deposits, sometimes, even beyond the deposit guarantee limit of ₺250 000. The ability of the CB to act as the *unconditional lender of last resort* to the banking system restores confidence in it and averts further bank runs.

Some argue that the ability of a CB to act as the unconditional lender of last resort to the banking system creates moral hazard. Obviously banks have no incentive to refrain from aggressive lending – lending to people with bad

---

[7]   For a bank, the loans it makes are its assets; loans are liabilities to borrowers.
[8]   Your deposits with a bank are assets for you, but liabilities for the bank.

credit at high IRs – if they believe that the CB will bail them out when their borrowers default. This puts the CB in a difficult position. If, during a panic, the CB does nothing and allows the banking system to fail, that failure will reverberate all through the economy. Since the banking system is the engine of money growth in the economy, the costs of closing down the banks will be borne by the society at large. The CB, in its role as lender of last resort, provides insurance to the banking system while being fully cognizant that this insurance breeds moral hazard.[9] That is why it adopts measures, like the RRR, and enacts prudential regulations[10] to control, as much as possible, the risk-taking of banks. Because of its pivotal role in maintaining the stability of the banking system, the CB has to decide when its lender of last resort function constitutes an efficient use of its deep pockets.[11]

1.1.4   The Government Budget and Bond Market

Kyber maintains an annual budget, which helps it keep track of how much it spends and how much it collects in taxes. If it spends more than it collects, it has a budget *deficit*. If it collects more taxes than what it spends, it has a budget *surplus* (Fig. 1.4). A government may have to run a deficit, for instance, if a disaster strikes and it has to provide disaster relief for the population. Governments can always deal with deficits by imposing more taxes. When a calamity hits, though, they often conclude that a disaster-hit citizenry would be unable to pay more taxes. A better option, then, is to borrow from the public instead of taxing it.

Kyber is willing to pay the public an annual IR on the amount of money it borrows from it. To facilitate borrowing, it has developed a market that makes it possible for people to buy government debt in the form of 'bonds'. Bonds are IOU certificates that denote the amount of money borrowed by the government, and for how long, and the rate of interest, the *coupon rate*, the government pays to those who hold its debt. When the bonds *mature*, it is time for the government to pay back the money it borrowed. Figure 1.5 is a depiction of a bond certificate. The holder of the certificate has lent the government Ŧ1 000, denoted as the bond's face value, for which she would receive a yearly interest of 5% (Ŧ50). When the bond matures on June 1, 2050, the holder of the certificate will get back her principal, the Ŧ1 000 she lent to the government. The FA sells bonds to banks and individuals through public auctions. The auctions take

---

[9]   Engel, *supra* note 6, at 22.
[10]   *See* Chapter 16.
[11]   Tamim Bayoumi et al., *Monetary Policy in the New Normal*, at 20, IMF Staff Discussion Note SDN/14/3, Apr. 2014.

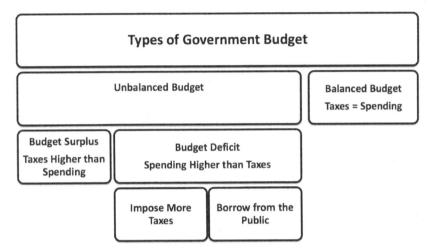

Figure 1.4   Government budget

place regularly. There are three steps to an auction: the announcement of the auction, the bidding for the bonds by individuals and banks, and the issuance of purchased bonds.

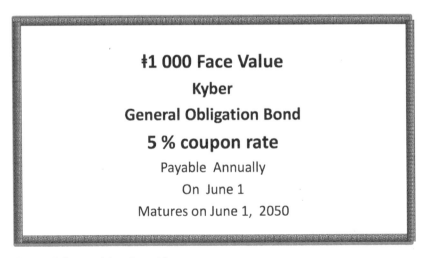

Figure 1.5   A bond certificate

The FA has designated certain banks to be the *primary dealers*[12] in the government bond market. An FA-designated primary dealer is a market maker. The dealer buys government bonds directly from the government, with the intention of reselling them to others, thus *making a market* for government bonds. The primary dealers, the *market makers*, are required to bid on a pro-rata basis in all FA auctions at reasonably competitive prices. After buying the bonds from the government, those who hold them can sell them in the *open market*, also called the *secondary market*. This secondary market for government bonds is a 'deep and liquid' market, which means that people active in that market can rapidly buy and sell a large amount of bonds with little impact on their prices.[13] In the open market, bonds may be sold above or below their face value. When bonds sell above their face value they sell 'at a premium'. When they sell below their face value they sell 'at a discount'. Bonds may sell at a premium or discount because of changes in the IRs. From the time of purchase, until the time buyers decide to sell their bonds, the prevailing IRs in the economy may have changed. In fact, in dynamic market economies, IRs rarely remain the same. They change based on changes in the benchmark IR set by the CB and the supply/demand dynamics in the bond market.

As mentioned above, a ₺1 000 face value bond that has a coupon rate of 5% will pay ₺50 to the bondholder every year (Fig. 1.5). If the market IR is 7%, and a bondholder wants to sell the bond, she will receive less than the amount she paid for it. When the prevailing IR in the economy is higher than the coupon rate, the bond's price has to drop so that investors can be enticed to buy the bond. Obviously, people will refuse to purchase a bond that offers a 5% return when they could invest their money in another asset and get the higher market rate of 7%. The lack of demand for the bond pushes its price down and the bond will sell at a discount. Conversely, a bond that offers a coupon rate that is higher than the prevailing market IR will sell at a premium. People should rush to buy bonds that offer higher coupon rates than the market IRs. As a result, the price of those bonds will increase and they will sell at a premium. In the open market, there is an *inverse relationship* between the market IRs and bond prices. When the IRs are up, bond prices are down. When the IRs are down, bond prices are up.

Overall, the factors that affect the prices of bonds in the open market have to do with the supply and demand for bonds and IRs associated with their maturity (Box 1.4).

---

[12]   In the United States primary dealers are big private banks, such as Barclays, Citigroup, Credit Suisse, Deutsche Bank, Goldman Sachs and HSBC.

[13]   BIS Committee on the Global Financial System, *How Should we Design Deep and Liquid Markets? The Case of Government Securities*, at 1, n. 1, Oct. 22, 1999.

BOX 1.4   FACTORS AFFECTING BOND PRICES

- Supply/demand for bonds
- Market IRs (when IRs down, bond prices up and vice versa)
- Their maturity

1.1.5   Government Debt as a Public Good

The bond *yield*, the return that investors expect to receive by holding a bond, has to do with the market IR associated with the maturity of that bond (Box 1.4). The yield curve shows how much money we can make by buying government debt. It is the chart of expected yields – the returns that investors hope to receive by holding bonds of different maturities. Figure 1.6 plots the yields of bonds that mature in 5, 10, 15, 20, 25 and 30 years. The yield curve is typically *normal, upward slopping*, because the longer one is willing to hold a bond, the higher the risk she takes on. She expects, therefore, a higher return on her investment. This makes sense because the further one looks into the future, the higher is the uncertainty that unanticipated events may derail the economy. Investors should be compensated for the risk they undertake by holding longer-term bonds. A *flat* yield curve is abnormal because it indicates that those who invest in long-term bonds will receive the same returns as those who invest in short-term bonds. Therefore, they will not be rewarded for extra risk they take on by investing in long-term debt. A flat yield curve indicates uncertainty, that something may be wrong with the economy, maybe an upcoming recession. An *inverted* yield curve is the most abnormal since it signals that short-term debt is expected to pay more than long-term debt. The anticipation that the IRs may fall in the future, owing to a potential economic contraction, causes the yield curve to invert. Financial forecasters are wary of inverted yield curves. Strongly inverted yield curves have been correlated with recessions.

The slope of the yield curve for government bonds is an indicator of a state's expected future economic performance. A normal yield curve indicates inflationary growth. A rising inflation dents the regular income that bondholders receive by purchasing bonds. When inflation is up the yield curve is normal because bondholders know that the longer they hold a bond the higher the chance is that their returns will be eaten up by increasing inflation. Therefore, the government has to offer them higher IRs to entice them to buy long-term, instead of short-term, bonds. Recessionary conditions, on the other hand, make bonds appealing because they offer a steady source income even in economic downturns. During recessions, people will not mind investing in long-term

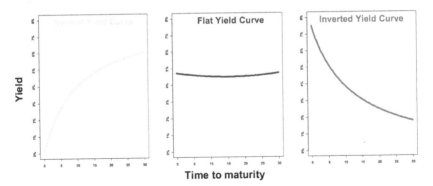

Figure 1.6   The yield curve

bonds even if those bonds offer lower yields than short-term bonds. This is especially so if they expect that bonds that will be issued in the future will offer even more meager returns. During recessions, therefore, the yield curve could be flat or inverted.

Besides the yield curve that depicts the expected returns on government bonds, other yield curves can be put together to help investors gauge the expected returns on corporate debt. Since corporations, whose profits fluctuate from year to year, are considered less creditworthy than the state, the yields offered by the bonds they issue are typically higher than those offered by government bonds. Companies pay a *risk premium* on the debt they issue to entice the public to invest in their debt rather than the safer government debt. Because Kyber has the ability to print its currency and to tax future generations to pay back its debt, government debt is the safest asset. In fact, holding short-term government bonds is considered as safe as cash. During an economic recession, people prefer to invest in government debt and will shun other more risky investments, such as corporate bonds or stocks. Because the state's debt is considered safe, it is also the most preferred kind of collateral in the economy. Collateral is a borrower's pledge of a specific asset (such as property, gold jewelry, stocks or government bonds) to a lender to ensure the lender that she will pay him back.[14] The fact that lenders prefer to hold as collateral government bonds, pieces of paper that certify that the government owes them money, instead of precious metals such as gold, tells us a lot about

---

[14]   The provision of collateral, in other words, protects a lender from a borrower's default. If a borrower fails to pay the principal and interest under the terms of the loan (i.e. defaults) it has to forfeit the asset she pledged as collateral. The lender becomes the owner of that asset.

the stature of the one and only state and the care it has put into developing the government debt market.

Kyber, in fact, views the establishment of the yield curve for the debt it issues as a financial infrastructure project – a fundamental building block of its economy. Since Kyber's debt is the safest asset, it is used to make economic policy and price all other debt in the economy. To calculate the IR for other borrowers, like businesses and households, one must take into account the government's risk-free rate and add to it a risk premium. The higher the risk of default of a borrower, the higher the risk premium she will have to pay.

The FA plays a central role in establishing and maintaining the yield curve. One of the tasks of the FA is to put together a *deep and liquid* government debt market by making available enough debt at various maturities to support active trading. Without active trading, bond prices may become volatile and unpredictable, and an unpredictable government debt market will generate uncertainty in other credit markets. As we explained before, the IRs for private lending are based on the risk-free rate enjoyed by the sovereign. Banks add a premium to the risk-free rate depending on the creditworthiness of each borrower. Therefore, if the rate enjoyed by the state fluctuates dramatically from day to day, this could cause high volatility and thus instability in the private lending markets.

In Chapters 3 and 4, we will demonstrate how, in the real world, the debt of certain states functions as a global safe asset, an asset everybody covets to acquire as a stable source of income. States, in fact, take pride when other states and private actors invest in their debt because they think of it as risk-free investment.

1.1.6   Tools of Economic Policy

The FA controls money by taxing, spending and borrowing from the public. The CB controls money by establishing the benchmark IR for the whole economy. Another tool of the CB, as we will see below, is the buying and selling of government debt, issued by the FA, in the open market. In fact, the coordination, between the FA and CB, on how to manage government debt is essential for the smooth functioning of the economy. Economic policies can be contractionary (tight), expansionary (lose) or neutral. Contractionary policies are implemented when the economy is growing at an unsustainable rate, creating risks of high inflation. Expansionary policies are used to treat economic downturns and alleviate recessions. Neutral polices are endorsed when the economy is growing at a sustainable rate but the CB is watchful for signs of accelerating inflation or deflation. Economic policies can never be completely neutral, though. This is because their target is an inflation rate of 2%. There is an inflation bias in economic policy because low to moderate inflation is considered supportive of growth.

The FA and CB control the money in the economy by manipulating the *monetary base* (MB) called also *high-powered money*. The MB is the sum of currency in circulation (C) and the total reserves (R) of banks, the official liquidity available in the financial system (MB = C + R; Box 1.5). Currency in circulation – the hand-to-hand money held by the public[15] – is currency not deposited with banks. The total reserves of banks are the money they deposit with the CB or money they hold as physical currency in their vaults (Box 1.3).

BOX 1.5   MONETARY BASE (MB) OR OFFICIAL LIQUIDITY

Total Reserves of Banks (R) + Money in Circulation (C) = MB

The MB is the *official liquidity*, how much money the public sector makes available in the economy. As seen above (Fig. 1.4), banks can also create private money by using the official MB to provide credit to individuals and firms. The money that banks create though the fractional reserve banking system is the money supply (MS) or *private liquidity* (Box 1.6). The government, the FA and CB can affect the MB – the official liquidity. However, they cannot directly affect the MS – the readiness of banks to lend (and people to borrow) – the private liquidity. In a market economy, it is willingness of people to borrow and banks to lend that *transmits* the official economic policies to the real economy.

BOX 1.6   MONEY SUPPLY (MS) OR PRIVATE LIQUIDITY

MB × Transmission Mechanism* = MS
*Willingness to Borrow & Readiness to Lend

1.1.6.1   Tools of fiscal authority

The FA controls the MB by taxing and spending (Box 1.7), but it does not have direct control over the MS. When the FA wishes to battle a runaway inflation, it must increase taxes or decrease spending. The more the FA taxes people, the

---

[15]   Milton Friedman and Anna Jacobson Schwartz, *A Monetary History of the United States 1867–1960*, at 50 (1963).

less the MB, the official liquidity in the economy, is. People whose income is decreasing owing to taxation should consume less and save more and their parsimony should shrink the incomes of producers who will produce less and contract the economy. A tight fiscal policy should force prices down and tame inflation, but at the risk of slower growth and higher unemployment.

BOX 1.7 TOOLS OF FISCAL AUTHORITY

Tax – Borrow – Spend/Invest

Contractionary policies can have unintended consequences, though. Some people may conclude that tax hikes are now a permanent feature of government policy. Therefore, they may decide to start saving an increasing percentage of their income to pay for future taxes. These savings should boost banks' reserves. Banks should, in turn, lend these excess reserves to increase their profits. In fact, their abundant reserves may tempt banks to espouse aggressive lending tactics, to invent schemes to lure less creditworthy individuals into borrowing. All in all, the ample availability of credit, owing to the rise in savings, may trigger an economic expansion rather than the contraction that the FA was aiming for.

The pursuit of an expansionary fiscal policy to battle deflation and a debilitating recession can also have side effects. Obviously, the less the FA taxes or the more it spends, the more the MB, the official liquidity in the economy, is. People whose income is growing because they pay fewer taxes may decide to consume more. This should boost business profits, lower unemployment and expand the economy. However, the FA may overshoot its goal and cut taxes too much. This could produce an exuberant consumption that accelerates inflation and erodes the savings base in the economy. At the other extreme, not all people whose income has increased owing to tax cuts would be eager to consume that extra income. They may decide, instead, to save it because they know that expansionary policies tend to be transitory. If the majority of people share this mindset, the FA's expansionary policy will probably fail.

Finally, the FA can affect the MB by borrowing (Box 1.7). Since short-term government debt is considered equivalent to cash, issuing short-term bonds is like printing currency. The FA can take advantage of the like-money properties of the short-term debt it issues. If it decides, for instance, to substitute some of its long-term debt with short-term debt, the MB should increase. If, on the other hand, it replaces some of its short-term debt with long-term debt, the MB must decrease. It is not guaranteed, however, that changes made in the composition of government debt will eventually cascade down to the economy and alter the behavior of the public.

Overall, it is hard to accurately predict the impact of fiscal policy on the economy. Fiscal measures are, therefore, considered imprecise tools of economic policy. The FA can change the MB but how this will affect the MS depends on how people and business react to a fiscally engineered expansion or contraction. An expansionary fiscal policy may boost inflation more than intended while a contractionary policy can really depress growth and dampen employment.

1.1.6.2 Tools of central banks

Monetary policies tend to have a more direct impact on the economy than fiscal policies. Central banks control the benchmark IR that they can increase to cool down the economy or decrease to spur growth. However, figuring out the IR that suits an economy is not easy. During an inflationary period, for instance, a small increase in the benchmark IR may not be sufficient to beat inflation. A drastic increase, on the other hand, may knock down inflation but also depress economic growth. Determining the exact IR that would produce desirable economic outcomes has to do with the skills, experience and luck of central bankers.

The interest rate

The CB, like the FA, can adopt expansionary or contractionary policies depending on the needs of the economy. The benchmark IR set by the CB (Box 1.8) affects, in normal circumstances, all of the IRs in the economy. If the economy is in recession, the CB can cut down the benchmark IR to encourage spending and investment. Decreasing the IR makes saving less enticing and spurs investment and consumption. The CB has to decide by how much to decrease the IR and for how long to achieve its goals. There is a danger that the CB may keep the IR too low for too long. In that case, the increase in consumption and borrowing may fuel inflation and unsustainable high prices, 'bubbles', in the housing and stock markets – 'asset bubbles'.

BOX 1.8 TOOLS OF CENTRAL BANK

- Benchmark **IR** → Up/Contractionary, Down/Expansionary
- Government **Bonds** → Buy/Expansionary, Sell/Contractionary
- **RRR** → Up/Contractionary, Down/Expansionary
- **Loans to Banks** → More/Expansionary, Less/Contractionary

When the economy is overheating, the inflation rate is above target, and the CB should increase the benchmark IR (Fig. 1.2). High IRs should entice people to save instead of borrowing. However, again the CB must decide by how much to increase the IR and for how long. A drastic increase in the IR may remedy high inflation but can also sink the economy into recession.

In normal circumstances, an IR hike should make people less willing to borrow and an IR cut should make them eager to spend and invest. These are not guaranteed outcomes, however. In a deflationary economy, even near-zero IRs may not be enough to entice people to consume and business to invest. This is especially so if people have been traumatized[16] by a prolonged recession and are pessimistic about the future. As a result, they are reluctant to borrow no matter how much the IRs decline. In an inflationary economy, in a similar fashion, people may be indifferent to IR hikes because they are irrationally exuberant[17] – they believe in never-ending growth. They do not hesitate to borrow no matter how much the CB keeps ramping up the IRs.

In summary, the CB can tweak the IR to accelerate or decelerate the economy, but how that tweaking will exactly affect the economy cannot be pre-determined.

Changing the RRR
The CB can change the MB by manipulating the RRR (Box 1.8). Manipulating the RRR targets the behavior of lenders, the banks. During a recession, for instance, banks tend to keep too much liquidity trapped in excess reserves (Box 1.3) because they fear that potential borrowers may become insolvent. If banks keep reserves above the RRR, instead of lending them, the CB can cut down the RRR. Reducing the RRR from 10 to 5%, for example, may convince banks to unload some of their excess reserves because, given the new RRR, they are now awash with cash. Conversely, the CB can increase the RRR when banks engage in risky lending behavior. An RRR hike will force banks to set more deposits aside as reserves and this should curb their appetite to lend.

Kyber's CB prefers not to make abrupt changes in the RRR though. Increasing the RRR may shock some banks, which will scramble for extra cash, and can cause an undesirable economic contraction. Decreasing the RRR may also give the wrong signal and unleash excessive lending. How exactly banks will behave when confronted with a changed RRR has to do with their outlook on the economy. The CB can manipulate the RRR to nudge banks to

---

[16]   Alan S. Blinder, *The Economy has Hit Bottom*, WSJ, July 23, 2009 (referring to 'traumatized consumers who have suddenly learned the virtues of thrift').

[17]   'Irrational exuberance' was a phrase used by the US Federal Reserve Board Chairman Alan Greenspan before the bursting of the dot-com bubble. *See* Alan Greenspan, *The Challenge of Central Banking in a Democratic Society*, Remarks at the Annual Dinner and Francis Boyer Lecture of the American Enterprise Institute for Public Policy Research, Dec. 5, 1996.

behave a certain way. However, in a market economy, it cannot command banks to slow down or accelerate lending.

Loans to banks
A CB can stimulate a sluggish economy by offering loans to banks (Box 1.8). A CB usually stands ready to lend to private banks because it expects that they will use these loans to expand their lending to businesses and individuals. Still, banks are the ones that make the decision whether to borrow from the CB. In principle, the lower the lending rate, the more willing a bank should be to borrow from the CB. The *discount rate* offered by the CB to entice banks to borrow from it may not be enough, though, if banks are not optimistic about the economy. If banks expect a large number of defaults on the loans they make, they may be reluctant to borrow from the CB even at a discount rate.

All in all, though, the discount rate is a potent monetary tool. During financial crises depositors typically withdraw their deposits and banks refuse to lend to each other. Loans granted by the CB can help many private banks weather tough economic times.

Buying and selling government bonds
Open market operations are another tool of monetary policy (Box 1.8, Fig. 1.8). Open market operations consist of the buying and selling of government bonds in the open (secondary) market. We must note here that a government entity, the CB, can buy, hold or sell the debt issued by another government entity, the FA. The CB cannot purchase these bonds directly from the FA though. Such direct buying of government debt from the FA would make it obvious that the government can be financed by its own CB. Yet, while the CB cannot buy government debt directly from the FA, it can buy such debt in the secondary market by placing an order with the primary dealers (Fig. 1.7).

The buying/selling of government bonds by the CB has a direct effect on the MB. For example, when the CB buys ł10 000 worth of government bonds, it writes a check to the bank, the primary dealer, from which it purchases the bonds. The bank can keep the check in its checking account at the CB or cash it and put the money in its vault. In both cases, the reserves of the bank have increased, which means that the MB has increased by ł10 000 (Box 1.5). The bank can use these reserves to make loans to businesses.

If banks use the money that the CB creates, by buying government bonds from them, to make loans to businesses and individuals, the CB's expansionary policy will stimulate the economy. However, if banks hold on to the injected cash and do not lend it further, the expansionary policy will probably fail (Fig. 1.8). The CB controls the MB, the official liquidity it makes available to the banking system. It has less control over the MS (Box 1.6) because banks decide whether to keep as reserves or lend the money the CB creates. When

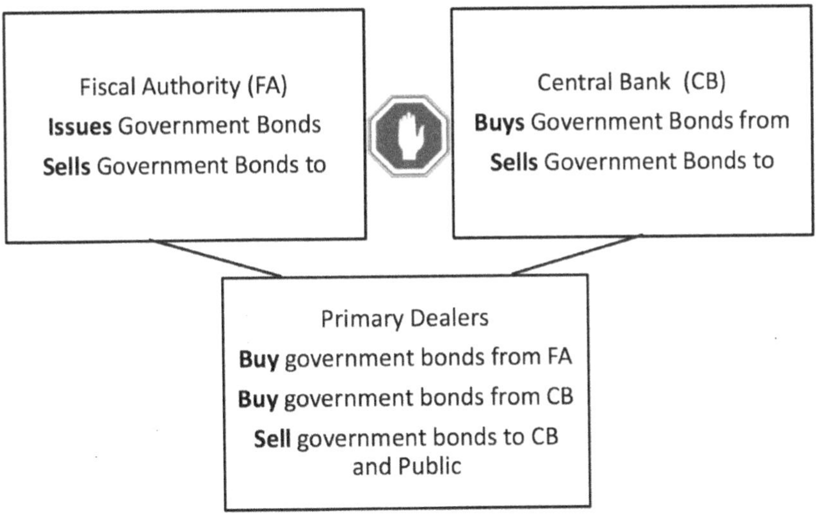

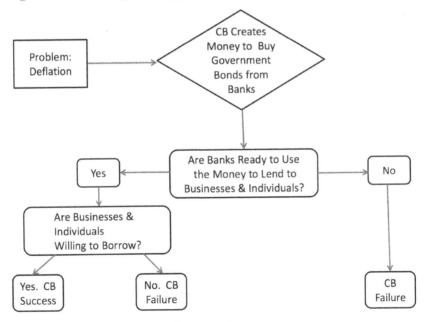

Figure 1.7   Management of government debt. The role of FA and CB

Figure 1.8   CB's open market operations

an economy is suffering from a recession, banks are typically reluctant to lend because of fears that borrowers might default. Potential borrowers are also unwilling to borrow and often withdraw money from banks. The CB is well aware that when the economy is deep into a recession the *transmission mechanism* (Box 1.6) from the MB to the MS will probably operate in an inefficient way.

In comparison with other monetary tools, the buying and selling of government bonds is the most precise one. Open market operations work directly on the MB by injecting or withdrawing liquidity from the economy. They are flexible and easily reversible since open market purchases can be reversed with open market sales and vice versa. Because buying and selling government debt is a convenient tool of monetary policy, if Kyber decides to run a conservative fiscal policy, balancing its budget and getting rid of debt, it can create a problem for its CB. When government debt becomes scarce, the CB will have to figure out some other securities to buy and sell to make monetary policy.[18] Unfortunately, there are no securities that are as safe as government bonds.[19]

In conclusion, the FA, by issuing bonds, the CB, by its bond buying or selling, and private actors, who may seek these bonds as a way to invest in safe assets, are the major players in the bond market (Box 1.9).

BOX 1.9   FACTORS AFFECTING THE PRICE OF GOVERNMENT BONDS

- Their **Maturity**
- **Supply** of bonds by FA
- **Demand** of bonds by CB and public
- Market **IRs**

1.1.6.3   Fiscal authority and central bank coordination

The FA and the CB have many tools at their disposal to control the economy. The FA taxes, spends and borrows (Fig. 1.9). The CB sets the benchmark IR, calibrates the RRR and the discount rate, the rate at which it lends to private banks (Fig. 1.9). Both the FA and the CB manage the government debt as the

---

[18]   This was an issue faced by the European Central Bank (ECB) in 2017 when the largest and economically most powerful country in Europe, Germany, balanced its budget, creating scarcity for its debt that was considered the most risk-free asset in Europe.

[19]   Maurice Obstfeld, *International Monetary System: Living with Asymmetry* 301, at 308–9, n. 8, in 'Globalization in an Age of Crisis: Multilateral Economic Cooperation in the Twenty-First Century' (Robert C. Feenstra and Alan M. Taylor, eds, 2014).

FA borrows money from the public, by issuing government bonds, and the CB may decide to buy or sell government debt, as it sees fit, to calibrate the economy (Fig. 1.9). As mentioned above, the CB can buy government debt, through the primary dealers, in the open market by creating money (Fig. 1.8). When the CB buys government debt, it *monetizes* it – it transforms it into money.

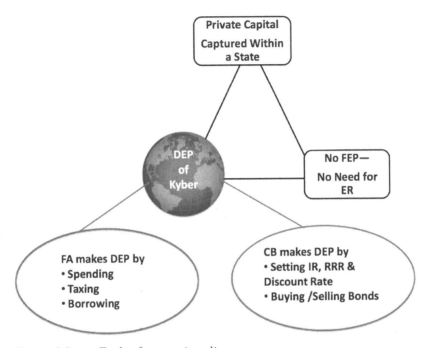

Figure 1.9   Tools of economic policy

The debt issued by the FA and bought by the CB is a liability for the FA but an asset for the CB. A consolidated balance sheet of the FA and CB would cancel this debt out (Fig. 1.10).

The question here is why would any state decide to manage its economic affairs through two entities – the FA and the CB – and then engage in the shenanigans of having its own CB create money to buy the debt issued by the FA? The answer is self-discipline. The state controls the printing press that enables it to create as much money as it wishes. However, having the power to print money is not always a blessing. The government knows that citizens are aware that the currency it prints, and passes on to them as a medium of exchange and store of value, is in essence plain paper with the state's insignia on it. If a natural disaster, an internal insurgency, a terrorist act were to destroy

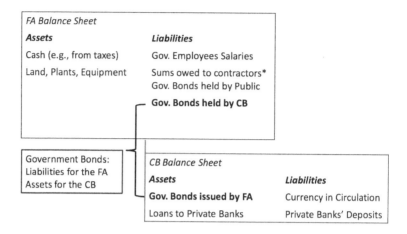

*companies that build highways, bridges etc.

Figure 1.10   Simplified balance sheets of FA and CB

the state, its paper currency would probably collapse with it. Kyber, in our example, is aware that the value of its currency depends on the faith people have in it. While currency can be printed in abundance, there is a limited amount of resources and, therefore, a limited amount of goods and services that can be made with these resources. Too much money chasing finite resources, goods and services can trigger uncontrollable inflation and deplete the currency's value.

The separation of powers between the FA and the CB is central for the long-term survival of the state. The FA spends on infrastructure, transportation, education, bread and circuses to keep the population happy. Some of these expenses are crucial for reducing internal opposition, terrorist activities and crime. The CB operates the government's printing press and can print currency incessantly to pay for all of the FA's expenses. Such incontinent money printing, though, will cause hyperinflation, the debasement of currency and possibly the dethroning of Kyber's government. Separating the FA from the CB is the institutional control that helps ensure the state's longevity. The state tries to preserve itself by assigning economic policy to two branches: the FA that is responsible for spending and the CB that prints the currency. The government has adopted legislation that plainly states that the CB is independent from the FA. The FA, in other words, cannot order the CB to print money to cover government expenses. The FA cannot even borrow directly from the

CB. The *overt* monetary financing of the government by its CB – the so-called 'helicopter money'[20] – because it is as close as we can get to creating money from scratch like when a helicopter drops money from the sky – is prohibited. However, while *overt* monetary financing is proscribed, *covert* monetary financing is still possible since the CB can buy government debt in the open market from the primary dealers. The primary dealers, by playing the role of intermediary between the FA and the CB, interject a degree of separation between the two branches of the same government (Fig. 1.7).

Obviously Kyber can get rid of its independent CB and command it to obey the FA. In fact, in emergency circumstances, it might just decide to do so by ordering the CB to buy government debt directly from the FA. In regular circumstances, though, the FA and CB prefer to collaborate at arm's length. The FA cannot order the CB to buy government debt to finance budget deficits. The CB does not have to monetize government debt if it believes that this is bad for the economy. There are limits to that independence, though.[21] The CB cannot be completely independent from the government because it is part of it.

1.2   A FRAMEWORK FOR ECONOMIC POLICY: THE FOUR SCENARIOS

In this section, we assume that a government's CB and FA coordinate to ensure that the economy grows at a sustainable growth rate. However, the FA tends to have the upper hand in this relationship – what is called *fiscal dominance*. This is because it makes the key economic decisions: how much to tax people and business and how much to spend and borrow. As we saw above, the government, through its fiscal branch, has the capacity to order the CB to print all of the money it needs for its spending. It refrains from doing so, though, because of fears that inflation will destroy the value of the paper currency it prints. The government has established the CB as an independent institution made up of experts whose job is to calibrate the money available in the economy to promote sustainable growth.

Figure 1.11 depicts the policy options of a CB by taking as a given the state of the economy and fiscal policy. The horizontal axis provides a snapshot of

---

[20]   Milton Friedman, *The Optimum Quantity of Money* 4–8 (2005 edition); Jordi Galí, *The Effects of a Money-financed Fiscal Stimulus*, at 2, Working Paper, Centre de Recerca en Economia Internacional (CREI), Aug. 2017; Adair Turner, *Debt, Money, and Mephistopheles: How Do We Get Out of This Mess?*, at 2, Occasional Paper 87, Group of 30, 2013.

[21]   On the limits of CB independence, *see* Rosa Lastra, *International Financial and Monetary Law* 2.104–2.158 (2015); Sarah Binder and Mark Spindel, *The Myth of Independence: How Congress Governs the Federal Reserve* (2017).

the economy. At the right side of the horizontal axis, we have a recessionary economy. In that economy, the private sector tends to be pessimistic; therefore, it does not actively seek new business opportunities. It refrains from borrowing and deleverages, sheds off debt, because it expects that the worst is yet to come. At the left side of the horizontal axis, we have a booming economy. In a booming economy, the private sector is eager to explore new opportunities by leveraging, taking on more credit.

The vertical axis summarizes the policies prescribed by the FA. The FA may be running a budget deficit or surplus or a balanced budget. A large fiscal deficit denotes fiscal largesse. A government will spend more than what it collects in taxes if it wishes to finance infrastructure projects, support education and welfare programs or fund current consumption. Small deficits, balanced budgets and surpluses, on the other hand, are demonstrative of fiscal restraint.

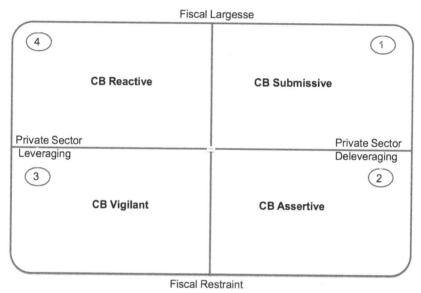

Figure 1.11   *The four scenarios: CB posture towards fiscal policy and private leverage/deleverage*

1.2.1   Economic Downturns (Scenarios 1, 2)

A government cannot always address a budget deficit through more taxation. When the economy is in bad shape, owing to a financial crisis, a trade conflict or an imminent war, a tax increase will trigger more pessimism and depress the economy even further. When the economy suffers, the private sector, businesses and households hoard money instead of investing and spending. Banks start charging higher IRs on the loans they give because of the anticipated high default rates. Citizens try to deleverage, pay down their debt, and accumulate savings to ensure that they have enough to survive an uncertain and austere future. Under these circumstances, Kyber has two options (Fig. 1.11).

1.2.1.1 Scenario 1: submissive central bank

To stimulate a deflationary economy, Kyber runs a budget deficit. The FA cuts taxes and increases spending to jumpstart the economy. In dire circumstances, the government is the spender and investor of last resort. It spends to restore the public infrastructure. In this way it employs people who are unemployed, because of the businesses that were destroyed, acting as the employer of last resort. In addition, the government hires private businesses for public works and subsidizes others that are crucial for the functioning of the economy but have suffered losses.

The government plans to finance the ensuing budget deficit by borrowing from the public. It realizes, though, that an already pessimistic public will be unwilling to buy all of the debt it issues. Some of the debt, therefore, is bought by its own bank, the CB. Given the dire economic circumstances, the CB is more than willing to conduct a loose policy and become the lender of last resort to its own government. When the economy is hit by deflation, and the FA takes action to reverse the economic downturn, the CB finances budget deficits as needed. The CB is *submissive* (Fig. 1.11); it gives in to the expansionary plans of the FA. It supports the FA so that the economy can grow again.

1.2.1.2 Scenario 2: assertive central bank

In scenario 2, the government is unable to run a large budget deficit even when the economy is in recession. Avoiding fiscal deficits during economic down-turns is known as austerity. The government, instead of increasing spending and cutting taxes to stimulate the economy, hikes taxes and reduces spending by curtailing essential social services. Governments that opt for austerity in tough times tend to be concerned about inflation. In our example, the many inflationary episodes in Kyber's history have made people aware that the money it prints, if printed excessively, can lose all of its value. The public is convinced that government debt and, even worse, the monetization of such debt by the CB, causes inflation and often hyperinflation.

To assuage peoples' fears the government must run a balanced budget or surplus. In fact, the obligation of the government to keep a balanced budget or, at least, to maintain a budget deficit of 3% of GDP, has been enshrined in the supreme law of the land, the constitution. In addition, a group of citizens, who call themselves 'bond market vigilantes',[22] tend to actively protest loose fiscal policies. They do so by selling off government bonds, when they determine that government debt is excessive. Those sell-offs trigger sharp declines in bond prices and the skyrocketing of bond yields (*see* Box 1.4). The FA is well aware that the debt it issues is sustainable until bond yields rise to the point of making it unsustainable. Since the FA has tied its own hands and is constricted by private actors, the CB is the only authority that can act.

The CB has many tools at its disposal. It can reduce the benchmark IR to zero or even introduce negative IRs.[23] Low IRs are good for debtors and should entice people and business to borrow, expanding the MS. The CB, because of its role as lender of last resort, may also lend money to private banks in exchange for even bad quality collateral.[24] The CB can finance corporations directly by buying their bonds. It can employ other unconventional monetary measures such as buying corporate stocks. In other words, when the FA is unable to take initiative, the CB becomes *assertive* (Fig. 1.11). It takes initiative to get the economy out of the slump.

It is unclear, though, whether CB's intervention will be sufficient to save the economy. If the private sector refuses to borrow, despite the low rates, CB's stimulus will remain trapped in the banking system. If businesses are not lured to borrow or banks are too cautious to lend, the CB's monetary expansion will be blocked. As mentioned above, the government, through its FA, is the borrower of last resort. If the government has abrogated that role by inserting in the constitution a clause that restricts fiscal deficits, the CB can attempt to revive the private sector by lending to private banks or even directly to corporations. After it exhausts those tools, though, the only thing it can do is to hope that the FA will find the will and the way to act.

In conclusion, in both scenarios 1 and 2 (Fig. 1.11), when recessionary forces squeeze the economy, the CB can deploy tools to stimulate the economy. When the government runs a budget deficit, the role of CB is somewhat easy: the borrower of last resort, the FA, and lender of the last resort, the CB, work hand-in-hand to revive the economy. The government runs a deficit, to provide employment and rebuild infrastructure, which is financed by its own CB. In scenario 2, though, it seems that the FA and the CB work at cross-purposes. The FA cannot do much because it has pledged not to run excessive deficits.

---

[22] The term was coined in the 1980s by Edward Yardeni. *See* Edward Yardeni, *Predicting the Markets: A Professional Autobiography* 19 (2018).

[23] On negative IRs, *see* Chapter 4, Section 4.3.2.

[24] *See* Jean-Pierre Landau, *Global Liquidity: Public and Private* 223, at 247, in Proceedings of Jackson Hole Economic Policy Symposium on 'Global Dimensions of Unconventional Monetary Policy,' Federal Reserve Bank of Kansas City, Aug. 22–24, 2013.

The CB then rebels and runs single-handedly an expansionary policy. Such policy will be successful if the private sector is eager to borrow the money the CB creates. If the private sector remains pessimistic about the economy, the CB's expansionary policy will be derailed. Eventually the FA may have to exploit some of the ambiguities in the legal rules to proactively engage with the CB.

1.2.2 Economic Upturns (Scenarios 3, 4)

1.2.2.1 Scenario 3: vigilant central bank
Under this scenario, the government runs a small deficit and inflation fluctuates around 2%. Almost all who wish to be employed are able to find jobs. Private credit may be moderate to high as people borrow to start businesses or buy homes. Because the fiscal policy is conservative, the CB refrains from actively intervening in the economy. The CB remains *vigilant* (Fig. 1.11), however, watching especially the growth of private credit, which could become unsustainable. Too much credit may trigger high inflation and asset bubbles.

1.2.2.2 Scenario 4: reactive central bank
In this scenario, inflation gets out of hand, exceeding the 2% target rate that the CB has set. People are irrationally exuberant, believing that prosperity can last forever. A technological breakthrough has generated beliefs that businesses will reap significant benefits from productivity gains and has propelled a buying frenzy in the stockmarket. The CB knows that excessive optimism in a booming economy can cause asset bubbles. Moreover, the FA is running a large budget deficit, adding more fuel to an already overheated economy.

Under these circumstances, the CB has to pull the reins in on the economy to keep it growing at a sustainable rate. It can do this by pursuing a tight policy, for instance, by hiking the benchmark IR to slow down the economy. A drastic increase of the benchmark IR, from 3 to 20%, for instance, can convince people to start saving instead of spending. A 20% IR can also reduce speculation in the stockmarket, as people will think twice before buying stocks on margin, i.e. borrowing to purchase stocks. A high IR should cool down an overheated housing market. People would hesitate to buy a house when they have to pay a 20% IR (plus the risk premium) on their loan.

A *reactive* CB that tries to discipline an FA that runs a large budget deficit (Fig. 1.11) makes the government look incoherent. The FA and the CB seem to work at cross-purposes when the CB raises the benchmark IR, to encourage people to save and fight inflation, while the FA cuts taxes, to give people more income, and fuels inflationary growth. Because of the CB's reactive stance, the FA will be hurt by the high IRs that would make it more difficult to finance government deficits. Unfortunately for the FA, it cannot instruct the CB to lower IRs. The independence of the CB, even if not enshrined in the constitution, is highly respected. The FA will have, therefore, to reduce its deficit, eventually. The CB, because of its independence, has the clout to restrain its own government. The independence of the CB, if respected, can help Kyber preserve the value of its currency and avoid potential economic pitfalls that can undermine its global reign.

2. The Trilemma

2.1 GLOBAL LIQUIDITY AND GLOBAL CAPITAL MARKETS

We move from the one-state world into a world of two states: Kyber and Nesis. Each state is controlled by a different government and prints its own currency. Kyber is printing the kobank (Ⱨ) and Nesis the netmon (ɯ). The two states trade actively with each other. There are no trade barriers, tariffs or quotas on the imports and exports of goods between them. Both countries have espoused the freedom of movement of capital, which makes up the *global private liquidity* (Table 2.1). People can move their money from one state to another freely. Large corporations, in fact, take advantage of the freedom of movement of capital and free trade. Some Kyber corporations have large operations in Nesis and vice-versa.

Because the two states trade and transact with each other, they have to adopt a FEP. They have to establish a price – an ER – of their currency in terms of the other state's currency. In addition, because they have endorsed the freedom of private capital, they cannot erect barriers to block the wealth that may enter or exit their borders. This decision further complicates their DEP, generating, as we will explain below, an intractable Trilemma.

In Chapter 1, we distinguished between *official liquidity*, the MB, and *private liquidity*, the MS, created by banks. Global official liquidity is the aggregate money the CBs of the two states make available to their residents (Table 2.1). The official liquidity of Nesis can be accessed by Kyber by the accumulation of netmons. Kyber's exporters to Nesis, who are paid in netmons, have to convert those netmons into kobanks, through Kyber's CB. Kyber's CB collects those netmons in its reserves and uses them, as needed, to pay for imports from Nesis, or to support the kobank in the foreign exchange (FX) market, as we will see below.

The economic policy of the two states, including the IRs that prevail in their respective economies, can be used to gauge the amount of global official liquidity. A high IR, a contractionary policy, of a state signals a reduction in the official liquidity of that state. A low IR, an expansionary policy, indicates an increase in the official liquidity. If both states pursue expansionary policies, global official liquidity will increase. The opposite will happen if both states

Table 2.1   Definitions of liquidity

Public (official) liquidity or MB	The money a CB makes available to the financial system equivalent to the money in circulation (C) plus private banks' reserves (R) (Box 1.5)
Private liquidity or MS	The money banks create through the factional banking system (Box 1.6)
Global public (official) liquidity	The public liquidity made available by both states
Global private liquidity	Money created through the cross-border lending of banks and other financial institutions
Market liquidity	How quickly assets can be converted into cash (or cash equivalents) with minimal or no loss of value. A deep and liquid market is one where investors rapidly execute large-volume transactions with little impact on prices

adopt contractionary policies. If the policies of the two states diverge – one state tightens while the other loosens – global official liquidity may remain unchanged. It all depends on whether the tightening of one state is offset by the loosening of the other.

Private liquidity has to do with the 'ease of financing', the availability of credit in the economy (Table 2.1). In a global financial system, private liquidity is created by the cross-border movement of capital put in motion by banks. A booming global economy is characterized by increasing global private liquidity as the banks of one state lend to the banks of the other state. During a global recession, banks are reluctant to lend and businesses deleverage, reducing global private liquidity. The two states have cyclical economies. This means that economic expansions are usually followed by contractions and so on. As a result, surges in the cross-border movement of capital, leading to abundance of global private liquidity, are followed by declines in the movement of capital and global liquidity shortages.

To propel the growth of global private liquidity, the two states have encouraged the development of global capital markets. Capital markets channel the savings of capital owners to those who need capital, such as businesses, individuals and governments. The global capital markets make it possible for investors of a rich country to put their money to work in a capital-starved country. Capital-poor countries offer higher returns than rich countries to entice wealthy individuals and institutions to invest in them.

The global capital markets consist of: (1) cross-border banking, when the banks of Kyber offer loans to banks and residents of Nesis (and vice versa); (2) the global bond market; (3) the global stock market; and (4) the global FX market. Companies and the two states have the option to borrow domestically or through the global bond market that gives them access to foreign lenders.

The global stock market facilitates the listing of companies' shares not only in the domestic stock exchange but also in the other state's exchanges. The global bond and stock markets, in other words, facilitate access to foreign capital. Additionally, the people of both Kyber and Nesis get the opportunity to purchase bonds and shares not only of domestic companies but also of foreign corporations.

The FX market, the currency market, was created initially to convert one currency into another for the facilitation of cross-border trade and investment. Since then it has grown significantly. Banks, companies and individuals can buy and sell the two currencies in that market. Some of this activity has to do with trade and cross-border investment. There are specialized companies, though, called hedge funds, that use the currency market to speculate on the value of currencies. Using the markets to speculate on the gyrations of currencies, bonds and stocks is legal. The global FX market is the largest financial market. An international network of exchanges and brokers all over the world facilitates the workings of that market.

2.2 FREE CAPITAL FLOWS OR CAPITAL CONTROLS?

The freedom of movement of private capital is the *status quo* in this two-state world. States have adopted the freedom of capital after many trials and errors that helped them conclude that it makes sense to unleash private wealth. Dismantling national barriers unlocks the 'animal spirits'[1] of private actors who seek opportunities to augment their wealth and improves the efficiency of allocation of capital. Profit-seeking capital holders vie to invest in the most productive places and projects in the world.

Some dissenters, in both Kyber and Nesis, argue, though, for the regulation of capital, the imposition of controls on capital inflows and outflows. Dissenters in Kyber are against the infusions of foreign capital because they make Kyber dependent on Nesis' wealth. They argue that states that need to import capital to finance their deficits live beyond their means by relying on the 'kindness of strangers'[2] for their growth. If, during a recession, these aliens decide to become less kind by withdrawing their capital, they will trigger

---

[1]   John Maynard Keynes, *The General Theory of Employment, Interest, and Money* 161 (1964). Keynes argued that many financial decisions are made owing to 'spontaneous optimism' rather than the careful calculation of costs and benefits. *See also* George Akerlof and Robert Shiller, *Animal Spirits: How Human Psychology Drives the Economy, and Why It Matters for Global Capitalism* (2009).

[2]   Mark Carney, *A Fine Balance*, at 6, Speech at the Manor House, London, June 20, 2017.

a crisis.[3] Some in Kyber believe also that keeping local private capital locked within Kyber's borders ensures indigenous growth. In a similar vein, elites in Nesis want to forbid foreigners from investing in certain sectors of the economy owing to national security concerns. Such sectors, the energy sector, the telecommunications sector and the internet, are key to national security and must be off limits to foreign investment.

The regulation of capital flows does not necessarily mean renouncing the freedom of capital. For states that start off with closed financial borders, it makes sense, for instance, to phase in the liberalization of capital over time. States can start by liberalizing foreign direct investment (FDI) first, that is investment in real assets, such as factories and land. FDI inflows are the most stable capital flows because they cannot be quickly liquidated and revert back to their country of origin during a crisis. They are also the most correlated with growth. After the liberalization of FDI, a state may consider liberalizing long-term portfolio flows. These are long-term investments by foreigners in its stock and bond markets. Finally, a state might consider liberalizing short-term portfolio flows, short-term investments in its markets. Short-term portfolio inflows, such as those invested in short-term corporate bonds, are the most fickle investments. These inflows, the so-called 'hot money', quickly become outflows when a state faces a crisis. Therefore, they are usually regulated more closely and, in some circumstances, even discouraged.

Capital flows can be regulated at their origin by the source state and, at the destination, by the recipient state.[4] Capital-rich states have the capacity, through financial regulation, to prevent capital flows to politically or economically unstable states. At the same time, though, most of these rich states do not have the incentives to curtail the freedom of capital owners. This is because such freedom enlarges the opportunities available to those who have exhausted lucrative opportunities at home and are keen on investing in new ventures abroad. States from which capital originates often leave the decision of whether to invest abroad to the risk-appetite of capital holders. Because source states adopt a *laissez faire* approach to the regulation of capital, it falls upon recipient states to decide whether they will welcome or block the private liquidity ready to gush into their borders.

If a state wishes to prevent foreigners from entering its domestic markets, it can chose from a garden variety of capital control measures. Some of these measures are mild, just aiming at discouraging capital inflows. Others are more

---

[3]   Edd Denbee et al., *Stitching Together the Global Financial Safety* Net, at 4, Financial Stability Paper No. 36, Bank of England, Feb. 2016.
[4]   IMF, *The Liberalization and Management of Capital Flows: An Institutional View* 28, Nov. 14, 2012.

intrusive, focusing on preventing foreign capital inflows. A state, for instance, can dissuade capital owners from moving in by reducing its IR. The CB of a state can also increase the RRR for banks that hold liabilities denominated in foreign currency, discouraging them from receiving foreign deposits. Capital control measures include taxes on capital inflows or ordering specific holding periods for stocks and bonds for foreigners who wish to invest in domestic markets.[5] More severe capital controls encompass the obligatory submission to the state of export earnings (in exchange for local currency) and the rationing of foreign exchange available to firms that import foreign goods. A state can restrict the availability of FX for import payments when it suspects that importers overstate the cost of imported goods to evade capital controls and send their money abroad.

States are particularly concerned when their banks and citizens are lured into borrowing in foreign currency. Such temptation may be strong since the financial systems of Kyber and Nesis are highly integrated, making global private liquidity easily accessible when the IRs abroad are lower than those at home. Short-term borrowing in foreign currency is a major source of economic instability, with implications for the security of a state. When a state or its residents borrow in foreign currency, the CB of that state becomes partially incapacitated in its role as lender of last resort because it cannot print foreign currency. To avoid becoming dependent on credit originating from foreign states, states can ban all loans to their residents from nonresidents.

A state can be clobbered by foreigners and its own citizens when they seek to move their wealth abroad. A state that fears the flight of domestic capital can impose taxes on the transfer of assets abroad. A state may even be tempted to erect permanent financial borders by empowering its CB to pre-approve each and every transfer of money to other states. In times of economic warfare, like that experienced in the 1930s, states are capable of going to exhaustive lengths to lock in private capital and to shield their economy from foreign intrusion.[6]

Capital controls are not foolproof.[7] In our two-state world, capital owners are not allegiant to any state. They are simply interested in maintaining their wealth and passing it on to their heirs. When capital controls are imposed, capital owners try to evade them by using loopholes in the legislation or by illegal means. If capital owners suspect that a state is likely to trap their wealth within its borders, they will not even think of investing in it. As a result, no

---

[5] *Id.* at 17.

[6] Ragnar Nurske, *International Currency Experience: Lessons of the Inter War Period* 206 (1944).

[7] Charles Engel, *Macroprudential Policy in a World of High Capital Mobility: Policy Implications from an Academic Perspective*, at 18, NBER Working Paper 20951, Feb. 2015.

matter how prudent it may be for a state to regulate capital, it may refrain from doing so, especially if it is a poor state in need of foreign capital.

2.3   THE BALANCE OF PAYMENTS

Kyber and Nesis keep track of their bilateral transactions by using the balance of payments (BOP) (Fig. 2.1). The BOP is a snapshot of all transactions of individuals, companies and the government of a state. On the BOP, transactions that cause the flow of money into a country (i.e. receipts) are marked as 'credits' while transactions that cause the flow of money out of a country (i.e. payments) are marked as 'debits'. As its name indicates, the BOP must balance; the sum of all debits (payments) must equal the sum of all credits (receipts). The BOP includes the current, financial and capital accounts. Figure 2.1 depicts the basic components of a BOP.

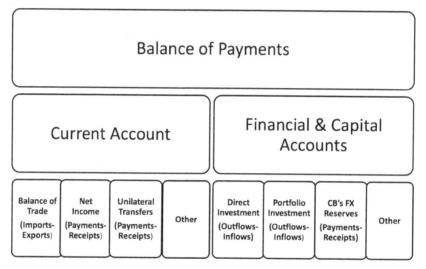

Figure 2.1   The BOP

The BOP reflects the strength of an economy. The debits/credits registered on it show: (1) how much capital we export versus how much capital we import; and (2) our country's *comparative advantage* over other countries, that is how much in goods and services we export versus how much we import.[8]

---

[8]   Milton Friedman and Anna Jacobson Schwartz, *A Monetary History of the United States 1867–1960*, at 58 (1963).

A country has a comparative advantage at producing, and thus exporting, something if it can produce it more efficiently than anyone else. Subtracting the value of our exports from the value of our imports is a way to measure the scope of our comparative advantage.

A large portion of the current account (CA)[9] is the balance of trade (BOT) that records the exports and imports of a state (Fig. 2.1). When we, the private and public sector of our state, import more goods and services than we export, we have a BOT deficit. When we export more than we import, we have a BOT surplus. Net income is the difference between payments we make to those who invest here and income we receive from our investments abroad (Fig. 2.1). It is worth noting here that the net income we receive from investing abroad, including interest payments from lending abroad, is not included in the capital account but in the CA.[10] Unilateral transfers include worker remittances: the difference between what foreign workers employed here send back to their home state and what our workers employed abroad send back here (Fig. 2.1). Remittances are very important for poor countries whose inhabitants have to migrate to other countries to find jobs. In summary, the CA helps us gauge our state's dependence on other states. A CA deficit indicates that a state is living beyond its means. It needs, therefore, infusions of capital from other states. These infusions are reflected in the financial and capital accounts of its BOP.

On the financial and capital accounts side, direct investment includes the difference between outflows (our acquisitions of foreign companies) and inflows (acquisitions of domestic firms by foreigners) (Fig. 2.1). Portfolio investment is the difference between outflows (our investment in foreign stocks and bonds) and inflows (the purchases of domestic stocks and bonds by foreigners) (Fig. 2.1). The CB's FX reserves are its holdings of foreign assets, such as foreign currency and foreign bonds. Our CB's FX reserves may go up or down depending on the payments our CB has to make in foreign currency, the foreign exchange it gets from exporters[11] and its earnings from holding foreign assets (e.g. interest earned on foreign-currency denominated bonds) (Fig. 2.1). Table 2.2 provides a simplified version of Kyber's BOP.

When the head of Kyber's FA presents the BOP to the rest of the government, they notice the following: Kyber imports more than it exports to Nesis, leaving it with a large BOT deficit of ₮1 000. The BOT is offset somewhat by the income Kyber receives by investing in Nesis' assets (₮500). Kyber has an

---

[9]   The composition of the CA is detailed in article XXX(d) of the IMF's Articles of Agreement. *See* Articles of Agreement of the International Monetary Fund, July 22, 1944, amended Jan. 26, 2016.

[10]   Art. XXX(d)(2), *id.*

[11]   Exporters usually convert the foreign currencies they receive by exporting goods into domestic currency.

Table 2.2   *Simplified BOP of Kyber*

	Credits	Debits
Exports	1 000	
Imports		−2 000
Income from invest. in Nesis	500	
Income paid to Nesis from invest. here		−200
Total credits and debits	1500	−2 200
Current account (CA) balance		700 (deficit)
Nesis direct invest. here (public + private inflows)	500	
Direct invest. in Nesis (public + private outflows)		−200
Nesis portfolio invest. here (public + private inflows)	550	
Portfolio invest. in Nesis (public + private outflows)		−250
Total credits and debits	1050	−450
Financial & capital accounts balance	600 (surplus)	
Statistical discrepancy	100	
Total balance: 700 balanced by 600 + 100		

overall CA deficit of ₭700 (Table 2.2). Nesis invests in Kyber much more than Kyber invests in Nesis: ₭500 + 550 in direct and portfolio investment versus Kyber's ₭200 + 250, which leaves Kyber with a financial account surplus of ₭600. The CA deficit (₭700), therefore, is balanced largely by the financial account surplus (₭600) (Table 2.2). Since Kyber imports more than it exports, it pays for those imports, using the money it receives from foreigners who purchase Kyber's assets (land, firms, stocks and bonds).[12] The ₭100 unaccounted for (Table 2.2) is attributed to accounting errors or transfers that went undetected. Maybe Kyber exported more to Nesis than the BOP recorded. Alternatively, some Nesis firms may have bought more assets in Kyber that were not reported and, thus, not recorded on the BOP. Some of these undetected transfers could be illegal.

Kyber's policy-makers are troubled by the CA deficit, a key gauge of the economy's health. They are particularly concerned that their country *spends more on foreign imports* (₭2 000) *than it earns from investing abroad* (₭500). Because of its CA deficit, some of the country's exports are paid by selling domestic assets – the land, firms, stocks and bonds that Nesis and its residents purchase in Kyber. In principle, a country that finances its CA deficit through

---

[12]   Kyber resembles the United States in this respect. The United States tends to have trade deficits with other states as it imports more goods than it exports. It usually has a financial account surplus. People bring their capital to the United States to invest in its deep and liquid markets.

the financial account diminishes its wealth in order to afford more goods and services now. Future generations may end up poorer when assets are sold to foreigners. Kyber is also alarmed because a large portion of the capital inflows into its economy is the hot money that tends to flee when investors panic.

Kyber wants to improve its CA. An obvious way to do so is to reduce its imports but this is difficult because some of these imports are crucial for growth. Asking people to consume less and save more is not considered polit-ically astute because it produces public discontent. Exporting more is another alternative, but Kyber has a weak export sector because of domestic market distortions including lack of new financing for investments and high labor costs that undermine the competitiveness of its export industries.

Borrowing from Nesis to finance the BOT deficit is not a viable long-term strategy. Borrowing abroad to finance a trade deficit may make sense if the money is used for productive purposes (e.g. to buy machines for factories) and not just for today's consumption (e.g. to import food and luxury items). Moreover, a state cannot entirely borrow its way to growth. When debt piles up, lenders become nervous because of the higher risk of default. To compen-sate for that risk, they demand higher and higher IRs for holding the debt of an over-indebted state until eventually that debt becomes unsustainable.

A more intelligent strategy for Kyber is to borrow from Nesis, at low IRs, and invest that borrowed money in projects there, provided that the rate of return on its investments in Nesis is higher than the rate of borrowing. A state can offset its trade deficit if its returns from investing abroad exceed the returns that foreigners receive from investing in that state. These higher returns – that register as income received from investing in Nesis (Table 2.2) – can help counterbalance the trade deficit. Borrowing at low rates to invest in projects abroad that produce higher returns than the rate of borrowing is a complex strategy though.[13] If the borrowed money does not yield the expected returns, Kyber can still be saddled with excessive debt.

Eventually, a state that runs chronic CA deficits will be forced to:

- consume less, import less, save more (which can hurt an economy whose growth is fueled by consumption);
- export more (which may be difficult if a country does not have a robust export sector);

---

[13] This strategy has been mastered by the United States, which is considered the venture capitalist of the world. *See* Pierre-Olivier Gourinchas and Hélène Rey, *From World Banker to World Venture Capitalist: U.S. External Adjustment and the Exorbitant Privilege*, 11, at 12, in 'G7 Current Account Imbalances: Sustainability and Adjustment' (Richard H. Clarida ed., 2007).

- generate more profits from investing abroad than foreigners receive by investing in that state (which may be unrealistic if a country has not much investment abroad or the whole world is suffering from recession).

Kyber obviously could go on hoping that its CA deficit will continue to be funded by its financial account surplus. Relying on the kindness of strangers,[14] however, to keep pouring money into Kyber to finance its spending cannot be a long-term strategy. If a crisis happens and strangers become less kind, financing the deficit will become harder. In fact, during crises, foreign financing usually dries up, destabilizing states' financial systems and their whole economies.

From the above, one could surmise that it is unwise for countries to run large and persistent CA deficits.[15] Not all deficits are signs of economic weakness though.[16] Under certain circumstances, a deficit may be the result of growing domestic economic opportunities financed by foreigners because of the shortage of indigenous capital. A state may also have a CA deficit when the prices for the goods it exports decline owing to a global recession.

Despite the fact that there may be good reasons for a country to run a CA deficit, such a deficit carries a stigma. States with chronic deficits are viewed as fiscally licentious, spendthrift organizations that constantly borrow to spend now. Their spending sprees often produce unsustainable debt and jeopardize the welfare of future generations. BOP surpluses do not carry the same stigma. Surpluses arise usually because of large domestic savings, that are successfully invested abroad, or a state's export-led growth strategy that, through subsides and cheap loans, has boosted its industries. It is hard to find fault with a state whose residents are thrifty and that thrives owing to the efforts it has put into strengthening the competitiveness of its export sector.

At the same time, there is an unholy symbiosis between surplus states and deficit states. Surplus countries export their surplus domestic savings by lending to deficit countries. The glut of savings of surplus countries is channeled, through the global financial markets, to deficit countries that are in dire need of financing. Surplus states take advantage of countries in need of financing, which makes it difficult for them to resist borrowing from their high-saving neighbors.[17] As a commentator has aptly put it, the high savings

---

[14]   *See supra* note 2.

[15]   Olivier Blanchard and Gian Maria Milesi-Ferretti, *(Why) Should Current Account Balances Be Reduced?*, at 5, IMF Staff Discussion Note, SDN/11/03, Mar. 1, 2011.

[16]   *Id.*

[17]   Raghuram G. Rajan, *Fault Lines: How Hidden Fractures Still Threaten the World Economy* 10 (2010).

of surplus states find outlet in countries that have 'the weakest policies or the least discipline'.[18] These countries borrow the savings offered to them at initially attractive IRs until, at some point, the debt becomes unsustainable and they give in to crisis. As we will see in the case study of Greece, the country's political elite lacked the will to restrain public borrowing. It sought to appease various rent-seekers through handouts enabled by debt instead of devising solutions for long-term growth.

This unhealthy symbiosis between surplus states and deficit countries is the root cause of economic conflict. Deficit countries have to rely on foreigners to finance their deficits. During a crisis, that financing is typically withdrawn, as capitalists pull back from these countries, making their situation even worse. On the other hand, surplus countries can keep their surplus 'for a long time, if not forever'.[19] Countries that maintain surpluses do not depend on the willingness of foreigners to finance domestic consumption and investment. Because of their savings and focus on exports, they are, in fact, considered safe havens during crises. Surplus countries also have more options during a global economic slowdown. They can rekindle their dormant domestic demand and refashion themselves as less export-dependent.

2.4 WHAT IS THE FAIR VALUE OF A CURRENCY?

2.4.1 Domestic Economic Policy and the Exchange Rate

The ER is the price of a currency in terms of another currency. Currencies may appreciate or depreciate vis-à-vis other countries' currencies. When the currency of a country strengthens, the people of that country feel richer as they can consume more goods from other countries or purchase vacations there. At the same time, though, the country's exports become dearer for other countries and this weakens the export sector. On the contrary, when the currency of a country depreciates, the people of that country feel poorer and cut down on imports. They opt to buy domestic goods and home vacations. However, as the country's goods become cheaper, its export sector should soar.

The MB of a state affects the ER of its currency. When the CB of a state creates money, increasing the liquidity in the economy – conducts expansionary monetary policy – the domestic IRs fall. This leads to capital outflows as investors migrate to states that offer higher IRs. In order to invest in other higher-yielding currencies, capital owners sell the currency of the state that offers low IRs and buy the currencies of states that offer higher IRs. As

---

[18] *Id.* at 10.
[19] Blanchard and Milesi-Ferretti, *supra* note 15, at 6.

a result, the low-yielding currency depreciates. At the same time, though, the state's low IR encourages its residents to borrow and invest, resulting in higher domestic growth. More importantly, the depreciated currency boosts the country's export sector. As exports increase, the economy should improve. A side effect of this abundance of money, though, may be the higher risk of inflation (Box 2.1). Things may become more complicated, in the long-run, if the monetary easing conducted by the CB is offset by the tightening of fiscal policy through an increase in taxes. Excessive fiscal tightening can certainly diminish the impact of monetary easing. This is why some sort of coordination between the FA and CB is required for the smooth functioning of an economy.

BOX 2.1   FEP IMPLICATIONS OF DEP: THE IMPACT OF MONETARY EASING ON THE ER

CB creates more money → IRs down →

> → Domestic borrowing/investment up
> → Capital outflows → Currency depreciation → Exports up
> → More growth, risk of inflation

If the CB decreases the liquidity in the economy, that is conducts contractionary monetary policy, domestic IRs should increase. This invites capital inflows as capital flows back to the state that offers higher IRs than other states. In order to invest in that state, capital owners should sell other currencies and buy that state's currency. The higher IRs, though, will discourage borrowing and dampen domestic growth. A stronger currency should also enfeeble the country's export sector. As exports decrease, the economy may suffer. A side effect of the shortage of money, owing to monetary tightening, is the higher risk of recession (Box 2.2). Things may become more muddled, in the long run, if the CB's tightening is counterbalanced by an expansionary fiscal policy. An expansionary fiscal policy can buffer some of the contractionary effects of tight monetary policy and help the economy avoid deflation. The coordination between the FA and CB, in this case, may be unavoidable.

BOX 2.2   FEP IMPLICATIONS OF DEP: THE IMPACT
OF MONETARY TIGHTENING ON THE ER

CB withdraws money → IRs Up →

→ Domestic borrowing/investment down
→ Capital inflows → Currency appreciation → Exports down
→ Less growth, risk of recession

2.4.2   Can Markets Determine the Fair Value of a Currency?

Some claim that there is a 'fair', 'proper', 'equilibrium' or 'long-term' value for each currency that is discoverable by the free markets.[20] This is because of the law of one price or purchasing power parity. According to the purchasing power parity, the same good should sell at the same price in two different states when priced in a common currency. The purchasing power parity makes sense in theory but, in reality, transportation costs, import taxes and other barriers may make purchasing power parity difficult to achieve. A currency, therefore, can be undervalued or overvalued versus another currency for a long period before it reaches purchasing power parity.

Currency traders try to discover the purchasing power parity of a currency in order to determine whether that currency may be cheap (undervalued) or expensive (overvalued) relative to its 'proper' value. When currencies deviate from their equilibrium long-term value – they are 'misaligned' – currency traders take advantage of this temporary misalignment to bet on the appreciation or depreciation of a currency. Betting on an expected appreciation, traders will accumulate a currency, driving its value up. Betting on a projected depreciation, traders will sell a currency, driving its price down. Traders think like this: when a currency appreciates, for a long time, relative to other states' currencies, the exports of that state should become expensive (relative to those of other states) and it will export less and less. Continuing currency appreciation eventually undermines growth. The state's CB, therefore, should loosen monetary policy by reducing the IR. Knowing that this is the likely move of the CB, currency traders will sell that state's currency, betting it will depreciate. If selling is not overdone, it should bring the currency back to its fair value (Box 2.3).

---

[20]   On the difficulties of determining the proper value of a currency, *see* T. Ashby McCown et al., *Equilibrium Exchange Rate Models and Misalignments*, Occasional Paper No. 7, Office of International Affairs, Department of the Treasury, Mar. 2007.

BOX 2.3   HOW MARKETS BRING A CURRENCY TO FAIR VALUE BY DEPRECIATING IT

Prolonged currency appreciation → Exports down → Speculators expect CB to drive IRs down → They sell currency → Currency depreciates

---

On the other hand, a state that experiences prolonged currency depreciation is likely to suffer from high inflation – since more and more money is necessary to buy the same amount of goods and services. High inflation undermines faith in the currency. Currency traders, therefore, expect the state's CB to tighten monetary policy by increasing the IR. They buy that state's currency, therefore, betting that the currency will appreciate. This way they strengthen the currency (Box 2.4).

BOX 2.4   HOW MARKETS BRING A CURRENCY TO FAIR VALUE BY APPRECIATING IT

Prolonged currency depreciation → Inflation up → Speculators expect CB to drive IRs up → They buy currency → Currency appreciates

---

The purchasing power parity has been popularized by the Big Mac Index developed by the *Economist* magazine, which shows the price of a McDonald's Big Mac hamburger adjusted for dollars in different countries. On January 30, 2013, a Big Mac was priced at $4.37 in the United States. In Norway, though, it was $7.84, making the Norwegian kroner seem like an overvalued currency by about 80% relative to the dollar. The Big Mac was priced at $3.51 in Japan, making the Japanese yen look like an undervalued currency by about 20% against the dollar.

Building on the purchasing power parity, economists have developed many models to help them gauge the 'correct' ER between two currencies. The nominal effective exchange rate (NEER) measures the value of a state's currency against the weighted average of the currencies of its trading partners. One would expect a state whose NEER has depreciated for a prolonged period of time to have a surplus. On the other hand, a continuing appreciation of a state's NEER means that its currency is becoming more expensive relative to the currencies of its trading partners. That state, as a result, should have a deficit.

Traders have developed many models that they use to determine currencies' 'true' value relative to other currencies in order to make the correct bets in the FX market. The plethora of models and estimates underlines the lack of consensus on how to evaluate the fair value of a currency. What makes appraising a currency even harder is that its 'proper' value is not set in stone. It fluctuates over time based on cyclical, structural and political factors. Structural factors are those that fundamentally change the economy of a state. Cyclical disturbances have temporary effects and the economy tends to return to its prior stage. An increase in the productivity of a state relative to other states, owing to the invention of a new technology, for example, should lead to an appreciation of its currency. In this case, the appreciation is driven by a positive change in the structure of that state's economy. It is, therefore, a sustainable appreciation and the currency must not be considered overvalued. Sometimes, though, it is unclear why currencies move the way they do or are stuck at a specific ER. Some have developed, therefore, a 'psychological theory' of ER fluctuations[21] that has to do with the sentiment of traders rather than the economic fundamentals of various states.

Political factors affect the value of currencies, especially when speculators assume the role of 'currency vigilantes'. Traders will sell a country's currency if they believe that political decisions that have nothing to do with the currency *per se* or the economy are likely to cause the devaluation of a state's currency. States are aware that traders judge their currency based on political risk. In 2018, for instance, when Kyber's leader decided to change the country's political system from a parliamentary democracy to a presidential system, amidst some public opposition, traders started en mass to sell that country's currency. Kyber's leader condemned the *shorting* of the currency, its speculative selling. He compared those shorting the kobank with terrorists who were using the currency as an economic weapon to discredit his country.[22]

2.5 STATE INTERVENTION IN THE CURRENCY MARKET: COOPERATION AND CONFLICT

States can be big players in the currency market when they intervene in it to influence the value of their currency. To make possible such intervention, the two states' CBs keep each other's currency as an asset in their FX reserves. Table 2.3 presents the simplified balance sheet of Kyber's CB that keeps Nesis' currency as an asset in its FX reserves.

Both CBs have concluded that a 4% IR is what is needed, in their respective economies, to maintain a stable inflation of around 2% while enjoying low unemployment. The two CBs communicate with each other. However,

---

[21] Nurske, *supra* note 6, at 118.

[22] Paraphrasing the statement of Turkey's leader Recep Tayyip Erdoğan. *See* Yeliz Candemir, *Turkey's Central Bank Announces New Measures to Boost Lira*, WSJ, Jan. 13, 2017.

Table 2.3   *Kyber's CB balance sheet*

Assets	Liabilities
Government bonds	Currency in circulation
Loans to private banks	Deposits of private banks
FX reserves (netmons, Nesis bonds)	
Assets – liabilities = capital	

each CB is solely responsible for making domestic policy. Each CB is free to change the domestic benchmark IR to achieve DEP goals – to keep the domestic economy developing at a sustainable growth rate. The manipulation of the IR to achieve DEP goals, though, affects the ER. In our two-state world, it has been proven, repeatedly, that states cannot change their IR without affecting their ER. It is an irrefutable fact that, given the freedom of capital, if one state increases its IR, so that it is higher relative to that of the other state, people will move their money to that state. The high demand for the currency of a country that offers a higher IR, in comparison with another country, helps its currency appreciate.

In the same vein, fluctuations of the ER of a state's currency in the FX market are reflected in the domestic IR, the DEP of that state. If, for instance, Nesis' companies happen to achieve a technological breakthrough, not available to Kyber, they will immediately become more valuable. People from Kyber should rush to buy the shares of these highly productive companies. As Kyberans flock to Nesis – exchanging their kobanks for netmons in order to buy stocks there – the netmon will appreciate. The high demand for the currency should, in turn, push Nesis' IRs up and increase the borrowing costs in that currency.

2.5.1   Cooperation: Why and How?

2.5.1.1 Simple intervention
The currency market is populated by a large number of traders that bet routinely on the appreciation or depreciation of currencies. At the same time, the two states have vowed not to let their currencies deviate significantly from the ₭1/ɯ1 ER. Both states can intervene in the FX market to ensure this *fixed* ER remains more or less unchanged.

When the kobank, for instance, depreciates significantly, more than 1%, versus the netmon, the CB of Kyber intervenes in the FX market to buy kobanks by selling netmons (Box 2.5). If it does not have enough netmons in its FX reserves to sell, it can borrow netmons from Nesis, through a *currency swap arrangement*, an agreement to borrow netmons from Nesis and pay it back in netmons at the same ER at a future date.

BOX 2.5 CB INTERVENES IN THE FX MARKET TO STOP DEPRECIATION

Threat: Currency depreciation → CB buys its currency by selling foreign currency → Currency scarcity → Currency appreciates

Nesis, whose currency has appreciated, can also intervene in the market by selling netmons to buy kobanks, creating an abundance of its currency and, thus, helping it depreciate (Box 2.6).

BOX 2.6 CB INTERVENES IN THE FX MARKET TO STOP APPRECIATION

Threat: Currency appreciation → CB prints its currency to buy foreign currency → Currency abundance → Currency depreciates

To increase their chances of success, the two CBs can coordinate a joint intervention in the FX market. The CB of Kyber buys kobanks (by selling netmons) and the CB of Nesis sells netmons by buying kobanks. Traders, taken aback by the zealous resolve of the two states to keep their mutually agreed fixed ER, should refrain from betting against it. These interventions in the FX market are not costless though. The CB of Nesis, which has to print more of its currency, conducts an expansionary DEP. The side-effect of an expansionary policy is inflation. The CB of Kyber, which has to buy its currency to prevent its depreciation, is pursuing a contractionary policy. This policy may lead to recession and deflation. To avoid these adverse repercussions, of their intervention in the FX market, on the domestic economy, the two CBs have decided to *sterilize*, offset their FX interventions with open market operations in the domestic bond market.

2.5.1.2 Intervention and sterilization

Kyber's CB, in order to sustain the value of the kobank, intervenes in the currency market to buy kobanks by selling the netmons it has accumulated in its FX reserves – a contractionary policy. The resulting scarcity of kobanks in the market prevents the currency's depreciation. At the same time, though, it reduces Kyber's MB. When Kyber's CB purchases kobanks, it removes them from circulation. The resulting scarcity of kobanks can have a deflationary effect on its economy – falling prices and increasing unemployment.

To offset this deflationary effect, Kyber's CB can sterilize the FX intervention by buying domestic government bonds. It buys those bonds by printing kobanks – switching now to an expansionary policy. The purpose of this *sterilization* operation is to ensure that the domestic economy is insulated from the FX intervention. This insulation, though, comes at the cost of wiping out some of the benefits of intervention. The expansionary policy, pursued for the purposes of sterilization, is likely to lower IRs, creating new pressure for the kobank to depreciate. Thus, Kyber's CB may have to intervene in the market multiple times to be able to hold up the currency's value. As long as the CB has enough netmons in its FX reserves, it can continue to intervene and neutralize that intervention to the extent that it suits its purposes (Box 2.7).

BOX 2.7   CB INTERVENES IN THE FX MARKET TO STOP DEPRECIATION: COMPLICATIONS

Threat: Currency **depreciation** → CB buys its currency by selling foreign currency → Domestic currency scarcity → Currency **appreciates**, but deflation risk

→ Prevent deflation by sterilization* → Currency abundance → **Depreciation** → **Repeat** intervention and sterilization

*Print currency to buy bonds.

Nesis, whose currency is appreciating, can also intervene in the market. Nesis' CB can intervene in the market to prevent the appreciation of its currency by selling netmons and buying kobanks. The printing of netmons, an expansionary policy, creates an abundance of them, preventing the currency from appreciating. Such an expansionary policy, though, generates risks of undesirable inflation. To offset the expansionary effect of its intervention in the currency market, Nesis' CB can, subsequently, switch to a contractionary policy by selling government bonds. The sale of government bonds helps withdraw liquidity from the economy and, thus, neutralize the inflationary impact of intervention in the FX market. Ironically, this contractionary DEP will undermine the expansionary foreign policy agenda pursued by the initial intervention in the currency market (Box 2.8).

BOX 2.8 CB INTERVENES IN THE FX MARKET TO STOP APPRECIATION: COMPLICATIONS

Threat: Currency **appreciation** → CB sells its currency by buying foreign currency → Domestic currency abundance → Currency **depreciates**, but inflation risk

→ Prevent inflation by sterilization* → Currency scarcity → **Appreciation** → **Repeat** intervention and sterilization

*Sell bonds to buy currency.

As we will see below in more detail, states are often confronted with the impossible trinity (Fig. 2.2). If their FEP is oriented toward maintaining a fixed ER, they will have difficulty pursuing an autonomous DEP. As a rule of thumb, when a country has a BOP deficit, its currency has to depreciate; when it runs a BOP surplus, its currency has to appreciate. If the deficit country and the surplus country want to keep the ER between their currencies fixed, they must intervene in the FX market to buy/sell their currencies, as needed, to achieve the mutually desirable fixed rate. These interventions, unless they are somehow sterilized, will have repercussions for domestic liquidity and, consequently, the domestic economy of states. If states are unwilling to accept those repercussions (deflation and unemployment in deficit countries, and inflation in surplus countries), they will not be able to maintain a fixed ER between their currencies. In general, when states have to choose between upholding a fixed ER and freedom to conduct the DEP of their choice, they opt for economic autonomy and let their ER fluctuate.[23]

2.5.2 Conflict: Competitive Devaluation

As we have seen above, Kyber is concerned about its CA deficit. Recognizing that borrowing is not a long-term strategy, it wants to increase its exports. Therefore, its CB adopts an expansionary policy by decreasing the benchmark IR from 4 to 3% (Box 2.9).

---

[23] Thomas Oatley, *International Political Economy* 223–4 (2012).

> ## BOX 2.9   HOW TO BOOST A STATE'S EXPORTS
>
> **Goal**: Increase exports by depreciating currency
>
> **Method**: CB decreases benchmark IR
>
> **Result**: Outflows of capital → Currency depreciates → Exports up

Decreasing the IR is expected to encourage companies to borrow to expand their presence in foreign markets. The decrease in the IR also leads to the outflow of capital that goes to Nesis, which offers a 4% IR (Box 2.9). There is no reason for investors to stay in Kyber when they can reap higher returns by putting their money in Nesis. The outflow of capital causes Kyber's currency, the kobank, to depreciate. Now ₭1 buys only ω0.5. The depreciation of the currency is good for Kyber, though. People feel poorer and, thus, do not buy as many imported goods as they did before. They prefer to buy domestic goods, powering up domestic industries. The depreciation of the currency also gives a boost to exporters (Box 2.9). Kyber's currency depreciation means that the netmon has appreciated. Now ω1 buys ₭2. Given the appreciation of their currency, people in Nesis feel richer. They buy Kyber goods and opt for vacations there. As a result, Kyber's CA deficit has started to shrink.

There are downsides to Kyber's engineered depreciation, though. Those in Kyber who import raw materials and other goods from Nesis are irate that they have to pay more for imports. Consumers also feel poorer. If they choose to buy imports, despite their now weakened currency, they will fuel inflation. The weakening currency makes domestic assets look cheaper, enticing foreigners to buy Kyber industries and properties. Despite these drawbacks, Kyber is content that its depreciating currency is helping to revive its export industry. At the same time, though, it is fearful that the kobank's depreciation may go too far. It is one thing for a currency to depreciate. It is quite another when it weakens to an extent that it completely loses its value. The rapid depreciation of a currency may produce a 'flight psychology' among foreign and domestic capital owners, who may fear that their savings in that currency are to evaporate.[24] If such flight psychology becomes entrenched, even a subsequent drastic increase in the IR is unlikely to convince capitalists to come back.[25]

The decision of Kyber to cut its IR has an impact on Nesis. Nesis is unhappy as the ensuing appreciation of its currency has dented its exports. Kyber's citizens buy fewer Nesis goods, which now, with their weak currency, seem

---

[24]   Nurske, *supra* note 6, at 163.
[25]   *Id.*

expensive to them. The bright spot is that as its currency has appreciated, businesses that import raw materials now pay half the price for these materials. Consumers are happier with an appreciating currency because they can buy foreign goods and afford cheap vacations abroad. Despite these advantages, the overall effect on the economy is negative. Nesis views its export sector as an engine of growth. It wants, therefore, to return to the previous ₦1/ա1 ER.

Nesis is enraged that Kyber reduced its IR, triggering the depreciation of its currency and boosting its exports. It protests against Kyber's policy and calls Kyber a 'currency manipulator'. Kyber, though, argues that it is acting like a responsible sovereign state. A hallmark of sovereignty is DEP autonomy. States have the freedom to change their IR, as needed, to calibrate their economy. The depreciation of its currency, Kyber argues, is simply an unintended consequence of its pursuing an autonomous DEP. Kyber refuses to change its domestic policy despite the impact on the FEP, the understanding it had with Nesis to maintain the fixed ER of ₦1/ա1.

Nesis retaliates. Its CB intervenes in the FX market to sabotage Kyber's strategy. It prints netmons, sells them and buys kobanks to stop the deprecia- tion of that currency. This tit-for-tat can continue *ad infinitum* as long as Nesis is eager to print netmons, thus stroking inflation, and Kyber is willing to do whatever it takes to keep a weak currency. Eventually, the two states must realize that engaging in currency conflict has too many unpredictable effects on their DEP. They may switch, therefore, to an overt trade war by imposing direct tariffs and quotas on imports. Imposing a tariff, a tax, on imported goods works just as well as currency depreciation. Eventually, the two states may even refuse to trade with each other and seek self-sufficiency.

2.6   THE IMPOSSIBLE TRINITY

The *Trilemma* or *impossible trinity* helps us conceptualize an economic reality: that the freedom of capital prevents states from simultaneously enjoying DEP autonomy and FEP stability through a fixed ER (Fig. 2.2).[26]

When capital is free to hop from state to state, a state can float its currency – let the market set the ER for its currency. A floating ER gives a state the freedom to use its DEP, for instance, the IR, to calibrate its economy. The state

---

[26]   Benjamin J. Cohen, *The Triad and the Unholy Trinity: Problems of International Monetary Cooperation* 245, at 260–3, in 'International Political Economy: Perspectives on Global Power and Wealth' (Jeffry A. Frieden and David A. Lake, eds, 2004). For an eye-opening analysis of the Trilemma, *see* Hélène Rey, *Dilemma not Trilemma: The Global Financial Cycle and Monetary Policy Independence*, Federal Reserve Bank of Kansas City Economic Policy Symposium 'Global Dimensions of Unconventional Monetary Policy', Aug. 22–24, 2013. *See also* Chapter 4, Section 4.2.

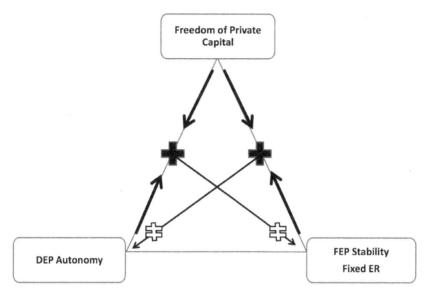

Figure 2.2   The Trilemma or impossible trinity

can decrease the IR during a recession to boost borrowing, investment and employment, or it can increase it to prevent accelerating inflation and asset bubbles. When a state does not have to manipulate its IR to support a fixed ER commitment, it can conduct an autonomous DEP according to the needs of its economy (Fig. 2.3).

States, though, have a 'fear of floating'. They tend to consider themselves sovereign and their currency the hallmark of their sovereignty. Therefore, they do not like it when markets are controlling the value of their currencies. States tend to tout their faith in free markets but, in practice, they do not really trust them to establish the right value for their currencies. They often point to historical evidence that indicates that the FX market is prone to disorder because of information imperfections. Such imperfections cause ERs to deviate, for prolonged periods, from their *fundamental* values, the values that truly reflect the performance of states' economies. Excessive volatility in the FX market, the result of rampant speculation about the 'right' value of currencies, generates uncertainty in international transactions and undercuts international trade. Large swings in the ER of a state's currency can abruptly change its status from a surplus state to a deficit state and vice versa.

Because of this 'fear of floating', states often decide to fix their ER. A fixed ER is good for international transactions and trade but deprives them of the freedom to conduct a DEP that fits their needs (Fig. 2.4). If speculators, for

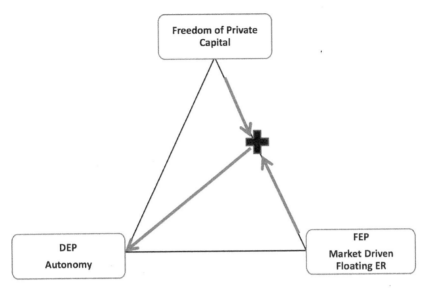

Figure 2.3   DEP + floating ER

instance, bet that a state's fixed ER cannot be maintained and its currency has to depreciate, they will sell that currency. If that state wishes to keep the fixed ER, it will have to buy back the currency that speculators are selling, shrinking its MB. It will also have to increase its IR to attract capital back. And it will have to do all this for the sole purpose of averting the depreciation of its currency. This type of contractionary DEP, pursued solely for serving an FEP agenda, could be bad for the domestic economy, especially if that economy is flirting with recession.

Overall, when states are concerned with internal stability (inflation or unemployment), they tend to pay more attention to their DEP. When they are more worried about their BOP imbalances, they cater more to their FEP and use the ER as a tool of economic policy. States can achieve some DEP autonomy while maintaining a fixed ER by imposing restrictions on capital movements. The chaotic feedback loop between the ER and the IR has to do with the freedom of capital – that capital can skip from state to state chasing the highest yields available. As we will see in Chapter 4, many states have adopted capital controls to secure some DEP independence and a more stable ER. In fact, certain states have been able to conduct a semi-autonomous DEP by using capital controls as a defense mechanism against the unpredictable movements of capital.

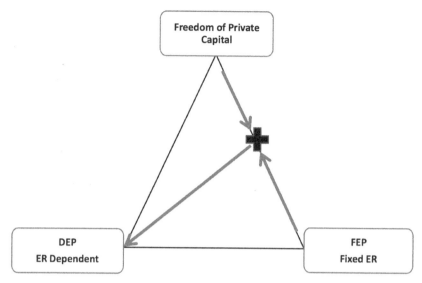

Figure 2.4   DEP + fixed ER

2.7   EXCHANGE RATE REGIMES

2.7.1   Fixed Exchange Rate Regimes

Based on the impossible trinity analyzed above, Kyber and Nesis have a decision to make. If they continue with the fixed ER of ⊬l/ɯ1, they will have to sacrifice their DEP autonomy (Fig. 2.4). DEP autonomy is cherished by these states because they wish to keep their economies growing at a sustainable rate. Fixing the ER at a specific rate, the so-called *hard peg*, also seems to contradict those states' endorsement of free markets. Adopting a fixed ER is an admission that a state can intervene in the market to fix its ER at a level it sees fit. An alternative to a hard peg is a *soft peg*, establishing a fixed ER *range* between two currencies and allowing the ER to fluctuate within that range.

2.7.2   Floating Exchange Rate Regime

If the two states decide to let their ER fluctuate based on the supply and demand dynamics for their currencies in the market, they can maintain their DEP autonomy (Fig. 2.3). The problem with a floating ER is that it generates uncertainty. States tend to see themselves as sovereign entities. Therefore, they dislike the unpredictability that markets bring when they value their currencies.

Large and abrupt swings in the ERs, brought by the free markets, can cause unexpected BOP imbalances that states could have a hard time correcting.

2.7.3 Managed Float Exchange Rate Regime

An alternative, to the extremes of fixed ER and floating ER, is the 'managed float', called by FX traders a 'dirty float'. Under a managed float regime, the CB does not, at least vocally, target a specific ER. However, it leaves open the door to intervene in the market when it determines that such intervention is necessary.[27] Kyber and Nesis can let their ER float based on the whims of the market. At the same time, though, they can declare they are ready to intervene in that market when the ER deviates substantially from the right ER as defined by them based on calculations that they may disclose, or not disclose, to the market.

Restrictions on the freedom of capital will probably be needed in this case when the managed float becomes unmanageable owing to rampant speculation in the FX market. Well-heeled traders have engaged multiple times in a battle of wills with governments that wish to keep a managed float. The unrelenting shorting of a currency by rich speculators has damaged the economies of many states. When wealthy private actors are bent on weakening a currency, capital controls, such as restrictions on the availability of currency for speculative purposes, could help preserve some DEP autonomy and some FEP stability.

2.7.4 Managed Float, Restricted Freedom of Capital and Precautionary FX Reserves

Many states are incapable of dealing with the impossible trinity even when they adopt capital controls. This is so particularly when market forces push strongly for the steep depreciation of their currency. An unpredictable event that shakes people's faith in the stability of a state can trigger a stampede of capital from that state. When capital rushes for the exits, almost all of a state's MB, close to M2, could be converted into foreign money, leading to the collapse of domestic currency.

A strategy that may help prevent such collapse is the *ex-ante* accumulation of FX reserves by a state. Such FX reserves, that a state accumulates and is ready to sell to stop the depreciation of its currency, act as a war chest safeguarding the external value of its currency (Fig. 2.5). A state that fears that markets may oversell its currency can prevent such overselling, at least

---

[27] *See* Atish R. Ghosh et al., *Exchange Rate Management and Crisis Susceptibility: A Reassessment*, at 3, IMF Working Paper WP/14/11, Jan. 2014.

temporarily, by keeping large, precautionary FX reserves, currencies of states that traders will probably buy when they sell off its currency. If Kyber, in our example, has accumulated large FX reserves, netmons, that it is willing to sell to buy back its currency, it can avert a massive depreciation of its currency for as long as its supply of netmons lasts.

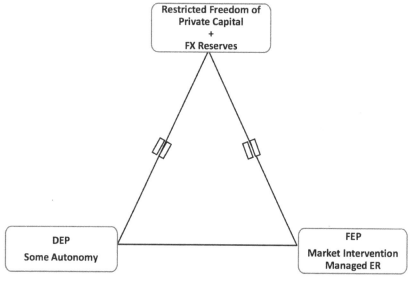

Figure 2.5   A possible trinity

Holding FX reserves insures a state against runs on its currency. A CB that has large FX reserves can provide foreign currency liquidity to domestic residents by acting as a *lender of last resort* in that foreign currency. Holding FX reserves can stop currency attacks in their tracks. Traders should stop betting against a state's currency when they know that the state is ready to use its reserves to buy its currency back, nipping currency attacks in the bud. However, maintaining FX reserves is not risk-free. Countries with large FX reserves face losses when the currencies they have accumulated to protect themselves against currency attacks depreciate and lose their value.

Because the accumulation of FX reserves is not risk-free, an effort has been made to determine the optimal amount of FX reserves that states need. Figure 4.1, in Chapter 4, summarizes commonsense guidelines for the accumulation of FX reserves that are rarely adhered to when states fret over the debauchment of their currency. States, when they can afford it, tend to be avid collectors of currencies of powerful states or precious materials, such as gold, above and beyond what these guidelines suggest. This manic collection is motivated by a primal fear. States hoard the currencies they believe are unlikely to lose their value and will be useful to them when they are under pressure from unpredictable events that random fate or other states inflict on them.

Precautionary FX reserves can increase the flexibility of a state but, in most cases, FX reserves will not be enough, by themselves, to secure a state's financial frontiers. As we will see in Chapter 4, most states do not have enough FX reserves to defend themselves if all their MS, close to M2, is eager to cross the border. Some states may have cooperative arrangements with other states that might help them fend off currency attacks. In the absence of hefty FX reserves and cooperative arrangements, only draconian capital controls can help safeguard a state. These controls come at the expense of private freedom, though.

A question we address in subsequent chapters is whether a state that achieves FEP stability by the close management of its ER and control of capital can be accused of manipulating its currency to achieve a competitive export advantage at the expense of other states. As we will see in Chapter 4, some have claimed that a protracted large-scale intervention in the FX market to maintain a fixed ER, for the purposes of achieving a CA surplus, should be considered currency manipulation. On the other hand, many states, throughout their history, have intervened in the currency market either directly or stealthily by altering their IR or the amount of liquidity they make available in their currency.

PART II

Economic strategies of states

3.　The United States as the global sovereign

3.1　THE PYRAMID OF STATES

3.1.1　The Global Sovereign

The UN Charter, the constitution of the post-World War II global order, is based on the sovereign equality of states.[1] Sovereign equality is the means through which weak states defend themselves, in the court of public opinion, against aggressions inflicted on them by dominant states. Because, despite what the UN Charter says, in the real world, states are far from equal. Many states are economically and militarily disadvantaged in comparison with other states. And this *de facto* feebleness cannot be remedied by simply calling them 'equal' to powerful states. Sovereign equality, though, still haunts our world as its myth system,[2] a system that empowers the weak to face off with the strong.

To be really sovereign, a state must be independent from other states in controlling a portion of the globe, its territory. Independence means the right to exercise, in that territory, the functions of state to the exclusion of any other state.[3] Making economic policy is one of the fundamental functions of a state. Not many states can claim they are independent in making that policy. In fact, most states' economic policies depend on the policy of the global sovereign, the United States. Some states that vie to become sovereign strive, therefore, to achieve with their currency what the United States has accomplished with the

---

[1]　Art. 2(1) of the UN Charter states that the United Nations is based on 'the principle of the sovereign equality' of its member states. Because they are sovereign equals, states must refrain 'from the threat or use of force against the territorial integrity or political independence of any state'. *See* art. 2(4), Charter of the United Nations and Statute of the International Court of Justice, June 26, 1945.

[2]　On myth systems, *see* W. Michael Reisman, *The Quest for World Order and Human Dignity in the Twenty-First Century: Constitutive Process and Individual Commitment* 93 (2012). *See also* Joseph Campbell, *The Power of Myth* (1991).

[3]　*Island of Palmas Case* (Netherlands, USA), II RIAA 829, at 838, Apr. 4, 1928. *See also* Rosa Lastra, *International Financial and Monetary Law* 1.29–1.55 (2015).

dollar: establish it as a universal means of exchange for trade and investment and a universal store of value.

Establishing a currency as the world's reserve currency – widely accepted, sought after and traded – is the epitome of a country's global preeminence.[4] The United States issues the *predominant reserve* currency. It has managed to cultivate a belief in other states and private actors that its currency, no matter the misfortunes that may fall upon our world, and unlike other paper currencies, stands the least chance of losing value. States believe that, in case of another world war, the United States, because of its military superiority, would likely win that war and that its currency would survive and remain the global reserve currency. Sovereignty is inextricably linked with military might, and military might is the result of wealth. The United States has accumulated substantial wealth that serves it well in asserting its sovereignty. Sovereignty, as we will see below, makes the United States the ultimate arbiter on where private capital is invested. The United States can inundate or starve other states of capital by simply tweaking its interest rate.

We adopt, in this study, a functional definition of sovereignty. It is the power of a state to prevent the encroachment on its autonomy by other states. To simplify matters we can divide sovereignty into internal sovereignty, the power of a state to make DEP independently from other states, and external sovereignty, the power of a state to make FEP without consulting with other states. As we saw in Chapter 2, because of the Trilemma, when capital is free, most states cannot achieve both an independent DEP and a stable FEP. Real sovereigns are states that conduct a DEP that fits their own needs. They then utilize that DEP to accomplish their FEP objectives.

Traits of sovereign states include: deep and liquid capital markets open to residents, foreigners and other states to participate freely in them, and the rule of law based on the sanctity of property and contracts. Free markets and the protection of property build trust that the sovereign is a safe haven, a place where other states and private actors can safeguard their assets without fearing expropriation. The United States has buttressed its sovereignty by creating public institutions and nurturing private financial organizations that have attained global legitimacy as unbiased umpires in financial affairs. These organizations include, as we will see below, credit rating agencies and global payment societies.

The prime reserve currency today is the US dollar. The bulk of international transactions are denominated and settled in dollars, and the populations of many states, and even states themselves, accumulate dollars. States collect

---

[4]   Arvind Subramanian, *Eclipse: Living in the Shadow of China's Economic Dominance* 35 (2011).

dollars for their FX reserves, more than any other currency, because they know that dollars are widely accepted internationally and likely to be useful to them when they face crises. The dollar accounts for 88% of global currency transactions[5] and more than 60% of states' FX reserves.[6] The 'global banking system runs on dollars'[7] since a huge amount of world debt, $9.7 trillion, is denominated in dollars.[8] It is the imperialism of the dollar that has elevated the status of the United States to that of the global sovereign.

The euro, the Swiss franc, sterling (UK), the yen (Japan) and the yuan (China) are considered reserve currencies since they exert influence beyond their borders. These currencies are less popular than the dollar, but they are still used by other countries as part of their FX reserves and by private actors to settle transactions. A less developed country, for instance, will keep in its FX reserves mostly dollars but also some euros, Swiss francs, yens and yuans. What makes these currencies reserve currencies is that they are issued by industrialized countries that have stable political systems and relatively advanced financial markets. Despite their status as reserve currencies, these currencies lag far behind the dollar and are unlikely to attain any time soon the status of the world's ultimate reserve currency. They have remained parochial currencies rarely used much beyond their immediate region. The financial markets of states that issue these currencies are not as deep and liquid as the US markets. The yuan, in particular, which has recently gained the status of reserve currency, is facing a tough road to predominance. This is because market participants still fret over China's semi-open markets and doubt its readiness to uphold the sanctity of property and contracts. Many reserve currencies are light years behind the dollar because they are issued by states that are middle powers uninterested in achieving the military might of the United States. The dollar is the world's chief reserve currency because the United States is still the world's only superpower. The United States is eager to maintain this superiority by spending lavishly on military technology. Lesser powers, including Japan, Saudi Arabia and European states, are allegiant to the United States because they are dependent on it for their security. The fact that the world's most vital commodity, oil, is priced in dollars has much to do with the US military dominance and the valuable security guarantees it showers

---

[5]   BIS, Triennial Central Bank Survey: Foreign Exchange Turnover in April 2016, at 3, Sept. 2016.

[6]   Claudio Borio, *More Pluralism, More Stability?*, at 2, Presentation at the Seventh High-Level SNB-IMF Conference on the International Monetary System, May 10, 2016.

[7]   Hyun Song Shin, *Global Liquidity and Procyclicality*, at 6, World Bank Conference 'The State of Economics, The State of the World', June 8, 2016.

[8]   *Id.* at 14.

upon oil-producing states, including Saudi Arabia, the swing producer in the oil market (Box 3.1).

BOX 3.1   THE PETRODOLLAR

For a state to be a *swing producer* in a commodity it must: (1) control the majority of global deposits in that commodity; and (2) have large spare production capacity. A swing producer is able to swiftly increase/decrease the supply of a commodity, at minimal additional cost to itself, giving it tremendous clout in pricing that commodity. Saudi Arabia's clout in the oil market has to do with its abundant spare capacity of oil. In 2018, it could produce 12 million barrels per day and could open/close its taps overnight, if needed, to adjust prices to its benefit. Its flexibility as a producer made it much more agile than the US oil giants that relied on offshore oil-drilling. US shale producers, similarly, needed several months of lead time to change their output to respond to swings in demand.

In the spring of 2018, four democratic senators asked US President Trump to leverage his personal relationship with Saudi Crown Prince Mohammed bin Salman to urge Saudi Arabia to use its swing capacity to increase world oil supplies before the start of the US summer driving season. In the meantime, a strong dollar, in combination with close to an $80 per barrel oil price, was wreaking havoc in many oil-dependent countries in Southeast Asia, Latin America and Africa. Since oil is priced in dollars, the strengthening of the dollar meant that other countries needed more units of their currency to buy oil. In Brazil, gasoline prices were up by 28% while the Brazilian real had fallen by 11% against the dollar. This prompted a crippling strike by truck drivers which ended with the intervention of the military. In Sudan high oil prices brought weeks of long overnight lines at gasoline stations while the government was scrambling to pay for fuel imports.

Source: Alison Sider and Georgi Kantchev, *Shale Surges, But Oil Market Power Swings Back to Saudis*, WSJ, May 28, 2018; Paulo Trevisani and Tom Fairless, *Steep Oil and Strong Dollar Make Toxic Brew for Global Economies*, WSJ, June 17, 2018.

Reserve-currency-issuing states, the core states, are, in terms of hierarchy, below the sovereign state (Fig. 3.1). Peripheral non-reserve-currency-issuing states are further down the pyramid. Given that global trade is conducted in reserve currencies, peripheral states are under constant pressure to convert their currencies into those currencies. Because of this pressure, they are avid accumulators of foreign exchange, especially dollars. Such accumulation makes them resilient and helps them avoid the risk of being excluded from the global markets (Fig. 3.1). Moreover, large FX reserves function as an insurance against currency attacks. As we have seen in Chapter 2, states with large reserves can intervene in the market to support their currency when it is under speculative attack. To collect the FX they need, states try to maintain trade surpluses. Not all states can keep such surpluses on a constant basis though. Fragile states, states with CA deficits, have scant FX reserves (Fig. 3.1). This, in combination with porous capital controls, makes it difficult for them to defend their economic borders. Their lack of control over their economy is often a source of political instability.

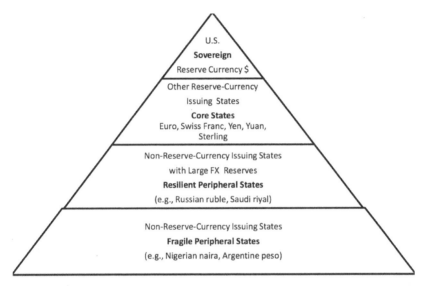

Figure 3.1   The pyramid of states

3.1.2   Privilege, Responsibility and Risks

3.1.2.1   The risk-free US debt
One of the privileges of the sovereign state is that, by simply managing its own economy, it has the capacity to disrupt the economic policies of other states. As a US Treasury secretary noted in 1971, the 'dollar is our currency, but it's your problem'.[9] The bond market of the sovereign showcases its global clout. The global sovereign sells debt in its own currency at auctions and does not have to enter into specific contracts with private creditors each time it issues

---

[9]   Statement of the US Treasury Secretary John Connally at the G-10 summit in Rome. On the G-7 and G-10 summits in the 1970s, *see* Chapter 9.

debt. Its debt is information-insensitive or immune to adverse selection problems. Investors simply do not care to scrutinize the specific terms of a bond issued by the sovereign. They know it is highly unlikely that the sovereign would default on its debt. The opposite is true for the debt of peripheral states. The bonds issued by them are much more detailed IOU instruments usually drafted by large law firms. They are sold by investment banks to interested investors rather than through public auctions.[10]

Many capital owners are eager to invest in the risk-free debt of the United States and, by the same token, in the debt of all reserve-currency issuing states. The enormous appetite for risk-free debt makes it easy for these states to finance themselves. In 2012, the global medium- to long-term government debt market was $40 trillion. Out of this, only 1.4% (about $600 billion) consisted of foreign-currency-denominated debt issued by peripheral states. The debt issued by core states, under their domestic laws, amounted to 83.2% of this $40 trillion. Most of this debt was issued by the United States, Japan and core European states.[11] It is true that almost all states can create a domestic market for their debt by requiring domestic investors, such as banks or public pension funds, to hold such debt. Yet not many states can create a global market for their debt, simply because they cannot make it attractive, 'safe-enough', for foreigners to hold.[12]

The role of the dollar as the predominant reserve currency forces the CBs of peripheral states to hold dollars or US bonds, the so-called Treasuries, in their FX reserves. The debt issued by the sovereign is the world's safest asset. The United States issues large quantities of debt and the US Treasuries market is the deepest and most liquid market in the world. In fact, nothing matches that market 'in size, liquidity, and freedom from risk'.[13] The US short-term government bonds (Treasury bills or T-bills) are considered the most money-like asset, an asset as liquid as cash. Because T-bills are highly liquid, they are the safest sort of collateral. Collateral is a borrower's pledge of a specific asset (such as property, jewelry, stocks or government bonds) to a lender to ensure him she will pay him back. Borrowers who can pledge T-bills as collateral are likely to find many eager lenders. The world runs on dollars and the global credit markets run on T-bills, the asset most sought after by lenders as the safest sort of collateral. As we will see below, during the 2008 financial crisis, the global credit markets ceased to function because of the low availability of

---

[10]   Anna Gelpern and Mitu Gulati, *The Wonder-Clause*, at 7, Georgetown Law Faculty Publications, 2013.

[11]   *Id.* at 6.

[12]   *Id.* at 8.

[13]   Alan Greenspan, *The Age of Turbulence: Adventures in a New World* 214 (2007).

T-bills. The scarcity of T-bills, which banks use as collateral for borrowing from each other, impaired the functionality of the interbank lending market.[14]

3.1.2.2 Exorbitant privilege and responsibility

Some have called the ability of the United States to borrow in its own currency the 'exorbitant privilege'. The United States can afford to borrow, while avoiding the debtor stigma, because it pays its creditors with the currency it prints – the dollar. This is a privilege that can be easily forfeited, though, if the United States mismanages the dollar. To give an example: after World War II, the dollar was indisputably the world's prime reserve currency. When a dollar scarcity threatened global growth, the United States opened its borders to imports from European states and Japan. This openness helped these states grow. Its high imports from other states made it possible for the United States to increase the global supply of dollars and solidify its status as global economic superpower. It transformed it also from a surplus state into a deficit state.

The United States ended up supplying the world with too many dollars by running recurrent and ever larger deficits. The ensuing 'dollar glut' created inflationary conditions worldwide and dented the world's faith in the dollar. Incessant dollar printing started to look like a weakness and undermined confidence in the ability of the United States to prudently manage its currency and the global economic system. Without adept handling, the dollar risked losing its status as the ultimate reserve currency. The United States eventually realized that it could not afford to inundate the world with dollars. It had to skillfully administer its currency to avoid both dollar gluts and dollar shortages. A way to supply the world with dollars is to run trade deficits, paying, for instance, for Chinese and European imports with newly minted dollars. Another way is debt – the T-bills; the world is eager to invest in them because they are the safest assets around.

Managing the dollar presents further difficulties because the currency has escaped US financial frontiers. Eurodollars are the dollars that circulate beyond the borders of the United States.[15] In 2015, the size of the eurodollar market was estimated to be $9 trillion and it was expected to reach $20–40 trillion by 2030.[16] During the 2008 crisis, the eurodollar credit market ceased to function because foreign private banks, which held eurodollar deposits, did not have enough dollars in their reserves to meet the huge demand for the US cur-

---

[14]   *See infra* Section 3.3.1.
[15]   These dollars circulated in Europe first. This is why they are called eurodollars.
[16]   *The Sticky Superpower*, Special Report: The World Economy, Economist, Oct. 3, 2015.

rency. The Federal Reserve System, the CB of the United States, therefore, had to supply not only domestic private banks but also foreign CBs with dollars.

3.1.2.3 Banker of the world

The status of the United States as the global sovereign provides it with other benefits. Since the 1950s, the United States has enjoyed a return on its external assets – its investments abroad – that is substantially higher than what foreign states receive by investing in US liabilities, the Treasuries. The United States has been acting as the banker of the world.[17] It borrows money from states that are willing to provide credit to it (e.g. China and the Gulf states) at low IRs because its debt is the world's safest asset. It subsequently uses this borrowed money to invest abroad in higher-risk but also higher-return assets.[18]

Being a world's banker entails risks though. During a crisis, capital holders 'fly to safety'. They sell off other states' assets and buy dollars and dollar-denominated assets. During a panic, foreign assets are sold off at fire-sale prices, resulting in the deterioration of the US foreign asset position. States that have invested in US assets, on the other hand, gain because the price of Treasuries, the global safe-haven asset, soars. The United States' 'exorbitant privilege' of reaping high returns from its assets abroad during normal times comes, inevitably, with an 'exorbitant duty': the onus of having to make payments, during bad times, to those who have insured themselves by investing in it.[19] According to an estimate, during the 2008 financial crisis, payments by the United States to the rest of the world amounted to 19% of US GDP.[20]

3.1.2.4 Dollar-denominated debt and global economic instability

The dependence of the world on the dollar is further associated with the function of that currency as the global financing currency.[21] In 2016, when the dollar strengthened by 1% it triggered a 0.5% decline in the quarterly growth rate of dollar-denominated cross-border debt. States and firms that obtain credit in dollars are affected by the ER of the dollar. When the currency of these states appreciates (versus the dollar) they are tempted to accumulate dollar debt. They run into trouble soon thereafter, when their currency depreci-

---

[17] Pierre-Olivier Gourinchas and Hélène Rey, *From World Banker to World Venture Capitalist: US External Adjustment and the Exorbitant Privilege* 11, at 25, in 'G7 Current Account Imbalances: Sustainability and Adjustment' (Richard H. Clarida ed., 2007).

[18] *Id.*

[19] *Id.* at 1.

[20] *Id.*

[21] Hyun Song Shin, *supra* note 7, at 9.

ates, making dollar-denominated debt much more difficult to repay.[22] Because the world 'runs on dollars', some have argued that it is the duty of the United States to act as the lender of last resort to the rest of the world. Since the United States prints the world's chief reserve currency, it is, in fact, the only entity that can act as the global unconditional and unlimited lender of last resort. As we will see below, the United States has taken over this role only partially, in a way that has benefitted a select number of states.

The United States' reluctance to act as the unconditional lender of last resort to all states causes financial instability. Many have argued that the stability of the international economic system is a global public good. All states, and their people, should benefit from the smooth functioning of such a system. A sovereign ready to supply the world with a stable economic system will be revered by many. Sovereigns benefit from the tributes, and the resulting legitimation they receive as providers of safety and security to others. Yet they do also benefit from some unpredictability and controlled instability. This unpredictability is embedded in the global economic system because of the pervasive ambiguity that exists about whether, during a crisis, the sovereign will be ready to assume, and for which states, the role of global lender last resort. Some unpredictability and some controlled, by the sovereign, instability is its way of rattling unruly allies and kneecapping, as needed, enemies.

3.1.3 The Control of Private Capital

3.1.3.1 The US risk-free rate

As we have seen in Chapter 1, the IR is a fundamental tool of economic policy. High IRs motivate people to save rather than consume. High IRs also discourage borrowing. Businesses are unlikely to borrow to expand their activities when IRs are high. In principle, when the Federal Reserve System (FRS), the United States' CB, increases the US benchmark IR, the US economy contracts. Usually the aim of a 'contractionary' or 'tight' monetary policy is to battle inflation. On the other hand, low IRs encourage people to consume more and save less as they conclude that it is not worth keeping their money in the bank. In addition, low IRs, encourage borrowing and risk-taking. When the IRs offered by banks are low, capital holders may be more willing to invest in the stock market in search for higher returns. The goal of this 'easy' or 'expansionary' policy, made possible by low IRs, is to boost growth.

The FRS calibrates the benchmark IR, the Federal Funds Rate (FFR), to regulate the US economy. In inflationary times, for instance in the late 1970s, the FRS increased the benchmark IR. During the Great Recession (2007–2009),

---

[22] *Id.* at 11.

on the other hand, it adopted a near-zero FFR to fight that recession and imminent deflation. Because the United States is the sovereign, its domestic IR policy inflicts externalities on other states. Those who own capital are keen on investing it in projects and places that produce high returns with minimal risk. Capital owners weigh the risks versus the returns of various investment opportunities. Investing in some countries is safer than in others. Countries where it is risky to invest offer higher returns than safe countries to compensate for the risk capital owners take by putting their money in them.

The United States, the global sovereign, is the world's safe haven. Capital flies to the United States during crises, because the US is seen as the country most likely to emerge the least scathed from them. Its attribute as safe haven enables the United States to set the global risk-free rate. Assuming that capital owners are free to invest anywhere in the world, they would prefer to invest in the United States, the world's safe haven for capital. This is so unless other countries are willing to offer them higher returns in terms of higher IRs or other benefits, such as tax breaks or lower labor costs, to offset the risk they take by investing in them. Typically, a country that wishes to attract capitalists to its economy sets its IRs higher than the US risk-free rate to entice them to invest in it. States have to re-evaluate their IR policy the moment the FRS decides to change the US benchmark IR.

That the United States indirectly ordains the IRs for the rest of states by setting its own IR, being the global IR maker, was evident in the years between 2008 and 2012 when the US IRs were near zero. Because they were unable to get a decent return on their capital in the United States, capital holders flew to other states in search for higher yields. However, this did not last for long. Rumors that the FRS was about to increase the FFR drained, subsequently, capital from these states. These abrupt and temporary transfusions of capital, based on the economic policy of the sovereign, are not always beneficial for other states. Sudden capital inflows can create asset bubbles (e.g. unsustainably high valuations in the stock and housing markets), leading subsequently to busts (sudden price drops in the markets) as capital is withdrawn. The hot money that crisscrosses national borders, based on the economic policy of the sovereign, is not the capital sought by many developing states. These states, instead, need steady inflows of capital that are invested in their long-term growth prospects.

The United States, the sovereign and a country with plentiful public and private capital, has been a major advocate of the idea that capital movements should be unrestricted. Capital owners should be able to move their wealth anywhere in the world irrespective of national borders. States should not, in principle, treat foreign capital holders any differently from domestic ones. If a US bank, for instance, wants to branch out into another country, it should not be subjected to more restrictive regulations than the domestic banks of that country. It comes as no surprise that countries with abundant capital – the United States and core states – are enthusiastic proponents of the freedom of movement of capital. Capital owners that have exhausted high-return investment opportunities in their home country can shop around the world for new opportunities to expand their own wealth and the sway of their country. Sometimes these investment opportunities arise because of laxer regulations in destination states. For instance, lax environment regulations, labor laws or a permissive tax code in a destination country can produce higher returns for capital owners. Globalization that took the world by storm in the 1990s and beyond had to do, in many cases, with these factors in destination countries.

The freedom of movement of capital sounds temptingly liberating. In practice, capital is free but where it ends up eventually depends on the US economic policy. By setting its own IR, the global risk-free rate, the United States resets the IRs for the rest of states (Box 3.2). A change in the US rate could swamp the world with capital or deplete it of it. Therefore, while, in principle, capital is free to move anywhere, the signal of where it goes is given by the sovereign state.

BOX 3.2 THE GLOBAL RISK-FREE IR IS THE BENCHMARK IR OF THE SOVEREIGN

The FRS Sets Global Risk-Free IR that impacts:

* Capital Flows
* Global Bond Market
* Global FX Market

During the Great Recession, when IRs in the United States were near zero, some complained that the FRS was engaging in 'financial repression'.[23] This was because the safest investments in the world, deposits with US banks and Treasuries, produced measly returns. Risk-averse capital owners had no other option but to get these meager returns by putting their money in the United

---

[23] Financial repression can be expressed in various ways including government control over the IRs, especially the imposition of negative real IRs, and restrictions on transfers of capital abroad. The cultivation of a captive domestic market for government debt, which is accomplished by asking financial firms and pension funds to hold such debt to meet their capital requirements, is also considered financial repression. *See generally* Carmen M. Reinhart and M. Belen Sbrancia, *The Liquidation of Government Debt*, NBER Working Paper 16893, Mar. 2011.

States. Higher returns were reserved for the more adventurous, those who could stand more risk by moving their capital to other states.

3.1.3.2 The US Government bond market

The US Treasury decides how much debt the United States must issue and for what duration. The US Treasuries, the US government bonds, have short-term (3- or 6-month), medium-term (2- or 5-year) and long-term (10- or 30-year) maturities. Capital owners consider holding US debt, and especially the short-term kind, risk-free. The 3- and 6-month US government bonds, the T-bills, are viewed as being as safe as cash with the added bonus that one receives interest by holding them.

The benchmark IR set by the FRS determines the IR the US government pays its creditors and it is used to price all other debt issued within its economy. US businesses and households that wish to borrow pay higher IRs than their government because they are more risky borrowers than it is. Likewise, foreign peripheral governments or foreign private actors who wish to borrow pay a higher IR than the US borrowing rate. Since US government bonds are some of the safest assets in the world,[24] private actors and peripheral states, when they issue debt, have to pay a risk premium on top of the risk-free rate that the US government pays. In other words, the IRs that the United States pays to those who hold its debt price the debt issued by all of the peripheral states (Box 3.2).

The US Treasury regulates the supply of US government bonds. As a rule, the more the US debt, the higher the IRs the United States pays to those who hold its debt. The supply of Treasuries is further regulated by the FRS, which may decide to intervene in the government bond market to buy or sell US bonds. As analyzed in Chapter 1, a CB's buying or selling its government's debt is one of the basic tools of economic policy. To deal with the Great Recession, for example, the FRS bought a large amount of Treasuries. In 2009 alone, it bought $300 billion worth of long-term US government bonds.[25] This purchase induced a scarcity of US bonds in the market. And that scarcity reduced the IRs that the United States had to pay on its debt.

Low IRs are good for debtors but bad for creditors. China, a large buyer of US debt for its FX reserves, was hurt by the low IRs offered on that debt. Moreover, the abundance of US dollars – the FRS had to issue dollars to buy the bonds – heightened inflation expectations around the world. In principle,

---

[24] As we will see below, the debt of some core states, such as Germany, is considered a safe asset, especially in the European region.

[25] Christopher J. Waller and Lowell R. Ricketts, *The Rise and (Eventual) Fall in the Fed's Balance Sheet*, Federal Reserve Bank of St Louis, Regional Economist, Jan. 2014.

when banks are flush with dollars they are eager to lend them to profit from them. But too much credit growth often causes inflation and asset bubbles followed by painful busts. During the Great Recession, foreign companies borrowed in dollars because the US IRs were much lower than the rates offered in their domestic economies. When United States economy rebounded and US IRs started to climb, these companies faced difficulties refinancing their debt.

In conclusion, how much debt the US Treasury issues and of what maturity and how the FRS deals with it (buying or selling government bonds) affects not only the US government bond market but also the bond markets of other states. It affects decisions that public actors and private players make about whether and when to issue debt and in which currency.

3.1.3.3 US intervention in the currency market

Depending on their economic circumstances and development needs, states may prefer a stronger (appreciating) or weaker (depreciating) currency versus other currencies. In tough economic times, when there is a looming global recession, states tend to engage in competitive devaluations, each country devaluing its currency to boost its exports. Countries can devalue their currencies by intervening in the FX market. In order to devalue its currency all a country needs to do is to sell its currency in the market by buying foreign currencies. How much currency it sells depends on how much depreciation it wants to achieve. Countries do keep in mind, however, that printing too much of their currency, in order to depreciate it, may eventually debauch it.

In the 1980s, the US Treasury and FRS intervened in the FX market to try to devalue the dollar by soliciting the reluctant participation of other states.[26] The United States has intervened in the FX market in other cases to accommodate the interests of other states. It helped, for instance, to stabilize the newly minted euro in 2000 by intervening in the currency market to support it. It put together a coalition of states that fended off the appreciation of the yen after the 2011 tsunami disaster in Japan. The US intervention helped stop the devaluation of currencies like the Mexican peso and the Brazilian real when speculators attacked them in the midst of economic crises. In general, US support for another country signals to the markets that speculation against that country's currency would be unfruitful. Similarly, the boycotting of a state, through the imposition of US economic sanctions, lends a helping hand to those who speculate against that state's currency. US economic sanctions against Russia in 2014 and Iran in 2010 did much to undermine those countries' currencies.

To date no private player has been willing to speculate aggressively against the dollar. While such speculation, the massive sell-off of dollars to buy some

---

[26] *See* Chapter 10.

other currency, has not happened yet, prudent policy-makers are right to be on the edge. A geopolitical shock that would signal the dethroning of the United States as the world's sovereign is not that far-fetched. Some argue that emerging powers, like China, will eventually antagonize the United States by selling all of the dollars and T-bills that they have amassed in their FX reserves in order to crush the dollar's value. While this is doubtful – China holds about $1 trillion of US debt,[27] the massive sell-off of which would hurt China first – the mere contemplation of such a risk is enough to jangle nerves.

Today, the US economic policy is not focused on ER targeting. Instead, the United States uses its IR and the bond market to strengthen or weaken its currency as needed. The FRS, for instance, can always buy Treasuries by creating dollars. The abundance of dollars helps cheapen the currency. On the other hand, selling Treasuries, by withdrawing dollars, creates dollar scarcity and makes the currency more expensive. Likewise, lowering the FFR should trigger dollar depreciation, but a higher FFR should produce dollar appreciation. In principle, capital owners should leave the United States for greener, albeit riskier, pastures when the US IRs are lower than the rates offered by other states and should come back to it when the US IRs are attractive in comparison with the IRs of other states. The United States has solved the Trilemma by insisting on the freedom of movement of capital, as this helps it achieve foreign policy objectives, and has used its DEP to trigger desirable changes in its ER and, consequently, the IRs/ERs of other states (*see* Fig. 2.3).

3.1.3.4 Extraterritorial reach of US private institutions

It is not only US public institutions, the Treasury and FRS which shape global economic conditions. Most of the big companies that run the global capital markets, by acting as intermediaries between capital owners and capital seekers, are located in the United States.[28] The same holds true with the credit rating agencies (CRAs),[29] the private companies that rate the creditworthiness not only of corporations but also of states. Three companies, 'The Big Three', dominate the credit-rating industry: Standard & Poor's and Moody's, both based in the United States, and Fitch, which has dual residence in the United States and the UK. The Big Three are the Nationally Recognized Statistical Rating Organizations in the United States. This means that they are relied upon to provide well-researched credit ratings that assist investors in making informed decisions about the risks involved in lending to various states.

---

[27] As of April 2019. *See* US Treasury, Major Foreign Holders of Treasury Securities, http://ticdata.treasury.gov.
[28] *See* Chapter 15.
[29] *Id.* Section 15.2.8.

Credit rating companies typically use the letters of the alphabet to designate the riskiness of various borrowers. An 'AAA' or 'AA' rating designates high-quality borrowers unlikely to default on their debt. An 'A' or a 'BBB' rating designates medium-quality borrowers. The bonds issued by high- to medium-quality borrowers are *investment-grade* bonds. Credit ratings such as 'BB', 'B' and 'CCC' are for low-quality borrowers likely to default on their debt. The bonds these borrowers issue are, therefore, non-investment-grade or *junk* bonds.

Institutional investors, like pension funds and insurance companies, the largest capital holders in the world,[30] typically have a mandate to invest only in investment-grade bonds. If any of 'The Big Three' downgrades a state's debt from investment-grade to junk, institutional investors will have to withdraw their capital from that state. This often means the withdrawal of millions, if not billions, of capital from the downgraded state. CRAs argue that their ratings are based on each state's economic fundamentals (Box 3.3). While this is in many cases true, the fact remains that three private companies, by rating the creditworthiness of states, carry tremendous influence over those states' economic destiny. To give an example, in 2016, everybody expected Turkey's government bonds to be downgraded to junk status by the CRAs, triggering a huge sell-off of these bonds – a $10 billion capital outflow from Turkey.[31]

BOX 3.3   WHO IS SOVEREIGN? THE VIEW OF THE CRAs

The factors that CRAs consider to evaluate states' creditworthiness provide insights into how markets distinguish between core states and peripheral states. These factors include:

- *The political environment of a state.* Debt repayment culture,* external and domestic security risks, legitimacy of institutions, social order, predictability of policy-making, perceived corruption, the rule of law and protection of property rights.
- *GDP, growth potential, fiscal assessment.* GDP per capita that reflects the tax base from which a state draws to repay debt; sustainable growth (i.e. no inflation or asset bubbles); diversified economy (dependence on a single cyclical industry for more than 20% of GDP makes a state look

---

[30]   *See*, e.g., OECD, Pension Markets in Focus 2017, at 11.
[31]   Isobel Finkel, *Turkey Faces Junk Status as Moody's Weighs Political Turmoil*, Bloomberg, Aug. 4, 2016.

vulnerable); the sources of financing of budget deficits (i.e. the debt burden of a state and how much domestic versus external debt it has).

- *External assessment. Status of currency* in international transactions (is the state's currency a reserve currency or, at least, an actively traded currency?); *external liquidity* (does the state have enough FX reserves** to meet private and public sector external obligations?); *external position* (is the state a net creditor or net debtor?).
- *Monetary assessment.* The ERR that guides FEP. A rigid FEP based on a *fixed* ERR and supported by heavy intervention in the FX market points to lack of DEP autonomy. On the contrary, a flexible FEP made possible by issuing a *reserve* currency or an *actively traded* currency points to substantial DEP autonomy. A *managed float* ERR supported by sporadic interventions in the FX market also provides some DEP autonomy. *Credibility of monetary policy* (e.g. does the CB strive for price stability? Does the CB have a long and established track record – more than 10 years of full independence and clear objectives?).

Notes: *CRAs have an uneasy relationship with countries that are serial defaulters or states whose governments tend to question the legitimacy of debt incurred by previous governments (owing to corruption or other issues). **CRAs look particularly into a state's *usable* FX reserves. Usable FX reserves are the most liquid reserves of states, for example foreign reserve currencies and gold.

Source: S&P Global Ratings, *Sovereign Rating Methodology*, Dec. 18, 2017; Arvind Subramanian, *Eclipse: Living in the Shadow of China's Economic Dominance* 60–1 (2011).

Companies that develop indexes tend to have an outsized impact on the economies of weak states. An index is a statistical device designed to measure the performance of stocks and bonds. For instance, the Dow Jones Industrial Average is an index designed to measure the performance of 30 well-established and financially stable US corporations that are representative of the US economy. The MSCI, a US private company, is in the business of putting together indexes to measure the performance of stock markets in various regions of the world. These indexes include: the MSCI World Index that measures the performance of stock markets of the developed world; the MSCI Emerging Markets Index that calculates the performance of stock markets of developing states; and the Frontier Markets Index that assesses the performance of equity markets of least developed states.

The inclusion or exclusion of the stock market of a state from an MSCI index can have a huge influence on its economy. Many investors that passively follow the MSCI indexes, for instance, often have the mandate to invest in developed states, because these are the safest places for capital, and to avoid emerging market states whose stock markets are much more risky and volatile. The decision of the MSCI to upgrade a state from emerging market to developed market, therefore, means the automatic flow of investors' money into that state. Conversely, the downgrading of a state from developed market to emerging market should trigger capital outflows from that state. And this happens just because the MSCI, a private company, decided to downgrade that state.

In 2016, China was eagerly anticipating its upgrade from emerging market to developed market. In order to convince the MSCI that it deserved that status, China had enacted a number of reforms and opened even further its capital markets to foreign investors. Unfortunately, the MSCI was not convinced that these reforms were enough to upgrade China and that country was still labeled an emerging market in 2016. During the same year, the MSCI upgraded Pakistan from frontier market to emerging market, citing the openness of its capital markets, and this triggered large capital inflows into that state.

The upgrades or downgrades of states by index companies are supposed to be based on the economic performance of states. Those who believe in statehood, though, are often taken aback when they realize that private companies, by merely creating indexes and deciding which states to include in what index, can trigger large capital inflows or outflows from states that like to call themselves sovereign. Index companies and the CRAs are obviously not the financial arms of the US government. At the same time, a state whose companies have the clout to rate the creditworthiness and, thus, *investability* of other states carries considerable weight in the global economy.

3.2 THE US ECONOMIC SYSTEM

3.2.1 Structure of the FRS

The FRS was established in 1914 as a response to a series of recurrent economic crises that had shaken peoples' faith in the stability of the financial system.[32] The FRS is supposed to be an independent CB immune to political pressure and private influence.[33] It is meant to work against market forces, when needed, to stabilize the economy[34] – responding to downturns with stimulus and to accelerating inflation with monetary tightening. It consists of a Board of Governors (BoG) and 12 Federal Reserve Banks (FRBs). The BoG has seven members appointed by the president and confirmed by the senate.

---

[32] Federal Reserve Act, 12 USC §221 et seq. The Federal Reserve Act was adopted, *inter alia*, 'to furnish an elastic currency' and to 'establish a more effective supervision of banking'.

[33] *See* James Forder, *'Independence' and the Founding of the Federal Reserve*, 50(3) Scottish Journal of Political Economy 297 (2003).

[34] Milton Friedman and Anna Jacobson Schwartz, *A Monetary History of the United States 1867–1960*, at 391 (1963).

The FRBs are hybrid institutions. They are structured as corporations[35] and function as regional CBs in their designated districts.[36] Private banks become members and owners of the FRB of their district by purchasing the shares issued by that FRB.[37]

Each FRB is managed by nine directors. Three directors (class A directors), who must be bankers, are appointed by the private banks, the members of each FRB. Another three directors (class B directors), who must represent the public, are appointed by the same private banks. The final three directors (class C directors) are appointed by the BoG by taking into consideration the interests of agriculture, commerce, industry, services, labor and consumers.[38] The BoG tries to ensure the fair representation of all interests in the FRBs. Undeniably, though, private banks have significant clout in the FRB of their district since they appoint six out of the nine directors at that FRB and own it as its share-holders. The ownership of the FRBs by private banks has led some to question the FRBs' independence.

The Federal Open Market Committee (FOMC) of the FRS is the decision-making body on monetary policy. The FOMC consists of 12 members: the seven members of the BoG, the president of the FRB of New York (FRBNY) and the presidents of four other FRBs who serve one-year terms on a rotating basis.[39] At the end of each FOMC meeting an announce-ment is made on whether the benchmark IR, the FFR – the rate at which banks lend to each other – has been raised, lowered or left unchanged. The FOMC assesses the future risks to the economy, for instance, whether higher inflation, lower productivity, trade disputes or other conflicts may affect the country's economic performance. The chair of FRS is the first among equals at the FOMC and the spokesperson of FRS.

The mandate of the FRS is to control inflation and achieve maximum employment.[40] This is a broad mandate that gives it leeway in policy-making. The FRS is an independent institution but does not take this for granted. Congress has threatened occasionally to rescind FRS' independence. The FRS' revenues consist of the income it receives from the securities it holds and the loans it makes to private banks. To safeguard its independence, the FRS does not receive any funding from the Treasury or Congress.

The FRS is supposed to be independent not only from the rest of the govern-ment but also from the banks it regulates. The FRS was developed, after all, to

---

[35]   12 USC §341.
[36]   12 USC §222–23.
[37]   12 USC §282. *See also* USC §501a.
[38]   12 USC §302–4.
[39]   12 USC §263.
[40]   12 USC §225a.

rein in the private banking interests[41] and to make sure that the financial system serves the public good. This is easier said than done. In 2014, there was much concern that the FRBNY, the FRB that holds a permanent seat at the FOMC, was compromised in its role as supervisor of big banks by failing to scrutinize their lending practices.[42] The Large Institution Supervision Coordinating Committee, established under the 2010 Dodd–Frank Act,[43] has taken over some of the supervision of private banks from the FRBs so as to reduce the conflicts of interests they face.

3.2.2   The FRS and the Control of Money

The banking system is central to the functioning of the US economy. Because banks 'borrow short and lend long' – there is maturity mismatch between their liabilities (deposits) and assets (the loans they make) – they are prone to bank runs. The United States has decided, therefore, to guarantee the deposits held in banks. The Federal Deposit Insurance Corporation (FDIC) provides insurance for up to $250 000 per depositor, per bank. The FDIC was established during the 1930s Great Depression. At the time, the only way to save the banking system from complete disaster was to guarantee the money deposited with both solvent and close-to-insolvency banks.

Another way to safeguard banks from bank runs is the RRR – namely how much money banks need to keep as reserves out of all of the money deposited with them. As analyzed in Chapter 1, the reserves banks are required to hold by law are called 'required reserves' (Fig. 1.3). As of January 17, 2019, the RRR for US private banks was: zero, for banks with deposits less than 16.3 million; 3% for banks with deposits between 16.3 and 124.2 million; and 10% for banks with deposits of more than 124.2 million.[44] The fact that banks are required to keep only a fraction of the money deposited with them and can lend the rest is the cornerstone of the fractional banking system. Fractional banking is the engine for money creation in the economy (Fig. 1.3). Banks are involved in asset transformation: they transform liquid, low-yield assets (short-term deposits) into less liquid, high-yield assets (long-term loans).

Banks can keep their reserves as deposits with the FRB of their district or hold them as physical currency in their vaults (Box 1.3). Banks borrow and lend to each other, as needed, to make sure that by the end of each business

---

[41]   Forder, *supra* note 33.

[42]   GAO, Large Bank Supervision: Improved Implementation of Federal Reserve Policies Could Help Mitigate Threats to Independence, GAO-18-118, Nov. 2017.

[43]   *See infra* Section 3.2.5.

[44]   BoG of FRS, Policy Tools, Reserve Requirements, https://www.federalreserve .gov.

day they meet the RRR. The IR that banks charge to lend to each other is the FFR. If, at the end of a business day, many banks cannot meet the RRR, the increasing demand for credit in the interbank lending market should trigger an increase in the FFR. A low FFR, on the other hand, indicates that the credit needs of banks are low. The FOMC sets the target for the FFR that, then, fluctuates based on the supply and demand for credit in the interbank lending market (Boxes 3.4 and 3.5).

BOX 3.4 THE IR AS A POLICY TOOL

- The FRS sets the *FFR*, the inter-bank lending rate
- The FRS lends to banks at *discount rate*, which is higher than the FFR
- The FRS pays an IR on reserves (IROR) that banks keep with it, which is lower than the FFR

The FRS uses the inflation rate to diagnose the health of the economy. It has determined that an annual inflation rate of around 2% is necessary to keep the economy functioning at a sustainable growth rate. This quantitative goal was adopted explicitly as a target at a 2012 FOMC meeting.[45] When inflation runs above 2%, it means that the economy is overheating and the FRS has to adopt contractionary policies to ensure that inflation remains under control. On the contrary, when inflation is below the 2% mark, it means that the economy may be entering recession and the FRS has to adopt expansionary policies to revive the economy (*see* Fig. 1.2). One way to calibrate the economy, to ensure that it grows at a sustainable rate, is the IR. As we mentioned, the FOMC sets the target for the FFR (Boxes 3.4 and 3.5). The target FFR, the rate at which banks lend to each other, is the benchmark for all IRs in the US economy.

BOX 3.5 TOOLS OF THE FRS

- FFR, discount rate, IROR
- RRR
- Open Market Operations

Another way to stimulate a sluggish economy is to offer discount loans to banks (Box 3.5). The FRS extends loans to banks hoping that they will use these loans to expand their lending. Discount loans can revive the economy

---

[45] FRS, Federal Reserve Issues FOMC Statement of Longer-run Goals and Policy Strategy, Press Release, Jan. 25, 2012.

only if banks are willing to use the FRS' *discount window*. The discount window functions as follows: the FRS sets the discount rate, the IR at which it is willing to provide credit to banks that is typically set above the FFR (Box 3.4), and banks decide whether to borrow from the FRS at that rate. The discount rate is an essential tool of economic policy during financial turmoil. When a crisis erupts, the interbank lending market may cease to function, as banks are suspicious that other banks may default and refuse to lend money to them. When the interbank credit market freezes, banks have no other option but to borrow from the FRS. The discount rate[46] is usually set 100 basis points (1%) above the FFR target[47] to encourage banks to use the interbank lending market first, before tapping the FRS discount window (Box 3.4). Healthy banks can borrow from the FRS at the discount rate but banks in trouble are charged an additional 0.5% above that rate.[48] The higher IR functions as a sort of penalty that troubled banks have to pay to borrow from the CB.

In addition to the required reserves, banks may be willing to hold excess reserves – reserves in excess of those required by law (*see* Box 1.3). High excess reserves mean that banks are anxious about the future. They are accumulating, therefore, excess reserves as an insurance against bad times, times when borrowers tend to default on their debt. The FRS can make monetary policy by exploiting banks' motives for holding excess reserves. If banks are awash with excess reserves, the FRS can reduce the RRR (Box 3.5). Such reduction should convince some banks to lend some of their excess reserves since, given the now reduced RRR, they are overloaded with cash. Conversely, when banks engage in risky behavior, the FRS can increase the RRR (Box 3.5). Banks that need to put more deposits aside as reserves, owing to the RRR hike, should refrain from aggressive lending. Most CBs, though, including the FRS, avoid making abrupt changes in the RRR. An unexpected increase in the RRR may shock some banks that would scramble for extra cash and this could cause economic contraction. A sudden reduction in the RRR may also send the wrong signal and unleash excessive lending.

The FRS, therefore, may abstain from tweaking the RRR. It may decide, instead, to alter the IR it pays banks that keep their reserves with it. By hiking the IR it offers on banks' reserves, the IR on reserves (IROR),[49] the FRS encourages them to maintain more reserves with it, pursuing, thus, a contractionary monetary policy (Boxes 3.4 and 3.5). Reducing the IROR, on the con-

---

[46]   In May 2019, the discount rate was 3%.

[47]   In May 2019, the FFR target range was 2–2.50%.

[48]   In May 2019, this rate was 3.50%.

[49]   12 USC §461(12). The FRS can further differentiate between two IRORs, the interest rate on required reserves and the interest rate on excess reserves, in order to fine-tune its monetary policy. *See* 12 CFR 204.10.

trary, should prompt banks to keep fewer reserves and lend the rest, expanding the economy. The IRs that the FRS pays on banks' reserves must be below the FFR (Box 3.4). Otherwise, banks will be incentivized to keep on holding their excess reserves rather than lending to each other.

Open market operations are the most flexible tool of monetary policy-making (Box 3.5). Open market operations directly affect the official liquidity. The FRS executes open market operations when it buys or sells government debt in the open market. In order to buy Treasuries, the FRS has to create dollars and this increases the MB (expansionary policy). If it sells Treasuries, on the other hand, it withdraws money from the economy (contractionary policy). Let us assume that the FRS is buying government bonds by creating dollars. This expansionary policy will be successful if the banks decide to lend the money the FRS prints. The FRS can certainly spew out any amount of dollars to bump up the MB, the official liquidity (*see* Box 1.5), but it has much less control over the MS, the private liquidity, as private banks decide whether to hoard as reserves or lend the newly printed dollars. During a recession, especially, the *transmission mechanism* (*see* Box 1.6) from the MB to the MS tends to function inefficiently because private banks may be reluctant to lend, even if the FRS is ready to create all the money they need for such lending.

The *money multiplier* measures the efficiency of the transmission mechanism (*see* Box 1.6) – the impact of a change in the MB on the MS. A money multiplier of 2.5% tells us that for a $1 increase in the MB, orchestrated by the FRS, the MS will increase by 2.5%. The money multiplier during the 1930s Great Depression fell from 6.5% in 1929 to 3.6% in 1933.[50] It was no wonder that the economy contracted during those years. The FRS can tinker with the MB and has the capacity to inject unlimited liquidity into the banking system. It has much less control, however, over the money multiplier – how banks and depositors react when it changes the MB.

The target FFR, the discount rate, the RRR, the IROR and open market operations are just the tools of monetary policy (Box 3.5). What influences markets most are the FRS' intentions, its grand strategy. The FRS' chairperson communicates that strategy to the public. Sometimes that communication is not crystal clear since the FRS, like other CBs, may decide to rely on surprise to move the economy in the direction that serves its objectives.[51]

---

[50]. David C. Wheelock, *Monetary Policy in the Great Depression: What the Fed Did, and Why*, at 17, Federal Reserve Bank of St Louis, Mar./Apr. 1992.

[51] CBs use 'indirect hints' or 'coded language' to state their policy intentions so as to retain 'plausible deniability' when the economy does not perform according to expectations. *See* Glenn D. Rudebusch and John C. Williams, *Revealing the Secrets of the Temple: The Value of Publishing Central Bank Interest Rate Projections* 247, at 248, in 'Asset Prices and Monetary Policy' (John Y. Campell et al., 2006). Some claim

The FRS has become, over time, more transparent about its goals and the tools it uses to accomplish them. On the 'Black Monday' of 1987, when the market suddenly collapsed, and after the 9/11, 2001 terrorist attacks, the FRS' message to the markets was loud and clear: it was willing to do whatever was necessary to save the financial system. Investors called this message the 'Greenspan put' after the FRS chairman, Alan Greenspan. It has encapsulated, since then, the belief that, if there is financial turmoil, the CB will step in to stem a descent into chaos. It is as if the FRS has provided market players with a *put option* – a financial instrument that protects those who hold it from losses during a market downturn. The belief that the FRS is ready to intervene in the markets, whenever needed, to curb losses thwarts market panics, but it also generates moral hazard and excessive risk-taking. Before the 2008 crisis, markets had faith that, when worse came to the worst, the FRS would be their lender of last resort. On the other hand, the FRS was not viewed as the right institution to gauge and deflate stock market bubbles by adopting preemptive contractionary policies.[52]

It takes time for monetary policy to have an effect on an economy. After the 2008 financial crisis, the FRS started to ease economic conditions aggressively. It reduced the FFR from 5.25% (September 2007) to almost zero (December 2008).[53] Despite this bold move and a \$4.4 trillion securities-buying program, the economy remained weak. The burst of the housing bubble, and ensuing mortgage defaults had generated large losses for many companies. Economic growth stalled as banks deleveraged and cut back lending and consumers cut down their spending to get rid of debt.

3.2.3 Management of Government Debt

The FRS is not the only institution that makes economic policy. The Treasury plays an equally pivotal role. As mentioned above, the FRS can boost the MB, the official liquidity, but it is incapable of forcing an increase in the MS. The MS expands only if private actors are willing to borrow the boosted MB. If

---

that CBs have an obligation to be secretive if secrecy boosts the effectiveness of their policy. *See* Daniel L. Thornton, *Monetary Policy Transparency: Transparent about What?*, Federal Reserve Bank of St Louis Working Paper 2002-028B, Sept. 2, 2003.

[52] Alan Greenspan, *Economic Volatility*, Remarks at the Symposium Sponsored by the Federal Reserve Bank of Kansas City, Aug. 30, 2002 ('We at the Federal Reserve considered a number of issues related to asset bubbles … [We concluded] it was very difficult to definitively identify a bubble until after the fact – that is, when its bursting confirmed its existence.').

[53] BoG of FRS, Effective Federal Funds Rate, retrieved from FRED, Federal Reserve Bank of St Louis, https://fred.stlouisfed.org.

private actors are not ready to borrow that official liquidity, because of their gloomy economic outlook, that liquidity will remain blocked in the banking system.[54] This is the moment when the Treasury steps in – as borrower of last resort – to borrow the blocked MB. It can do so by issuing debt. Since the private sector is reluctant to borrow, banks can make money by lending to their government. The banks' demand for government bonds should push bond prices up and yields down. Thus, the government can borrow cheaply to finance a fiscal deficit bound to be created as it tries to stimulate the economy.[55]

The government has a dual role, in other words: the FRS is the lender of last resort that provides credit to banks, when necessary, and to its own government. The Treasury is the borrower of last resort. The Treasury can borrow, as necessary, the MB created by the FRS in order to finance fiscal deficits, the purpose of which is to invigorate a sluggish economy. As the Treasury taxes less and spends more, the public should also eventually spend more and this should jump-start economic activity.

The US Treasury is privileged in comparison with regular countries' finance ministries. This is because the T-bills it issues (e.g. 1-, 3- and 6-month T-bills) are considered as safe as cash. Since investors view T-bills as equivalent to cash, when the Treasury issues them it creates money that directly expands the MB. During the 2007–2009 Great Recession, market participants invested in T-bills, despite their scant returns, because of the liquidity and safety they provided. In an economy, where short-term government debt is treated as equivalent to cash, the CB is incapacitated from making monetary policy by buying or selling short-term debt, as this would be equivalent to exchanging one form of cash for another. When T-bills and cash are viewed as interchangeable, the FRS can make policy only by targeting longer-term debt – buying or selling medium- to long-term government bonds. In the same vein, the Treasury, by taking advantage of the like-money properties of T-bills, and changing the composition of its debt (from short-term debt to long-term debt and vice versa), can change the MB. Switching from issuing T-bills to longer-term bonds implies that the Treasury is tightening economic conditions. Inversely, switching from issuing longer-term bonds to T-bills means that the Treasury is expanding the economy.

The Treasury was the driving force of US economic policy during World War II.[56] Issuing government bonds was an easy way to finance that war. The FRS supported the Treasury's war effort by keeping IRs at low levels: that

---

[54]   Richard C. Koo, *The Escape from the Balance Sheet Recession and the QE Trap: A Hazardous Road for the World Economy* 73 (2015).
[55]   *Id.* at 67.
[56]   Friedman and Schwartz, *supra* note 34, at 561.

was 3/8 of 1% on T-Bills[57] and 2.5% on long-term bonds.[58] Whenever IRs rose above those targeted levels, the FRS would immediately execute open market purchases. Those purchases reduced the availability of government bonds in the market, driving their prices up and their yields down (*see* Box 1.4). The FRS made sure to create sufficient dollars to buy the amount of Treasuries that would prevent the IRs from rising. This transformation of government debt into dollars – the monetization of government debt – demonstrates that a CB cannot be independent from the government in all circumstances. In a state of emergency, like a war, the CB becomes submissive. It conducts monetary policy to meet the financing needs of its government (Fig. 3.2).

The FRS role as the financier of the government was also evident during the Korean War (Fig. 3.2). The FRS tried again during that war to keep IRs down through open market purchases of government debt, guaranteeing in this way the cheap funding of government's war effort. Such purchases, which were conducted by creating new dollars, increased the money supply so much that, between 1950 and 1951, the Consumer Price Index, a measure of inflation, rose by 8%. Because inflation was rearing its ugly head, the FRS decided to assert control over monetary policy by abandoning its commitment to the low IR policy that was useful to the Treasury. Asserting CB independence during a war was a radical idea though. US President Truman wrote a letter to the chairman of the FOMC that, in a didactic tone, demanded low IRs on government debt as this was essential for the successful conclusion of war effort.[59]

High inflation, a side-effect of expansionary policies, made it clear that the FRS can lose its grip on the economy if its primary goal is to ease government financing through low IRs. In principle, when markets are deluged with government bonds, they should force bonds' yields up and their prices down. This should be enough to make any government reconsider whether it is worth issuing additional debt. However, if, in order to prevent IRs from rising, a CB keeps on buying its government's bonds by churning out new money, it will certainly fuel inflation and undesirable credit growth. The spat between the FRS and Treasury about which institution should lead economic policy terminated in 1951. The two institutions signed an accord on March 4, 1951[60]

---

[57] *Id.* at 577.

[58] *Id.* at 581.

[59] Robert L. Hetzel and Ralph F. Leach, *The Treasury–Fed Accord: A New Narrative Account*, 87 Federal Reserve Bank of Richmond Economic Quarterly Review 33, at 40 (2001).

[60] Joint Announcement by the Secretary of the Treasury and the Chairman of the Board of Governors, and of the Federal Open Market Committee of the Federal Reserve System, Press Release, Mar. 4, 1951.

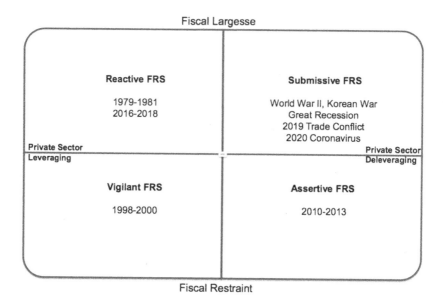

*Figure 3.2   FRS posture towards fiscal policy and private legerage/
deleverage*

agreeing that, in principle, the successful financing of government must go hand-in-hand with a decline in the monetization of government debt.[61]

Each time the Treasury issues bonds to the public to deal with a budget deficit, the supply of bonds goes up, which causes bond prices to fall and yields to rise. If the FRS thinks that high IRs are bad for the economy, it will monetize the government debt, as needed, by buying bonds in the open market. When the FRS buys up bonds, their supply in the market shrinks, their prices increase and the IRs should go down. If the FRS, however, keeps buying the bonds the Treasury issues, through money creation, it will risk high inflation. Therefore, the Treasury and the FRS have to reach an understanding, at some point, on how to manage government debt. When an FA plans to issue lots of debt, for instance, it should have some insight into the CB's readiness to purchase that debt. The fact that a country's CB can buy the government debt that market participants spurn – it can act as a lender of last resort to its own government – lowers a government's borrowing costs. It also impairs 'market discipline' since it incapacitates market players from punishing a profligate government by refusing to buy its bonds and making its debt burden unbearable.

---

[61]   *Id.*

In early 2016, the FRS still held $2.5 trillion in Treasuries[62] – the legacy of the extreme measures it took to address the 2008 financial crisis. The profits it made by holding these securities were submitted to the Treasury.[63] In effect, one branch of government was paying another branch – the government was paying itself – for having debt. The important thing to keep in mind here is that a government's debt held by its own CB is, in essence, an accounting entry that represents a claim of a branch of government, the FRS, on another branch, the Treasury (*see* Fig. 1.10). When assessing the sustainability of a government's debt, therefore, it makes sense to look at the net debt. A country's debt burden may look substantially smaller when we deduct from it the debt held by its own CB. The 2015 US debt-to-GDP ratio fell from 89 to 67% after deducting from it the Treasuries held by the FRS.[64] Similarly, Japan's debt-to-GDP ratio dropped from 234 to 94% after excluding from it bonds held by the Bank of Japan.[65]

3.2.4   Exchange Stabilization Fund

Another way for the Treasury to regulate the economy is the management of the ER between the dollar and other currencies. The Treasury has been granted the freedom to actively intervene in the FX market by using, at its discretion, the Exchange Stabilization Fund (ESF).[66] As of October 2018, that fund held assets worth about $95 billion.[67] The ESF began operations, in April 1934, financed by $2 billion out of the $2.8 billion of Treasury profits realized by depreciating the dollar against the gold (from $20.67 to $35 per ounce of gold). This occurred in an international environment ridden with discord. Britain had abandoned the gold standard[68] and had depreciated the pound against the dollar, prompting the United States to retaliate. The ESF was modeled after Britain's Exchange Equalization Account that had been in place since 1932. The United States viewed the Exchange Equalization Account as a secretive

---

[62] Federal Reserve Statistical Release, H.4.1, Factors Affecting Reserve Balances, Jan. 28, 2016.

[63] The FRS submits these profits to the Treasury based on a practice it has adopted since 1947. Peter Conti-Brown, *The Institutions of Federal Reserve Independence*, 32(2) Yale Journal of Regulation 257, at 284, n. 103 (2015).

[64] McKinsey Global Institute, *Debt and (Not Much Deleveraging)*, at 34, Feb. 2015.

[65] *Id.* at 33.

[66] *See* 31 USC §5302. The ESF was established by a provision of the Gold Reserve Act of January 31, 1934.

[67] Department of the Treasury, Office of Inspector General, Audit of the Exchange Stabilization Fund's Financial Statements for Fiscal Years 2018 and 2017, at 7, Dec. 7, 2018.

[68] *See* Chapter 7.

body that was skillfully employed by Britain to weaken the pound in the inter-war years.[69]

The ESF was supposed to operate in secrecy, mimicking the practices of British and French stabilization funds. The secretary of the Treasury, under the supervision of the president, was, therefore, the only administrator of the fund.[70] This ensured that transactions in foreign currency, including those that made losses, remained hidden from public view. Secrecy empowered the Treasury to conceal other ESF operations too, such as loans to foreign countries that were central to US foreign policy. The ESF became more transparent in the mid-1970s through an amendment of the Gold Reserve Act. Now any ESF loan to a foreign entity or government, for more than 6 months, requires the President to give Congress 'a written statement that unique or emergency circumstances require the loan or credit'.[71] Furthermore, the Treasury has to provide the House and Senate Banking Committees with a monthly statement on all agreements made or renewed, all transactions and all projected liabilities of the ESF.[72] Further disclosure was ordered by the Mexican Debt Disclosure Act of 1995. The Act was adopted when Congress objected to the President granting $20 billion in medium-term loans to Mexico, which was undergoing, at that period, a severe financial crisis.

The ESF is not funded by the federal budget. Its income consists of the interest it receives from holding foreign securities. The fact that the ESF is financially independent means that the Treasury enjoys considerable autonomy in the conduct of FEP. The FRS works with the Treasury to execute that policy. To facilitate the work of the ESF, the FRS has agreed to *warehouse* foreign exchange on behalf of the Treasury. Warehousing takes place when the Treasury sells the foreign currency it has accumulated to the FRS for dollars while, at the same time, agreeing to repurchase this currency at a future time. Warehousing foreign exchange at the FRS makes it possible for the Treasury to obtain the dollars it needs to lend to foreign governments or to sell in the market to depreciate the dollar as needed.[73] The warehousing transactions between the FRS and Treasury are, in essence, a way to provide dollars to the Treasury by using foreign currency as collateral. Because of this, they could be considered illegal, given that the law prohibits the direct financing of the

---

[69]   Anna J. Schwartz, *From Obscurity to Notoriety: A Biography of the Exchange Stabilization Fund*, 29(2) Journal of Money, Credit, and Banking 135, at 137 (1997).
[70]   C. Randall Henning, *The Exchange Stabilization Fund: Slush Money or War Chest?* 53, Institute of International Economics (1999).
[71]   31 USC §5302(b).
[72]   31 USC §5302(c).
[73]   Henning, *supra* note 70, at 50.

government by the FRS.[74] Warehousing has not been used since 1992. Despite this, it remains an option, an *aid memoire* of the teamwork required to operate a government.

The ESF's first incursion into the currency market occurred on September 5, 1934 when it supported the dollar against the French franc. The EFS was also used to implement the 1936 Tripartite Agreement between the United States, Britain and France. The three countries adopted the agreement to effectuate the joint devaluation of their currencies against the gold, the reserve asset at that time.[75] The Treasury entered additionally into several bilateral stabilization agreements through which it extended ESF credit to foreign governments.[76] During World War II, the mission of the ESF was to provide dollars to countries deemed worthy of US assistance because of their contribution to the war effort. The ESF provided dollars, in exchange for gold, to the Soviet Union and concluded agreements with China to exchange gold, silver and yuans for dollars.[77]

During the 1960s, the ESF was used by the Treasury to intervene in the currency market to defend the dollar. The United States borrowed from foreign CBs foreign currencies to buy dollars held abroad in order to stem the dollar's devaluation against the gold. Buying dollars in the open market, by using borrowed foreign currencies, induced dollar scarcity and stemmed the free fall of the dollar.[78] In October 1978, when the dollar reached record lows against the German mark and the Japanese yen, the Treasury and FRS, in coordination with other states, executed a $30 billion intervention in the FX market. The Treasury issued foreign-currency denominated debt to obtain German marks and Swiss francs. It subsequently used these currencies to buy dollars in order to prop up the dollar's value (Box 3.6).[79]

---

[74] The FRBs can buy 'any bonds, notes, or other obligations which are direct obligations of the United States ... but *only in the open market*' (emphasis added). 12 USC §355(1). *See also* Fig. 1.7.

[75] *See* Chapter 7.

[76] Henning, *supra* note 70, at 14.

[77] Schwartz, *supra* note 69, at 147.

[78] *See* Chapter 9.

[79] Henning, *supra* note 70, at 26.

BOX 3.6   INTERVENTION TO STOP $ DEVALUATION

Goal: Prevent $ depreciation

Tool: Create $ scarcity: Buy dollars by selling foreign currency* → Too few
$ → Price $ Up

Note: *Problem: Treasury and FRS do not have foreign currencies to sell. Solution: Borrow
currencies from foreign CBs or issue foreign-currency denominated bonds.

In 1979–80, when the dollar appreciated, the Treasury took advantage
of that appreciation to buy foreign currencies cheaply. It used these foreign
currencies to pay down the foreign-currency denominated debt it had issued
before. Buying foreign currencies when the dollar appreciated was a judicious
strategy. The Treasury's goal was to reduce its dependence on foreign CBs
each time it needed to defend the dollar. Building a stash of FX reserves,
a war chest, alleviated the pressure of having to desperately look for foreign
currencies in times of need.[80] However, reserve accumulation is never risk free.
The currency and bonds of other states are of lower quality than those of the
United States. The Treasury disliked the fact that, by holding such currencies
and bonds, it was in essence extending credit to foreign states and taking on the
risk of potential future depreciation of their currencies.

During the 1980s, the United States was combating, yet again, an undesirable dollar appreciation that was hurting the competitiveness of its exports.
Between October 1979 and February 1981, the Treasury and FRS purchased
roughly $7 billion worth in foreign currencies by selling dollars in order to
devaluate the dollar.[81] The United States' intervention in the FX market escalated in 1989 when $20.7 billion was sold in an attempt to weaken the dollar
to beef up export competitiveness. Some $10.3 billion out of this $20.7 billion
came from the ESF.[82]

By the late 1980s, though, the FRS started to worry that its close collaboration with the Treasury in the FX market was undermining its reputation as
an independent CB. The FRS was particularly alarmed because the Treasury's
FEP was affecting DEP. The large-scale interventions in the FX market
that the FRS was performing at the behest of the Treasury looked more like
currency manipulation rather than nudging the markets in the right direction.
Interventions targeting at curbing the dollar's ascent compelled the FRS to
implement an expansionary policy even if it had officially committed to doing

---

[80]   *Id.* at 28.
[81]   *Id.*
[82]   *Id.* at 5.

exactly the opposite. Selling dollars to buy large amounts of foreign curren-cies, an easy monetary policy, was inconsistent with the tight policy the FRS had pledged to adopt to fight inflation.

3.2.5 The Dodd–Frank Act

The 2010 Dodd–Frank Wall Street Reform and Consumer Protection Act[83] adopted after the 2008 financial turmoil gave the FRS board oversight powers over financial institutions. The Act was adopted to: promote US financial stability, by strengthening accountability and transparency in the financial system; terminate the 'too big to fail' financial institutions; protect the US taxpayer by ending bailouts; and shield consumers from abusive financial services practices.

3.2.5.1 What is an SIFI?

The Federal Stability Oversight Council (FSOC), established under the Act, is charged with the task of determining whether a company is 'too big to fail', a so-called systemically important financial institution (SIFI).[84] The FSOC has 10 voting members including the secretary of the Treasury, who chairs the council, the chairperson of the FRS and the Comptroller of the Currency.[85] Bank holding companies, any company that has control over a bank,[86] that have more than $250 billion in assets are deemed systemically important.[87] The FSOC can additionally designate a non-bank company as systemically impor-tant if that company experiences material financial distress or if its nature, scope, size, scale, concentration, interconnectedness or a mix of its activities could pose a threat to financial stability.[88] Such companies come under the direct supervision of the FRS and are subject to higher prudential standards. The FSOC initially designated the American Insurance Group (AIG),[89]

---

[83]   Dodd–Frank Wall Street Reform and Consumer Protection Act, 12 USC §5301 et seq.

[84]   12 USC §5321.

[85]   *Id.*

[86]   *See* 12 USC §1841(a)(2)(A).

[87]   12 USC §5331(a)(1). Initially, to qualify as an SIFI a bank had to have more than $50 billion in assets. This was amended to $250 billion by the Economic Growth, Regulatory Reform, and Consumer Protection Act that came into effect on May 24, 2018. The BoG still has discretion to apply stricter standards to banks whose assets are equal to or greater than $100 billion. *See* 12 USC §5331(a)(1)(C).

[88]   12 USC §5323.

[89]   It rescinded that designation in 2017.

General Electric Capital Corporation,[90] MetLife[91] and Prudential Financial as such companies.

3.2.5.2   Living wills

Once an institution is labeled an SIFI, it is subject to intense scrutiny. All SIFIs must submit annual resolution plans, known as living wills, to the FRS.[92] The purpose of these living wills is to ensure that SIFIs can be easily sold or shut down if they fail. The BoG and FDIC determine whether the resolution plans submitted by SIFIs are credible.[93] If they conclude that an SIFI's plan is deficient, that institution must submit an amended plan by making changes to its business operations and corporate structure, as necessary, to facilitate the implementation of the plan.[94] If the SIFI fails to resubmit a credible plan, the BoG and the FDIC may jointly impose stringent capital, leverage or other liquidity requirements, and even restrictions on the growth, activities and operations of the SIFI and its subsidiaries.[95] The BoG and FDIC, in consultation with the FSOC, may also jointly order an SIFI to divest certain assets or cease some operations in order to smooth out its future potential resolution.[96] The details of living wills remain hidden from the public. Each living will has two sections: a public section and a confidential one. The confidential section, which provides insights into the financial strengths and weaknesses of SIFIs, is not released to the public.

3.2.5.3   Liquidation of companies

The Dodd–Frank Act vests the Treasury with the orderly liquidation authority. This means that the Treasury can take over a financial company that is in danger of defaulting or in actual default when that default could cause systemic damage to the economy. If the Treasury, backed by the FRS and the FDIC,[97] concludes that a company is on the verge of default or has defaulted and that its failure 'would have serious adverse effects on financial stability',[98] it can trigger the resolution of that company. The process starts when the Treasury

---

[90]   It rescinded that designation in 2016.

[91]   MetLife challenged its designation as an SIFI in the courts and won. The court called the designation 'fatally flawed'. *See MetLife, Inc. v. Financial Stability Oversight Council*, 177 F.Supp.3d 219 (2016).

[92]   12 USC §5365(d)(1).

[93]   12 USC §5365(d)(4)(A).

[94]   12 USC §5365(d)(4)(B).

[95]   12 USC §5365(d)(5)(A).

[96]   12 USC §5365(d)(5)(B).

[97]   12 USC §5383(a)(1)(A).

[98]   12 USC §5383(b).

files a petition with US District Court for the District of Columbia.[99] The hearing takes place behind closed doors and the court has 24 hours to rule on the Treasury's petition. If the petition is not arbitrary and capricious, the court must approve it.[100]

3.2.5.4 Stress tests

The FRS conducts annual stress tests to determine whether SIFIs have enough capital 'to absorb losses as a result of adverse economic conditions'.[101] Initially, all bank holding companies with at least $50 billion in assets were subject to stress tests. After the adoption of the Economic Growth, Regulatory Reform, and Consumer Protection Act in 2018, bank holding companies with less than $100 billion in total assets do not have to endure stress testing.[102]

The FRS performs annually the Comprehensive Capital Analysis and Review (CCAR) to assess whether bank holding companies have sufficient capital to continue operations in times of economic stress.[103] Through the CCAR, the FRS scrutinizes the capital adequacy of banks including their plans for dividend payments and share buybacks. In 2014, the FRS blocked the planned dividends and share buybacks of five systemically important banks[104] because it concluded that such capital distributions would have made them unfit to withstand adverse economic events.

3.2.5.5 Capital requirements

All banks are required to hold, in addition to the required reserves, capital equivalent to 7% of their risk-weighted assets – i.e. the loans they make weighted by how risky they are.[105] Furthermore, firms considered to be global systemically important banks (GSIBs)[106] are subject to an additional capital surcharge. Capital surcharges are imposed not only to make banks safer, so that taxpayers do not have to bail them out during a crisis, but also to discourage them from becoming too big to fail in the first place. The surcharges imposed on GSIBs can range from 1.0 to 4.5% of each firm's risk-weighted

---

[99] 12 USC §5382(a)(1)(A)(i).

[100] 12 USC §5382(a)(1)(A)(iii)–(v).

[101] 12 USC §5365(i).

[102] *See supra* note 87.

[103] FRS, Supervision Stress Tests and Capital Planning, Mar. 7, 2017.

[104] Citigroup, HSBC, Royal Bank of Scotland, Citizens Financial Group and Santander.

[105] FRS, Federal Reserve Board Approves Final Rule to Help Ensure Banks Maintain Strong Capital Positions, Press Release, July 2, 2013.

[106] As of 2018 these banks were: Bank of America, Bank of New York Mellon, Citigroup, Goldman Sachs, JP Morgan Chase, Morgan Stanley, the State Street Corporation and Wells Fargo.

assets. The exact percentage imposed on each bank is based on its financial situation, which may change over time.[107] The 2016 capital surcharge levied on JP Morgan Chase, the biggest US bank, was 4.5%, making its overall capital requirements 11.5% of its risk-weighted assets.

The FRS was the first CB that required foreign banks operating within its jurisdiction to have enough capital to withstand adverse financial conditions on their own rather than relying on their parent company in their home country. Foreign banking companies with US assets of $50 billion or more are required to establish a US intermediate holding company. This intermediate holding company is subject to the capital, liquidity and risk management requirements that apply to similar US bank holding companies.[108] The rule was adopted despite concerns that other countries may endorse similar rules resulting in the fragmentation of global banking. Banks claimed that they would be unable to maintain global operations if every country in which they operated demanded that their subsidiaries must have enough capital to weather financial turbulence on their own. The EU fought against the adoption of the rule because it was bound to curtail the activities of European banks in the United States and threatened to retaliate in kind.

3.2.5.6 The Volcker rule

The Dodd–Frank incorporates the Volcker rule, named after the former FRS chairman Volcker who proposed it. The rule is based on the premise that commercial banking should be separated from investment banking. Commercial banks, the banks that accept deposits from the general public, should not use these deposits to engage in high-risk investing activities. These activities, which involve placing bets on the direction of the markets, should be reserved for investment banks. The separation between commercial banking and investment banking was articulated first in the 1933 Glass–Steagall Act, which was repealed in 1999[109] when the banking business was deregulated. The 1933 Act banned commercial banks from owning investment banks and vice versa.

---

[107] FRS, Federal Reserve Board Approves Final Rule Requiring the Largest, Most Systemically Important US Bank Holding Companies to Further Strengthen their Capital Position, Press Release, July 20, 2015.

[108] FRS, Federal Reserve Board Approves Final Rule Strengthening Supervision and Regulation of Large US Bank Holding Companies and Foreign Banking Organizations, Press Release, Feb. 18, 2014.

[109] The 1932 Glass–Steagall Act consisted of four provisions that were incorporated into the 1933 Banking Act. The 1999 Gramm–Leach–Bliley Act repealed two of the provisions that separated commercial banking from investment banking. 12 USC §1841–50 (amended 1999).

The Volcker rule, embodied in the Dodd–Frank Act, aims to separate investment banking from commercial banking by prohibiting the involvement of commercial banks in investment banking activities likely to create conflicts of interest for them. The Act bans commercial banks from the proprietary trading of securities. Commercial banks can no longer engage in securities trading for themselves using other people's money – their depositors' money.[110] The Act further limits commercial banks' investment in hedge funds[111] and private equity funds[112] because of the speculative nature of such investments.[113] Banning proprietary trading and limiting commercial banks' speculative activities was expected to reduce the likelihood of their failure during a crisis. Commercial banks, though, can still engage in trading, on behalf of their customers, for risk-mitigating hedging activities, and can still do underwriting[114] or engage in market making.[115] These broad exceptions make the implementation of the Volcker rule quite difficult.

Separating proprietary trading, which is prohibited under the Volcker rule, from market making, which is still a legitimate activity under the exception to the rule, is like splitting hairs. A market maker is a bank that takes on the risk of holding a certain number of shares of a particular security in order to facilitate trading in that security. Market makers create a market by quoting both a buy and a sell price for a security. They make money by buying the security at a lower price than they sell it at. Because this is the way a market maker makes a profit, it is difficult to disentangle market making from proprietary trading. Both a market maker and a proprietary trader make money by buying a security at a lower price than the price they sell it; what separates one from the other is their intention. Market makers buy and sell to facilitate the creation of a market for a security; proprietary traders buy and sell for themselves. In 2016, fears that market making may be deemed proprietary trading and, thus, prohibited under the Dodd–Frank Act led some commercial banks to forgo trading altogether.

---

[110] 12 USC §1851(a)(1)(A).

[111] Hedge funds are usually structured as LLCs. Their goal is to produce high returns for those who invest in them no matter the markets' performance. For more details on hedge funds, *see* Chapter 15, Section 15.2.5.

[112] Private equity firms are investment vehicles for the very wealthy. They invest in start-up companies or they borrow to buy out already existing companies. For more details on private equity firms, *see* Chapter 15, Section 15.2.6.

[113] 12 USC §1851(a)(1)(B).

[114] Underwriting is a process through which banks help companies raise capital by selling stocks or bonds in the markets.

[115] 12 USC §1851(d).

3.2.5.7 Effects of regulation

The Dodd–Frank Act did not bring about the downsizing of big banks, despite the myriad rules that were put in place to encourage them to break up. Most banks maintained their pre-crisis size but they stopped growing. In the 1990s, the world's 10 biggest banks had assets of just $3.6 trillion, an amount equal to 16% of global GDP. This amount skyrocketed to $25 trillion (40% of global GDP) by 2008 before it fell to $16 trillion (35% of global GDP) by 2016.[116] Some large banks closed down their subsidiaries in foreign countries. Others refrained from capital-intensive activities, such as trading financial instruments, and opted for safer business (e.g. underwriting new companies and advising wealthy clients). By 2017, there was concern that the Dodd–Frank Act might have gone too far and was impeding market functionality.[117] The enactment of the 2018 Economic Growth and Regulatory Reform Act[118] generated fears, on the other hand, that the lighter rules adopted under it to lessen the regulatory burden of Dodd–Frank would erode the hard-won financial stability.

3.3 SAVING THE SOVEREIGN: THE 2008 FINANCIAL CRISIS AND ITS SPILLOVERS

3.3.1 The Crisis

The 2008 financial turmoil started when a housing boom turned into a housing bust. At the epicenter of the crisis were the asset-backed securities (ABS) and, more specifically, the mortgage-backed securities (MBS) (Table 3.1 and Fig. 3.3).

Faith in MBS faltered when the housing market crashed and mortgage defaults skyrocketed, especially defaults on subprime mortgages – mortgages granted to buyers with poor credit. The US government-sponsored enterprises (GSEs), known as Fannie Mae and Freddie Mac, were hurt by the housing bust. The GSEs are public–private partnerships (PPPs): they are owned by both the government and private investors. Their purpose is to support home ownership, a foundation of the US economy.[119]

A typical financial crisis occurs when depositors run on banks. The queue of depositors in front of a bank or an ATM to retrieve their deposits is the

---

[116] *Chop Chop: Big Banks*, Economist, Jan. 30, 2016.
[117] See US Department of the Treasury, A Financial System that Creates Economic Opportunities: Banks and Credit Unions, June 2017.
[118] *See supra* note 87.
[119] Niall Ferguson, *The Ascent of Money: Financial History of the World* 282–3 (2008).

Table 3.1   *Definitions of ABS, MBS and SPVs*

ABS	ABS are securities that make it easier to invest in debt. Investment banks package together similar loans (e.g. auto loans) into securities that they subsequently sell to investors. The securitization of debt transforms it from an illiquid asset into a liquid one, a security, which can be traded in the markets
MBS	MBS are ABS secured by mortgages (Fig. 3.3). During the 2008 financial crisis, it became evident that many of these MBS were worthless because of the burst of the housing bubble that led to many mortgage defaults
SPV or special purpose entity	An SPV is usually established as an LLC. Because it is an LLC, it can be used by capital holders to sponsor a risky project without putting all their assets at risk. Many SPVs have been used to hide the debt of companies that establish them. Corporations have used SPVs to move their debt off their balance sheet into an SPV to avoid disclosing the true extent of their indebtedness. SPVs have been used to camouflage the ownership of assets and, thus, facilitate tax evasion

classic depiction of a bank run. The 2008 financial crisis was triggered, though, because banks ran on other banks.[120] The motto that guided banks during that

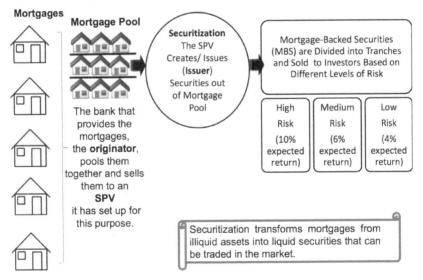

Figure 3.3   *Mortgage-backed securities*

[120] Gary Gordon, *Slapped in the Face by the Invisible Hand: Banking and the Panic of 2007*, Paper Prepared for the Federal Reserve Bank of Atlanta's 2009 Financial Markets Conference 'Financial Innovation and Crisis', May 11–12, 2009.

financial meltdown was: 'I won't lend to you even though I think you're okay because I am not sure others will lend to you either'.[121] Banks became wary of lending to other banks, especially when the collateral for the provision of credit consisted of MBS. MBS were labeled 'toxic' during the crisis because they were losing value rapidly.

The FRS and Treasury worked together to address the crisis. However, even with such close collaboration fears persisted that the situation was out of hand. As the chairman of the FRS put it at the time: the United States needed 'a strong, well defined, *ex ante*, clear regime' to address the crippling crisis,[122] but such regime did not exist. The joint appearance of the Treasury secretary and chairman of the FRS before the Senate Banking Committee on September 23, 2008 showcased their close collaboration. On May 23, 2009, the Treasury and FRS issued a joint statement through which they tried to clarify, for themselves and the public, the division of their responsibilities – the '2009 Treasury-Federal Reserve Accord'.[123] The accord was an effort to explain the FRS' fiscal initiatives, particularly its lending high-quality bonds (T-bills) to financial institutions by accepting as collateral the moribund MBS. The fear that the FRS may eventually run out of T-bills led the Treasury to adopt, on September 17, 2008, the Supplementary Financing Program.[124] The program enabled it to issue T-bills on behalf of the FRS. Given that the FRS could run out of T-bills as it was lending them to institutions in trouble, it could use the T-bills made available through the Supplementary Financing Program to conduct its policy.

3.3.2   The Interest Rate as a Policy Tool

On August 17, 2007, the FRS lowered the discount rate by 50 basis points (0.5%) so that banks could borrow from it more easily given that many of them were unable to obtain credit in the interbank lending market. Furthermore, it expanded the duration of loans it offered to banks from overnight to 30 days with the possibility of renewal.[125] Starting in September 2007, the FOMC announced a series of reductions in the target FFR. In late 2008, it introduced

---

[121]   FRS, Meeting of the Federal Open Market Committee, at 4, Oct. 28–29, 2008 [hereinafter FOMC October 2008].

[122]   FRS, Meeting of the Federal Open Market Committee, at 51, Sept. 16, 2008.

[123]   Joint Statement by the Department of the Treasury and the Federal Reserve, The Role of the Federal Reserve in Preserving Financial and Monetary Stability, Mar. 23, 2009.

[124]   US Treasury, Treasury Announces Supplementary Financing Program, Press Release, Sept. 17, 2008.

[125]   GAO, Federal Reserve System: Opportunities Exist to Strengthen Policies and Processes for Managing Emergency Assistance, at 17, GAO-11-696, July 2011.

the zero interest rate policy by setting the FFR range between 0 and 0.25%. When the FFR is around 0, the IROR should be even lower and this should incentivize banks to boost lending (Box 3.4). In addition, the FRS adopted unconventional measures: it eased economic conditions by printing dollars to buy large amounts of Treasuries and MBS.

The FRS was straightforward when it communicated its policies to the public. The 2011 FOMC statement left no doubt that 'exceptionally low levels' for the FFR should be expected until, at least, mid-2013.[126] The mid-2013 deadline was revised to late 2014 at the January 2012 meeting,[127] and to mid-2015 at the September 2012 meeting.[128] Eventually the FOMC abandoned calendar-based guidance. Instead, it started placing emphasis on the recuperation of the economy. In December 2012, it announced that, as long as the unemployment rate remained above 6.5% and inflation below 2.5%, monetary stimulus would continue.[129] Subsequent FOMC statements released all through 2013 reiterated that thresholds indicating economic recovery had to be crossed before hiking the IRs. During the December 2013 meeting, the FOMC clarified that the FFR would remain between 0 and 0.25%, especially if inflation hovered below the 2% target. This was to be the case even if unemployment dropped below 6.5%.[130] Overall, the FRS clearly communicated its strategy for reviving the economy. By 'tying its hands', that is publicly announcing specific, numerical goals for inflation and unemployment that had to be achieved before withdrawing monetary stimulus,[131] the FRS convinced the public that the growth of the US economy was its top priority.

3.3.3   The FRS as Lender of Last Resort

The FRS fulfilled its role as lender of last resort because it stood ready to take risks to stabilize the financial system that market participants loathed to take. It played that role by making available ample credit and accepting as collateral assets of questionable quality.[132] To paraphrase Bagehot, the FRS treated the 2008 crisis as a type of disease it could not risk starving.[133] It was ready to provide bankers with cash even against bad-quality collateral.

---

[126] FRS, Minutes of the Federal Open Market Committee, Aug. 9, 2011.
[127] FRS, Federal Reserve Issues FOMC Statement, Press Release, Jan. 25, 2012.
[128] FRS, Federal Reserve Issues FOMC Statement, Press Release, Sept. 13, 2012.
[129] FRS, Federal Reserve Issues FOMC Statement, Press Release, Dec. 12, 2012.
[130] FRS, Federal Reserve Issues FOMC Statement, Press Release, Dec. 18, 2013.
[131] *See* Mark Carney, *Remarks at the CFA Society*, Toronto, Dec. 11, 2012.
[132] GAO, *supra* note 125, at 83.
[133] Walter Bagehot, *Lombard Street: A Description of the Money Market* 25 (1873, reprinted in 1979).

The FRS boosted liquidity by buying long-term government bonds and the infamous MBS through a series of so-called quantitative easing (QE) policies. QE policies aimed to 'ease' the quantity of money available in the economy. The FRS first round of QE (QE1) was an attempt to prevent the collapse of housing credit market, the market most affected by the bursting of the housing bubble. Mortgaged-backed securities, especially those issued by the GSEs, accounted for more than 80% of the assets purchased during QE1. These purchases helped build up the excess reserves of private banks. On November 25, 2008, the FRS announced that it was planning to purchase $100 billion of GSEs' debt and $500 billion of MBS issued by those GSEs and private banks.[134] On March 18, 2009, a new wave of purchases was announced – $100 billion of GSEs' debt, $750 billion of MBS and $300 billion of long-term Treasuries.[135]

On November 3, 2010, the FRS unleashed the second round of QE, QE2. QE2 was necessary because household spending remained constrained owing to 'high unemployment, modest income growth, lower housing wealth, and tight credit'.[136] Between November 2010 and June 2011, the FRS purchased $600 billion in long-term Treasuries[137] – an amount almost equal to the amount of new government bonds issued during that period. The FRS' aggressive buying of government bonds increased their price and decreased their yield. The scant returns offered by Treasuries pushed market players to shift their money to the stock market, lifting companies' values and creating fears of a stock market bubble. Many capital holders fled the United States for the emerging markets in search of higher yields. The low IRs in the United States put a downward pressure on the dollar, a boon for US exporters.

QE2 was not as successful as expected and the FRS had to adopt even bolder measures. Those measures included the 'Maturity Extension Program', the so-called 'Operation Twist', that was announced on September 21, 2011.[138] Under Operation Twist, the FRS sold $400 billion in short-term government bonds, bonds with remaining maturities of 3 years or less, and bought the equivalent amount of long-term government bonds, bonds with remaining maturities of 6–30 years.[139] This engineered scarcity of long-term bonds

---

[134] FRS, Federal Reserve Announces it will Initiate a Program to Purchase the Direct Obligations of Housing-Related Government-Sponsored Enterprises and Mortgage-Backed Securities Backed by Fannie Mae, Freddie Mac, and Ginnie Mae, Press Release, Nov. 25, 2008.

[135] FRS, FOMC Statement, Press Release, Mar. 18, 2009.

[136] FRS, FOMC Statement, Press Release, Nov. 3, 2010.

[137] *Id.*

[138] FRS, Federal Reserve Issues FOMC Statement, Press Release, Sept. 21, 2011.

[139] *Id.*

forced their yields down. As a result, short-term yields moved even closer to zero.[140] Operation Twist helped lift the economy[141] but it also had undesirable side-effects. The flattening of the yield curve (*see* Fig. 1.6), the result of the narrowing of the spread between long-term and short-term yields, dented the profitability of banks. Banks make money by borrowing short (from depositors at low IRs) and lending long (to borrowers at higher IRs). When there is not much of a spread between short-term and long-term yields, the profitability of banks suffers.[142]

The third and final round of QE, QE3, was announced on September 13, 2012. The FRS stated that it would purchase $40 billion of MBS per month as long as the 'outlook for the labor market does not improve substantially'.[143] QE3 was further expanded, on December 12, 2012, when the FRS announced that it would continue to buy $45 billion of long-term Treasuries per month but would no longer offset, sterilize, these purchases by selling short-term Treasuries.[144]

QE3 was different from QE1 and QE2 because the FRS, instead of committing to buying a fixed amount of securities by a certain date, declared that it would keep on buying until the labor market improved. The promise that QE could continue indefinitely, if needed, made it clear that the FRS was ready to satisfy all of the financing needs of the government.[145] QE3 increased the FRS' securities holdings from $2.6 trillion in 2011 to about $4.4 trillion in 2014. An S&P Global Ratings analysis concluded that QE3 must have worked because of the creation of 1.9 million jobs and reduction of unemployment by 1.3%.[146]

By 2014, the FRS was holding more than $2.5 trillion of US government bonds – about 19% of the 13.2 trillion US debt market – and about $1.8 trillion in MBS, its assets reaching the unprecedented amount of $4.4 trillion. In the future, it would have to figure out how to disentangle itself from the command-and-control bond market it had single-handedly created (*see* Box 3.7). If the FRS were to switch, at one point, to a contractionary policy by selling the securities it had bought during the crisis all at once, the US IRs would increase sharply. In fact, on May 22, 2013, when the FRS chairman

---

[140] *See* Koo, *supra* note 54, at 82–3.

[141] *Id.* at 83.

[142] *Id.*

[143] FRS, Federal Reserve Issues FOMC Statement, Press Release, Sept. 13, 2012.

[144] FRS, Federal Reserve Issues FOMC Statement, Press Release, Dec. 12, 2012.

[145] Paul McCulley and Zoltan Pozsar, *Helicopter Money: Or How I Stopped Worrying and Love Fiscal–Monetary Cooperation*, at 24, GIC Global Society of Fellows, Jan. 7, 2013.

[146] Beth Ann Bovino, *Should the Fed Consider Income Inequality When Setting Monetary Policy?*, S&P Global Research & Insights, Aug. 30, 2016.

hinted at 'tapering off' QE,[147] the US IRs rose abruptly in anticipation of the end of 'easy money'. This 'taper tantrum' of market participants demonstrated how addicted to easy monetary conditions they had become.[148] The FRS, therefore, proceeded cautiously. On December 18, 2013, it announced the slowing down of purchasing of MBS (from $40 billion to $35 billion per month) and Treasuries (from $45 billion to $40 billion per month). The FRS, though, kept up its existing policy of reinvesting the principal payments it received from its holdings of MBS and Treasuries, thus maintaining an expansionary stance.[149] In early 2017, the bloated MB, which was the result of the FRS' large asset purchases, remained mostly unchanged. It was in 2018 when the FRS stopped reinvesting the proceeds of its maturing bonds (Box 3.7) and started to wind down its easy policies.

BOX 3.7   QUANTITATIVE EASING (QE) VERSUS OVERT MONETARY FINANCING

During a financial panic, the FRS can always expand the economy by buying Treasuries and creating dollars, boosting the official liquidity to stimulate the economy. How can the FRS 'drain' the liquidity, the money it injects into the financial system during a crisis, when the economy recovers? If the FRS holds the Treasuries it buys until maturity, the Treasury will have to make a payment to the FRS. This is a transaction between two branches of the same government which does not affect the liquidity the FRS created by buying Treasuries in the open market. If the dollars created are not drained out of the financial system, QE becomes overt monetary financing of the government, or 'helicopter money'.

In fact, a way to monetize government debt is for the CB to hold a certain amount of that debt in perpetuity, reinvesting in new debt when the existing debt on its balance sheet reaches maturity. In 2018, the FRS decided to *wind down* QE. It stopped reinvesting in new Treasuries when the Treasuries it held matured.

Source: Richard C. Koo, *The Escape from Balance Sheet Recession and the QE Trap: A Hazardous Road for the World Economy* 91–110 (2015); Adair Turner, *Debt, Money, and Mephistopheles: How Do We Get Out of This Mess?*, Occasional Paper 87, Group of Thirty, May 2013.

---

[147] Ben S. Bernanke, *The Economic Outlook*, Testimony before the Joint Economic Committee, US Congress, May 22, 2013.

[148] Koo, *supra* note 54, at 91.

[149] FRS, Federal Reserve Issues FOMC Statement, Press Release, Dec. 18, 2013.

In addition to QE, the FRS could have used other unconventional policies. It could have introduced negative IRs the way Japan's CB and the European Central Bank (ECB) did shortly thereafter. It could have targeted households by promising to keep mortgage rates at low levels for an extended period so as to prop up the housing market. It could have bought foreign assets – such as foreign government bonds or currency – to force the dollar down and boost exports. In the post-crisis recessionary world, CBs around the world were desperate to convince a jaded public that they had infinite tools to battle what seemed to be an entrenched deflation.

3.3.4 Treasury and FRS Coordination

The FRS was not the only institution conducting rescue operations. The Treasury took action to remove toxic assets from the market, resorting even to nationalization of companies when run-of-the mill assistance was inadequate. On October 3, 2008, the United States adopted the Emergency Economic Stabilization Act[150] which authorized the Treasury to establish the $700 billion Troubled Asset Relief Program (TARP). The purpose of that program was to purchase or insure up to $700 billion in troubled assets owned by financial institutions.[151] The terms 'troubled asset'[152] and 'financial institution'[153] were purposefully left vague in the Act to give the Treasury the flexibility it needed to decide what assets to buy and which institutions to save.

The first program launched under TARP was the Capital Purchase Program. Through this program, the Treasury invested $205 billion in 707 financial institutions,[154] and acquired majority stakes in the AIG, an insurance company, and US automakers. The government ended up owning 60.8% of General Motors, an automobile maker, and 74% of General Motors Acceptance Corporation, the financial arm of General Motors that was later renamed Ally Financial.[155] The government holdings of these companies were reduced or eliminated later through public share offerings. By June 21, 2013, the total TARP disbursements amounted to $419.97 billion[156] and the losses from

---

[150] The Emergency Economic Stabilization Act of 2008, 12 USC §5201 et seq.
[151] The Dodd–Frank Act of 2010 reduced the overall amount of TARP to $475 billion. *See* 12 USC §5201 note.
[152] 12 USC §5202(9).
[153] 12 USC §5202(5).
[154] GAO, *supra* note 125, at 14.
[155] Baird Webel, *Troubled Asset Relief Program (TARP): Implementation and Status*, at 3, CRS, June 27, 2013 [hereinafter GRS TARP].
[156] *Id.* at 5.

that program were expected to be $28.78 billion.[157] On October 14, 2008, the Treasury invoked the systemic risk provision of the Federal Deposit Insurance Act,[158] which makes it possible for it to provide assistance to banks. It directed the FDIC to adopt the Temporary Liquidity Guarantee Program, through which it guaranteed more than $600 billion of newly issued debt for banks.[159]

The FRS adopted more than 12 emergency programs under section 13(3) of the Federal Reserve Act.[160] Section 13(3), as articulated at the time,[161] granted the FRS a large amount of discretion in emergency situations. The FRS could in 'unusual and exigent' circumstances give loans to any 'individual, partnership or corporation' as long as these loans were backed with collateral. The FRS used section 13(3) to bail out a number of SIFIs. These institutions included the AIG, Bear Sterns, an investment bank, and the GSEs – Fanny Mae and Freddie Mac. Using section 13(3) to save 'too big to fail' firms attracted the ire of Congress and the public, who disapproved of using government, taxpayers' money to save large corporations that seemed to have been incapable of prudently managing their assets. Most rescue programs were executed by the FRBNY. They involved the establishment of special purpose vehicles (SPVs) structured as limited liability companies (LLCs; *see* Table 3.1). These SPVs received FRBNY loans that they used, in turn, to purchase the toxic assets of troubled SIFIs. Putting together SPVs, which served as a sort of intermediary between the FRBNY and distressed SIFIs, was a way to separate the FRBNY rescue programs from its normal operations.

A big rescue operation was the bailout of Bear Stearns, an investment bank. Bear Stearns suffered from a run when other banks refused to do business with it because of rumors of its impending collapse. On March 14, 2008, the FRS authorized the FRBNY to provide a $12.9 billion loan to Bear Stearns. The loan made it possible for the bank to avoid bankruptcy and to continue operating.[162] On March 16, 2008, it was announced that JP Morgan

---

[157] *Id.* at 6.

[158] 12 USC §1823(a)(4)(G).

[159] GAO, *supra* note 125, at 14.

[160] 12 USC §343(3).

[161] Section 13(3) of the Federal Reserve Act was amended by the 2010 Dodd–Frank Act. Today the BoG can authorize section 13(3) emergency lending only under broad-based eligibility programs and after receiving the approval of the Treasury (section 13(3)(B)(i)). In other words, the FRS can no longer provide loans to individual firms as it did in 2008. Some have argued that the FRS could outmaneuver this restriction by 'creating an across-the-board lending facility that is really a single firm bailout in disguise'. *See* David A. Skeel, Jr, *The New Financial Deal: Understanding the Dodd–Frank Act and its (Unintended) Consequences*, at 9, Paper 329, University of Pennsylvania Legal Scholarship Repository, Oct. 2010.

[162] GAO, *supra* note 125, at 178.

Chase, an investment bank, would acquire Bear Stearns. According to the Treasury: 'Ultimately, only JP Morgan Chase was willing to consider an offer of a binding commitment to acquire the firm and to stand behind Bear's substantial short-term obligations'.[163] The FRS and Treasury played an active role in structuring the transaction, which took the form of a merger. Under the Share Exchange Agreement between JP Morgan and Bear Stearns, JP Morgan received $95 million newly issued shares of Bear Stearns common stock (amounting to 39.5% of the outstanding shares) in exchange for JP Morgan shares. The share exchange was completed before the scheduled (April 8, 2008) meeting of Bear Stearns shareholders who were to vote on the merger.[164] The FRBNY facilitated the acquisition by providing a $28.82 billion loan that was used to buy the majority of toxic assets of Bear Stearns. The rescue operation was structured as an SPV called Maiden Lane, an LLC. The FRBNY provided a $28.82 billion loan and JP Morgan a $1.15 billion loan to Maiden Lane. Maiden Lane used the cash from these loans to purchase assets, mostly the toxic MBS, of Bear Stearns.[165] The purpose of Maiden Lane was to acquire the assets of Bear Stearns and manage them in a way that would make possible the repayment of the FRBNY and JP Morgan loans.

The government's bailout of the AIG, an insurance firm, totaled approximately $182 billion. That included an $85 billion FRBNY-backed revolving credit facility that was supplemented by a $49.1 billion loan from the Treasury under the TARP. The total FRBNY support for AIG (including the $85 billion revolving credit facility) was $133.3 billion.[166] The FRBNY received in exchange 77.9% equity interest in AIG 'for Treasury', practically nationalizing that company. On January 16, 2009, the FRBNY announced the establishment of a trust – the AIG Credit Facility Trust – to oversee the 77.9% equity in the company 'in the best interests' of the Treasury. Based on the trust agreement, the trustees had the mandate to sell AIG stocks 'in a value maximizing manner' after getting the approval of FRBNY, which, in turn, had to consult with the Treasury.[167] The role assumed by the FRBNY in the establishment of the trust was criticized by Congress because it eschewed the typical separation

---

[163] Timothy F. Geithner, *Actions by the New York Fed in Response to Liquidity Pressures in Financial Markets*, Testimony before the US Senate Committee on Banking, Housing and Urban Affairs, Apr. 3, 2008.

[164] Marcel Kahan and Edward Rock, *How to Prevent Hard Cases from Making Bad Law: Bear Stearns, Delaware and the Strategic Use of Comity*, 58 Emory Law Journal 713, at 719–21 (2009) (the shareholders challenged the merger agreement in court but they did not prevail).

[165] GAO, *supra* note 125, Appendix IV.

[166] Congressional Oversight Panel, The AIG Rescue, Its Impact on Markets, and the Government's Exit Strategy, at 2, June 10, 2010.

[167] *Id.* at 81.

of powers between the FA (assigned to the Treasury) and the MA (assigned to the FRS).[168] It seemed incompatible with FRS independence to have one of its banks, the FRBNY, manage the Treasury's stake in a US company.[169]

Other facilities structured as SPVs, which the FRBNY put together for the rescue of AIG, included Maiden Lane II and Maiden Lane III. Through Maiden Lane III, the government paid all holders of credit default swaps (CDS) (*see* Table 3.2) issued by the AIG. Congress criticized the Treasury's handling of AIG's default and especially its failure to negotiate 'haircuts' (discounts on the amounts the AIG owed to holders of CDS). Many argued that AIG's creditors should have borne some of the cost of AIG's default and that the burden of rescuing that company should not have fallen solely on the US taxpayer. The Special Inspector General for the TARP criticized the secrecy surrounding Maiden Lane III, especially the initial failure of the government to disclose the holders of CDS that were benefitting from AIG's bailout.[170] It was revealed, eventually, that those that benefitted from AIG's rescue included not only large US banks (e.g. Goldman Sachs and Merrill Lynch) but also foreign banks (e.g. Societé Générale, Deutsche Bank).[171] The US government eventually made $22.7 billion from the interest payments on the loans it granted to AIG and the eventual public sale of the AIG stock it acquired when it nationalized the company.

In 2011, AIG sued the US government, claiming that its nationalization during the crisis was illegal. The Court of Federal Claims concluded that the terms of AIG's bailout involved 'plain violations of the Federal Reserve Act'[172] since there is nothing in that Act that permits the FRS to 'take over a private corporation and run its business as if the Government were the owner'.[173] The court acknowledged, however, that 'if the Government had done nothing, the shareholders would have been left with 100% of nothing'.[174] In other words, while the court disapproved of the methods that the government used to bail out AIG, it did not see an alternative to the bailout.

---

[168] *Id.* at 154–5.

[169] *Id.*

[170] SIGTARP, Factors Affecting Efforts to Limit Payments to AIG Counterparties, at 31, SIGTARP-10-003, Nov. 17, 2009.

[171] *Id.* at 20.

[172] *Starr Int'l Co. v. United States*, Court of Federal Claims, No. 11-779C, 121 Fed. Cl. 428, at 436, June 15, 2015.

[173] *Id.* at 434.

[174] *Id.* at 436.

Table 3.2   *Definitions of derivatives and CDS*

Derivatives	Derivatives are *financial contracts* whose value is 'derived' from an asset. Investors use derivatives as an *insurance* against unexpected movements in the IRs, ERs and commodity prices or against a debtor's default. Traders use derivatives to *speculate* on the price movements of IRs, ERs and commodities or on the default of a borrower
CDS	A *credit default swap* is a type of derivative. It is executed as a bilateral contract between a swap *dealer* and its customer, a *creditor*. The creditor pays the dealer a periodic fee in order to insure itself against the potential default of a borrower. This fee is paid until the debt matures. If the borrower does not default, the dealer profits from the fee and the creditor gets back the debt principal from the borrower minus the fee already paid to the dealer. If the borrower defaults, the dealer must pay the creditor the amount of debt left unpaid by the borrower. During the financial crisis, companies that issued CDS, like the AIG, could not honor their obligations because of the high number of defaults

On December 12, 2007, the FRS put together the term auction facility (TAF)[175] to address the continuing stress in the interbank lending market.[176] Banks borrow from the FRS when they cannot obtain credit from each other. The discount rate at which the FRS offers loans to banks is higher than the FFR (Box 3.4). This higher IR penalizes banks that do not have good enough credit to borrow from other banks. During the crisis, though, because of the prevailing uncertainty, the interbank lending market froze as most banks refused to lend to each other. Despite this severe credit crunch, banks hesitated to borrow from the FRS because of the stigma attached to such borrowing. The TAF was used to remove that stigma by making available discount loans to all banks through competitive auctions.[177] Because of the auction format, each bank did not have to approach the FRS individually for a loan.[178] The program was open to the US branches of foreign banks as well. Some of the foreign banks that benefitted from it included: Barclays (UK), Societé Générale (France), Dresdner Bank (Germany) and the Mitsubishi Financial Group (Japan). The top 25 global banks received more than 70% of the loans granted under the program.[179] The total amount of credit extended under the TAF amounted to $3.8 trillion.[180]

---

[175] The TAF was based on 12 USC §347b, which authorizes the FRS to provide loans to banks through its discount window.

[176] GAO, *supra* note 125, at 17.

[177] *Id.* at 18.

[178] *Id.* at 19.

[179] *Id.* Appendix XIII, at 231.

[180] *Id.* at 232.

Media outlets filed requests for information under the Freedom of Information Act[181] asking the FRS to provide details about the loans it granted to banks through its discount window and other *ad hoc* emergency programs. The FRS and the Clearinghouse Association, a private association of banks, claimed that releasing that information would deter banks from taking advantage of the discount window in the future. The courts agreed with the media, though, and ordered the FRS to disclose the information related to its emergency programs.[182] The release of the information in 2011 revealed the extent to which some big foreign and domestic banks had benefitted from the largesse of the US government.

Another market that counted on the government for its survival was the repo market. The repo market is the market for repurchase (repo) agreements. Repos are a way for large depositors to receive returns on their deposits with banks. A large company, for example Google, may have $1 million of spare cash deposited with a bank. To earn a return on this cash, it can conclude a repurchase agreement with the bank: Google buys T-Bills from the bank and the bank agrees to repurchase these T-Bills in the future at a price above the original price Google paid to buy them. This way Google receives a guaranteed return on the money it keeps with the bank. The T-bills that the bank sells to Google, with the promise to buy them back in the future, act as a sort of collateral for the transaction.

To address the scarcity of T-bills, which debilitated the functioning of the repo market, the FRS instituted on March 11, 2008 the Term Securities Lending Facility.[183] Financial institutions could use the facility to exchange, for a fee, the securities they held, for example the toxic MBS, for T-bills. The government funds available under the Term Securities Lending Facility amounted to $2.3 trillion.[184] The program benefitted mostly global US and foreign banks.[185] Another facility established on March 16, 2008, the Primary Dealer Credit Facility,[186] expanded discount window lending to primary dealers to help them address the lack of liquidity in the markets. Five big banks borrowed 82.5% of the total amount of Primary Dealer Credit Facility loans.[187]

---

[181]   The Freedom of Information Act, 5 USC §552 et seq.

[182]   *Bloomberg, L.P. v. Board of Governors*, 601 F.3d 143 (2d Cir. 2010), cert. denied *Clearinghouse Association v. Bloomberg*, 131 S.Ct. 1674 (2011); *Fox News Network, LLC v. Board of Governors*, 601 F.3d 158 (2d Cir. 2010), cert. denied *Clearing House Association v. Fox News Network*, 131 S.Ct. 1676 (2011).

[183]   GAO, *supra* note 125, Appendix XIV.

[184]   *Id.* at 240.

[185]   *Id.*

[186]   *Id.* Appendix XI.

[187]   *Id.* at 216.

Table 3.3   *Definition of currency swaps*

Central bank currency swaps (CBCSs)	CBCSs are reciprocal currency arrangements between two CBs to swap their currencies. They consist of two transactions: (1) CB Z agrees to sell its currency to CB Y in exchange for Y's domestic currency at the prevailing market rate; (2) at the same time, the two CBs enter into a binding agreement that obliges CB Y to buy back its currency on a specified date at the same exchange rate. CBCSs make it possible for CBs to make available to their domestic private banks another country's currency. Swap arrangements can be concluded during a crisis or can be permanent

The loans disbursed, all through the life of the facility between March 17, 2008 and February 1, 2010, amounted to approximately $9 trillion.[188]

3.3.5   The FRS as Global Lender of Last Resort

The FRS supported not only foreign private banks but also foreign governments. Based on article 14(1)[189] of the Federal Reserve Act, the FOMC concluded swap arrangements with select foreign CBs to address dollar scarcity in foreign markets. Under these swap arrangements, the FRS exchanged dollars for foreign currency and foreign CBs agreed to buy back their currency at a future date (Table 3.3).

These currency swap arrangements provided the dollar transfusions that made it possible for foreign CBs to support their private banks. Foreign private banks held a large amount of dollar-denominated assets – bonds and other securities. However, they did not hold significant amounts of dollars and could not borrow dollars from other private banks as the interbank credit market was not functioning owing to the lack of clarity about which banks were still creditworthy. Dollars were in high demand during the crisis, as investors were speedily redeeming their dollar-denominated securities for cash. The FRS extended swap lines in unlimited amounts[190] to CBs of developed countries – the ECB and the CBs of Switzerland, Australia, Canada, Denmark, the UK, Japan and New Zealand. It also established for the first time in its history swap lines with the CBs of four other countries – the CBs of Brazil, South Korea, Mexico and Singapore.

---

[188] *Id.* at 216–17. For a list of all emergency programs, *see* GAO, *supra* note 125, at 3.

[189] 'Any Federal reserve bank may ... purchase and sell in the open market, at home or abroad, either from or to domestic or foreign banks ... cable transfers'. 12 USC §353. The FRS has interpreted cable transfers to mean foreign exchange.

[190] Experience with Foreign Currency Liquidity-providing Central Bank Swaps, ECB Monthly Bulletin, at 67, Aug. 2014.

At the FOMC meeting of October 2008, there was extensive discussion on whether to extend swap lines to developing countries. As an FOMC member pointed out, the last thing the FRS wanted was for the CBs of various states to gang up on it demanding swap lines as their right.[191] The FRS outlined criteria for selecting countries worthy of swap arrangements. They included the size of a country's economy, its systemic importance in the global financial system and good economic fundamentals. There was broad support for establishing swap lines with Mexico, Brazil, South Korea and Singapore because of those countries' large economies and Singapore's role as a major financial center.[192] These countries were unlikely to approach the International Monetary Fund (IMF), an international organization, for financial assistance because of the stigma attached to requesting such assistance.[193] Eventually, the FRS granted four temporary swap lines of up $30 billion each to Brazil, Mexico, Korea and Singapore.[194]

The names of the countries that requested swap lines but were rejected by the FRS were redacted from the minutes of the 2008 FOMC meeting.[195] According to media reports, these countries included India, Indonesia, Peru and the Dominican Republic. In the case of India, the rejection seems to have been based on that country's financial system, which was not that developed and integrated into the global system.[196] For the rest of states, there was concern that they might not be able to settle the swap when due – give back the dollars they had received from the FRS to get back their currency. Some suggested that the US government extended a helping hand to certain large developing countries to ensure their support at the first ever summit of heads of state of the Group-20 (G-20) – the group of 20 states with the largest economies worldwide. During that 2008 summit, the US financial leadership was expected to come under attack, particularly from European countries.[197] Others argued that the designation of a country as 'swap-worthy' had to do with the magnitude of the exposure of the US banking sector to that country.[198]

---

[191] FOMC October 2008, *supra* note 121, at 42.

[192] *Id.* at 10.

[193] *Id.* at 25.

[194] FRS, Federal Reserve, Banco Central do Brasil, Banco de Mexico, Bank of Korea, and Monetary Authority of Singapore Announce the Establishment of Temporary Reciprocal Currency Arrangements, Press Release, Oct. 29, 2008.

[195] FOMC October 2008, *supra* note 121, at 30.

[196] *Id.* at 29.

[197] Hyoung-kyu Chey, *Why Did the Federal Reserve Unprecedentedly Offer Swap Lines to Emerging Market Economies during the Global Financial Crisis? Can we Expect them Again in the Future?*, at 6–8, Discussion Paper 11–18, GRIPS, Jan. 2012.

[198] Joshua Aizenman and Gurnain Kaur Pasricha, *Selective Swap Arrangements and the Global Financial Crisis: Analysis and Interpretation*, at 1, NBER Working Paper

The eligible CBs borrowed $1 trillion from the FRS.[199] The ECB made the most use of its swap line, accounting for 80% of that amount. Brazil, Canada, Singapore and New Zealand did not draw on their swap lines. The FRS' arrangements with European countries were eventually cemented as permanent bilateral swap agreements that could be tapped during future crises. For instance, the arrangement between the ECB and the FRBNY took effect through two virtually identical agreements. One was a standing agreement between the FRBNY and ECB to exchange their currencies, as needed, to supply liquidity in dollars.[200] The other had to do with providing liquidity in euros.[201]

During the crisis, the FRS played the role of lender of last resort, the CB of CBs, for a select number of countries. The scale of dollar lending to other CBs could not be accomplished by any another organization but by the institution that creates dollars, the FRS. However, the FRS backed off from assuming the role of global unconditional and unlimited lender of last resort. It picked and chose which CBs to support based on US interests. The rest of states, unless they had some sort of self-insurance, i.e. large FX reserves, were left to agonize over the domestic repercussions of the global crisis.

3.3.6   Spillovers of US Policy

The FRS was not the only CB that pursued near-zero IRs and large purchases of assets. The Bank of England and the ECB followed similar paths soon thereafter, to try to stimulate growth in their own stagnating economies. The outcome of these policies was the fall of IRs in much of the developed world and depreciation of many core countries' currencies. The United States, the sovereign, the first country to launch an aggressive QE as a cure for the crisis, had legitimized these policies. Some were apprehensive that, if every country adopted its own QE, the resulting tit-for-tat depreciations would set off currency wars. As the dollar and the euro were falling, for instance, some states intervened in the FX market to prevent the ensuing appreciation of their currencies. Switzerland intervened aggressively in the market to stop the appreciation of the Swiss franc against the euro, which was falling rapidly owing to the ECB's QE policies.[202]

14821, Mar. 2009.
[199] GAO, *supra* note 125, Appendix IX, at 205.
[200] US Dollar–Euro Swap Agreement, Jan. 16, 2014.
[201] Euro–US Dollar Swap Agreement, Jan. 16, 2014.
[202] *Why the Swiss Unpegged the Franc*, Economist, Jan. 18, 2015.

As QE took the developed world by storm, the total global liquidity increased from $18 trillion in 2003 to $35 trillion in 2014.[203] The global FX reserves, a measure of *official* global liquidity, expanded from $3.2 trillion in 2003 to over $12 trillion in 2014.[204] Foreign-currency-denominated bonds issued by emerging market states, an estimate of global *private* liquidity, increased from $638 billion in 2003 to $2.6 trillion in 2014.[205] The aggressive easing and plummeting of IRs in the developed world pushed capital owners to seek higher yield opportunities in other countries. The influx of hot money into countries like China, South Korea, Brazil, Indonesia, Thailand and Vietnam generated fears of inflation there. Many states, in order to defend themselves, introduced capital controls that found renewed legitimacy under the rubric 'capital flow management' measures.

Much of the hot money that flew to the developing world reverted back to the United States when the US moved, first out of all developed countries, to increase its IRs. When the FRS indicated its plans to tighten in 2013, the yields of US bonds spiked abruptly amid complaints from the developing world that US tightening would trigger large capital outflows and destabilize their economies. These complaints were brushed aside by US authorities. The president of the FRB of Atlanta made it clear that it was not the responsibility of the United States to adjust its policies to fit those of other states. It was the job of other states to take the US policy as a given and adjust their policies if they needed to.

> You have to remember that we [the FRS] are a legal creature of Congress and that we only have a mandate to concern ourselves with the interest of the United States. Other countries simply have to take that as a reality and adjust to us if that's something important for their economies.[206]

The FRS slowed down its easing programs all through 2014. On December 16, 2015, it increased the target range for the FFR from 0–0.25 to 0.25–0.50%.[207] It is hard to fathom that hiking the US benchmark IR by a mere 0.25% can spread havoc to the rest of the world but this is, in fact, what transpired. After

---

[203] The aggregate domestic liquidity of three countries and a region (US, EU, UK and Japan) is used here as a proxy of global liquidity. *See* Tao Sun, *The Impact of Global Liquidity on Financial Landscapes and Risk in the ASEAN-5*, at 5, IMF Paper No. WP/15/211, Sept. 29, 2015.

[204] *Id.*

[205] *Id.*

[206] Statement of Dennis Lockhart (President of the FRB of Atlanta), *see* Simon Kennedy et al., *Fed Officials Rebuff Coordination Calls as QE Taper Looms*, Bloomberg, Aug. 26, 2013.

[207] FRS, Federal Reserve Issues FOMC Statement, Press Release, Dec. 16, 2015.

the FRS guided the IRs higher in December 2015, and announced that four additional rate hikes should be expected in 2016, capital poured out of the developing world and headed back to the United States, strengthening the dollar. Countries with weak fundamentals (e.g. high inflation, budget and CA deficits) experienced large capital outflows.[208] Some states (e.g. Peru, Chile, Colombia, Angola, Zambia and Ghana) increased their IRs, as they anticipated the lift-off of the US IRs, to stem capital outflows. The FRS did not proceed with all of the IR hikes it was contemplating though. It lifted the FFR range again a year later, on December 14, 2016, from 0.25–0.50 to 0.50–0.75%.

All through 2015, the appreciation of the dollar, owing to expectations of continuing tightening, resulted in the depreciation of other countries' currencies. This had a huge impact on the dollar-denominated debt market – the states and companies that borrow in dollars. As we have seen, when US IRs are near zero, many states and foreign companies tend to borrow in dollars. It was estimated that, by 2014, non-financial companies outside the United States had borrowed more than $9 trillion.[209] The FRS' QE had reduced the yields on the Treasuries to such an extent that it pushed banks and other financial institutions to switch from buying Treasuries to buying the debt of foreign states and companies.[210] Foreign companies were able to borrow in dollars through their offshore subsidiaries, despite efforts of their governments to restrict access to dollar credit. Chinese and South Korean companies, for instance, were able to bypass domestic regulations and borrow in dollars through their subsidiaries in less-regulated jurisdictions across the world. Many financial firms were engaging in a lucrative *carry trade* – borrowing dollars cheaply in the United States and then lending them, at higher IRs, to firms in other countries. The ubiquity of the bond market, which made it possible for firms to borrow in other countries' currencies, had weakened national policies that sought to restrict dollar credit.[211] Companies like Russia's Gazprom, a gas company, and Brazil's Petrobras, an energy company, were able to issue dollar-denominated bonds through their subsidiaries in Luxembourg and the Cayman Islands. In addition, countries, like Brazil, Turkey and South Africa, whose exports were lower than their imports, balanced their deficits by borrowing in dollars.

It eventually became obvious that, owing to a pessimistic global economic outlook and a slowdown in China, the largest of the emerging markets, the FRS could not afford to raise IRs as quickly as it had anticipated by the end

---

[208] *See generally* UN Department of Economic and Social Affairs, *World Economic Situation and Prospects 2016*, at 2–4.

[209] Robert N. McCauley et al., *Global Dollar Credit: Links to US Monetary Policy and Leverage*, at 5, BIS Working Paper No. 483, Jan. 2015.

[210] *Id.* at 20–21.

[211] *Id.*

of 2015. In fact, on March 16, 2016, the FRS stated that any further rate hikes had to take into account the global economic and financial developments.[212] Policy-makers noted that the sharp appreciation of the dollar and the growing spreads between investment-grade debt and junk debt demonstrated that markets had added an extra 0.75% of tightening to the official 0.25% rate increase.[213] If the planned additional rate increases were to be 'amplified' in similar ways, the world, including the United States, could easily fall back into recession.[214] The FRS was mostly apprehensive about setting off another US recession, as the strong dollar could dent the competitiveness of US export sector and choke off nascent growth. From mid-2014 all through 2015, foreign currencies had weakened on a trade-weighted basis by 22% against the dollar. The Japanese yen had fallen by 16% and the euro by 20%. The dollar's strength, fueled by expectations of higher US rates, surprised the FRS. The FRS chair explicitly cited the strength of the dollar as an important factor to bear in mind before proceeding with more rate hikes.[215]

The Treasury also made it clear that it was not happy with the depreciation of other countries' currencies. In April 2016, it created a 'Monitoring List' of countries suspected of engaging in currency manipulation – that is intervening in the currency market to depreciate their currency at the expense of the dollar. Under the 1988 Omnibus Trade and Competitiveness Act[216] the Secretary of the Treasury must annually analyze the ER policies of foreign states in order to evaluate whether any of them are manipulating their currency to gain an unfair trade advantage.[217] To be included in this list of infamous currency manipulators, a country has to meet two out of three criteria:

- significant trade surplus with the United States (more than $20 billion);
- material CA surplus – larger than 3% of its GDP;
- intervention in the markets to depreciate its currency – repeated purchases of dollars amounting to more than 2% of its GDP over a year.[218]

---

[212] FRS, Federal Reserve Issues FOMC Statement, Press Release, at 2, Mar. 16, 2016.

[213] Lael Brainard, *What Happened to the Great Divergence?* at 7, Speech at the 2016 Monetary Policy Forum sponsored by the University of Chicago Booth School of Business, Feb. 26, 2016.

[214] *Id.*

[215] FRS, Transcript of Chair Yellen's FOMC Press Conference, at 6, Mar. 18, 2015.

[216] The 1988 Omnibus Trade and Competitiveness Act was strengthened in 2015 by the Trade Facilitation and Trade Enforcement Act. *See* 19 USC §4301 et seq.

[217] 19 USC §4421(a)(2)(ii).

[218] The Treasury has quantified the criteria included in the 2015 Trade Facilitation and Trade Enforcement Act. *See* US Department of the Treasury, *Foreign Exchange Policies of Major Trading Partners of the United States*, at 1–2, Apr. 29, 2016.

The countries that made it to the monitoring list in 2016 were China, Japan, South Korea, Taiwan and Germany.[219] However, because none of the countries met all three criteria, they were not subject to US sanctions. Investors are well aware of the asymmetric power of the United States vis-à-vis the rest of the world. Therefore, they take the pronouncements of US officials on the overvaluation of the dollar at face value. Market participants noted the 2016 US dissatisfaction with the dollar's appreciation. As a result, the dollar fell. It appreciated again, by the end of 2016, when the FRS adopted a more aggressive tightening stance.

---

[219] *Id.* at 2.

4. The core and the periphery

4.1 STRATEGIES OF CHINA

4.1.1 Accumulation of Reserves

On August 5, 2019, the United States called China a currency manipulator,[1] triggering fears that the trade conflict between the old superpower and the emerging one was soon to become a full blown currency war. On August 5, China let the yuan depreciate below the 'key psychological threshold' of 7 yuans (renminbi, RMB) to the dollar, generating speculation that China was planning to respond to punitive US trade tariffs on almost all of its goods by devaluing its currency.[2]

The United States first labeled China a currency manipulator in the early 1990s. That label was prompted by a steep devaluation of the yuan. In 1993, $1 dollar bought only 5.76 Chinese yuans; in 1994, it bought as many as 8.61 yuans. China at the time was branding itself as the world's manufacturer and that fueled expectations of yuan's appreciation. However, China was reluctant to let the yuan strengthen as this would harm its exports. It intervened in the markets to ensure that the yuan would remain at a level that would guarantee its future growth.

The People's Bank of China (PBOC) intervention to prevent the yuan's appreciation involved several steps:

- The PBOC, through state-owned banks, bought dollars from Chinese exporters in exchange for yuans.
- The bank used these dollars to buy T-bills and Treasuries to build up its FX reserves, its war chest.
- Exchanging yuans for dollars put too many yuans in circulation, risking domestic inflation. The PBOC sold bonds to the public to sterilize its

---

[1]   US Treasury Department, Treasury Designates China as a Currency Manipulator, Press Release, Aug. 5, 2019.
[2]   Joanne Chiu and Steven Russolillo, *China's Yuan Breaches Critical Level of 7 to the Dollar, Prompting Trump Critique*, WSJ, Aug. 5, 2019.

intervention in the currency market, that is wipe out the excess yuans it was creating.

- The increasing government debt pushed IRs up. High IRs on domestic debt were not sustainable because the Chinese state was bent on holding T-bills in its FX reserves, no matter their low yields in comparison with the IRs it had to pay on its own debt.
- To address the problem of high IRs that stemmed from its sterilization efforts, the PBOC fixed domestic IRs at low levels. This was not costless. Low IRs made it easier to borrow, risking bubbles in the housing sector and stock market. Low IRs had another adverse effect: financial repression. Households that received low IRs on their deposits felt compelled to save even more to offset their low-yielding savings.[3]

Between 2014 and 2019, China's FX reserves fluctuated around $3 trillion, reaching at one point $4 trillion. China's reserve accumulation has become a model for many developing states. Self-insurance by accumulating FX makes sense because of the lack of a global lender of last resort. In Chapter 3, we examined how the United States has opted to be a limited lender of last resort to a select number of states. Additionally, international organizations, like the IMF,[4] do not have the resources or the mandate to act as global and unconditional lenders of last resort.

China's large accumulation of reserves, which include a large amount of dollar assets, has raised national security concerns in the United States. Some are worried about the repercussions on the dollar if China one day resolves to sell, all at once, its dollar-denominated assets. Others have even speculated that China, and other states that hold large amounts of dollar-denominated assets in their reserves,[5] could collaborate to guarantee an offshore 'global dollar', a dollar functioning outside the US financial system.[6] The independence of this global dollar could be made possible by a payment system dissociated from the US payment system.[7] While this seems like a far-fetched scenario at the moment, it cannot be totally disregarded as a potential security threat. The US anxiety over the dollars held by third countries has prompted the IMF

---

[3]   C. Randall Henning, *Choice and Coercion in East Asian Exchange Rate Regimes*, at 8, Working Paper No. 12-15, Peterson Institute for International Economics, Sept. 2012.

[4]   For the establishment and evolution of the IMF, *see* Chapters 8 and 13.

[5]   In 2019, it was estimated that $6 trillion in US government debt was held overseas, *see* US Treasury, Major Foreign Holders of US Treasury Securities, http://ticdata .treasury.gov.

[6]   *The Sticky Superpower*, Special Report: The World Economy, at 13–14, Economist, Oct. 3, 2015.

[7]   *Id.*

to examine how much FX reserves countries really need. It has argued that a common sense formula can be concocted to determine the amount of reserves countries should ideally keep. China and developing countries have retorted, though, that the FX needs of states cannot be reduced to a one-size-fits-all formula. They have urged the IMF to instead devise country-specific method-ologies to assess the adequacy of each and every country's reserves.[8]

In April 2015, the IMF published a formula (Fig. 4.1) that has been used by financial analysts to assess the adequacy of countries' FX reserves.[9] The IMF has acknowledged that countries may have different reasons for keeping large reserves, such as maintaining a capability for unilateral intervention in the FX market to stabilize their ER, instilling confidence in their currency and thwarting attacks against it, and responding to shocks and disorderly market conditions. The IMF has conceded that the accumulation of reserves as a pre-cautionary measure against future unpredictable events lessens the likelihood of BOP crises in emerging-market economies.[10] States need precautionary reserves especially because the FRS is not ready to provide swap lines to all countries in times of crisis, and because the IMF credit lines are not automatic and unconditional. The IMF, though, has also pointed out that some states may have 'mercantilist motives' for holding large reserves. States can use their reserves to intervene in the FX market to depreciate their currency and improve their exports at the expense of other states.[11]

States with **Fixed ER** Need Enough FX Reserves to Cover:		States with **Floating ER*** Need Enough FX Reserves to Cover:	
30 %	of their Short-Term Debt	30 %	of their Short-Term Debt
20%	of their other Liabilities	15%	of their other Liabilities
10%	of their MS (M2)	5%	of their MS (M2)
20%	of their Exports	5%	of their Exports

*States that let their ER float based on market sentiment need less reserves because they do not have to intervene in the market to maintain a fixed ER.
See IMF, *Assessing Reserve Adequacy: Specific Proposals*, at 19, Apr. 2015.

Figure 4.1   How much FX reserves do states need?

---

[8]   IEO, *International Reserves – IMF Concerns and Country Perspectives*, at 16 (2012).

[9]   IMF, *Assessing Reserve Adequacy – Specific Proposals*, Apr. 2015 [hereinafter IMF Reserve Adequacy].

[10]   *Id.* at 6.

[11]   *Id.* at 8, n. 8.

The IMF has concluded that, at a minimum, reserves must provide: export cover (sufficient FX reserves to cover exports in case of lack of global demand); short-term debt and other liabilities cover (enough FX reserves to cover all of a country's short-term debt and other liabilities); and M2 cover – FX reserves should cover about 5–20% of the M2 in case of outflows of bank deposits held by residents.[12] The IMF has assigned specific weights for estimating the adequacy of state reserves (Fig. 4.1). These weights are not set in stone. Countries can customize them to fit their needs based on whether:

- they impose capital controls – states that use capital controls need fewer reserves since capital controls prevent, even if somewhat ineffectively, the outflow of capital;[13]
- they are commodity exporters – states that rely on the export of commodities need more FX cushions to address global recessions that drive down demand for commodities;[14]
- they are credit-constrained – states that cannot obtain financing in the global markets need more FX reserves as buffers.[15]

In 2016, China was subjected to probing speculative attacks[16] aimed at testing its resolve to defend the yuan. Speculators, including many US-based hedge funds, were trying to determine the readiness of the government to pay the price for sustaining the fixed dollar/yuan ER. An accurate assessment of state's FX reserves is a pre-condition for launching a successful currency attack. If a country has more reserves than speculators predict it has, and it is ready to sell them to prevent the depreciation of its currency, the speculative attack will fail.

On February 10, 2016, Hayman Capital, a hedge fund, sent a letter to its clients explaining why it was betting against the yuan. The letter was leaked to the press to increase the probability that the projected yuan devaluation would indeed happen. The hedge fund used the IMF formula (Fig. 4.1) to assess whether China had adequate FX reserves. Based on the formula, it concluded that China needed $2.7 trillion worth of reserves to fend off a currency attack.[17] It then, by making certain assumptions, concluded that Chinese FX

---

[12] *Id.* at 19.

[13] *Id.* at 20.

[14] *Id.* at 23.

[15] *Id.* at 32.

[16] On probing currency attacks, *see* Paul Krugman, *Are Currency Crises Self-Fulfilling?*, 345, at 357, in 11 NBER Macroeconomics Annual (Ben S. Bernanke and Julio J. Rotemberg, eds, 1996).

[17] J. Kyle Bass, *The $34 Trillion Experiment: China's Banking System and the World's Largest Macro Imbalance*, at 10, Hayman Capital Management, Feb. 10, 2016.

reserves that could be quickly liquidated to avert a currency attack were about $2.1 to $2.2 trillion.[18] China, therefore, could not afford to continue 'burning' reserves, selling its dollar reserves to buy back its currency, and would eventually have to succumb to speculative pressure and let its currency depreciate.

Others contested whether the IMF formula was the appropriate way to calculate the amount of FX reserves China needed.[19] This was because China was not the typical emerging market country. It maintained a CA surplus and, as a creditor nation, had a large financial account surplus. China implemented capital controls and was transitioning from a fixed ER to a floating ER. Taking into account these Chinese idiosyncrasies, it probably needed less than $1.5 trillion in reserves to hinder a currency attack.[20] China's $3.2 trillion reserves, of which more than $2.1 trillion were estimated to be liquid, quickly convertible into cash, were more than enough to ensure that it could withstand a protracted currency attack.[21]

The big unknown in the currency market in 2016 was whether China would be able to manage the orderly depreciation of its currency. Some actively bet that short-sellers would get the upper hand and that the yuan would collapse.

4.1.2   Exchange Rate Targeting

In 2005, China claimed that it was changing its strategy of pegging the yuan to the dollar. Instead it would maintain, from then on, a managed peg to a basket of major currencies. In 2009, when the US crisis hit the rest of the world, China re-pegged the yuan to the dollar. On December 11, 2015, the PBOC re-signaled its hope of establishing a flexible peg to a basket of currencies. De-pegging the yuan from the dollar and tying it to a basket of currencies at the time the dollar was appreciating was a way to weaken it. This was expected to help the Chinese economy, which was experiencing a slowdown and could not afford to deal with the imported appreciation of its currency owing to the dollar peg.

The yuan is one currency that trades under two symbols: as CNH in the offshore market and CNY in China mainland. The PBOC fixes at 9:15 a.m. every day the *onshore* value of yuan (CNY) within a trading band of ±2%.[22] Traders can use this 'fixed' yuan/dollar rate to trade within the established

---

[18]   *Id.*

[19]   Sheeraz Raza, *Michael Pettis: Here is Why Kyle Bass is Mistaken on China*, ValueWalk, Feb. 25, 2016.

[20]   *Id.*

[21]   *Id.*

[22]   The trading band has changed over time. *See* John Clark, *China's Evolving Managed Float: An Exploration of the Roles of the Fix and Broad Dollar Movements in*

trading band. The PBOC has stated that it sets the fix after it consults with major foreign and Chinese banks. These banks submit yuan/dollar prices to the PBOC based on the trading of the yuan/dollar the previous day. The PBOC then averages them to calculate the 'central parity' rate or midpoint.[23] The PBOC intervenes in the market to keep the ER from drifting more than 2% above or below the midpoint. The *offshore* yuan, on the other hand, is freely tradable in Hong Kong. There is no offshore trading band and no commitment of the PBOC to intervene in the offshore market.

Because the onshore ER is highly regulated but the offshore ER is market-determined, there is usually a spread between CNY and CNH. When CNH trades higher than CNY, it makes sense for China's onshore importers to bring their CNY to Hong Kong where they can convert them into dollars at the CNH higher rate. On the other hand, if CNH trades lower than CNY, it makes sense for China's exporters to convert their dollars into yuans on the mainland rather than in the offshore market.

The China Foreign Exchange Trading System, an agency managed by the PBOC, announced in 2015 that the yuan would loosely follow a basket of 13 currencies.[24] It clarified further that 'referring' to a basket of currencies did not mean 'pegging' the yuan to that basket. The yuan would not 'mechanically' follow the ER index of currencies included in the basket. Market supply and demand for the currency was another important reference.[25] Many understood this to mean that the PBOC would be able to select, based on market conditions, whether to anchor the yuan on the US dollar or the basket of 13 currencies.[26]

Singapore's monetary management has been a model for China's PBOC. Singapore's ER policy is a hybrid between a fixed ER and a floating ER system. The Monetary Authority of Singapore uses the ER, not the IR, to calibrate the economy. However, it does not keep its ER fixed, the way other countries that target the ER do. The Singaporean dollar is managed against a trade-weighted currency *basket* and can fluctuate based on an undisclosed *band*. This makes possible the short-term appreciation or depreciation of the

---

Explaining Daily Exchange Rate Changes, at 5–6, FRBNY Staff Report No. 828, Nov. 2017.

[23] *Id.* at 5.

[24] The weights (%) of the 13 currencies in the basket are: US dollar, 26.4; euro, 21.4; yen, 14.7; Hong Kong dollar, 6.6; Australian dollar, 6.3; Malaysian ringgit, 4.7; Russian ruble, 4.4; UK pound, 3.9; Singaporean dollar, 3.8; Thai baht, 3.3; Canadian dollar, 2.5; Swiss franc, 1.5; and New Zealand dollar, 0.7. *See* Yuko Gomi, *A New Renminbi Index: The CFETS RMB Index*, Eyes of IIMA, No. 3, Jan. 12, 2016. *See also* CFETS, The Launch of the RMB Index Helps to Guide Public View of RMB Exchange Rate, Press Release, Dec. 11, 2016.

[25] *Id.*

[26] *Bending, Not Breaking: China's Currency*, Economist, June 4, 2016.

currency based on market conditions. The monetary authority intervenes in the market when the ER moves outside its prescribed band by buying or selling foreign currencies as needed to steer the ER back into the band. The ER band is periodically reviewed by the authority to ensure that it is consistent with the fundamentals of the Singaporean economy. If those fundamentals change, the authority allows the ER band to *crawl* upwards or downwards, as needed. It uses this *basket, band and crawl* system[27] to provide general guidance on the anticipated ER fluctuation and to reduce the need of constant meddling in the market.

4.1.3   China and the Trilemma

The yuan was one of the world's top-performing currencies for most of 2015. The subsequent deceleration of the Chinese economy, though, pointed to its weakening. By the end of 2015, many expected that China would have to intervene in the market to devalue its currency to address a domestic economic slowdown. Yuan's devaluation could benefit Chinese exporters and counter a possible deflation by increasing the price of imports. Given the extensive QE programs that were operating in full force in Japan and the EU, the PBOC could not afford to abstain from monetary easing.

Currency devaluation to boost export competitiveness entails costs though. If China, Asia's biggest economy, were to devaluate, other countries would be likely to follow its example, sparking a currency war and erasing any advantage that China might have gained by devaluating. Moreover, given that capital was already flowing out of China, lured by the prospect of higher US IRs, yuan's depreciation would hasten more outflows. The weakening of the yuan would hurt Chinese firms that had piled up about $1 trillion in foreign debt. Furthermore, China was attempting, at that point, to establish the yuan as a global reserve currency. A depreciating yuan could have torpedoed that effort. In fact, in order to boost yuan's credibility, China had kept a steady ER against the dollar despite the 2008 financial turmoil. The IMF's verdict that the yuan was no longer undervalued, which came out on May 26, 2015, added to yuan's credibility.[28]

Speculation that the yuan would depreciate, though, took the markets by storm in the early days of 2016, when the relationship between yuan's closing price and the fix the next morning suddenly broke down. On January 7, 2016,

---

[27]   MAS, *Singapore's Exchange Rate-Based Monetary Policy*, http://www.mas.gov .sg/.
[28]   IMF Staff Completes the 2015 Article IV Consultation Mission to China, Press Release No. 15/237, May 26, 2015.

the PBOC reduced the fix more than the markets expected based on its previous practice.[29] What ensued was a gigantic scuffle between the PBOC and currency traders about who was in control over how far and fast the yuan would depreciate. Hayman Capital Management, a hedge fund, made it public that it was betting against the yuan. It had put 85% of its portfolio in trades expected to pay off only if the yuan depreciated.[30]

On January 12, 2016, China fired back. The PBOC ordered state-owned banks to buy so many yuans in the offshore Hong Kong market, where speculators placed their bets against the yuan, that the IR for borrowing yuan overnight[31] shot up to 66.8%[32] making it close to impossible to finance short positions (i.e. borrowing yuans to sell them so as to devalue the currency). The PBOC's forceful reaction alarmed short-sellers who were betting that the currency would decline. Some scaled back or exited their short bets, claiming that they could not afford to take on the Chinese state. China used approximately $10 billion per month, in 2016, to prop up its currency.[33] Some even alleged that sudden spikes of trading in the offshore FX market indicated further undisclosed intervention. The intervention to jack up the yuan was not costless. By engineering an artificial scarcity of yuans in the offshore market, China reduced the appeal of its currency as a reserve currency.

The PBOC took additional measures to curb speculation against the yuan. It asked foreign banks that were trading in yuans in the offshore market to start maintaining yuan reserves with it.[34] Because most foreign banks could not meet the PBOC prescribed RRR, they had to suspend their trading activities. The PBOC further ordered three private foreign banks, the Development Bank of Singapore, Standard Chartered Bank and Deutsche Bank, to suspend some of their yuan trading operations in an effort to thwart excessive speculation against the currency.[35]

---

[29] Lingling Wei and Anjani Trivedi, *Why China Shifted its Strategy for the Yuan, and How it Backfired*, WSJ, Jan. 7, 2016.

[30] Juliet Chung and Carolyn Cui, *Currency War: US Hedge Funds Mount New Attacks on China's Yuan*, WSJ, Jan. 31, 2016.

[31] The Hong Kong Inter-bank Offered Rate, HIBOR, the standard benchmark IR in the offshore market.

[32] Saumya Vaishampayan and Lingling Wei, *Surge in Offshore Yuan Borrowing Rate Suggests China Intervention*, WSJ, Sept. 11, 2016.

[33] *The Yuan's Weakness is a Dilemma for China's Central Bank: How Far to Fall?*, Economist, Dec. 1, 2016.

[34] *China Orders Foreign Banks to Set Aside Reserves for Forex Forward Trading*, WSJ, July 6, 2016.

[35] *China: Central Bank Limiting Yuan Trading Operations*, Stratfor Situation Report, Jan. 8, 2016.

In order to stem the outflows of domestic capital, the dominant credit card issuer in the country, China UnionPay, started to enforce the existing $5 000 per-transaction cap on the amount cardholders could transfer to overseas accounts.[36] It further imposed a new annual limit of 100 000 yuan ($15 200) on overseas withdrawals of cash through UnionPay cards.[37] Additional capital controls were put in place later, such as restrictions on how much money multinational companies could get out of China and tighter restrictions on foreign takeovers by Chinese firms. By the end of 2016, for instance, multinational companies could *sweep* only $5 million worth of yuans in and out of the country, a drastic reduction from the previously allowed amount of $50 million.[38] Capital controls were not China's FEP instrument of choice. It endorsed them because it was under siege by those who were shorting its currency. Capital controls hurt an economy, closing it off from the rest of the world and driving capital into offshore and unregulated jurisdictions.

China's main priority, after the 2016 currency attack, was to further unshackle the yuan from the dollar by reducing the dollar's influence on its FEP. In December 2016, as the dollar was rapidly appreciating against the yuan, the PBOC expanded the number of currencies in the basket it was already using to calibrate yuan's value from 13 to 24.[39] It also reduced the weight it assigned to the dollar in that basket from 26.4 to 22.4%.[40] Chinese leaders declared that maintaining the yuan's 'basic stability' was the most important monetary task for 2017.[41] Ironically, the recipe for achieving that basic stability was to add some mild volatility and unpredictability to the currency's ER so as to wrong-foot traders hoping to make a fortune from abrupt currency movements. By early 2018, it was apparent that China had been successful in defending its currency. China's endorsement of selective but stringently enforced capital controls along with domestic growth and better global economic conditions had worked in its favor.[42]

The 2016 speculation against the yuan came at a time when the Chinese government was attempting to readjust the economy. That involved a battle on many fronts including dealing with a heavily indebted banking system and

---

[36]   Wei Gu, *China UnionPay Clamps Down on Foreign Insurance Purchases*, WSJ, Feb. 3, 2016.

[37]   *Id.*

[38]   James T. Areddy and Lingling We, *Foreign Companies Face New Clampdown for Getting Money out of China*, WSJ, Dec. 1, 2016.

[39]   CFETS, Public Announcement of China Foreign Exchange Trade System on Adjusting Rules for Currency Baskets of CFETS RMB Indices, Press Release, Dec. 29, 2016. *See also supra* note 24.

[40]   *Id.*

[41]   Lingling Wei, *China Retools in Push to Stabilize Yuan*, WSJ, Dec. 29, 2016.

[42]   *How China Won the Battle of the Yuan: Stable Hands*, Economist, Jan. 11, 2018.

navigating a transition from export-led growth to indigenous growth through the boosting of wages, pensions and social spending.

China has resolved to deal with the impossible trinity[43] by imposing capital controls[44] and using its precautionary FX reserves to stem attacks against its currency. Large FX reserves and capital controls have given it the freedom to calibrate the IR to address domestic recessionary conditions and to intervene in the FX market to stabilize the value of the yuan (*see* Fig. 2.5). China has used its reserves and capital controls to defend itself against foreigners and its own residents when they sell off yuans and yuan-denominated assets to buy foreign assets and currencies.

4.1.4   A Taste of Sovereignty

To establish the yuan as *the* prime global reserve currency, foreigners must view it as indispensible for the conduct of international transactions and a store of value. Investors will not accumulate yuans the way they accumulate dollars unless there is some way they can invest them to generate returns. People hold currencies for transactional, speculative and precautionary purposes. For the yuan to acquire the status of the prime global currency, it must become the vehicle for international trade and investment and the means of storing wealth.

In 2016, the IMF decided to include the yuan in the SDR (Special Drawing Rights) basket,[45] its basket of global reserve currencies, boosting its international prestige. The IMF's decision to include the yuan in the SDR basket was 'an important milestone in the integration of the Chinese economy into the global financial system'.[46] It was, indeed, a crowning moment of China's FEP. China had spent years enacting measures to internationalize the use of yuan. By 2015, invoicing in yuan accounted for 24.6% of China's merchandize trade and

---

[43]   *See also* Joshua Aizenman, *The Impossible Trinity – from the Policy Trilemma to the Policy Quadrilemma*, at 8, Working Paper, Economics Department, University of California Santa Cruz, Mar. 2011.

[44]   Capital controls are never perfect. Many capital owners take advantage of the loopholes in capital control measures or use illegal means to hide their riches from their home states. China's elite is no different. *See* Clark Gascoigne, *US$400 Billion Smuggled into China from Hong Kong through Trade Misinvoicing since 2006*, Global Financial Integrity, Press Release, Jan. 7, 2014; Clark Gascoigne, *Chinese Economy Lost $3.79 Trillion in Illicit Financial Outflows since 2000, Reveals New GFI Report*, Global Financial Integrity, Press Release, Oct. 25, 2012.

[45]   On the SDR, *see* Chapter 13, Section 15.2.

[46]   IMF, IMF Adds Chinese Renminbi to Special Drawing Rights Basket, Press Release, Sept. 30, 2016.

this figure was expected to be 46% by 2020.[47] When transactions are invoiced and settled in yuan, Chinese firms transfer the foreign exchange risk to their trading counterparts. The use of the yuan for trade settlement helps China, and those who trade with it, address potential dollar shortages. Furthermore, the yuan has been the second-most-used currency in trade finance[48] and in 2015 it overtook the Japanese yen and became the fourth most used currency for international payments.[49] The China International Payments System has been instrumental in mainstreaming the yuan. The System is viewed as a challenge to SWIFT, the world's largest payment system.[50]

Yuan's global dominance is further abetted by the willingness of other states to accumulate yuans. By 2016, more than 60 foreign CBs had invested in yuan assets.[51] By 2018, the official holdings of yuan were estimated at $202 billion, still a small share of $11 trillion global reserves.[52]

A state cannot really assert economic autonomy if it does not have a domestic bond market that is deep, liquid and coveted by foreigners for its safe and predictable returns. In 2019, China's $13 trillion bond market was the second in the world.[53] Foreigners owned only 2% of that market[54] but, as we will see below, China's inclusion in global bond indexes was expected to bring large capital inflows to it. There is nothing more empowering for a state than its ability to borrow from foreigners in its domestic currency. The United States has the luxury of running large deficits because it pays for its debt by simply using its currency. These deficits have provided the world with dollars and have helped establish the dollar as the prime global reserve currency.

China has expanded its offshore bond offerings. The so-called dim sum bonds issued in Hong Kong are denominated in yuan. The bank HSBC was the

---

[47]   *Renminbi Internationalization: The Pace Quickens*, Standard Chartered, June 10, 2015.

[48]   SWIFT, RMB Now 2nd Most Used Currency in Trade Finance, Overtaking the Euro, Press Release, Dec. 3, 2013.

[49]   The five currencies most used to make international payments are the US dollar (44.82%), the euro (27.20%), the sterling pound (8.45%), the yuan (2.79%) and the yen (2.76%). *See Renminbi's Stellar Ascension: Are You on Top of It?*, at 5, RMB Tracker, SIBOS (2015).

[50]   *See* Chapter 15, Section 15.2.9.

[51]   Patrick Graham and John Geddie, *Yuan Reserves Set to Rise by $500 Billion Over 5 Years: Banks*, WSJ, Feb. 25, 2015.

[52]   Most CBs still accumulated dollars in their FX reserves – $6.6 trillion out of the total amount of disclosed reserves of $11 trillion. IMF, IMF Releases Data on the Currency Composition of Foreign Exchange Reserves Including Holdings in Renminbi, Press Release, Mar. 31, 2019.

[53]   After the US bond market ($41 trillion). BIS, Summary of Debt Securities Outstanding, June 4, 2019, https://www.bis.org/statistics.

[54]   *Id.*

first corporation to issue dim sum bonds followed by McDonalds, a fast-food chain.[55] In 2012, China started to issue yuan-denominated bonds in Taiwan – the Formosa bonds.[56] Yuan-denominated bonds are now trading in the UK, Luxembourg, Germany, France and all of Southeast Asia. In 2014, the UK became the first state to issue yuan-denominated debt.[57] China has further made it possible for foreigners to issue *onshore* yuan-denominated bonds – the Panda bonds. The first company to issue such bonds was Daimler,[58] a German car company.

The internationalization of yuan has brought other perks, such as international *seigniorage*. Seigniorage is the difference between the face value of a currency and its production costs. It is captured, at the international level, when foreigners hold a country's currency.

All in all, a globalized yuan makes it possible for China to join the United States and some other reserve-currency issuing states as the maker rather the than taker of global economic policy.[59] The increasing internationalization of the yuan should enable China to use its financial system to penalize its enemies, the way the United States is doing today. Moreover, the rise of another economic behemoth may curb US zeal to financially ostracize unpalatable states.[60] This is because China is well positioned to take advantage of the frustration of states that scramble for alternatives when afflicted by US sanctions and persistent dollar shortages. States treated as pariahs by Western states and financial institutions can escape the dollar world, to some degree, by finding refuge in the yuan.

China maintains swap agreements with many marginalized countries. These agreements help bring together a constituency of states that may view it as a benevolent hegemon. On July 18, 2014, the PBOC and the CB of Argentina renewed their 2009 currency swap agreement. The size of the swap was $11 billion (70 billion yuan/90 billion pesos).[61] The renewal made it possible for Argentina to bolster its foreign reserves by paying for Chinese imports with yuans, and helped it squash speculation about the peso's devaluation. At the time, Argentina could not obtain dollar financing in the bond market and was struggling to support its currency with its dwindling dollar reserves.

---

[55] Chris Brummer, *Soft Law and the Global Financial System: Rule Making in the 21st Century* 14 (2012).

[56] *Id.* at 20.

[57] *Id.* at 23.

[58] *Id.* at 12.

[59] *Id.* at 7.

[60] *Id.* at 25.

[61] Peoples Bank of China, *Highlights of China's Monetary Policy in 2014*.

In December 2015, a shortage of US dollars prompted Zimbabwe to endorse the yuan as an alternative legal tender to the dollar.[62] Zimbabwe had abandoned its own dollar in 2009 after a yearly hyperinflation of 500 billion% that caused the collapse of its currency, rendering it worthless. It subsequently started using foreign currencies, including the US dollar. Zimbabwe's imports, though, far exceeded its exports. Because of this, it could not obtain the dollars it needed through its export sector. To make matters worse, foreign capital inflows dried up because of the US and EU economic sanctions imposed on the country, which is a perennial abuser of human rights. The continuing dollar shortages wreaked havoc on Zimbabwe's economy. In 2015, consumer prices fell by 3% as companies resorted to layoffs and wage reductions. However, as the West was isolating Zimbabwe, China came to its rescue. It became Zimbabwe's largest trading partner and, by providing it with yuans, a monetary benefactor.

If China plans to establish the yuan as *the* global reserve currency, the currency that will substitute for the dollar, it will face an uphill battle though. Printing the global reserve currency confers privileges but entails risks. It is unclear whether China may be willing to provide the world with ample yuan liquidity by running deficits instead of surpluses. Printing too many yuans to support global liquidity needs is risky because it can trigger inflation and currency devaluation. This in turn can shake people's faith in the stability of a reserve currency, as the United States found out the hard way in the 1970s.[63]

4.1.5   Escaping the Dollar World: the Obstacles

4.1.5.1   Financial dependence

As we explained in Chapter 3, an index is a statistical device designed to measure changes in the behavior of an economic variable. The consumer price index measures changes in the prices consumers pay to buy goods and services. A change in the index upwards or downwards signifies the rise or decline of inflation. The Dow Jones Industrial Average is a securities index that measures the performance of stocks of 30 large companies that are representative of the US economy. The Standard & Poor's 500 assesses the performance of stocks of the largest 500 US companies. Index developers can shape the global financial markets because they are the *de facto* arbiters of how investors allocate their money in those markets. In 2017, about $11.7 trillion in investment funds

---

[62]   *Zimbabwe to Make Chinese Yuan Legal Currency after Beijing Cancels Debts,* Guardian, Dec. 21, 2015.
[63]   *See* Chapter 9.

were tracking indexes managed by the Standard & Poor Dow Jones company.[64] The MSCI indexes were followed by $11 trillion in funds.[65]

A US private firm, MSCI, develops many indexes including the MSCI Emerging Markets Index, which consists of shares of large companies in 24 emerging markets representing 10% of world market capitalization. MSCI announced on June 20, 2017 that it would include the shares of 222 large Chinese companies in the MSCI Emerging Markets Index.[66] Shares of companies located in mainland China were previously excluded from that index. This was because MSCI disapproved of the lack of transparency of the Chinese capital markets and restrictions faced by foreigners seeking to invest in them. The inclusion of Chinese companies in the MSCI index in 2017 was expected to attract large amounts of capital to China's stock market, at least an estimated $17 billion in passive foreign investment.

Index makers are instrumental in the configuration of the bond market as well. In 2017, China boasted the world's third largest government bond market yet Chinese bonds were not included in any major global indexes. On March 1, 2017, Bloomberg was the first company to come up with two new hybrid fixed income indexes[67] that included yuan-denominated Chinese bonds. However, it was still not ready to include China's bonds in its Bloomberg Barclays Global Aggregate Index.[68] Chinese government bonds were not included in Citi's World Government Bond Index or GBI-EM Global developed by JP Morgan, two other major bond indexes. US index companies claimed they excluded China's bonds owing to the country's capital controls and the difficulties encountered by foreigners willing to invest there. The exclusion of Chinese bonds from global indexes developed by major US investment banks inhibited the flow of foreign capital into China's bond market. It was in 2018 that Bloomberg announced that it was adding Chinese bonds in its Global Aggregate Index. As a result, big institutional investors poured approximately $35.9 billion (229.4 billion yuans) into the Chinese bond market. All in all, by

---

[64] S&P Global, S&P Dow Jones Indices Releases Annual Survey of Assets, Press Release, June 29, 2017.

[65] MSCI, *Global Indexes: Delivering the Modern Index Strategy* (2017).

[66] MSCI, Results of MSCI 2017 Market Classification Review, Press Release, June 20, 2017. In 2019, it was revealed that China's inclusion was probably the result of Chinese pressure on MSCI. *See* Mike Bird, *How China Pressured MSCI to Add its Market to Major Benchmark*, WSJ, Feb. 3, 2019.

[67] The Global Aggregate + China Index; and EM Local Currency Government + China Index.

[68] Bloomberg Launches New Fixed Income Indices Covering China Bonds, Bloomberg Press Release, Mar. 1, 2017.

May 2018, foreign investors' holdings of Chinese bonds reached 836 billion yuan – 1.7% of the estimated $12 trillion Chinese government bond market.[69]

4.1.5.2 Strategic misalignment

The dollar is the world's chief reserve currency because the United States is still the world's only superpower. The United States maintains this superiority by spending lavishly on its military. Lesser powers, like Japan, Saudi Arabia[70] and the European states, are allegiant to the United States because they are dependent on it for their security. The fact that almost all commodities, including oil, are priced in dollars has much to do with the military dominance of the United States and the security it is ready to provide to the rest of the world. Whether China would be able to develop such strong allegiances in its own neighborhood and globally is still at play. China seeks to gain effective control over a number of disputed islands in the South China Sea (e.g. Paracel islands, Spratlys and Scarborough Shoal), generating animosity among its neighbors.[71] On the other hand, in East Asia, the yuan has become the *de facto* alternative to the dollar. Malaysia, Thailand, Singapore, the Philippines and South Korea have already formed a loose yuan block with China.[72] The yuan is a component of the currency baskets of these countries but has not yet surpassed the dollar, which remains the chief anchor currency in Asia.[73]

China has expanded its influence in Latin America. The China Export–Import Bank and the Inter-American Development Bank (IDB) have jointly established a $1.8 billion equity fund to support investment in Latin America and the Caribbean.[74] By 2014 China's overseas direct investment (ODI) was $900 billion out of which $106 billion was direct investment in Latin American

---

[69] Shen Hong, *Foreign Investors are Biggest Buyers of Chinese Government Debt*, WSJ, June 14, 2018.

[70] For the special relationship between Saudi Arabia and the United States, *see* David E. Spiro, *The Hidden Hand of American Hegemony: Petrodollar Recycling and International Markets* 90–91 (1999).

[71] *See*, e.g. *The South China Sea Arbitration* (Philippines v. China), PCA Case No. 2013-19, July 12, 2016. On January 22, 2013, the Philippines instituted arbitral proceedings against China under Annex VII of the UN Convention on the Law of the Sea (UNCLOS). The Philippines contested the lawfulness of actions taken by China in the South China Sea. China adopted the stance of non-acceptance and non-participation in the proceedings. The court ruled against China. China called the arbitral award null and void.

[72] Henning, *supra* note 3, at 4.

[73] Ming Zhang, *Internationalization of the Renminbi: Developments, Problems and Influences*, at 9, Paper No. 2, CIGI Series New Thinking and the New G20, Mar. 2015.

[74] IDB, China Eximbank Join Forces to Set up Infrastructure Facility and a Public–Private Investment Fund for Latin America and the Caribbean, Press Release, Mar. 28, 2011.

and Caribbean countries.[75] China is the largest trading partner of Chile, Peru and Brazil. In 2017, Chinese companies invested $21 billion in Brazil, including the purchasing of power plants, an electricity distributor and ports.[76] China has expanded its investment in many countries in Africa and strategic states in the Indian Ocean, including the Maldives[77] and Sri Lanka.[78]

China's overseas lending reached $700 billion in 2019, rendering it the world's largest official creditor – more than twice as big as the World Bank and the IMF combined. While China has been depicted as a rapacious lender,[79] it has engaged since 2000 in 140 debt write-offs and restructurings.[80] This makes it more of a long-term, strategic lender. It seems that the purpose of Chinese official lending is not to capture other countries in 'a debt trap',[81] but to establish the goodwill and high-level relationships that produce long-term alliances.

The New Development Bank, a multilateral development bank operated by the BRICS states – Brazil, Russia, India, China and South Africa – is based in Shanghai.[82] The Asian Infrastructure Investment Bank, which some view as a rival to the IMF and World Bank – the two most important global economic institutions – aims to facilitate yuan lending and to boost the internationalization of the yuan.[83]

By 2018, China was not merely catching up with the United States in terms of improving its military technology. It was making strides in quantum technologies, big data, artificial intelligence and communication networks. This alarmed the United States,[84] which was keen on maintaining its competitive

---

[75] David Dollar, *China's Investment in Latin America*, at 2, Geoeconomics and Global Issues, Paper 4, Brookings Institution, Jan. 2017.

[76] *China Moves into Latin America: Bello*, Economist, Feb. 3, 2018.

[77] *China–Maldives Friendship Bridge Opens to Traffic*, Xinhuanet, Aug. 31, 2018.

[78] Maria Abi-Habib, *How China Got Sri Lanka to Cough up a Port*, NY Times, June 25, 2018.

[79] *Id.*

[80] Sebastian Horn et al., *China's Overseas Lending*, at 32, Working Paper No. 2132, Kiel Institute for the World Economy, June 2019.

[81] Agatha Kratz et al., *New Data on the 'Debt Trap' Question*, Rhodium Group, Apr. 29, 2019, www.rhg.com.

[82] Art. 1, Fortaleza Agreement on the New Development Bank, July 15, 2014. *See also* Hongying Wang, *From 'Taoguang Yanghui' to 'Yousuo Zuowei:' China's Engagement in Financial Minilateralism*, at 3, CIGI Paper 52, Dec. 2014.

[83] *See* Chapter 17, Section 17.4.

[84] IISS, Military Balance 2018 (Feb. 14, 2018). According to 2018 US defense posture, 'China is a strategic competitor using predatory economics to intimidate its neighbors while militarizing features in the South China'. *See* Summary of the 2018 National Defense Strategy of the United States of America, Sharpening the American Military's Competitive Edge, at 1, 2018.

edge in technology, a key for military dominance. In 2019, the US–China rivalry escalated to a full-blown trade war. The US President issued an executive order limiting the exports of technology to countries deemed foreign adversaries.[85] The executive order did not specifically name China but the language used was a copy of past US warnings about China's potential exploitation of technology to sabotage Western infrastructure. Furthermore, the United States cracked down on Huawei, a Chinese private technology firm and the frontrunner in building the world's 5G internet.[86] The Commerce Department specified that US firms could sell products to Huawei only after obtaining a license. Approval of such licenses would start from the 'presumption of denial'.[87] This was an earth-shattering decision given Huawei's heavy dependence on components made by US firms and the previous US wholehearted endorsement of globalized supply chains.[88]

4.2   STRATEGIES OF THE PERIPHERY

4.2.1   Dependence on Dollar-denominated Debt

Typically, during recessions, as the wealth of businesses and people declines, states' revenues drop and their spending increases. States make payments to the unemployed and spend to improve the public infrastructure so as to boost the economy and offset the lack of private spending. During recessions, states also usually levy fewer taxes as they strive to rekindle private demand. This produces budget deficits that are financed by borrowing in the domestic and foreign markets. States that do not have a developed banking sector or a vibrant

---

[85]   US Executive Order on Securing the Information and Communications Technology and Services Supply Chain, May 15, 2019, https://www.whitehouse.gov. This was in addition to the National Defense Authorization Act for Fiscal Year 2019 that explicitly banned US agencies and recipients of federal grants from doing business with five Chinese companies and US contractors using these companies' equipment. The blacklisted Chinese companies were Huawei, ZTE Corporation, Hytera Communications Corporation, Hangzou Hikvision Digital Technology Company and Dahua Technology Company. *See* DoD, GSA, and NASA are issuing an interim rule amending the Federal Acquisition Regulation to implement section 889(a)(1)(A) of the John S. McCain National Defense Authorization Act for Fiscal Year 2019 (Pub. L. 115-232), Aug. 13, 2019, www. regulations.gov.
[86]   Joshua Brustein, *Trade War Threatens to Divide the World's Smartphone Makers*, Bloomberg, Jan. 10, 2019.
[87]   US Department of Commerce, Department of Commerce Announces the Addition of Huawei Technologies Co. Ltd. to the Entity List, Press Release, May 15, 2019.
[88]   *See also* Henry Farrell and Abraham Newman, *Weaponized Interdependence*, Apr. 4, 2018, https://henryfarrell.net.

domestic bond market tend to borrow from foreigners. Many developing countries borrow from foreign capital holders, not only during recessions but also in periods of growth, because of the scant domestic capital.[89] Developing states entice foreign capitalists to invest in them by offering them higher IRs on the debt they issue, lower labor costs or weaker environmental restrictions than developed states. Private capital imports are vital for the growth of many states because the official foreign aid provided by international organizations and non-profit entities is quite limited.

States import capital by borrowing from foreign banks. Other forms of capital infusion are investments by foreigners in the stock and bond markets of states – the so-called portfolio flows. Foreign direct investment, buying an already existing business or building a new factory in a state,[90] is the most secure type of financing because those who put their money in real assets are the least likely to flee at the first sign of economic downturn.

Attracting private capital is not easy. East Asia attracts much more capital than Sub-Saharan Africa. Capitalists tend to favor the rapidly industrializing developing states rather than those stuck in underdevelopment and rife with conflict. Capital holders weigh carefully what they will get by investing in a state versus the risks of such investment. Such risks include political risk that stems from a fragile government and a fragmented social fabric. Capitalists will not invest in a state if they believe that their investment may be expropriated. They also flee states when they sense resentment against 'imperialistic' foreign capital.

A state that depends on foreigners to finance its development can never be fully autonomous. Foreign capital flows to developing states, especially portfolio flows, tend to be quite erratic.[91] One day a state may be showered with money because of its growth potential, only to be shunned the next owing to a newfound concern about its unsustainable private or public debt, especially foreign-currency-denominated debt. Many developing states have difficulty obtaining credit in their own currency because that currency is considered weak. During an economic downturn, weak currencies tend to depreciate to the point of losing their value. From creditors' perspective, currency depreciation is a sort of default for which they cannot really seek relief in courts.[92]

---

[89] Thomas Oatley, *International Political Economy* 300 (2012).

[90] *Id.* at 301.

[91] *Id.* at 303.

[92] *See The Oscar Chinn Case* (Britain v. Belgium), 1934 PCIJ (Ser. A/B) No. 63, para. 100, Dec. 12, 1934. US courts have upheld the right of the government to change the currency system of the country, *see Norman v. Baltimore & Ohio Railroad Co.*, 294 U.S. 240, 304 (1935). A similar case emerged in the international arena, *see Case of Certain Norwegian Loans* (France v. Norway), (1957) ICJ Reports 9, July 6, 1957.

Today the majority of debt issued by developing states is dollar-denominated. Issuing debt in dollars transfers the risk of currency depreciation from the creditors to the state that issues the debt. If that state's currency depreciates against the dollar, it would need many more units of its currency to pay back its dollar-denominated debt. That may not seem like an issue, as countries can print as much of their currency as they need. At the same time, though, states cannot engage in a printing frenzy as this would rapidly devalue and debauch their currency.

Large amounts of short-term dollar-denominated debt, the so-called capital flows bonanzas,[93] present a problem for developing states when the dollar strengthens against their currency. Currency depreciation boosts exports but also increases the debt burden of states that have large amounts of dollar debt. The amount of dollar-denominated debt can reach staggering proportions. In 2015, for example, dollar credit to non-banks outside the United States was $9.8 trillion.[94] Emerging-market economies accounted for $3.8 trillion of this amount.[95]

Developing countries have to manage their economic affairs carefully when their economies are booming, their currency is appreciating and foreign lenders are knocking on their door to sell them dollar-denominated credit. The high influx of capital into their economies strengthens their currency and makes debt repayment look easy. At the same time, though, their export sector may be sinking as other states can no longer afford to import goods from a state with an appreciating currency. This can cause an economic slowdown followed by the severe depreciation of their currency, making it difficult for them to service their external debt.

4.2.2   Periphery and the Trilemma

As we mentioned before, capital tends to gravitate to the United States because investors view it as a safe haven. When US IRs are low, though, capital holders are tempted to invest in more risky states. In 2010, for instance, when the

---

Investors are unlikely to recover depreciation losses they incur *before* the date a government expropriates their investment. *See* Charles Proctor, *Mann on the Legal Aspects of Money* 633 (2012).

[93]   IMF, *Annual Report on Exchange Arrangements and Exchange Restrictions*, at 58 (2014) [hereinafter IMF Exchange 2014]. *See also* Carmen M. Reinhart and Vincent R. Reinhart, *Capital Flow Bonanzas: An Encompassing View of the Past and Present*, NBER Working Paper No. 14321, Sept. 2008.

[94]   Robert N. McCauley et al., *Dollar Credit to Emerging Market Economies*, at 27, BIS Quarterly Review, Dec. 2015.

[95]   *Id.* at 30.

yields on US government bonds were close to zero, Zambia, whose bonds were yielding 5.4%, all of a sudden became an attractive place to invest. Overall, how capital behaves has to do with the IR of the United States. This renders the majority of states dependent on the US DEP (Fig. 4.2).

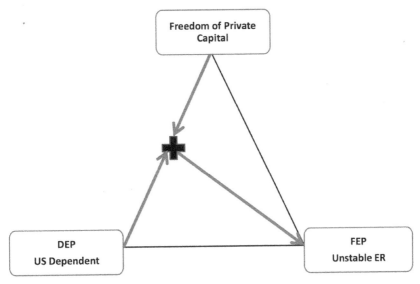

Figure 4.2   Trilemma of open developing states

The surge of capital inflows to developing states that took place between 2009 and 2010 had to do with the near-zero US IRs, as the country was trying to recover from the Great Recession. These flows started to reverse in 2013 and, more dramatically, by the end of 2016 because of the expected tighter US economic policy. By 2018, many developing states' currencies had depreciated significantly against the dollar. This increased investors' anxiety about the ability of these states to pay down their dollar-denominated debt and led to a massive sell-off and thus the rapid depreciation of many of these states' currencies.

When a developing state is dealing with a currency attack it often finds itself stuck between the Scylla and Charybdis. It can defend its currency, which is rapidly depreciating, by hiking its IRs. This may stem the outflow of capital but the higher IRs, a contractionary policy, will harm its already deteriorating economy. Alternatively, it can let market-driven speculation drive the currency lower. In that case, it will have to deal with the repercussions of a weakening currency, including expensive imports, higher inflation and bloated foreign debt. Usually developing states try to defend their currency using their FX reserves, only to find out that they do not really have enough of them to stem a rapid depreciation.

Developed states and developing countries grapple with crises differently. In the developed world, economic cycles are addressed by counter-cyclical measures.[96] A looming recession is treated by engineering expansion, and an inflationary economy is deflated through contraction. Open developing states can ill-afford the luxury of counter-cyclical economic policies because they have to be vigilant about how the US IRs affect the flows of private capital. The direction of capital flows can have a large impact on the value of their currency which, in turn, has ramifications for their whole economy.[97]

To shield themselves against the excessive volatility of their currency, developing states tend to peg it to a global reserve currency, frequently the dollar. Some of them have adopted *de facto* managed floats. They allow their ER to float but also intervene in the currency market to adjust it when this suits their goals. However, not all countries can manage their ER successfully. Only countries with large FX reserves can guarantee, to some extent, the sustainability of a fixed ERR or a managed float.

4.2.3   The Trap of Fixed Exchange Rate

4.2.3.1 Case study of Argentina

In 1991, Argentina passed the Convertibility Law, which established a fixed ER of 1 Argentinean peso/$1. The law was adopted as a panacea for the high inflation and an independent currency board was established to supervise its implementation. The function of the board was to maintain the full and complete convertibility of pesos into dollars on demand at the fixed rate. Argentina could not impose foreign exchange controls or other restrictions that could hamper the fixed peso/dollar ER.[98] The board kept sufficient dollars, as reserves, to guarantee the parity between the two currencies. New pesos could be created only when the board had in its possession the dollars required to back them up. The board was unable, in other words, to conduct active economic policy. Because of the fixed ER, it imported, by default, the policy of the anchor state, the United States.

The creation of the board propped up confidence in the peso and inflation fell from an annual rate of 800% in the early 1990s to less than 5% in 1994. However, when the dollar appreciated in the late 1990s, owing to the increase

---

[96] Luc Laeven and Fabián Valencia, *Systemic Banking Crises Database: An Update*, at 15, IMF Working Paper WP/12/163, June 2012.

[97] Poonan Gupta, *Capital Flows and Central Banking: The Indian Experience*, at 2–3, World Bank Policy Research Paper 7569, Feb. 2016.

[98] Proctor, *supra* note 92, at 873.

of US IRs, the peso, which was pegged to it, strengthened in tandem. The peso's rapid appreciation priced Argentinean exports out of foreign markets and triggered a recession. In 2001, the unemployment rate reached 20%, prompting the government to alter the peg. The peso's peg was changed from a pure dollar peg to a dollar/euro peg. In June 2001, the government created a separate lower ER to support the export sector. Toying with the peg did not please investors, who started to short the peso, betting it would depreciate. Argentina tried to prop up its currency by selling its dollar reserves. Almost 40% of the country's reserves were exhausted during the first months of 2001 to fend off the currency attack. This contractionary policy, put in place to defend the peso, exerted even more pressure on the economy.[99] Eventually in January 2002, the government repealed the Convertibility Law and suspended the on-demand conversion of pesos into dollars.[100] It also defaulted on its $155 billion debt, most of which was denominated in dollars.[101] Because of that default, Argentina was expelled from the global bond indexes and ostracized by the bond market.

The country had amassed a large amount of debt that was difficult to restructure as it was spread among 152 series of bonds, governed by eight different laws, denominated in various currencies and held by 700 000 bond-holders around the world, including pension funds, hedge funds and banks.[102] Eventually, the government managed to restructure the majority of its debt. Certain bondholders, however, opted out of that settlement and sued Argentina in the United States. In 2012, a US-based court ruled that Argentina would have to pay in full the minority of holdout bondholders, those who had refused to participate in the debt restructuring.[103] The country was embroiled in additional litigation with a number of multinational companies that had invested in it but had disputes with the government and were demanding damages. The ICSID tribunals,[104] which were put together to arbitrate some of these cases under the

---

[99] Oatley, *supra* note 89, at 334.

[100] Proctor, *supra* note 92, at 875.

[101] Oatley, *supra* note 89, at 334.

[102] Mauro Megliani, *Sovereign Debt: Genesis – Restructuring – Litigation* 373 (2015).

[103] For more details, *see* Chapter 15, Section 15.2.5.

[104] The International Center for Settlement of Investment Disputes (ICSID) is a global arbitration institution established to resolve disputes between states and foreign investors. It is funded by the World Bank (WB), an international lending organiza-tion, and located at the WB headquarters in Washington, DC. *See* Convention on the Settlement of Investment Disputes between States and Nationals of other States, Mar. 18, 1965, 4 ILM 524 (1965).

Bilateral Investment Treaties (BITs)[105] between Argentina and the home states of foreign companies, awarded damages to these companies in dollars.[106] This was because of the numerous legal precedents of awarding damages in convertible currencies and the severe devaluation of the peso that made awarding damages in that currency worthless. By January 2014, Argentina had to pay $980 million[107] to various companies that claimed that Argentina had breached the BITs it had signed with their home countries.

By 2012, Argentina's FX reserves were only $30 billion – less than 6 months' worth of imports. The government was already restricting imports, which led to shortages of goods, and trying to stop the outflow of capital. While the official ER was 8.5 pesos/1 dollar, the black market ER had climbed to a record high of 16 pesos/1 dollar. On July 2014, Argentina, in an attempt to de-dollarize its economy, signed a currency swap agreement with China that made it possible for it to bolster its reserves by paying for Chinese imports with yuans.[108] However, the road ahead was steep. Most of the debt of the country was denominated in dollars. The high inflation rate and repeated defaults[109] had created doubts about whether the peso would ever again be able to hold its value.

4.2.3.2   Case study of Nigeria

In September 2015, JP Morgan, a private bank, removed Nigeria from its emerging market bond index. This was a blow to the Nigerian government and triggered the sell-off of Nigerian government bonds. Insurance companies and pension funds, which passively follow indexes, invest only in countries included in those indexes. The removal of a country from an index therefore causes an automatic disinvestment from that country. The

---

[105] BITs include arbitration clauses because foreign investors prefer not to use the domestic courts of their host state. They fear that these courts may be biased against them. Critics have called the BITs' arbitration clauses 'gunboat arbitration' alluding to past practices when creditor states sent their gunboats to debtor states to force them to pay back their debts. *See* José E. Alvarez, *The Once and Future Foreign Investment Regime* 607, 612, in 'Looking to the Future: Essays on International Law in Honor of W. Michael Reisman' (Mahnoush H. Arsanjani et al., eds, 2011).

[106] *See*, e.g. *Compañiá de Aguas del Aconquija S.A. and Vivendi Universal S.A. v. Argentine Republic*, ICSID Case No. ARB/97/3, paras 8.4.4, 8.4.5, Aug. 20, 2008. The tribunal cited the *Lighthouses Arbitration* (France v. Greece), 12 RIAA 155, 23 ILR 65, July 24, 1956. *See also National Grid v. Argentine Republic*, UNCITRAL Tribunal Award, Nov. 3, 2008.

[107] Cecilia Olivet and Pia Eberhardt, *Profiting from Crisis: How Corporations and Lawyers are Scavenging Profits from Europe's Crisis Countries*, at 12, Transnational Institute and Corporate Europe Observatory, Mar. 2014.

[108] *See supra* Section 4.1.4.

[109] *See* Chapter 15, Section 15.2.5.

rapid outflows of capital increased the IRs that Nigeria had to pay on its foreign-currency-denominated debt and put pressure on its currency, the naira, to depreciate. All of this coincided with the plummeting of global oil prices, causing a deep recession in Nigeria, a country dependent on oil exports. The collapse of oil prices set off, in turn, a severe dollar shortage given that oil transactions are priced in dollars.

Nigeria faced additional problems because its currency is pegged to the dollar. Nigeria wished to keep that currency peg (₦198/$1) so as to maintain its credibility with the credit rating companies and to facilitate paying down its dollar-denominated debt. In order to support the naira, the CB of Nigeria had to buy nairas in the currency market by selling its reserves. Other measures adopted included reducing imports and imposing limits on the amounts charged on credit and debit cards denominated in foreign currency. In January 2016, the CB had to suspend all dollar sales at the country's foreign exchange bureaus. It eventually, however, succumbed to the short-sellers and let the currency float and severely depreciate.[110]

Capital controls are always available to developing states like Nigeria that wish to stop capital outflows. However, they are rarely the solution for states that are keen on convincing capital holders that they are open to foreign investment. Furthermore, when capital controls are imposed, they tend to be porous. Even China, a staunch believer in capital controls when needed, had difficulties both in stemming inflows when the yuan was strong in the early 2010s and in curtailing outflows when the yuan was depreciating in 2016. Many developing states have a hard time controlling their financial borders because many transactions are conducted in cash, which is difficult to trace. Rich institutions and individuals can, moreover, find refuge in numerous states, such as Switzerland and Luxembourg, where a plethora of intermediaries from law firms to banks are ready to assist them in moving out and hiding their wealth from their home states.

4.2.4   Flipping the Pyramid

In 2019, the global FX reserves totaled $11 trillion, up from $1.4 trillion at the end of 1995.[111] Developing states maintain large FX reserves to:

* self-insure against shocks that imperil their current and capital accounts;
* stabilize their ER;

---

[110] Paul Wallace, *Nigeria's Central Bank Finally Throws in Towel on Naira Peg*, Bloomberg, June 14, 2016.

[111] IMF, IMF Releases Data on the Currency Composition of Foreign Exchange Reserves Including Holdings in Renminbi, Press Release, Mar. 29, 2019.

- signal economic strength so that credit rating companies do not lightheart-
edly downgrade their credit scores and index firms do not eject them from
popular indexes; and
- intervene in the market to depreciate their currency to boost their exports.[112]

In fact, intervening in the FX market to strategically weaken their currencies
to boost their exports is a matter of economic survival for many of these states.
Without a CA surplus they will be unable to accumulate the FX reserves they
need to defend their currencies in times of trouble. As mentioned before, the
IMF has developed criteria (Fig. 4.1) that should help determine the amount
of FX reserves states really need. In practice, though, no amount of reserves
can really protect a state that is under a severe currency attack – when not only
foreigners but also its own residents are ready to grab their money and leave.[113]
Developing states have learnt the hard way that having ample FX reserves
guarantees their economic stability. Because of their limited DEP autonomy,
their capability of having an even semi-effective economic agenda depends on
those reserves. As of 2019, $6 trillion, out of the total $20 trillion US debt,[114]
approximately 30%, was held by various states as a safe asset expected to
become useful to them when the world or luck turned against them.

India, which has adopted a managed float since the mid-1990s, has been
using its FX reserves to calibrate its ER. Between 2003 and 2008, the country
took advantage of capital inflows to accumulate reserves by printing its
currency to buy dollars while partially sterilizing domestic money growth.
In addition, it adopted regulations to temper the inflows of capital while it
encouraged outflows. During the sudden stop of capital inflows between 2008
and 2009, and again in 2013, the Reserve Bank of India tightened monetary
policy by increasing IRs. It used the reserves it had accumulated between
2003 and 2008 (about $280 billion) to intervene in the currency market to buy
back its currency, preventing in this way its steep depreciation.[115] In 2013,
when expected higher US IRs lured capital back to the United States, the
Reserve Bank used $13 billion of its reserves to prop up the Indian rupee.[116]
Additionally it encouraged capital inflows, especially those coming from
non-resident Indians, but restrained capital outflows.[117] India views its reserves

---

[112] Gupta, *supra* note 97, at 14.
[113] Jean-Pierre Landau, *Global Liquidity: Public and Private* 223, at 241, in
Proceedings of Jackson Hole Economic Policy Symposium on 'Global Dimensions of
Unconventional Monetary Policy', Federal Reserve Bank of Kansas City, Aug. 22–24,
2013.
[114] *See supra* note 5.
[115] Gupta, *supra* note 97, at 25.
[116] *Id.* at 26.
[117] *Id.* at 9.

as a strategic asset that helps it, to some extent, deal with external adverse shocks. By 2019, it had accumulated $420 billion in reserves.[118]

India has striven to modernize its economic policy-making by shifting from ER targeting to inflation targeting, following the example set by developed countries. On February 20, 2015, the Reserve Bank of India and the government signed an inflation-targeting agreement.[119] According to that agreement, the objective of monetary policy is 'to primarily maintain price stability, while keeping in mind the objective of growth'.[120] The Reserve Bank of India has to adhere to a 'flexible inflation target' of 4% (within a band of ±2%).[121] The bank has to report to the government every 6 months on the causes of inflation and provide an inflation forecast.[122] If at any time it misses its target – inflation exceeds 6% or is below 2% for three straight quarters[123] – it must report to the government on the causes of its failure, propose remedial action and provide the timeframe within which it plans to achieve the inflation target.[124] India hopes to revamp its economic policy by stockpiling reserves and nurturing the development of a deep and liquid domestic bond market. The ability to borrow in its own currency will certainly free it from the tyranny of ER targeting and help it focus on domestic policy-making.[125] India, like many other states, has learnt the lesson that economic resilience stems from a big stack of FX reserves. As of 2019, Brazil, China, India, Korea, Taiwan and Mexico had the largest amounts of FX reserves in the world that they used as cushions against external shocks that could adversely impact their BOP (Table 4.1).

Developing countries have additionally tried to get the upper hand in their relationship with US private firms that constantly pronounce judgments on their economic fate. In January 2017, Indonesia announced that it was severing its ties with JP Morgan Chase, a US private bank. Indonesia decided to exclude the bank from its list of primary dealers for government bond auctions. The dispute had to do with a report issued by the bank about the global repercussions of the 2016 US presidential election. In that report, JP Morgan downgraded the shares of Indonesian companies stating the obvious: that the US election outcome had increased the emerging market risk pre-

---

[118] Reserve Bank of India, 32nd Half Yearly Report on Management of Foreign Exchange Reserves: October 2018–March 2019, Press Release, May 21, 2019.
[119] Government of India and Reserve Bank of India, Agreement on Monetary Policy Framework, Feb. 20, 2015, https://www.finmin.nic.in.
[120] Preamble, *id.*
[121] Art. 2, *id.*
[122] Art. 5, *id.*
[123] Art. 6(a), *id.*
[124] Art. 6(b), *id.*
[125] Gupta, *supra* note 97, at 2.

Table 4.1   *FX reserves as a percentage of short-term debt and GDP,*
                   2019[1]

Countries	Reserves as percentage of short-term debt	FX reserves as percentage of GDP
Brazil	547%	19%
China	252 %	23%
India	356%	14%
Korea	311%	24%
Mexico	273%	14%
Taiwan	261%	79%

Note: [1] US Department of the Treasury, *Report to Congress: Macroeconomic and Foreign Exchange Policies of Major Trading Partners of the United States*, at 20, May 2019.

miums and this was to trigger capital outflows from the developing world. This common sense assessment was accompanied by a steep downgrade of Indonesian companies' shares. The bank, in essence, urged investors to sell those shares. On November 14, 2016, the day after the report was published, the yield on Indonesia's 10-year government bond jumped up 0.466% – the highest intraday jump since January 2011. The increase in the premium that the government had to pay on its debt angered it and prompted it to fire the firm.[126]

The government clarified that its treatment of JP Morgan did not mean that it was closing itself off to financial assessment. Firing the company was, instead, a way of registering its displeasure with JP Morgan's incorrect assessment of its economy. Indonesia, at that point, had a small deficit – 1.8% of GDP – and had achieved a trade surplus of 8.8%, the highest level since 2011. The external debt of the country was also much lower than of that its peers.

JP Morgan was taken aback by Indonesia's response. On January 16, 2017, the bank upgraded Indonesia from 'underweight' to 'neutral',[127] an upgrade probably prompted by the government's reaction to the pervious downgrade, since nothing much had changed in terms of Indonesia's economic fundamentals.[128]

Developing states aspire to graduate from the periphery to the core by accumulating FX reserves, but most of them, owing to their large CA deficits, are unable to maintain an adequate amount of safe assets for the proverbial rainy day. This makes it difficult for them to address BOP fluctuations and forces

---

[126] I. Made Sentana et al., *Indonesia Plans New Rules for Market Reports after JP Morgan Downgrade*, WSJ, Jan. 7, 2017.

[127] *Indonesia, One of Five 'Fragile' Emerging Markets, Looks Stronger Now*, Economist, Jan. 21, 2017.

[128] *Id.*

them to resort to borrowing from countries with surpluses. Piling up debt is not the way to grow, though. The redistribution of global currency reserves, through the credit markets, is a 'wasteful method of capital supply',[129] especially when borrowing is not 'earmarked for specific productive purposes'.[130]

4.3 STRATEGIES OF JAPAN

4.3.1 The Export-led Model of Growth

Japan, China and Germany are often cited as states that have pursued aggressively the export-led model of growth. Between 1970 and 1995, the United States and Japan were locked in a battle as the US manufacturing sector found it increasingly difficult to compete with Japanese exporters. Threats of trade war led to the strengthening of the yen in 1971–73 and 1977–78. Eventually, the 1985 Plaza accord[131] cemented a mutual understanding on the right ER between the two currencies and achieved the goal of the US government, which wanted to curb Japanese imports into the United States. The yen appreciated from ¥260/$1 in February 1985 to ¥150/$1 in the summer of 1986. This sharp appreciation led to recession and deflation in Japan. The Bank of Japan (BOJ) cut the benchmark IR in 1986 to stimulate the economy and stem the climbing of the currency. The loose monetary policy backfired, triggering bubbles in the housing and stock markets. When the BOJ had to increase the IR in 1989 to curb speculation, the bubbles burst, driving the economy into recession. This was the beginning of the lost Japanese decade: the 1990s.

It is easy to trace the Japanese lost decade to the Plaza accord and the unrelenting policy of the United States, which sought the strengthening of Japan's and Germany's currencies to help its own export sector. Some have attributed the Japanese lost decade to the US 'mercantile' pressure on Japan and the 'dependent' policy pursued by the BOJ.[132] While the BOJ decreased IRs to stimulate growth and offset the strengthening of the yen, it avoided direct meddling in the currency market and shied away from a direct confrontation with the United States.[133] Others have pointed out, though, that Japan's

---

[129] Ragnar Nurske, *The International Currency Experience: Lessons of the Inter-War Period* 93 (League of Nations, 1944).

[130] *Id.*

[131] *See* Chapter 10.

[132] Ronald I. McKinnon et al., *The Syndrome of the Ever Higher Yen, 1971–1995: American Mercantile Pressure on Japanese Monetary Policy* 341, at 342, in 'Changes in Exchange Rates in Rapidly Developing Countries: Theory, Practice, and Policy Issues' (Takatoshi Ito and Anne O. Krueger, eds, 1999).

[133] *Id.*

reliance on the export-led model of growth was the real cause of its economic troubles. Countries that rely on exports for growth become dependent on other states to buy their goods and services. When foreign demand slows down, export-dependent states inevitably bump into recessions. Japan should have tried to advance its non-tradable goods sector and foster its services industry to kindle domestic consumption instead of counting on the American consumer for its growth.[134]

4.3.2   How Japan Lost More than a Decade

After the 1985 Plaza accord, the yen appreciated continuously with the exception of a brief period in 1989, after the bursting of the Japanese bubble. Some attributed this continuous appreciation to the 'syndrome of the ever-higher yen'[135] – markets' conviction that the yen would continue to strengthen owing to the US pressure. When the yen reached ¥84/$1 in 1995, the US Treasury realized that the continuing deflation in Japan, brought about by its strong currency, was not sustainable. This prompted it to work with the BOJ to weaken the yen. As a result, the yen depreciated, at one point in 1998 reaching ¥144/$1. In 1999, the Treasury reversed course, and the yen appreciated, despite Japan's ¥3 trillion intervention in the market.[136]

In 1998, Japan passed a law that guaranteed the independence of the BOJ from the government. The BOJ vowed to stop deflation and bring back economic growth[137] by adopting a zero interest rate policy.[138] The bank focused on the nominal IR, which it was able to drive close to zero. This was not enough, though, to revive growth as the real IR, the IR adjusted for inflation, remained quite high.[139] The bank attempted to further inflate the economy through QE – by purchasing large amounts of government bonds. It also intervened in the currency market to sell ¥35 trillion to depreciate the currency.[140] Despite these

---

[134] Raghuram G. Rajan, *Fault Lines: How Hidden Fractures still Threaten the World Economy* 64 (2010).

[135] McKinnon, *supra* note 132.

[136] Richard C. Koo, *The Escape from Balance Sheet Recession and the QE Trap: A Hazardous Road for the World Economy* 188 (2015).

[137] Takatoshi Ito and Frederic S. Mishkin, *Two Decades of Japanese Monetary Policy and the Deflation Program* 131, at 140, in 'Monetary Policy under Very Low Inflation in the Pacific Rim' (Takatoshi Ito and Andrew K. Rose, eds, 2006).

[138] *Id.* at 131.

[139] *Id.* at 132.

[140] Takatoshi Ito, *Interventions and Japanese Economic Recovery*, Conference on 'Macro/Financial Issues and International Economic Relations: Policy Options for Japan and the United States', Ford School of Public Policy, University of Michigan, Oct. 22–23, 2004.

efforts, the Japanese consumer remained reluctant to spend and businesses unwilling to invest. To address the lack of private spending, the government took on the role of spender of last resort. As the government borrowed to spend, a large portion of that debt was bought by the BOJ – a classic case of monetization of government debt.

Abeconomics was a new policy adopted in 2012 by Japan's new prime minister, Shinzō Abe. It consisted of three arrows: (1) expansionary monetary policy by the BOJ; (2) flexible fiscal stimulus; and (3) structural reforms. In April 2013, the BOJ fired the first of the three arrows by vowing to achieve 2% inflation in a stable manner within 2 years.[141] A pact was signed between the BOJ and the government that spelled out that monetary policy would be complemented by the appropriate fiscal policy and structural reforms to ensure that Japan exits deflation.[142] The 2% inflation target was an improvement, after years of failing to establish such a clear target, but it was still short of what some economists believed was necessary to help Japan exit economic stagnation.[143] To achieve 2% inflation, the BOJ declared that it would double the MB in two years. It projected that the MB, which stood at ¥138 trillion by the end of 2012, would reach ¥200 trillion by the end of 2013 and ¥270 trillion by the end of 2014.[144] This was to be achieved by open market operations, more specifically, by purchasing Japanese government bonds (about ¥50 trillion a year) and corporate bonds.[145] The BOJ even ventured to purchase exchange-traded Funds (ETFs).[146] An ETF is a basket of thousands of stocks bundled together in a single fund that trades in major markets like an ordinary stock.

In 2014, as the inflation rate of 2% continued to be elusive, the BOJ increased its purchases of Japanese government bonds to ¥80 trillion per year. It also tripled the amount of purchases of ETFs.[147] It even announced a scheme that made it look like the central planner of the economy. In addition to the

---

[141] Bank of Japan, The 'Price Stability Target' under the Framework for the Conduct of Monetary Policy, at 1, Press Release, Jan. 22, 2013.

[142] Ministry of Finance and Bank of Japan, Joint Statement of the Government and the Bank of Japan on Overcoming Deflation and Achieving Sustainable Economic Growth, Press Release, Jan. 22, 2013.

[143] A target inflation range of 3–4% could have assertively conveyed BOJ's intention of moving away from deflation. *See* Ben S. Bernake, *Japanese Monetary Policy: A Case of Self-Induced Paralysis?*, 149, at 159, in 'Japan's Financial Crisis and its Parallels to US Experience' (Adam S. Posen and Ryoichi Mikitani, eds, 2000).

[144] BOJ, Introduction of the 'Quantitative and Qualitative Monetary Easing', at 1, n. 1, Press Release, Apr. 4, 2013.

[145] *Id.* at 1–2.

[146] *Id.* at 2.

[147] BOJ, Expansion of the Quantitative and Qualitative Monetary Easing, Press Release, Oct. 31, 2014.

already existing program of buying ETFs at the pace of ¥3 trillion per year, it decided to buy ETFs composed of stocks issued by firms that were proactively investing in Japanese physical and human capital.[148] Since such ETFs did not exist at the time, the BOJ was obviously nudging the financial sector to put together the type of ETFs it was prepared to buy. It was also indirectly urging companies to make investments in human and physical capital if they wanted their shares to be included in such ETFs. By 2016, the BOJ already owned one-third of the government bond market, 2% of the stock market and about half of the ETFs by value. It was estimated that if it continued to purchase government bonds at the pace of ¥80 trillion per year, it would end up owning two-thirds of government debt by 2020. The government would, in effect, owe money to itself – an obvious monetization of government debt. In 2016, Japan's public debt was about 240% of its GDP. Market participants were not concerned about this seemingly unsustainable debt burden because it was yen-denominated and one-third of it was owned by the BOJ and the rest mostly by Japanese residents.

On January 29, 2016, the BOJ announced the negative interest rate policy (NIRP), which came into effect on February 16, 2016. The bank made it clear that it was ready to cut IRs further into negative territory if that was necessary to revive the economy.[149] The NIRP was not considered an unconventional policy at the time. The ECB was already charging private banks 0.4% on the deposits they kept with it.[150] Negative IRs are supposed to work as follows: encouraging banks to lend instead of keeping excess reserves; discouraging savers from saving and enticing them to spend; convincing businesses to borrow and increase investment; and most importantly, devaluing a country's currency and boosting its exports.

However, negative IRs were not very successful in the case of Japan. The yen fell initially but then it quickly rebounded. On February 5, 2016, only a week after the announcement of negative rates, it was stronger against the dollar than before the NIRP. When the BOJ started to charge banks for the excess reserves they kept with it, it was hoping that they would stop hoarding cash and resume lending to jumpstart the economy. Instead of investing at home, though, banks decided to invest overseas in a search for higher yields. The US government debt offered positive yields because the United States was the only economy in the developed world that showed signs of growth.

---

[148] BOJ, Establishment of 'Special Rules for Purchases of ETFs to Support Firms Proactively Investing in Physical and Human Capital', Press Release, Mar. 15, 2016.
[149] BOJ, Introduction of 'Quantitative and Qualitative Monetary Easing with a Negative Interest Rate', Press Release, Jan. 29, 2016.
[150] Furthermore, the CBs of Denmark and Switzerland charged banks 0.75% on their reserve balances, while the CB of Sweden charged them 1.1%.

To address the revolt of financial institutions against negative rates, the BOJ decided to take a firmer 'control of the yield curve'. It did so by announcing that only short-term government debt would offer negative yields while the yields on the 10-year bond would remain positive.[151] This was a relief for pension funds and insurance companies. These firms invest in long-term government debt and use the returns from that investment to meet their obligations to the people they insure and pensioners.

Overall, for two decades, the BOJ took drastic measures to change the deflationary mindset of businesses and consumers in Japan – a mindset that it viewed more as a psychological handicap rather than as an economic problem.[152]

4.4   THE EUROZONE

4.4.1   The Eurocrisis

The birth of the European Union (EU) in 1951 was propelled by the desire to stop European nations from going to war against each other. Many hoped that the European Community that started as an economic and trade partnership could one day become a political union, something like the United States of Europe.[153] The eurocrisis, which devastated the EU periphery and led to a continent-wide deflation, derailed the dream of European unity.

The EU's establishment and evolution have taken place through a number of international treaties.[154] In 1999, certain EU states decided to abandon their national currency in favor of the euro, a common European currency. States converted their currencies into the euro at mutually agreed fixed ERs. Entry

---

[151] BOJ, New Framework for Strengthening Monetary Easing: 'Quantitative and Qualitative Monetary Easing with Yield Curve Control', Press Release, Sept. 21, 2016.

[152] Haruhiko Kuroda, *The Role of Expectations in Monetary Policy: Evolution of Theories and the Bank of Japan's Experience*, at 9, Speech at the University of Oxford, June 8, 2017.

[153] *See*, e.g. J.H.H. Weiler, *The Transformation of Europe*, 100 Yale Law Journal 2403 (1991). *See also* Elli Louka, *Conflicting Integration: The Environmental Law of the European* Union (2004).

[154] Treaty Establishing the European Economic Community (EEC Treaty or Treaty of Rome), Mar. 25, 1957, *reprinted in* 298 UNTS 11. The EEC Treaty was followed by the Single European Act, Feb. 17, 1986; Treaty on European Union (Maastricht Treaty), Feb. 7, 1992; Treaty of Amsterdam, Oct. 2, 1997; Treaty of Nice, Feb. 26, 2001; Treaty of Lisbon, Dec. 13, 2007. These treaties have been consolidated. *See* Consolidated Versions of the Treaty on European Union (TEU) and the Treaty on the Functioning of the European Union (TFEU), OJ C 326/1, 26.10.2012 [hereinafter Consolidated Treaties and Protocols].

into the eurozone, the group of states whose currency would be the euro, was reserved for states that met the criteria included in a regulation called 'Stability and Growth Pact'.[155] These criteria, which were supposed to be the same for all states, included a deficit-to-GDP ratio of less than 3% and a debt-to-GDP ratio of less than 60%. Germany, whose currency was used to model the euro, and economically the strongest state in EU, was justifiably concerned that high budget deficits and debt would invite speculative attacks against the euro. Germany was, at the time, the *de facto* IR-setter in Europe[156] as other states were watching closely the IRs set by the German CB to establish their own. Because of its dominance, Germany succeeded in inserting the deficit and debt limits in the treaties that established the eurozone. By 2008, a mixture of states had been accepted in the eurozone, including export-oriented, highly industrialized states like Germany, the *de facto* sovereign in Europe, other core states (e.g. Netherlands) and peripheral states, the so-called PIIGS (Portugal, Ireland, Italy, Greece and Spain).

Germany's insistence on the adoption of the Stability and Growth Pact made sense because of the Trilemma analyzed in Chapter 2 (*see* Fig. 2.2). When capital is free to criss-cross national frontiers, as it is the case in the EU, which is based on the freedom of movement of capital, states cannot maintain a fixed ER – through the euro – while, at the same time, enjoying DEP autonomy (e.g. the freedom to sustain a large budget deficit to address unemployment). States that wanted to adopt the euro were expected to shackle their DEP so that they could pursue, together, a successful FEP (*see* Fig. 2.4) targeted to the survival of the euro and, hopefully, its establishment as one of the world's reserve currencies.

The deficit and debt ceilings that were supposed to safeguard the euro were quickly undermined by the states that insisted on their adoption. In 2003 Germany, the instigator of the Stability Pact, and France, one of the founding members of the eurozone, violated the deficit ceilings. The European Commission, the executive branch of the EU, took action against France and Germany but eventually they prevailed.[157] Political interference that made possible the violation of the Stability Pact by the most powerful EU countries strengthened beliefs that the pact was unenforceable.[158] The Stability Pact

---

[155] *See infra* Section 4.4.3.2.

[156] Jean Pisani-Ferry, *The Euro Crisis and its Aftermath* 24 (2011).

[157] *See* Council of the European Union, 2546th Council Meeting, Economic and Financial Affairs, Press Release, Nov. 15, 2003; Council of the European Union, 2634th Council Meeting, Economic and Financial Affairs, Press Release, Jan. 18, 2005.

[158] Céline Allard et al., *Toward a Fiscal Union for the Euro Area*, at 8, IMF Staff Discussion Note, Sept. 2013.

was further watered down in 2005[159] to an extent that it became 'no more than a gentlemen's agreement of non-intervention' in the economic affairs of states.[160] In fact, even after the eurocrisis, many EU member states continued to engage in creative accounting[161] to fudge their real national debt and budget deficit numbers. Playing fast and loose with the rules was one of the reasons why, when the 2008 financial crisis hit the world, the eurozone was woefully unprepared.

The crisis started in Ireland in early 2009 when a property bubble burst, the banking sector collapsed and the country entered into recession. Greece was next to crumble owing to high deficits and debt. In April 2010, the CRAs downgraded the Greek debt to junk status, making it impossible for the country to refinance it in the bond market. As the ground was fertile for a pan-European crisis, France and Germany issued the Deauville Declaration that sent shockwaves throughout the global markets.[162] In that declaration they acknowledged, for the first time, that private creditors could be 'bailed in', that is suffer large losses, when a eurozone state was on the verge of default. That acknowledgement caused widespread panic because, before Deauville, investors harbored the belief that the eurozone was a single entity bound to become, at some future time, a political union. They assumed, therefore, that eurozone states would prefer to bail each other out in times of economic trouble rather than risk the credibility of the euro by allowing for a state's default. Because of these assumptions, they had appraised peripheral states' bonds as high-quality debt commanding low risk premiums. As disillusioned bondholders sold off the bonds of the periphery, the price of peripheral debt plunged and its yields soared to unsustainable levels.[163]

---

[159] It was amended to give states latitude in addressing 'economic bad times'. *See* article 5, Council Regulation No. 1055/2005 of 27 June 2005 amending Regulation (EC) No. 1466/97 on the strengthening of the surveillance of budgetary positions and the surveillance and coordination of economic policies, OJ L 174/1, 7.7.2005.

[160] European Parliament, Committee of Economic and Monetary Affairs, MEPs Hear Views of Leading Figures on the Greek Fiscal Crisis, Press Release, Apr. 14, 2010.

[161] *See* Jürgen von Hagen and Guntram B. Wolff, *What do Deficits Tell us about Debt? Empirical Evidence on Creative Accounting with Fiscal Rules in the EU*, 30(12) Journal of Banking & Finance 3259 (2006). *See also* Timothy C. Irwin, *Accounting Devices and Fiscal Illusions*, IMF Staff Discussion Note SDN/12/02, Mar. 28, 2012.

[162] Franco-German Declaration, Statement for the France–Germany–Russia Summit, Deauville, Oct. 18, 2010.

[163] Arturo C. Porzecanski, *Borrowing and Debt: How do Sovereigns Get into Trouble?* 309, at 320, in 'Sovereign Debt Management' (Rosa Lastra and Lee Buchheit, eds, 2014).

In November 2010, Ireland formally requested financial assistance and eventually received a EUR85 billion loan from the EU. Ireland used that loan to bail out its banks. The Irish banks in turn used the loans given to them by their government to pay back the UK and German banks from which they had borrowed. This prevented the failure of UK and German banks and their likely bailout by their governments at the expense of the Irish state and its taxpayers.[164] In 2011, Portugal received a EUR78 billion emergency loan. In June 2012, Spain asked for financial assistance. As things were spiraling out of control, the ECB declared that it was ready to do whatever it took to preserve the euro.[165] This declaration was enough to stop the sell-off of peripheral states' bonds and contain the eurocrisis.

4.4.2   European Central Bank in Crisis Mode

4.4.2.1   Containing the crisis

The euro-system is a subgroup of the European System of Central Banks.[166] It includes the ECB, based in Frankfurt, and the National Central Banks (NCBs) of states that have adopted the euro and function as ECB's branches. The ECB is the only CB that can create euros. Its goal is to maintain price stability at an inflation rate below but close to 2%.[167] Achieving full employment is a secondary goal.[168] Since 2014, with the establishment of the Single Supervisory Mechanism within it, the ECB aims to supervise financial institutions so as to foster the soundness and stability of the financial system.[169] The ECB has been established as an independent institution from other EU institutions and national governments.[170] Its capital is the aggregate capital of the CBs of all EU member states, amounting to EUR10 trillion. The NCBs are the shareholders of the ECB. Its shares are distributed to the NCBs based on their paid-in capital. That capital is calculated based on a key that reflects each state's population and GDP (Table 4.2).

---

[164]   Martin Sandbu, *Europe's Orphan: The Future of the Euro and the Politics of Debt* 102 (2015).

[165]   ECB, Speech by Mario Draghi at the Global Investment Conference in London, Press Release, July 26, 2012.

[166]   *See* arts 282(3), 127, 130, TFEU, *supra* note 154.

[167]   Art. 127(1), TFEU, *id.*

[168]   *Id.*

[169]   Regulation (EU) No. 468/2014 of the European Central Bank of 16 April 2014 establishing the framework for cooperation within the Single Supervisory Mechanism between the European Central Bank and national competent authorities and with national designated authorities, OJ L 141/1, 14.5.2014.

[170]   Art. 130, TFEU, *supra* note 154.

Table 4.2   *Select countries' contributions to the ECB*[1]

CBs	Capital paid to ECB (EUR)	Capital key percentage
CB of Germany	1 988 229 048	18.37%
CB of France	1 537 811 329	14.20%
CB of Italy	1 277 599 809	11.80%
CB of Spain	902 708 164	8.33%
CB of Netherlands	440 328 812	4.06%
CB of Greece	187 186 022	1.72%
CB of Portugal	177 172 890	1.63%
CB of Ireland	127 237 133	1.17%

Note: [1] ECB, Capital Subscription, Jan. 1, 2019.

The Governing Council is the decision-making body of the ECB. It consists of the governors of the CBs of the eurozone states (19 states) plus the six members of the ECB's Executive Board.[171] The Executive Board is responsible for implementing the monetary policy adopted by the Governing Council. Members of the Executive Board are nominated by the heads of states of the eurozone countries by a qualified majority vote.[172] They serve for a non-renewable eight-year term[173] and are not supposed to represent their own country. They must work, instead, for the benefit of the eurozone as a whole. Since the beginnings of the ECB, there has always been at least one representative from Germany, France and Italy who have served on the Executive Board.

The Governing Council of the ECB makes decisions by two-thirds majority. The governors of the five largest economies share four votes[174] while the remaining 14 governors share 11 votes based on a rotating system. Not all countries have the same authority in the ECB. There is a 'Germanization' of the ECB, which creates a feeling of bias against peripheral countries.[175] The ECB is based in Frankfurt and there are many more German nationals on its staff than French, Italians and Spanish combined. In 2017, out of the 2 900 ECB staff on fixed-term contracts, 29% were German and 7% French.[176] The

[171] Art. 10, Protocol (No. 4) on the Statute of the European System of Central Banks and of the European Central Bank [hereinafter ECB Statute], Consolidated Treaties and Protocols, *supra* note 154.

[172] Art. 11, *id.*

[173] *Id.*

[174] Art. 10, *id.* The largest countries are Germany, France, Italy, the Netherlands and Spain.

[175] Tom Fairless and Patricia Kowsmann, *ECB's German Skew Raises Questions over Draghi's Successor*, WSJ, Mar. 20, 2018.

[176] *Id.* These data were not public; they were put together by the WSJ.

oversized weight of Germany within the ECB is reflected in the behavior of the markets. During the eurocrisis, market participants refrained from taking ECB's announcements at face value unless there was a signal that the German CB was on board. Investors had a hard time figuring out how to react to the decisions of the ECB when the president of the German CB publicly challenged the soundness of those decisions. The fervor with which the German CB sought often to sabotage the official ECB position led some to proclaim that the German bank should not be allowed to derail the euro.[177]

To address the crisis, the ECB adopted in May 2010 the Securities Markets Program (SMP) through which it bought the government bonds of distressed eurozone countries. The program was necessary because the exceptional circumstances in the financial markets were hampering the effective conduct of the ECB's policy.[178] There were strong disagreements between the ECB and the German CB on the adoption of the SMP, which led to the resignation of the president of the German CB from the ECB's Executive Board. Eventually, the SMP was terminated in September 2012. As of February 21, 2013, the ECB held EUR218 billion worth of bonds of distressed eurozone countries that it had bought because of the SMP.[179] In comparison, the FRS had bought a much larger amount of US bonds – a total of $1.7 trillion between 2008 and early 2010[180] – during a time when the ECB seemed to be in denial even about the existence of a crisis.

As the sell-off of peripheral states' bonds continued, the ECB surprised the markets by stating that it was ready to do whatever it took to save the euro.[181] That simple statement triggered a surge of bond buying by hedge funds covering short positions – bets on the declines of Italian and Spanish bonds. Institutional investors, such as pension funds, started to return to the bond markets of debtor states. The ECB subsequently announced the Outright Monetary Transactions (OMTs), the purchase of bonds of peripheral troubled states. The goal of that program was to provide 'a fully effective backstop to avoid destructive scenarios'[182] that were circulating in the markets about

---

[177] *See*, e.g. George Soros, *Europe's Future is not up to the Bundesbank*, FT, Apr. 11, 2012.

[178] Para. 2, Preamble, Decision of the European Central Bank of 14 May 2010 establishing a securities market program, OJ L 124/8, 20.5.2010.

[179] 14.2 billion, Ireland; 33.9 billion, Greece; 44.3 billion, Spain; 102.8 billion, Italy; and 22.8 billion, Portugal. *See* ECB, Details on the Securities Holdings Acquired under the Securities Market Program, Press Release, Feb. 21, 2013.

[180] Steve Meyer, *Recent Federal Reserve Monetary Policy*, Jan. 14, 2011, http://www.federalreserve.gov.

[181] *See supra* note 165.

[182] ECB, Mario Draghi Introductory Statement to the Press Conference, Press Release, Oct. 4, 2012.

the break-up of the eurozone. The OMTs were, in essence, a way to finance distressed peripheral states. Those who buy a state's debt finance that state for the full value of debt they hold. The OMTs were in tune with the EU founding treaties. These treaties prohibit the ECB from buying states' debt in the primary market.[183] However, there is nothing mentioned in them that prevents the ECB from purchasing a state's debt in the open market.[184] The buying and selling of government debt is practiced by many CBs around the world, including the FRS, and it is an effective tool of monetary policy. The treaties, furthermore, grant significant discretion to the ECB in the conduct of monetary affairs.[185]

The ECB announced that it was ready to use OMTs to buy the bonds of financially troubled states if those states were already receiving financial assistance from European institutions[186] and were complying with the strict conditions imposed on them in exchange for such assistance.[187] The announcement was intentionally vague regarding the amount of bonds it was ready to buy, leaving open the possibility of unlimited purchases. The prospect of unlimited purchases of government bonds by the ECB, the only entity that can print euros at will, was meant as a warning to the markets. The ECB was threatening that it was ready to print an unlimited amount of euros to buy the bonds of peripheral states that market players were massively selling off. When confronted with such a threat, speculators backed off.

The OMTs were challenged at the German Federal Constitutional Court by a number of German nationals. The court referred the case to the European Court of Justice (ECJ) asking it for a preliminary ruling[188] on the legality of the OMTs. More specifically, the German court asked the ECJ whether the ECB, by adopting the OMTs:

- exceeded its policy mandate and made policy that is under the purview of states;
- engaged in monetary financing of governments that is prohibited under article 123 of the founding treaties.[189]

---

[183] Art. 123(1), TFEU, *supra* note 154.

[184] *But see* Willem H. Buiter and Ann Sibert, *How the Eurosystem's Treatment of Collateral in its Open Market Operations Weakens Fiscal Discipline in the Eurozone (and what to do about it)*, at 5, CERP Discussion Paper No. 5387, Dec. 2005; Matthias Ruffert, *The European Debt Crisis and European Union Law*, 48 Common Market Law Review 1777, at 1777–88 (2011).

[185] *See* art. 18, ECB Statute, *supra* note 171.

[186] These were the EFSF and ESM.

[187] See *supra* note 182.

[188] *See* Art. 267, TFEU, *supra* note 154.

[189] *See* Art. 123, *id.*

At the ECJ proceedings, the ECB explained that the spike in the yields of government bonds of peripheral states undermined its 'ability to implement monetary policy through the usual channels for monetary policy transmission'[190] (e.g. the IR). Because of this, it had to intervene in the open market as the 'unbearable increase' of IRs in some states did not reflect 'the macroeconomic reality of those states'.[191] The fragmentation of government debt market – meaning the dramatic increase in the bond yields of peripheral states when compared with the drop in the yields of core states (Box 4.1) – was preventing the transmission of 'signals' that the ECB uses to make policy.[192] The bank had to adopt, therefore, an unconventional monetary policy measure, namely the OMTs.[193] The purpose of OMTs was not to finance debtor states but to 'unblock' the ECB's policy channels and preserve the singleness of its policy.[194]

BOX 4.1   EUROCRISIS AND THE TRILEMMA

During the eurocrisis, eurozone states could not rely on their NCBs to engineer domestic expansion by creating euros. These banks were subordinated to the ECB, the only entity that can print euros. Eurozone states had lost their DEP autonomy because they had fixed their ERs by adopting the euro. During the crisis, investors fled the bond markets of peripheral states and bought the bonds of core states, especially the German government bonds, the *bunds*, because Germany is considered a safe haven in Europe. The run on the government bonds of the periphery led to the skyrocketing of their yields, making it punitive for these states to refinance their debt. The only tool left for economic policy-making was taxes. Peripheral states had to increase taxes, if they were highly indebted, to pay back their debt. The rapid increase in taxes and cuts on spending led to recession and contraction of their economies (Fig. 4.3).

---

[190]   Para. 104, Opinion of the Advocate General, Cruz Villalón, *Gauweiler et al. v. Deutscher Bundestag* (Request for a Preliminary Ruling), Case C-62/14, Jan. 14, 2015 [hereinafter Opinion of the Advocate General].

[191]   Para. 121, *id.*

[192]   Para. 104, *id.*

[193]   *Id.*

[194]   *Id.*

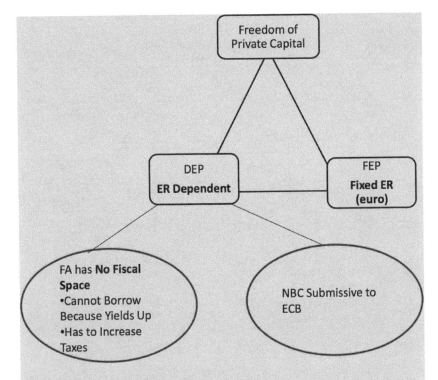

Figure 4.3   Trilemma of the Euro-periphery

On the other hand, core states had considerable *fiscal space* (Fig. 4.4). Their role as safe havens during the crisis meant that the yields of their bonds dramatically fell, reducing their borrowing costs. In fact, Germany, the chief core state in the eurozone, was able to borrow at negative real yields. During the crisis, Germany saved EUR100 billion, or 3% of its GDP, owing to the falling yields on its debt. Because their borrowing costs fell so drastically, core states did not have to increase taxes to deal with the calamities brought by the financial panic (e.g. the collapse of some of their banks). Core states had, in fact, the fiscal space to reduce taxes to kindle domestic economic expansion that could spill over to other states and speed up global economic recovery. Most of them made the deliberate choice, though, not to use that fiscal space.

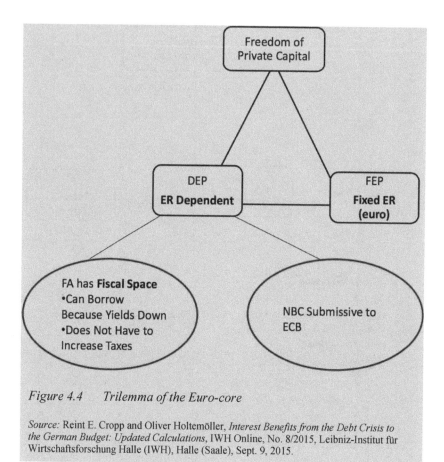

Figure 4.4   Trilemma of the Euro-core

Source: Reint E. Cropp and Oliver Holtemöller, *Interest Benefits from the Debt Crisis to the German Budget: Updated Calculations*, IWH Online, No. 8/2015, Leibniz-Institut für Wirtschaftsforschung Halle (IWH), Halle (Saale), Sept. 9, 2015.

The ECJ is assisted by the advocates general. The role of the advocates general is to review the written and oral submissions of the parties to a dispute and deliver a balanced opinion on how to resolve it. Advocates general are not involved in the ECJ's deliberations. Their opinions are not binding on the Court, but they tend to be highly detailed and reasoned and, consequently, highly influential. The advocate general, after examining the arguments and counterarguments in this case, concluded that:

- the ECB should be afforded 'a broad discretion' in framing and implementing its policy;[195]

---

[195]   Paras 110–11, *id.*

- the bank had to maintain the transmission channels of its policy in order to achieve the goal of price stability[196] enshrined in the EU founding treaties;
- the transmission channels of monetary policy can be disrupted by global political and economic crises;[197]
- when the regular channels of transmission of monetary policy, such as the IRs, are disrupted, the ECB has to intervene in the market to unblock those channels;[198]
- article 18(1) of ECB's Statute permits the ECB to operate in the financial markets by buying and selling marketable securities[199] (including government bonds) and furthermore, it is common knowledge that CBs intervene in the government debt market to make monetary policy;[200]
- the selectivity of the OMTs, which applied only to financially troubled states, did not detract from their legality. Selectivity was the 'logical consequence' of OMTs that sought to remedy the fragmentation in eurozone debt market – the high yields on peripheral debt in comparison with the yields on core states' debt.[201]

The court agreed with the advocate general and ruled that the OMTs were lawful.[202] Probably because of the political and legal uproar that was created, though, OMTs were never used. Eventually, as the eurozone was sinking into deflation and stagnation, the ECB adopted QE policies following in the footsteps of the FRS. In comparison with the FRS, though, the ECB was slow in realizing that its failure to achieve the 2% inflation rate made it look ineffectual and undermined its mandate to act as CB for all European states.

4.4.2.2 Expansionary policies
To beat deflation, on December 8, 2016 the ECB reduced its benchmark IR, the deposit facility rate, below zero, to minus 0.4%. Banks, in other words, were charged a 0.4% IR on their excess deposits with the ECB. Receiving negative yields on their reserves should have motivated banks to lend to business and households. This hardly happened in Europe, however.

---

[196] Para. 112, *id.*
[197] Para. 115, *id.*
[198] Para. 116, *id.*
[199] Para. 113, *id.*
[200] Para. 194, *id.*
[201] Paras 152–3, *id.*
[202] *Gauweiler et al., v. Deutscher Bundestag*, Case C-62/14, June 16, 2015. On June 21, 2016, the Federal Constitutional Court of Germany used the ECJ decision to rule against the German plaintiffs, *see* Bundesverfassungsgericht (Federal Constitutional Court of Germany), Constitutional Complaints against the OMT Programme of the European Central Bank Unsuccessful, Press Release No. 34/2016, June 21, 2016.

On January 22, 2015, the ECB put in motion a large-scale QE program – the asset purchase program (APP)[203] inspired by the FRS' QE programs. The Public Sector Purchase Program consisted of buying EUR60 billion worth of bonds (later increased to 80 billion) issued by eurozone states and other public agencies[204] on a monthly basis. Not all states were eligible for this APP. The bonds of debtor states were eligible for purchase only if those states had successfully passed a review conducted by their creditors on their fulfilling the conditionality requirements of their bailouts.[205] In addition, the ECB could only buy bonds rated investment-grade by the CRAs. Some of the peripheral states' debt was rated junk at the time. The ECB, therefore, would have to waive its investment-grade requirement in order to purchase those states' bonds.

The purchase of bonds of eurozone states was based on their capital key: how much capital each state contributed to the ECB. This meant that the ECB had to conduct larger purchases of bonds of creditor states, since their capital contributions to the ECB were significantly larger than those of debtor states (Table 4.2). Buying bonds based on its capital key, rather than states' needs, was a political decision that favored creditor states. Creditor states, the majority at the ECB, were against its buying the risky debt of the periphery. Buying such debt could have generated losses for the ECB if debtor states defaulted. Additional restrictions, and exceptions to those restrictions, made sure that the ECB's bond purchases favored the states that least needed them. For example,

1. The ECB could not purchase more than one-third of each state's outstanding debt.[206] Because the bank had already purchased bonds of debtor states through the 2010–2012 SMP, it had to buy more of the bonds of creditor states through the APP.
2. The ECB could not buy bonds offering yields below its own 'deposit-facility rate', which stood at −0.4%. This meant that it could not buy the bonds of states offering even more negative yields. As a result, the ECB could not purchase German bonds, yielding −0.5%, despite Germany's status as a safe haven in Europe and Germany's large contributions to the ECB. In December 2016, that restriction was waived to make it possible for

---

[203] ECB, ECB Announces Expanded Asset Purchase Programme (including Technical Annex), Press Release, Jan. 22, 2015 [hereinafter ECB APP].

[204] *See* Benoît Cœuré, *Embarking on Public Sector Asset Purchases*, Speech at the Second International Conference on Sovereign Bond Markets, Frankfurt, Mar. 10, 2015.

[205] Para. 4, Technical Annex, ECB APP, *supra* note 203.

[206] ECB, Mario Draghi Introductory Statement to the Press Conference (with Q&A), Press Release, Sept. 3, 2016.

the ECB to buy more German bonds.[207] The ECB suffered losses when it bought these negative-yielding bonds. However, this did not trouble the creditor states on its board. They would rather have the ECB buy their bonds, even at a loss, than allow it to purchase the higher-yielding but riskier bonds of the periphery.

Despite the fact that the APP was adopted with the intention to emulate the success of the FRS' QE programs, it was not as helpful to states that were experiencing financial distress. In December 2016, Portugal needed the APP program much more than Germany since its 10-year bond yielded 4%, the highest yield in the eurozone after Greece. On the other hand, Germany was operating at full employment and the yields on German debt were mostly negative.

In June 2016, to further ease monetary conditions, the ECB started to buy investment-grade bonds of established eurozone private companies including telecommunications, insurance and utility companies.[208] While it did not state how much corporate debt it was willing to buy, most expected that it was targeting to purchase between EUR5 billion and EUR10 billion of corporate bonds per month in a market estimated to be worth around EUR600 billion. By July 2016, the ECB had accumulated EUR3.26 trillion in assets. Some EUR1.3 trillion out of the EUR3.26 trillion had to do with its QE operations.[209]

4.4.2.3 Saving banks

The ECB, like other CBs, lends money to private banks against adequate collateral, typically *investment-grade bonds* issued by governments. The regular ECB financial operations are the main refinancing operations and the longer-term refinancing operations (LTROs). Through these operations, each NCB provides liquidity to its country's private banks, at IRs set by the ECB Council, against adequate collateral.[210] Before the crisis, the ECB provided credit to private banks by accepting readily as collateral bonds issued by any eurozone state. Any bank that held bonds issued by any eurozone state could always turn to the ECB for its financing. This constituted a huge credit upgrade for many peripheral states.

---

[207] ECB, ECB Adjusts Parameters of its Asset Purchase Programme (APP), Press Release, Dec. 8, 2016.

[208] ECB, ECB Announces Details of the Corporate Sector Purchase Programme (CSPP), Press Release, Apr. 21, 2016.

[209] Consolidated Financial Statement of the Eurosystem as of 22 July 2016, https://www.ecb.europa.eu.

[210] Article 18.1, ECB Statute, *supra* note 171.

Before their entry into the eurozone, these states, like most of the periphery, had difficulty issuing debt in their national currency. Endorsing the euro as their currency bumped up peripheral states' creditworthiness, since their debt was immediately accepted as collateral by one of the world's most credible CBs. Adopting the euro, in other words, enabled peripheral European states to finance themselves at the low IRs that are usually reserved for core states.

During the financial crisis, the ECB continued to grant loans to the private banks of the periphery, as many of these banks faced major liquidity shortages. The private banks of Ireland, Italy, Spain and Greece, for instance, absorbed the majority of the 3-year LTRO[211] granted by the ECB in 2011, amounting to EUR1.1 trillion.[212] Since the ECB is prohibited from providing direct support to governments,[213] a large portion of the financing it provided to private peripheral banks through these LTROs was used to buy their governments' debt. By buying the bonds of their governments, peripheral banks that were not in the best financial health themselves were supporting their countries that had lost access to the global bond market.

ECB's refinancing operations of banks faced a stumbling block, however, when the CRAs started to downgrade the debt issued by peripheral states. During the crisis, the Greek, Portuguese and Irish bonds were rated junk. Instead of stopping the infusion of funds into those states' private banks, the ECB decided to waive the requirement that the bonds it accepted as collateral must be investment-grade.[214] In this way it was able to defend the banking sector of the periphery, despite the massive short-selling of the debt of peripheral states. However, this waiver policy, which was supposed to benefit the periphery, was eventually weaponized to discipline it as well. The waiver granted to Greece was withdrawn, for instance, in 2012. That year the ECB decreed that Greek government bonds would be temporarily ineligible as collateral for ECB credit.[215] The Greek bonds became again eligible only after Greece's creditors certified that the country was complying with the conditions

---

[211] Typical LTROs extend credit to private banks for 3 months. The 3-year LTROs were an unconventional monetary policy. *See* Matthieu Darracq-Paries and Roberto De Santis, *A Non-Standard Monetary Policy Shock: The ECB's 3-year LTROs and the Shift in Credit Supply*, ECB Working Paper No. 1508, Jan. 2013.

[212] European Commission, European Financial Stability and Integration Report 2012, at 17, Apr. 2013 [hereinafter Stability and Integration Report].

[213] Art. 125, TFEU, *supra* note 154.

[214] Based on its post-2008 policy, the ECB kept the minimum credit threshold for the collateral it accepted at investment-grade level (BBB). *See* ECB, Jean-Claude Trichet, Speech before the European Parliament, Press Release, Mar. 25, 2010.

[215] ECB, Eligibility of Greek Bonds Used as Collateral in Eurosystem Monetary Policy Operations, Press Release, Feb. 28, 2012.

they had imposed on it as a *quid pro quo* for its bailout.[216] The ECB used its economic might, as lender of last resort, to discipline debtor states throughout the eurocrisis.

4.4.2.4 Enforcement of debt contracts

Banks excluded from the ECB's regular refinancing operations, because they lack adequate collateral, can still receive emergency liquidity assistance (ELA).[217] ELA support is provided, in exceptional circumstances and on a case-by-case basis, to temporarily illiquid banks that are solvent.[218] Greek private banks had to tap into the ELA in 2015 when a newly elected Greek government conflicted with creditor states. During that crucial period of negotiations between Greece and its creditors, the ECB decreed again that Greek government bonds would be unacceptable collateral for ECB credit.[219] The ECB's Governing Council was 'fairly evenly split' in making that decision.[220] Owing to the rotating voting system that came into effect in 2015, the Greek, Cypriot, Irish and French CB governors were unable to cast a vote at that 2015 ECB meeting.

Since the ECB was refusing to accept Greek government bonds as collateral, the Greek banks had to tap into ELA. Greek banks were in really bad shape as capital was fleeing Greece at a rapid pace. The Greek CB was responsible for making the decision on whether and when to provide ELA to the Greek banks. However, it also had to inform the ECB's Governing Council within two working days after making that decision.[221] The Governing Council's role is to evaluate whether the ELA provided by an NCB may be at odds with 'the objectives and tasks' of the Eurosystem.[222] The Governing Council can restrict or discontinue the ELA, provided by an NCB to domestic private banks, by a two-thirds majority vote if it determines that the ELA is incompatible with the objectives of the Eurosystem.

---

[216] ECB, ECB Announces Change in Eligibility of Debt Instruments Issued or Guaranteed by the Greek Government, Press Release, Dec. 19, 2012.

[217] Approval of the governing board of the ECB is needed when the amount of ELA provided exceeds certain thresholds, *see* ECB, ELA Procedures, Oct. 17, 2013 [hereinafter ELA Procedures].

[218] *Id.*

[219] ECB, Eligibility of Greek Bonds Used as Collateral in Eurosystem Monetary Policy Operations, Press Release, Feb. 4, 2015.

[220] Transparency International EU, *Two Sides of the Same Coin? Independence and Accountability of the European Central Bank* 51 (2017) [hereinafter ECB Independence].

[221] *See supra* note 217.

[222] *Id.*

All through the eurocrisis, the ECB Council used the threat of cutting off the ELA to pressure states to accept the conditions demanded by their creditors. It pressed Ireland to accept the restructuring of its debt proposed by the EU in 2010 by threatening to stop the provision of ELA to the Irish banks. The ECB forced a resolution of the Cypriot financial crisis by announcing, on March 25, 2013, that it was ready to discontinue the ELA unless Cyprus was ready to agree to the privatization of its banking sector.[223] When Greece chose to put to a referendum the conditionality demanded by its creditors on June 25, 2015, the ECB froze the ceiling of ELA provided to Greek banks to EUR90 billion,[224] an amount woefully inadequate to address the run on the Greek banking system. That decision taken amid circumstances of high political uncertainty and raging rumors about 'Grexit'– the exit of Greece from the eurozone – intensified the run on the Greek banks. Given the freezing of ELA and collapsing faith in its banking system, the Greek government had to resort to capital controls. As people started to queue in front of ATMs to collect their daily allotment of EUR60, the government capitulated to the demands of its creditors, ending the financial and political drama that captivated the world in 2015.

Many criticized the ECB for the role it played in the Greek crisis. Its decision to withdraw regular financing from the Greek banks because of the inability of the Greek state and its creditors to find a compromise was obviously a pressure tactic to speed up the conclusion of an agreement acceptable to creditors. Its decision to freeze the ELA at EUR90 billion certainly intensified the run on the Greek banks. Because of the limited and conditional assistance it made available, the ECB did not function as a lender of last resort to Greece. The lender-of-last-resort function involves unconditional and unlimited lending until faith is restored in the economy of a state. The ECB, on the contrary, made it a habit to warn debtor states that it was willing to accept their debt as collateral for lending to their banks only if these states were ready to comply with the demands creditors made.

In hindsight, it should not have come as a surprise that, in the conflict that was raging in the eurozone between creditors and debtors, the ECB placed itself in the camp of creditors. The ECB is made up of European states the majority of which, at the time, were creditor states. These states were unwilling to make concessions and, in fact, some pushed for Grexit. Given the staunch resistance of creditors, the ECB could not do much. In the words of its pres-

---

[223] ECB, Governing Council Decision on Emergency Liquidity Assistance Requested by the Central Bank of Cyprus, Press Release, Mar. 21, 2013.
[224] ECB, ELA to Greek Banks Maintained at its Current Levels, Press Release, June 28, 2015.

ident: 'And we [ECB] did it ... always acting on the assumption that Greece will be a member of the euro area. There was never a question. And that is *what makes us [ECB] different from the ones who said, "You should have cut ELA a long time ago"*. They [creditor states] wanted us not to respect our mandate, deciding who should be a member of the euro area and who should not.'[225]

Another task of the ECB that made it look like it had been captured by the creditors was its participation in the troika, the fearsome trio that included the European Commission and the IMF. The purpose of the troika was to ensure that debtors actually implemented the conditionality demanded by their creditors. Being part of the troika pushed the ECB to take sides and hurt its image as an independent CB.[226] The ECB, additionally, compromised its independence when it unilaterally reprimanded and urged the elected governments of Ireland,[227] Spain[228] and Italy to adopt fiscal consolidation and labor reforms if they wished to obtain its continuing support.[229]

All in all, during the crisis, the ECB treated some states as sovereigns and others as lesser states. Because of the ECB's structure and the power dynamics of that period, this should have been expected. In a union torn between creditors and debtors, and in which creditors had the upper hand, the ECB had to side with the creditors, no matter its internal doubts and consternation.

4.4.3   Conditionality, Surveillance and Sanctions

4.4.3.1   Emergency mechanisms
The eurocrisis tarnished the reputation of the EU as a polity of equals. Even proponents of European unity started to have doubts about the merits of preserving a union that looked like a supranational organization controlled by a club of creditors. The European Council, the decision-making organ of the EU, consists of the heads of state of all EU member states. These are

---

[225] ECB, Mario Draghi Introductory Statement to Press Conference (with Q&A), Press Release, July 16, 2015. Emphasis added.

[226] ECB Independence, *supra* note 220, at 17.

[227] In 2014, the European Ombudsman chastised the ECB for its lack of transparency citing specifically the failure to disclose the letters it sent to the Irish authorities. *See* European Ombudsman, Governing Council of the ECB has Wasted an Opportunity for Openness and Transparency, Press Release, Mar. 7, 2014. The correspondence between the ECB and the Irish authorities was eventually published on the ECB website.

[228] In 2014, the ECB published the letter it sent to the Spanish prime minister.

[229] *See* European Court of Auditors, *Financial Assistance Provided to Countries in Difficulties*, at 48, Special Report No.18, 2015.

supposedly the masters of the treaties,[230] the kings comparable with the kings of the early nineteenth-century constitutions.[231] Based on the EU treaties, the states that make the European Council are equals. During the crisis, though, the inherently unequal dynamic between creditors and debtors transformed the Council into an echo-chamber of creditors. The difficult political decisions on how to address the crisis were made at the bilateral level by France and Germany and were quickly rubber-stamped at inter-governmental summits. France, however, quickly found itself playing second fiddle to Germany as the German chancellor became, for all practical purposes, the *de facto* leader of the European Union.

The eurogroup, the group of financial ministers of the eurozone, worked tirelessly to resolve the crisis, but its informal character[232] and lack of transparency undercut much of the legitimacy of its leadership. The European Commission, which is considered the EU executive, ended up playing a marginal role when the eurozone was in panic mode. The same holds true with the European Parliament, the only body directly elected by the populations of EU states.

The European Financial Stabilization Mechanism (EFSM) was the first institution created to address the crisis. This was a EUR60 billion fund established in 2010 and available to countries facing difficulties.[233] The European Financial Stability Facility (EFSF) was put together subsequently as a company with a lending capacity of EUR440 billion. It was created outside the EU system exclusively by eurozone states to deal with the crisis on a temporary basis.[234] The EFSF was incorporated in Luxembourg and an agreement, signed between the company and the eurozone states outlined its functions.[235]

---

[230] *See* paras 231, 235, English translation of the judgment of the federal constitutional court of Germany on the Lisbon Treaty, Federal Constitutional Court of Germany (BVerfG), 2 BvE 2/08, June 30, 2009, http://www.bverfg.de.

[231] Jürgen Habermas, *The Crisis of the European Union: A Response* 44 (2012).

[232] Art. 1, Protocol No. 14, TFEU, *supra* note 154.

[233] Council Regulation (EU) No. 407/2010 of 11 May 2010 establishing a European Financial Stabilisation Mechanism, OJ L 118/1, 12.5.2010. A similar mechanism was adopted in 2002 to assist non-eurozone member states. *See* Council Regulation (EC) No. 332/2002 of 18 February 2002 establishing a facility providing medium-term financial assistance for Member States' balances of payments, OJ L 53/1, 23.2.2002.

[234] ECOFIN, Note of the General Secretariat of the Council No. 9614/10, May 9, 2010. For the articles of incorporation of the company, *see* European Financial Stability Facility, Société Anonyme, Memorial Journal Officiel du Grand-Duché de Luxembourg C-No. 1189, at 57026, June 8, 2010.

[235] EFSF Framework Agreement between Belgium, Germany, Estonia, Ireland, Greece, Spain, France, Italy, Cyprus, Luxembourg, Malta, Netherlands, Austria, Portugal, Slovenia, Slovakia, Finland and the European Financial Stability Facility, July 7, 2010 [hereinafter EFSF Agreement].

Some doubted the legality of this arrangement[236] while others viewed it as a brilliant combination of EU law and private international law.[237]

The European Stability Mechanism (ESM) that was put in place in 2012 replaced the EFSF. This is a permanent body with ammunition of EUR700 billion, out of which EUR500 billion are available to troubled states and banks.[238] The ESM was established outside the EU framework, though, as an international organization headquartered in Luxembourg.[239] The ESM's capital of EUR700 billion is divided into 7 million shares, each share having a nominal value of 100 000.[240] The shares are available to states for subscription based on their share of paid-in capital contribution to the ECB (Table 4.2).[241] Based on the ESM's contribution key, Germany has the highest number of shares (1 900 248) followed by France (1 427 013) and Italy (1 253 959).[242] The paid-in capital contribution to the ESM is EUR80 billion and the remaining EUR620 billion is callable capital.[243] The ESM Board of Governors consists of the ministers of finance of eurozone states. Certain decisions of the board require unanimity, such as whether to assist a eurozone state;[244] the rest is made by qualified majority.[245] Qualified majority is defined in the ESM treaty as 80% of the vote cast – with voting rights equal to the number of shares allocated to each country.[246] Since Germany holds about 27% of ESM shares, it can veto

---

[236] *See*, e.g. Giuseppe Bianco, *The New Financial Stability Mechanisms and their (Poor) Consistency with EU Law*, European University Institute Working Paper, RSCAS 2012/44 (2012).

[237] *See*, e.g. Bruno De Witte, *Using International Law in the Euro Crisis: Causes and Consequences*, Working Paper No. 4, Centre for European Studies University of Oslo, June 2013.

[238] Treaty Establishing the European Stability Mechanism, Feb. 2, 2012 [hereinafter ESM Treaty].

[239] The creation of the ESM required a modification of article 136 of TFEU, *supra* note 154. *See* European Council Decision of 25 March 2011 amending Article 136 of the Treaty on the Functioning of the European Union with regard to a stability mechanism for Member States whose currency is the euro, OJ L 91/1, 6.4.2011. Both the TFEU amendment and the ESM Treaty were challenged before the ECJ. *See Thomas Pringle v. Ireland*, Case C-370/12, Nov. 27, 2012.

[240] Art. 8(1), ESM Treaty, *supra* note 238.

[241] *See* Annex I and II, *id.*

[242] *Id.*

[243] Art. 8(2), *id.*

[244] Art. 5(6), *id.*

[245] Art. 5(7), *id.*

[246] Art. 4(5), *id.*

decisions made by qualified majority.[247] Nevertheless, the establishment of the ESM was legally challenged in Germany.[248]

Financial assistance, through the ESM, is available to eurozone states on the condition of their ratification of the Fiscal Compact.[249] A memorandum of understanding between the debtor state and the ESM must enumerate the conditions and surveillance procedures a state must submit to in order to get assistance. In 'exceptional cases an adequate and proportionate form of *private sector involvement*'[250] could be part of an ESM program. This means that private bondholders may be asked to incur losses if the ESM decides to get involved in restructuring the debt of a state that is on the brink of default.

4.4.3.2   Squeezing fiscal autonomy

The Maastricht Treaty, one of the founding treaties of the EU, sets forth the excessive deficit procedure.[251] This procedure is triggered when countries exceed the 3% deficit-to-GDP ratio or 60% debt-to-GDP ratio as elaborated further in the Stability and Growth Pact that imposes sanctions when countries exceed these ceilings.[252] Before the crisis, the Stability Pact was not really working. About 100 violations of the 3% rule by many countries, including Austria, Belgium, France, Germany, the Netherlands, Poland and the UK, went unpunished.[253] The sanctions included in the Stability Pact were hard to enforce. Countries refrained from seeking to impose financial penalties on others when they knew they could be violators one day.[254]

---

[247]   Art. 5(7), *id.*

[248]   *See* official English translation of the German court's ESM decision, BVerfG, 2 BvR 1390/12, Sept. 12, 2012, http://www.bundesverfassungsgericht.de.

[249]   Para. 5, Preamble, ESM Treaty, *supra* note 238. *See also infra* section 4.4.3.4.

[250]   Para. 12, Preamble, *id.* Emphasis added.

[251]   Art. 126, TFEU, *supra* note 154.

[252]   *See* Council Regulation (EC) No. 1466/97 of 7 July 1997 on the strengthening of the surveillance of budgetary positions and the surveillance of economic policies, OJ L 209/1, 2.8.1997 (the preventive arm of the Stability Pact); Council Regulation (EC) No. 1467/97 on speeding up and clarifying the implementation of the Excessive Deficit Procedure , OJ L 209/6, 2.8.1997 (the corrective arm of the Stability Pact) [hereinafter Stability Pact].

[253]   Jean Tirole, *The Euro Crisis: Some Reflexions on Institutional Reform*, at 225, n. 6, Banque de France Financial Stability Review, No. 16, Apr. 2012.

[254]   ECB, *A Fiscal Compact for a Stronger Economic and Monetary Union*, at 81, ECB Monthly Bulletin, May 2012.

The Stability Pact was amended in 2011 by the so-called 'six-pack' – five regulations and one directive:

- two regulations on preventing[255] and correcting[256] violations of the Stability Pact;
- a regulation on sanctions imposed on violators of the Stability Pact;[257]
- a regulation on the prevention and correction of macroeconomic imbalances;[258]
- a regulation on sanctions imposed on states with excessive macroeconomic imbalances;[259] and
- a directive on budget requirements.[260]

The 2011 amended Stability Pact has two arms: the preventive arm and corrective arm. The aim of the preventive arm is to ensure that governments do not overshoot the debt and deficit limits.[261] The corrective arm strengthens the excessive deficit procedure.[262] In 2011, for the first time, a specific regulation was exclusively devoted to sanctions imposed on eurozone countries that violate the preventive or corrective arm of the Stability Pact. These sanctions are triggered automatically, on a recommendation by the Commission, unless the Council decides by a qualified majority to reject that recommendation (what is called 'reverse qualified majority voting').[263]

---

[255] Regulation (EU) No. 1175/2011 of the European Parliament and of the Council of 16 November 2011 amending Council Regulation (EC) No. 1466/97 on the strengthening of the surveillance of budgetary positions and the surveillance and coordination of economic policies, OJ L 306/12, 23.11.2011 [hereinafter Preventive Regulation].

[256] Council Regulation (EU) No. 1177/2011 of 8 November 2011 amending Regulation (EC) No. 1467/97 on speeding up and clarifying the implementation of the excessive deficit procedure, OJ L 306/33, 23.11.2011 [hereinafter Corrective Regulation].

[257] Regulation (EU) No. 1173/2011 of the European Parliament and of the Council of 16 November 2011 on the effective enforcement of budgetary surveillance in the euro area, OJ L 306/1, 23.11.2011 [hereinafter Sanctions Regulation].

[258] Regulation (EU) No. 1176/2011 of the European Parliament and of the Council of 16 November 2011 on the prevention and correction of macroeconomic imbalances, OJ L 306/25, 23.11.2011.

[259] Regulation (EU) No. 1174/2011 of the European Parliament and of the Council of 16 November 2011 on enforcement measures to correct excessive macroeconomic imbalances in the euro area, OJ L 306/8, 23.11.2011.

[260] Council Directive 2011/85/EU of 8 November 2011 on requirements for budgetary frameworks of the Member States, OJ L 306/41, 23.11.2011.

[261] Preventive Regulation, *supra* note 255.

[262] Corrective Regulation, *supra* note 256.

[263] Art. 6(2), Sanctions Regulation, *supra* note 257.

Every state is required to make significant progress towards its medium-term budgetary objective (MTO).[264] This MTO differs from state to state, but all states have to achieve a budget 'close to balance or in surplus position, while providing a safety margin with respect to the 3 % of GDP government deficit ratio'.[265] States must submit their medium-term budgetary plans annually for multilateral fiscal surveillance under the European Semester.[266] The European Commission issues a warning if a state experiences significant deviation from the MTO.[267] The Council recommends corrective action to the state which must adopt that action within specific deadlines.[268] Sanctions of up to 0.2% of GDP can be inflicted on states that fail to correct their excessive deficits.[269]

It has been argued that the Stability Pact has operated in a lopsided fashion because it punishes countries with excessive deficits but does nothing to discipline states with excessive surpluses. This asymmetric functioning – compelling countries with deficits to adopt contractionary policies but lacking clout over countries with fiscal space[270] – skews economic policy against growth. Moreover, while European governments have tied their hands by adhering to strict deficit and debt ceilings, which discourage counter-cyclical stimulus,[271] the ECB focuses single-mindedly on fighting inflation even at the cost of inhibiting growth and employment. Many have lamented the fact that European regulations place so many constraints on states that they neuter their capacity to deal effectively with crises. Constricting regulations, which are supposed to be applied uniformly across states, are marred further by implementation inconsistencies and lack of clarity on how exceptions to the rules are determined.

4.4.3.3   Correction of imbalances

In the aftermath of the crisis, the EU adopted new regulations for preventing and correcting the macroeconomic imbalances of its member states. The regulations define imbalances broadly to include high levels of indebtedness in the private sector, high unemployment, asset bubbles, trade deficits or surpluses, and CA deficits or surpluses. Countries that have *excessive* macroeconomic

---

[264]   Art. 2a, Preventive Regulation, *supra* note 255.
[265]   *Id.*
[266]   Not later than April 30, *see* art. 4(1), *id.*
[267]   Art. 6(2), *id.*
[268]   *Id.*
[269]   Art. 6, Sanctions Regulation, *supra* note 257.
[270]   EFB, Annual Report, at 47 (2017). *See also* Jesper Jespersen, *The Stability Pact: A Macroeconomic Straightjacket!* 45, in 'The Price of the Euro' (Jonas Ljungberg, ed., 2004).
[271]   Benjamin J. Cohen, *Toward a Leaderless Currency System* 142, at 149–50, in 'The Future of the Dollar' (Eric Helleiner and Jonathan Kirshner, eds, 2009).

imbalances have to undergo the excessive macroeconomic imbalances procedure. This means they could be fined for not correcting their imbalances.[272]

The impulse to correct the macroeconomic imbalances of states is right, but the enforcement of the macroeconomic imbalances regulation has remained erratic. The Commission has been aggressive in pursuing countries with excessive CA deficits, but has refrained from taking action against countries with excessive surpluses. The US Treasury has admonished the lopsided application of the macroeconomic imbalances procedure[273] that has failed to address the large external surpluses of countries like Germany.[274] In Germany, though, a country where trade surpluses are hailed as proof of industrial prowess, calls to reduce such surpluses are dismissed as jealous attacks against the country's exceptional economic performance. If the United States were to ever take action against Germany, the way it took action against China in 2019,[275] it could inflict a large blow to the eurozone and to the by-default hegemony of Germany in that zone.[276] Given the many animosities among European states, the European project was alive and well only because of the continuing support of the United States.[277]

That support seemed to be eroding during the Trump presidency. The US president vociferously condemned Germany's large trade surpluses and its paltry contributions to the security of Europe through the Trans-Atlantic alliance, NATO. NATO and an integrated EU made it possible for Germany to cut down defense spending and to export to rich neighboring states, piling up large CA surpluses. Some branded Germany a 'taker' in the world – importing stability and wealth from its neighboring states and the United States but offering nothing to them in return.[278]

4.4.3.4 Balanced budgets and the debt break

The Fiscal Compact was adopted as the key to guaranteeing economic stability in Europe. The compact was adopted as an international treaty by member

---

[272] *See* art. 3, Regulation 1174/2011, *supra* note 259.

[273] US Department of the Treasury, *Report to Congress on International Economic and Exchange Rate Policies*, at 10, Oct. 30, 2013. *See also* Claus D. Zimmermann, *A Contemporary Concept of Monetary Sovereignty* 170 (2013).

[274] US Treasury, *id.* at 25.

[275] *See supra* Section 4.1.5.

[276] *Berlin's Economic Power Creates 'New Fear of Germany' Across EU*, DW, Nov. 20, 2019.

[277] *See*, e.g. Deidre Berger, *In Spite of It All, America: A Transatlantic Manifesto in Times of Donald Trump – A German Perspective*, The German Marshall Fund of the United States, No. 34, Oct. 2017.

[278] Philip Stephens, *Donald Trump, Italy and the Threat to Germany*, FT, June 7, 2018.

states of the EU,[279] except for the UK and the Czech Republic, which refused to sign it. Eurozone states have to ratify the Fiscal Compact in order to receive financial assistance from the ESM in times of need.[280] The premise of the compact is that the 'structural' budgets of states (Box 4.2) 'shall be balanced or in surplus'.[281] The European Commission is in charge of assessing whether states' budgets are balanced budgets.[282] In case a state deviates from a balanced budget a correction mechanism, the so-called 'debt break', is triggered automatically, forcing that state to correct the deviation.[283] Exceptions are allowed only temporarily and only in exceptional circumstances,[284] such as unusual events outside the control of a state that have an impact on its finances or periods of severe economic downturn.[285]

BOX 4.2   STRUCTURAL DEFICIT V. CYCLICAL DEFICIT

A state violates the compact when it records a structural budget deficit. A *structural* budget deficit is different from a *cyclical* budget deficit. A cyclical deficit reflects the current state or cycle of an economy, for instance, a recession that has decreased tax receipts. A structural deficit has to do with the fundamentals of an economy. We say that a state has a structural deficit if that deficit persists even when its economy recovers and is at almost full employment. Economic fundamentals that produce structural deficits can include an ageing population or a high level of poverty that fuels public spending. Structural deficits do not always mean that an economy is in bad shape. A government may intentionally decide to maintain a structural deficit by increasing spending to invest in infrastructure and boost future productivity and growth.

The Fiscal Compact is unusual for an international treaty because it specifies exactly how states are to incorporate it into their domestic order. State parties have the obligation to transpose the Fiscal Compact 'through provisions of

---

[279] Treaty on Stability, Coordination and Governance in the Economic and Monetary Union (called informally Fiscal Compact), Mar. 2, 2012.

[280] Preamble, *id.*

[281] Art. 3(1)(a)(b), (d), *id.* This rule is considered respected if the structural deficit is 0.5% of GDP; or, alternatively, if the structural deficit is 1% of GDP, the debt-to-GDP ratio is below 60% and long-term risks to fiscal sustainability are low.

[282] Art. 3(1)(b), *id.*

[283] Art. 3(1)(e), *id.*

[284] Art. 3(1)(c), *id.*

[285] Art. 3(3)(b), *id.*

binding force and permanent character, preferably constitutional, or otherwise guaranteed to be fully respected and adhered to throughout the national budgetary processes'.[286] In other words, states have to amend their constitution, or adopt rules that are hierarchically superior to ordinary legislation, to embed the Fiscal Compact in their domestic order. These hierarchically superior rules must serve as an anchor for the national budgetary process.

The debt break included in the compact is copied from the German constitution. Germany adopted the debt break after its reunification in an effort to curb public spending. Whether the debt break can actually discipline states depends on how they use it. When implementing its own break, Germany attempted to manipulate it to give itself more fiscal space.[287]

Overall, the complexity of the Fiscal Compact and the 'micromanagement' of the European states by the Commission, which is in charge of the enforcement of the Compact, have caused political tension and acrimony in the European Union.[288]

4.4.3.5 Surveillance of states

Additional legislation placed national budgets under Union surveillance.[289] Starting in 2013, and each and every year thereafter, by October 15, states must submit to the Commission and eurogroup their draft budgets for the following year.[290] The Commission must examine these draft budgets and give an opinion on each of them by November 30.[291] If the Commission 'identifies particularly serious non-compliance' with the Stability Pact, it must request the non-compliant state to submit a revised budgetary plan.[292] This request is not binding on states. However, if the Commission labels a draft budget

---

[286] Art. 3(2), *id.*

[287] *See* Achim Truger and Henner Will, *The German 'Debt Brake' – a Shining Example for European Fiscal Policy?*, Working Paper, No. 15, Institute for International Political Economy (Sigrid Betzelt et al., eds, 2012).

[288] Agnès Bénassy Quéré et al., *Reconciling Risk Sharing with Market Discipline: A Constructive Approach to Euro Area Reform*, at 9, Policy Insight No. 91, Center for Economic Policy Research, Jan. 2018.

[289] Regulation (EU) No. 473/2013 of the European Parliament and of the Council of 21 May 2013 on common provisions for monitoring and assessing draft budgetary plans and ensuring the correction of excessive deficit of the Member States in the euro area, OJ L 140/11, 27.5.2013 [hereinafter Regulation 473]; Regulation (EU) No. 472/2013 of the European Parliament and of the Council of 21 May 2013 on the strengthening of economic and budgetary surveillance of Member States in the euro area experiencing or threatened with serious difficulties with respect to their financial stability, OJ L 140/1, 27.5.2013 [hereinafter Regulation 472].

[290] Art. 6, Regulation 473, *id.*

[291] Art. 7(1), *id.*

[292] Art. 7(2), *id.*

non-compliant with the Stability Pact and the non-compliant state does not submit a revised budget, the Commission can use that as evidence of recalcitrance when deciding whether that state should undergo the excruciating excessive deficit procedure. A state undergoing the excessive deficit procedure must present to the Commission and the Council an 'economic partnership program' describing the policy measures and structural reforms it needs to undertake for 'an effective and lasting correction of the excessive deficit'.[293] The state must report to the Commission regularly on the measures it has taken to correct its excessive deficit.[294] A state's non-compliance with its obligations under the excessive deficit procedure may trigger economic sanctions.

States that experience severe financial difficulties or are receiving assistance on a precautionary basis are subject to an even more rigorous, 'enhanced' surveillance procedure.[295] States that emerge from financial assistance programs are subject to 'post-program surveillance'. These states are subjected to economic surveillance until they pay back, at the minimum, 75% of the loans they have received from other states, the EFSM, ESM or EFSF.[296]

There is no question that EU surveillance undermines the economic independence of member states. Some have claimed that this repression of national economic autonomy may strengthen states' resolve to build a political union. To this date, the opposite has happened. States subjected to surveillance because they exceed deficit or debt limits resent the tutelage they have to endure that lays bare their impotence as states. This is particularly so because a single state is the *de facto* European sovereign. This has crushed previously entrenched beliefs that the EU is a partnership among equally sovereign states.

4.5 CONCLUSION

Many have called the years between 2007 and 2016 a lost decade for the developed world. The private sector was deleveraging and preferred to save rather than invest. Tepid borrowing and consumer demand triggered deflation and an economic malaise dubbed 'secular stagnation'.[297] Savings were invested in safe assets – risk-free government debt, the debt issued by the United States and a handful of core states. Because only a few countries were trusted to supply risk-free assets, and because of the law of supply and demand – the

---

[293] Art. 9, *id.*
[294] Art. 10, *id.*
[295] Arts 3–4, Regulation 472, *supra* note 289.
[296] Art. 14, *id.*
[297] Lawrence H. Summers, *U.S. Economic Prospects: Secular Stagnation, Hysteresis, and the Zero Lower Bound*, Keynote Address at the NABE Policy Conference, 49(2) Business Economics 65 (2014).

Table 4.3   *Bond yields by country, July 2016*

Country	3 Year	5 Year	10 Year	15 Year	30 Year
Switzerland	−1.08	−1.01	−0.61	−0.36	−0.10
Japan	−0.32	−0.35	−0.25	−0.12	0.06
Germany	−0.68	−0.59	−0.16	−0.09	0.37
Netherlands	−0.61	−0.46	0.05		0.50
Finland	−0.61	−0.46	0.10	0.35	0.52
Austria	−0.54	−0.43	0.15	0.12	0.83
France	−0.56	−0.39	0.15	0.49	0.92
Belgium	−0.57	−0.46	0.19	0.53	1.03
Sweden		−0.36	0.11		
Denmark		−0.35	0.06		0.46
Ireland	−0.31		0.44	0.74	1.19
Spain	−0.06	0.23	1.19	1.53	2.26
Italy	−0.01	0.31	1.27	1.57	2.29
United States	0.67	0.95	1.39		2.16

Source: Bloomberg Global Development Sovereign Bond index.

supply of such assets was low, but the demand was high – IRs fell.[298] In some cases, in fact, the IRs dipped into negative territory (Table 4.3).

The anxiety of savers, who sought risk-free returns, was particularly acute in the eurozone. In 2016, the eurozone, as a whole, had a CA surplus of 3%. This was because of Germany's large surplus (above 6%) and the austerity measures adopted by debtor states that had to shrink their deficits. In the past, countries with surpluses, like Germany, were able to export their savings to countries with deficits, which in turn were more than willing to borrow these savings. Now the whole eurozone was saving instead of spending and investing. Therefore, there was not enough demand for the savings put aside by surplus states.

All through the crisis, developed states adopted an array of measures, including large bond-buying programs and benchmark negative rates, to entice business to borrow and invest and to bring their economies back to growth. In the eurozone, the ECB was the only institution ready to do something to spur growth since states had tied their hands with inflexible fiscal rules. The ECB rose to the task by adopting an *assertive* monetary policy stance (Fig. 4.5). It bought government debt to unleash liquidity in the market. It also bought

---

[298]   ECB, Mario Draghi Addressing the Causes of Low Interest Rates, Speech at the Annual Meeting of the Asian Development Bank, Press Release, May 2, 2016.

corporate debt, directly financing various corporations. It even guided IRs to negative territory. Because of this assertive policy, it attracted the ire of surplus states, especially Germany, which doubted that monetary easing was the way to ignite growth. The push and pull between the ECB and the German CB, ECB's largest and richest shareholder, caused a lot of friction in Europe.

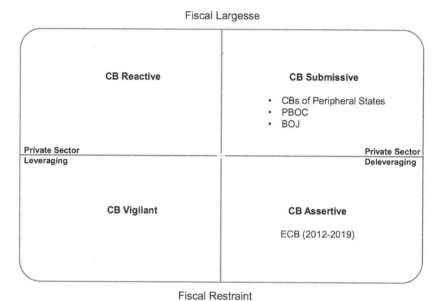

Figure 4.5   *CBs' posture towards fiscal policy and private leverage/ deleverage*

The Japanese government and the BOJ were in agreement that expansionary policy was what the economy needed (Fig. 4.5). The BOJ worked closely with the government, not because it did not treasure its independence, but because of the chronic domestic deflation that made necessary such collaboration. In 2013, the BOJ and the government announced a joint effort to return the country to growth. In July 2016, the BOJ hinted that it was ready to adopt OMF or 'helicopter money' by buying government debt, not in the secondary market as it is the custom, but directly from the government. When the government announced a fiscal stimulus package on July 27, 2016, rumors abounded that it was to be financed by the BOJ.[299] Enacting a tax cut financed by money cre-

---

[299] Chelsey Dulaney, *Japanese 'Helicopter Money' Prospect has Yen Traders on Edge*, WSJ, July 27, 2016.

ation[300] demonstrates how synchronized government policies must be to battle a persistent deflation. During times of war, deflation and private deleveraging, CBs are willing to coordinate with FAs, especially if FAs have fiscal space and are ready to use it to jumpstart the economy.

The tepid growth that afflicted the developed world in the aftermath of 2008 created fears that the 'Japanese syndrome' of chronic deflation would become the global norm. Some proposed that the cure for chronic deflation was reflation. Central banks needed to stop obsessing about the inflationary impact of easy money and focus on reflating the global economy. Such reflation could break 'the deflationary psychology' of the public.[301] Economists advocated flexible inflation targets and the 'intelligent and flexible' interpretation of those targets.[302] A flexible inflation target, between 2 and 3%, like that adopted by the Reserve Bank of Australia, was expected to lessen CBs' fixation on a single inflation number and to give them more leeway in policymaking.

The developing world faces many economic challenges. Because developing states are takers rather than makers of global policy, they have relied on the close collaboration between their CB and FA to address periods of economic malaise. Many developing states face acute problems of poverty and financial underdevelopment. This motivates them to adopt 'pro-cyclical' fiscal policies – they spend too much when the economy is booming and cut back on spending during bad times. Developing states usually operate under fiscal dominance, the CB being simply the bank of the FA printing the currency needed for the government. Fiscal dominance is unquestionably the cause of the high inflation encountered in many developing states and the lack of convertibility of their currencies.

Even states that have liberated their CB from the grab of the FA do not enjoy full economic independence. This is because the CBs of developing states have to synchronize their policies with the US policy even if domestic economic conditions dictate a completely different approach. Developing states have urged the United States to take into account the spillovers of its policies on them and the FRS seems to have listened to some of those concerns. The truth, though, has always been that the FRS is the CB of the United States. In times of trouble, it has to put US interests first.

Developing states are also at a disadvantage because the United States, the only real lender of last resort, is unwilling to play that role for all states. This has driven some of these states to run CA surpluses to collect the FX

---

[300] *See* Ben S. Bernanke, *Some Thoughts on Monetary Policy in Japan*, Remarks before the Japan Society of Monetary Economics, Tokyo, Japan, May 31, 2003.
[301] *Id.*
[302] Adair Turner, *Debt, Money, and Mephistopheles: How Do We Get Out of this Mess?*, at 20, Occasional Paper 87, Group of 30, 2013.

reserves they need to defend their currency when it is under attack. In 2016, the whole world was watching as China, one of the largest FX accumulators, was fending off speculative attacks against its currency while attempting to loosen its dependence on the dollar. Fragile developing states, states with scant FX reserves and large deficits, have no other option but to accommodate, at their peril, the economic policies of the sovereign.

PART III

Searching for world order: conflicts, truces and peace

5. Coordination and conflict

5.1 CONVERGENCE AND DIVERGENCE OF ECONOMIC POLICIES OF STATES

States have occasionally coordinated their fiscal and monetary policies and cooperated for the global management of economic affairs. They have concluded in many cases, however, that coordinating with others will not produce the best outcomes for them. This sounds counter-intuitive. One would expect that, in principle, coordination or at least some form of cooperation should benefit all owing to the spillovers of various DEPs and FEPs on other states. As a rule, the economic policies of core states spill over to other states. Those states' reaction to these policies, such as the accumulation of large FX reserves for self-insurance, has the potential to spill back to core states. For instance, in the mid-2000s the high foreign demand for dollars and T-bills spilled back to the United States by driving down US IRs. These low IRs contributed, in turn, to the US housing bubble, which put in motion one the worst financial disasters in modern economic history.

We elaborate here on four scenarios of economic policy. Under scenarios A and B all states are en route to adopting similar economic policies – that is to expand their economies (Scenario A) or fight global inflation (Scenario B). Their policies, therefore, converge. The question is whether they will coordinate to achieve the best outcomes out of this convergence or choose to compete and free ride on others. Under Scenarios C and D we examine the potential for coordination and conflict when states' policies diverge. Under Scenario C the sovereign wishes to expand but other states fear that more growth would fuel inflation. Under Scenario D, the sovereign adopts contractionary measures to beat domestic inflation, but others wish to expand their underdeveloped economies.

5.1.1 Scenario A (Convergence)

Owing to tepid global growth, all states scramble to develop their economies. This can be achieved by orchestrating a gradual monetary easing starting with the sovereign. The sovereign's expansion should leak to other states, helping them expand their own economies. If the pursuit of global expansion is coordinated and consistently telegraphed to the markets, states may be able to avoid the outcome of private capital prancing from state to state in pursuit of the highest IRs available. States may also be able to avoid a trade war which usually takes place when lower IRs, adopted to encourage borrowing, cause the depreciation of currencies.

In the alternative scenario of conflict, all states wish to grow their economies but their efforts are uncoordinated. When a state, for instance, lowers its IRs to devalue its currency, its neighbor immediately does the same and the two states are engulfed in tit-for-tat devaluations. Since all states are trying to cheapen their currencies simultaneously, the ER becomes increasingly unable to generate the desired expansion. States, therefore, may start restricting imports from other states or impose capital controls.

5.1.2   Scenario B (Convergence)

Under Scenario B, fighting global inflation is a priority for all states. States in this case have an incentive to free-ride as they may benefit from the spillovers of the sovereign's contraction without having to tighten their own economies as much. At the other extreme, each state adopts its own contractionary policies, which, in combination with the tightening of the sovereign, turn the anticipated global slowdown into a global recession. Coordination is the logical course of action here as it may help avert a severe global slump.

5.1.3   Scenario C (Divergence)

Under Scenario C, the sovereign pursues expansion, because of anemic domestic growth, while other states follow neutral policies. The expansionary policy of the sovereign results in the depreciation of its currency and the appreciation of other countries' currencies. This boosts the exports of the sovereign at the expense of other states. In addition the low IRs of the sovereign fuel a credit boom that spills over to developing states. Many developing states and their private companies borrow in dollars because of the low US IRs, increasing their vulnerability to future IR hikes. Unless the sovereign is prepared to coordinate with others, its engineered expansion is likely to inflict negative externalities on them.

Chances are that a sovereign that craves expansion will not cooperate with others to limit the spillovers of its policy. An enlightened sovereign, on the other hand, might see some benefits from coordinating. In that case, it would phase in expansion carefully and in stages so that it minimizes the negative externalities it inflicts on others. The sovereign may adopt prudential regulation to ensure that its financial firms do not engage in aggressive lending practices in other states to take advantage of the higher IRs there. A sovereign that pursues expansion, as a response to a financial crisis, may be incapable of self-restraint though. In this case, many states will face difficulties. If they increase their IRs to curtail capital inflows and prevent unsustainable credit booms their currencies will appreciate, reducing their exports. Lower IRs, on the other hand, would support the export sector but may cause domestic economic instability.

5.1.4   Scenario D (Divergence)

In Scenario D, the sovereign follows neutral policies but other core states, whose economies are performing badly, wish to expand by lowering their IRs. In that case, the currency of the sovereign should strengthen, reducing its exports. The currencies of other states should weaken, boosting their export potential. The sovereign will certainly resent losing market share owing to its appreciating currency and might wish to orchestrate a more gradual appreciation in coordination with other states. Coordination of the IR policies of states should curb capital inflows to the sovereign and may make unnecessary the adoption of capital control measures or tariffs on imports of goods and services.

All of the scenarios that we examined above are obviously crude scenarios. Their purpose is to simplify and thus clarify the potential repercussions of coordination and conflict among states. In reality, monetary policies interact at the domestic level with fiscal policies. It is not uncommon for a state to adopt fiscal expansion (tax cuts) while at the same time pursuing a tight monetary policy so as to preemptively avoid the expected overheating of its economy. In this case, the contractionary policy adopted by the CB points to a strong currency but the expansionary fiscal policy entails deficits and indicates a weaker currency. The unclear outcome of these seemingly contradictory domestic policies may be amplified by the policy reactions of other states. What we have, in most cases, therefore, is a muddled international scene as states try to adjust their policies to that of the sovereign but also try to escape from the constraints imposed on them by that policy.

The chapters in this section provide a historical overview (*see also* Table 5.1) of the global economic policy from the 1920s until today by tracing the evolution of four global institutions: the IMF and three coalitions of the world's largest economies: the Group of 7 states (G-7),[1] the Group of 10 states

---

[1]   Canada, France, Germany, Italy, Japan, the UK and the United States.

(G-10)[2] and the Group of 20 states (G-20).[3] These groups do not have a legal personality. They are, in essence, lobbying groups of large states that urge the rest of world to endorse their preferred polices. The groups tend to coalesce in times of crisis but, in normal times, produce nothing more than 'agreeing to disagree', non-binding declarations or toothless statements.

5.2   MERCANTILISM AND CURRENCY MANIPULATION: THE WTO AND IMF

As we saw in Chapter 4, the United States tends to label states currency manipulators when they intervene in the market for a prolonged period of time to buy dollars by selling their currency in order to devalue that currency and increase their exports to the United States. At the same time, core states and the sovereign have used low or near-zero IRs to boost growth. This strategy, used extensively during the Great Recession (2007–2009) and beyond, cheapened their currency and boosted their exports, generating an uproar in the developing world over the unfairness of using DEP to achieve FEP objectives.

The sovereign, because of its global clout, also has the ability to move the ER through simple verbal announcements. When, on January 24, 2018, the US Treasury Secretary declared during a Davos meeting that a weaker dollar was good for US trade, the dollar tumbled to a 3-year low against the basket of US trading partners' currencies.[4] The question we address in this section is to what extent a unilateral intervention in one direction in the currency market by a state can be labeled currency manipulation given that: (1) currency manipulation is possible through other channels, including the conduct of DEP; and (2) no state is more adept than the sovereign at unilaterally changing the ER between its currency and other currencies.

As we will see in Chapter 9, after the collapse of the Bretton Woods system, countries can choose the ER policy they prefer as long as they do not peg their currency to gold. Countries can peg their currencies to another currency or a basket of currencies; they can choose a purely floating rate; or they can opt for a managed float that implies some intervention in the currency market.[5]

---

[2]   The G-10 is made of up 11 states: the G-7 plus Belgium, the Netherlands, Sweden and Switzerland.

[3]   Argentina, Australia, Brazil, Canada, China, France, Germany, India, Indonesia, Italy, Japan, Mexico, South Korea, Russia, Saudi Arabia, South Africa, Turkey, the UK, the United States and the European Union.

[4]   Matt Clinch, *A Weaker Dollar is Good for the US, Treasury Secretary Mnuchin Says*, CNBC, Jan. 24, 2018.

[5]   *See* art. IV(2)(b), Articles of Agreement of the IMF, July 22, 1944, as amended, effective January 26, 2016 by the Board of Governors Resolution No. 66-2, Dec. 15, 2010.

Most countries have intervened in the FX market to stop a depreciation or appreciation of their currency that they consider harmful to their economy. States have tried to figure out how to employ the IMF, the global institution charged with preserving monetary stability, to discipline countries, including the sovereign, if need be, if these countries manipulate their currency with the intention of securing a competitive advantage over other countries.

One of the purposes of the IMF is to promote 'exchange stability', maintaining 'orderly exchange arrangements' among states and avoiding 'competitive exchange depreciation'.[6] Member states of the IMF are obliged to 'avoid manipulating exchange rates or the international monetary system *in order to* prevent effective BOP adjustment or to gain an *unfair* competitive advantage over other states'.[7] As we analyze in subsequent chapters, the IMF has had difficulties labeling states currency manipulators because it is hard to prove that a state is manipulating its ER with the intent to ('*in order to*') gain an unfair competitive advantage. It is difficult to come up with evidence, moreover, that a state has obtained an *unfair* competitive advantage as a result of its currency manipulation. To give an example, on October 8, 1982, Sweden announced a 16% devaluation of the krona in order to improve the competitiveness of Swedish industry. Because the rest of the Nordic countries complained, the Executive Board of the IMF met formally to ponder the Swedish devaluation. The Board took no action though.[8] Since Finland retaliated in kind against Sweden's devaluation, the IMF decided not to weigh into the economic conflict between the two states.

Since the IMF Articles of Agreement are not that helpful in addressing competitive devaluation, some have proposed that the World Trade Organization (WTO) could be used to bring action against states that manipulate their ER to gain advantages in trade. If a WTO Dispute Settlement Body (DSB) concludes that a state has manipulated its ER to achieve a trade advantage, that state will have to stop the manipulation. Otherwise, states adversely affected by that manipulation could take countermeasures in the form of tariffs or countervailing duties against that state.

More specifically article XV(4) of the GATT,[9] the global agreement that encourages free trade, could be used to take action against currency manipula-

---

[6]   Art. I (iii), *id.*

[7]   Art. IV 1(iii), *id.* Emphasis added.

[8]   *See* Andreas F. Lowenfeld, *International Economic Law* 636 (2011) (Lowenfeld mentions, however, that there was a 'general understanding' within the IMF and the international financial community that Sweden had acted contrary to Article IV(1)(iii)). *See also* IMF Annual Report 1983, at 28, 65, 104.

[9]   General Agreement on Tariffs and Trade (GATT) 1994, Apr. 15, 1994, Marrakesh Agreement Establishing the World Trade Organization, Annex 1A, 1867 UNTS 187, 33 ILM 1153 (1994) [hereinafter GATT].

tors. Based on this article a state must not, 'by exchange action', 'frustrate the intent' of the provisions of the GATT. A country's undervalued currency is in essence a subsidy to its industry[10] or could be considered a tariff on imports from other states. Subsidies and tariffs *frustrate* the intent of the GATT, which is based on free trade. The question, then, becomes how easy it would be for a DSB to determine that a country maintains an undervalued currency that frustrates GATT's intent.

Article XV(9) of the GATT, on the other hand, provides that nothing in the GATT can preclude the use by a state of exchange controls or exchange restrictions in accordance with the Articles of Agreement of the IMF. The WTO DSBs are mindful that if they are to find that an exchange restriction which a state adopted in accordance with the IMF Articles of Agreement frustrates the intent of the GATT, they will create dissonance and confusion within the international economic system. This is especially so because the GATT defers to the IMF on ER issues. Article XV(2) of the GATT mentions that states should accept the determination of the IMF as to whether an 'action' by a state 'in exchange matters' is in accordance with the IMF Articles of Agreement. Therefore, it is unlikely that a WTO DSB will be willing to declare that actions of states that have to do with management of their ER violate the GATT when the IMF has given its blessing for such actions.[11]

Let us assume here, for the sake of argument, that a WTO DSB does find that a state has manipulated its currency. That state, then, obeys the DSB ruling and refrains from intervening in the FX market to calibrate the value of its currency. Is there anything else that this state can subsequently do to improve what it sees as its deteriorating BOP? Article XII(1) of the GATT provides that a state 'may restrict the quantity or value of merchandise permitted to be

---

[10]   However, for a measure to be considered a subsidy it must provide advantages to a specific industry or group of industries. An undervalued currency helps the whole export sector and not specifically an industry or group of industries. *See* Charles Proctor, *Mann on the Legal Aspect of Money* 602 (2012), referring to the specificity test that must be met for a measure to be considered subsidy. *See also* art. 2, Agreement on Subsidies and Countervailing Measures, Apr. 15, 1994, Marrakesh Agreement Establishing the World Trade Organization, Annex 1A, 1869 UNTS 14.

[11]   *See* Robert Howse, *Towards an Equitable Integration of Monetary and Financial Matters, Trade and Sustainable Development* 285, at 297, in 'The Rule of Law in Monetary Affairs' (Thomas Cottier et al., eds, 2014); *India – Quantitative Restrictions on Imports of Agricultural, Textile, and Industrial Products*, WHO Panel Report, WT/DS90/R, para. 2.4., Apr. 6, 1999 [hereinafter WTO-India]. The WTO Panel relied on IMF expertise for determining that India's monetary reserves were adequate and not threatened by a serious decline. *See also Dominican Republic – Import and Sale of Cigarettes*, WHO Panel Report, WT/DS302/R, Nov. 26, 2004 (for an extensive discussion on the interface between the IMF Articles of Agreement and the GATT provisions).

imported' if this is necessary 'to safeguard its external financial position and its BOP', including preventing an imminent threat of a serious decline in its monetary reserves.[12] With regard to article XII(1), the WTO DSBs tend, again, to defer to the IMF's judgment for determining whether import restrictions adopted by a state to safeguard its allegedly scant FX reserves are in conformity with the Articles of Agreement of the IMF.[13]

Indubitably states can comb through the founding documents of the IMF and WTO to try to call attention to other states' manipulation of the monetary system. The reason that the WTO dispute settlement process has yet to be used to bring legal action against states with regard to the ER is that all states are more or less 'guilty' of some sort of currency manipulation (indirectly through their DEP or directly through intervention in the market). More specifically, the global sovereign, whose mere pronouncements are viewed by market participants as prophesies on the future direction of global economic policy, would have a hard time asserting with a straight face that the rest of the states are manipulating their currencies to its disadvantage.

---

[12]   Article XII(1)(a), GATT, *supra* note 9.
[13]   *See supra* note 11.

Table 5.1   Historical overview of the international economic system[1]

	Gold standard (1819–1914) to gold-exchange standard (1925–31)	Bretton Woods System (1944–73)	Post-Bretton Woods Period (1973–today)
ER	ER of each currency 'per ounce of gold'	Dollar pegged to gold. Other currencies pegged to $	Floats, managed floats, pegs
Capital controls?	No	Yes	Yes
Institutions	Bank of England – gold standard; No central institution – gold-exchange standard	IMF	IMF; Regional/bilateral arrangements G-7, G-10 and G-20
DEP versus ER stability	ER stability>DEP	ER stability> DEP	Advanced economies often opt for inflation targeting (DEP priority); Developing economies often opt for ER targeting (FEP priority)
Global Liquidity (GL)	GL determined by gold	GL formally determined by gold but, in practice, by the dollar	– GL determined by the dollar – euro, yen, sterling, yuan are reserve currencies but not substitutes for dollar
Safety net	None; Self-insurance (gold reserves)	IMF; Self-insurance (gold and dollar reserves)	IMF and regional/bilateral agreements; Self-insurance (FX reserves)

Note: [1] *See also* IMF, Strengthening the International Monetary System – A Stocktaking, at 8, Mar. 2016.

6.   The gold standard

Before World War I, Britain was the uncontestable economic sovereign that exercised its power through the administration of the gold standard. Britain was already on the gold standard in 1819 and many countries believed that they could emulate its economic success by adopting the gold standard themselves. In 1873, the United States discontinued the bimetallic silver/gold standard and endorsed the gold standard in an act[1] that some called the 'Crime of 1873'.[2] A crime was committed, claimed those who abhorred the gold standard, because how much money could become available in the US economy became dependent on the stock of a single metal, gold. Limited gold supplies put a lid on monetary expansion and, as a result, on the growth potential of the economy.

A country was on the gold standard if its CB specified a fixed ER between the domestic currency and gold and was willing to buy and sell gold at this fixed ER. The CBs of gold-standard countries held in their reserves gold and were ready to convert local currency into gold on demand. In addition to gold, the British pound, and, to a much lesser extent, the German mark and the French franc, were part of countries' FX reserves. States, though, felt more secure holding gold rather than other states' currencies.[3] The adoption by a state of the gold standard signaled to capital owners that the state was monetarily stable – it had sufficient gold reserves to convert its currency into gold as needed. The gold standard eliminated uncertainty in global transactions since countries had their ERs fixed through the gold. The elimination of the ER risk encouraged world trade that fueled the first globalization.

Britain's hegemony during this period stemmed from the fact that investors treated the pound sterling as equivalent to gold. This fueled growth and guaranteed the preeminence of Britain's capital markets. States and private actors primarily used London for their financial transactions because they believed in the stability and liquidity of sterling, its quick conversion into gold on demand.

---

[1]   The Coinage Act of 1873, Public law 42-131, 17 Stat. 424.
[2]   Milton Friedman, *Money Mischief: Episodes in Monetary History* 50, 60 (1994).
[3]   Benjamin J. Cohen, *Organizing the World's Money: The Political Economy of International Monetary Relations* 211 (1977).

It was difficult for other states to compete with the British financial pedigree and the depth of British financial markets.[4]

The endorsement of the gold standard by a number of major states prompted a semi-automation of economic affairs. States that tied themselves to the gold standard could no longer print domestic currencies at will betting that monetary expansion would make it possible for their economies to grow faster. Their money creation was constricted by the gold they kept in their reserves. States had to be vigilant because they had promised to convert their currencies into gold, but their gold reserves could change from day to day. Gold reserves had to be adjusted upwards or downwards on a daily basis based on the inflows or outflows of capital. If a country had a BOP deficit, its CB had to contract the money supply by converting currency into gold. That gold had to be transferred to foreign CBs, as needed, to meet the country's foreign obligations. Obviously, deficit countries, which were losing gold, were eager to get that gold back. They usually accomplished this by increasing their IRs so as to entice capital holders to come back to them. Contractionary policies are usually implemented to cool down an overheating economy. Their side-effect is the shrinking of business investment and employment. In the gold standard era, states desperate to get their gold back had to conduct such policies.

The gold standard lays bare the tradeoffs states must be willing to make to address the Trilemma. The gold-standard states had to conduct their DEP in a way that guaranteed the success of FEP – the fixed ER of their currency to gold (*see* Fig. 2.4). This meant that gold-losing states had to adopt a contractionary DEP, for example increasing their IRs, in order to attract fleeing gold back. Gold-receiving states, on the other hand, could lower their IRs to spur business investment, propel demand and increase employment. This expansionary policy of gold-receiving countries was expected to spill over to gold-losing countries. Expected higher demand in surplus countries was to stimulate global growth and boost demand for the exports of deficit countries, helping them eliminate their deficits. Eventually deficit countries were to become surplus countries, starting the cycle all over again. The elegance of the gold standard was based on this simple automaticity. All a CB had to do was to observe the gold flows and adjust the DEP as needed.

However, that famed automaticity did not work as expected.[5] While, in theory, the gold standard was supposed to dictate the rules of the game among states, in reality, their CBs disobeyed these rules when this was what they

---

[4]   Barry Eichengreen, *Hegemonic Stability: Theories of the International Monetary System* 220, at 224, in 'International Political Economy: Perspectives on Global Power and Wealth' (Jeffry A. Frieden and David A. Lake, eds, 1996).

[5]   Ragnar Nurske, *The International Currency Experience: Lessons of the Inter-War Period* 66–7 (League of Nations, 1944).

needed to do to prop up the domestic economy.[6] States were aware then, as they are now, that the contraction or expansion of the money available in an economy – the money supply – affects prices, incomes and employment. They concocted, therefore, various techniques, such as direct intervention in the FX market, swap arrangements, barriers on gold exports and sterilization operations, to buffer the impact of gold flows on their economy and maintain some autarky in the conduct of DEP.[7] Some of these techniques were successful in shielding them from the whims of the global gold flows[8] and helped them achieve some DEP independence. Sterilization operations, through which CBs tried to neutralize the effects of gold flows on the domestic money supply, were very much *de rigueur* during this period. As a commentator correctly put it, central bankers were the reluctant champions of the gold standard.[9] Central banking was invented, after all, to protect states from external shocks, including those caused by the depletion of their gold reserves, and to help them secure some independence in DEP making.[10]

States had to manipulate the gold standard because they were not ready to have their people 'crucified on the cross of gold'.[11] The limited global supply of gold often dictated contractionary DEPs when states were losing gold, and this resulted in low growth and high unemployment. Obviously, capital-rich states were better equipped to skirt crucifixion than others. The world was split between core, capital-exporting countries and periphery, capital-recipient countries. The pyramid of states illustrated in Chapter 3 – monetary sovereign at the top, in this case Britain, core countries in the middle and periphery countries at the bottom – was as real then as it is now.

There is a power asymmetry between surplus (creditor) states and deficit (debtor) states. Surplus countries have by definition surplus capital. They have the option, therefore, to free or restrict capital flows based on their DEP objectives. Britain was at the time an economic superpower. A change in its domestic IR signaled to capital owners whether to invest in Britain or seek higher returns in other states.[12] Deficit (debtor) countries, on the other hand, were dependent on foreign capital imports. They had less control over these imports and, consequently, the gold flows to their economies.

---

[6]   *Id.*

[7]   *Id.* at 84.

[8]   *Id.* at 85.

[9]   *Id.* at 105.

[10]   *Id.*

[11]   *See* William Jennings Bryan, *Cross of Gold*, Speech Delivered at the Democratic National Convention, Chicago, July 9, 1896 ('You shall not press down upon the brow of labor this crown of thorns! You shall not crucify mankind upon a cross of gold!').

[12]   Cohen, *supra* note 3, at 212.

When Britain and the rest of the European states were embroiled in World War I, it was the United States' turn to become the safe haven for capital. As a result, the country experienced large gold inflows. These inflows stopped when the United States entered the war. In September 1917, the United States prohibited all gold exports without the permission of the FRS and Treasury.[13] The United States was not the only country that loathed losing gold. All states were obsessed with maintaining their gold reserves. As a result, during that war, the gold standard collapsed as the world's monetary standard, and was replaced by floating ERs. Paper currency could be sold for another paper currency at the price available in the market, but not for gold.

---

[13]   Milton Friedman and Anna Jacobson Schwartz, *A Monetary History of the United States 1867–1960*, at 220 (1963).

7. From World War I to World War II

After World War I, states decided to restore the gold standard. That was not easy. During the war, when the gold standard was suspended, countries printed vast amounts of their currency to support their war needs. The gold standard dictates that a state's money must be backed up by its gold reserves. States revered the gold standard but, at the same time, were reluctant to withdraw money from circulation despite their lacking adequate gold reserves to support the money supply. States knew that a contractionary shock of such a magnitude would have a recessionary impact on their economies, which were just starting to recover from a prolonged war. Furthermore, the 1917 Bolshevik revolution, in combination with universal suffrage, was an eye-opener for many states. Governments realized, with a new sense of urgency, that gold outflows dictating economic contraction risked social disruption that was at odds with their re-election prospects. Many states, as a result, engaged in 'beggar thy neighbor' strategies by doing anything they could to lure gold flows from other states. Devaluing the national currency to boost exports and building a CA surplus was a popular strategy employed to boost gold reserves. Given that many states opted for this strategy, economic conflict was unavoidable.

The post-World War I economic landscape was, indeed, gloomy. European countries were bickering over how to deal with the reluctance of Germany to pay for war damages. Germany, on the other hand, eventually succumbed to hyperinflation that led to the decimation of its currency.[1] The economies of France and the UK were marred by debt, as they had borrowed heavily from the United States to pay for war expenses. The United States was the only country in relatively good shape as it had escaped the physical destruction of the war and was now the world's biggest creditor.

The 1920 Brussels Conference was a half-hearted attempt to forge some sort of international cooperation. Thirty-nine countries sent delegates to the conference, but since they participated in their private capacity as bankers or economic experts,[2] the conference did not produce any legally binding outcome.

---

[1] On the economic condition of Germany after World War I, *see generally* William C. McNeil, *American Money and the Weimar Republic: Economics and Politics on the Eve of the Great Depression* (1986).

[2] Louis W. Pauly, *The League of Nations and the Foreshadowing of the International Monetary Fund*, at 7, Essays in International Finance No. 201, Department of Economics, Princeton University, Dec. 1996.

The Cannes Conference took place in January 1922 to do the preparatory work for the Genoa Conference held later that year.[3] At the Cannes Conference it was recognized that a united effort by the world powers was necessary to remedy the paralysis of the European system. That effort had to include the removal of all obstacles to trade, the provision of substantial credits to weaker countries and the cooperation of all nations in the restoration of normal prosperity.[4] Despite these well-intended pronouncements, the conference was unable to map a road out of the global economic quagmire.

The 1922 Genoa Conference was relatively more productive. It made a breakthrough by urging states to adopt the gold-exchange standard in lieu of the gold standard. The conference proposed centralizing and coordinating the demand for gold to avoid the problems generated by the 'simultaneous and competitive efforts of a number of countries to secure' gold. Instead of scrambling for gold, countries were asked to include in their FX reserves the currencies of states that could easily be exchanged for gold.[5] Gold reserves had to be centralized in major financial centers – the gold centers of world (e.g., London, New York).[6] Peripheral countries that subscribed to the gold-exchange standard could regulate their ER by buying and selling 'gold exchange' – currencies easily convertible into gold – instead of gold itself.[7]

Despite this unambiguous endorsement of the gold-exchange standard, the Genoa conference failed to stop economic competition among states. Some peripheral states that were lacking gold had no other option but to keep the currencies of the big powers in their FX reserves. Yet the dominant states, the UK, France and the United States, engaged in a fierce competition to secure gold since holding other currencies was viewed 'as damaging to the prestige of a great or even moderately great nation'.[8] Core states with undervalued currencies that sought to strengthen their BOP by boosting their exports clashed with states with overvalued currencies that retaliated against them by imposing import restrictions. The currency conflict soon escalated into a global trade war. With no clear sovereign in sight, states hoarded gold and other tangible resources that could be useful during a crisis.

---

[3]   Resolutions Adopted by the Supreme Council at Cannes as the Basis of the Genoa Conference, Jan. 1922, 1922 Cmd. 162.

[4]   *Id.*

[5]   Res. 11(1)(d), (3), Genoa Financial Commission Report, at 678, Apr. 20, 1922, *reprinted in* Federal Reserve Bulletin, June 1922.

[6]   Res. 11(2), *id.*

[7]   Res. 11(5), *id.*

[8]   Ragnar Nurske, *The International Currency Experience: Lessons of the Inter-War Period* 42 (League of Nations, 1944).

The architecture of the gold standard was founded on the coordination of policies of gold-losing countries and gold-gaining countries. These countries were supposed to preserve the international equilibrium by 'meeting each other half way', including adjusting prices, imports and exports, and through the short-term money market.[9] Meeting each other half way was certainly not the name of the game in the interwar years. The world was divided into winners and losers. Winners were the creditor states that had accumulated most of the existing gold (the United States, France and the UK).[10] Losers were the debtor states that had experienced a drastic reduction of their gold reserves (Germany, Italy and Japan).[11]

In 1925, the UK returned to the gold standard by authorizing the convertibility of the sterling into gold at the pre-war ER. By adopting the pre-war ER, the UK sought to re-establish itself as the undisputable economic sovereign. The price for that re-establishment was steep. At the pre-war ER to the gold, the sterling was overvalued by 10%. France, on the other hand, returned to the gold standard (*de facto* in 1926 and *de jure* in 1928) at one fifth of its pre-war ER to the gold.[12] This undervalued the French franc by as much as 25%. The result of the interplay between an overvalued pound and an undervalued franc was the drain of gold from the UK to France.

The United States was the big creditor and the debtors were the conflict-ridden European states. Capitalists were escaping Europe for the promise of the new world. In July 1927, the governors of CBs of the UK and Germany and the US Undersecretary of the Treasury met in Long Island, United States to try to find some common ground.[13] The United States promised to reduce its domestic IRs to stem gold inflows but that promise was not kept. On the contrary, the FRS tightened monetary policy in 1928 to avert a speculative stock market bubble. Domestic prerogatives proved again to be stronger than the commitment to global policies.

In 1929, some prominent New York City bankers developed an initiative, the so-called Young plan after the name of the banker who proposed it, to instill order in the global economic space. They ventured into ordaining the global

---

[9]   *Id.* at 87.

[10]   By the end of 1932, the United States and France together possessed 63% of the world's gold and competed fiercely against each other to attract gold. Barry Eichengreen, *Hegemonic Stability: Theories of the International Monetary System* 220, at 234, in 'International Political Economy: Perspectives on Global Power and Wealth' (Jeffry A. Frieden and David A. Lake, eds, 1996).

[11]   Nurske, *supra* note 8, at 90.

[12]   Kenneth Moure, *Undervaluing the Franc Poincare*, 49 The Economic History Review 137 (1996).

[13]   Stephen V. O. Clark, *Central Bank Cooperation 1924–31*, at 123–4 (FRBNY, 1967).

economic system based on the principles of the US central banking system.[14] They believed that an international CB composed of the world's prominent CBs was the way to regulate the economic relationships among states.[15] In 1929, the United States had already imposed high tariffs on European imports. Because of these high tariffs, the UK and France were unable to export enough to pay back their war debt to the United States. The only way for these countries to get out of debt was for Germany to compensate them for the damages it had inflicted on them during the war.

The bankers and industrialists, who initiated the negotiations for the establishment of the Bank of International Settlements (BIS), believed that the economic integration of states would prepare the way for political integration and a lasting peace. The US private sector, US corporations and banks, which possessed the capital resources, were to be the leaders of that integration.[16] On March 2, 1929, the BIS was established. The BIS was to play the role of the global CB for national CBs. Its first task was to administer the German reparation payments that were to be financed through the US bond market. Germany sold bonds in the market so as to make the reparation payments it owed to France and the UK. These countries, in turn, could use the German payments to pay back their debts to the United States. It was hoped that this global churning of debt would reduce animosities and bring about economic peace among states.

The US stock market crash of 1929 was followed by the 1931 German crash. Germany suspended payments on its foreign debt, imposed capital controls and went off the gold standard. As the financial panic spread to the UK, gold holders left it for France and the United States. The Bank of England intervened in the FX market, under the 'strictest secrecy', to stem gold outflows,[17] and the FRS cooperated closely with it to the point of being reproved by Congress for exceeding its mandate and making global economic policy.[18] Eventually the UK abandoned the gold standard on September 21, 1931. The United States did the same in 1933.

Half-hearted attempts at international cooperation were the trademark of the 1930s. On June 20, 1931, US President Hoover adopted the so-called Hoover moratorium that postponed payments on war debt for a year. Hoover clarified that the moratorium did not mean that the debt was cancelled. Instead, the

---

[14]   Frank Costigliola, *The Other Side of Isolationism: The Establishment of the First World Bank, 1929–1930*, 59 Journal of American History 602 (1972).

[15]   *Id.* at 603.

[16]   *Id.* at 605.

[17]   Michael D. Bordo et al., *The Historical Origins of US Exchange Market Intervention Policy*, at 14, NBER Working Paper 12662, June 23, 2006.

[18]   *Id.* at 15.

postponed debt was to be paid back over a period of 10 years with an interest of 4%. According to Hoover, the moratorium on debt, by thwarting the 'collapse of Germany', ensured that the US profited from the maintenance of agricultural markets and the prevention of panic and unlimited losses.[19]

In 1933, US President Roosevelt called for a World Economic Conference. The hope was that such a conference could produce an agreement that would stabilize the international economic system. The conference that was convened in London, between June 12 and July 27, 1933, with the participation of 66 states, was eventually sabotaged by the country that called for it – the United States. The US President sent a message to the conference, on July 3, 1933, making it clear that the United States was not planning to attend. As Roosevelt put it, the world could not afford to be 'lulled by the specious fallacy of achieving a temporary and probably an artificial stability in foreign exchange'.[20] The United States was not ready, at that point, to stabilize the ERs between the dollar, the pound and the French franc. It was fearful that such stabilization could cause dollar overvaluation and exacerbate the Great Depression. Given the precarious global conditions, most states held the belief that unilateral currency manipulation made much more sense than developing a consensus on temporary currency stabilization.

In 1933, the United States was in the throes of the Great Depression. Between August 1929 and March 1933, the money supply had fallen by one-third, causing a severe deflation. As the crisis intensified, people started to lose their faith in the dollar and to convert their dollar-denominated assets into gold. Because the United States was on the gold standard it had to increase its IRs to stop the drain of gold out of the country. However, an IR hike during an economic depression was certain to cripple the economy. In March 1933, the gold holdings of the FRBNY fell below the legal limit.[21] The FRBs of Illinois, Massachusetts, New Jersey and Pennsylvania went on bank holidays.[22] The FRS, which was set up to ensure that a financial crisis would not bring panic, joined the commercial banks 'in the most widespread, complete, and economically disturbing restriction of payments than had ever been experienced in the history' of the United States, contracting the economy even further.[23]

---

[19]   Herbert Hoover, Statement on Signing the Foreign Debt Moratorium Resolution, Dec. 23, 1931.

[20]   Franklin D. Roosevelt, Wireless to the London Conference, July 3, 1933.

[21]   Milton Friedman and Anna Jacobson Schwartz, *A Monetary History of the United States 1867–1960*, at 326 (1963).

[22]   *Id.* at 327.

[23]   *Id.* at 328. According to Friedrich Hayek, during the Great Depression the FRS 'pursued a silly deflationary policy'. *See* Diego Pizano, *Conversations with Great*

It was time for drastic measures, and the demonetization of gold was one of them. On March 6, 1933, by executive order, US President Roosevelt prohibited gold exports and FX transactions in gold given that 'extensive speculative activity' had resulted 'in severe drains of the nation's stocks of gold'.[24] Furthermore, on April 5, 1933, the United States prohibited the hoarding of gold coin, gold bullion and gold certificates, criminalizing the possession of monetary gold in its territory.[25] People had to surrender their gold to the government at the price of $20.67 for every ounce of gold. After the nationalization of gold, the dollar depreciated significantly (from $20.67 to $33 per ounce of gold). It was abundantly clear that the government had offered minimum compensation for confiscating private gold.

The US Gold Reserve Act, adopted on January 30, 1934, prohibited the possession of gold except under license. The Act gave the president the power to devalue gold by up to 40% which he exercised by devaluating the dollar to $35 per ounce of gold.[26] This devaluation made possible the printing of $3 billion of new dollars.[27] Out of this $3 billion, $2 billion were put into a stabilization fund, the ESF, which was placed under the control of the Treasury. The Treasury could use the ESF to intervene in the currency market, as needed, to achieve an ER that would favor the United States.[28] The United States was not the only state to set up such a fund. The UK had its own stabilization fund[29] and France, which eventually devalued the franc on September 26, 1936, used the money it created through that devaluation to establish a similar fund.

From the perspective of the United States, the demonetization of gold was a matter of economic survival – a response to the competitive devaluations employed by other states to boost their exports. After it demonetized gold, the country started to acquire it as a commodity. This shrunk the global availability of gold and aggravated the situation of states that were still on the gold standard. These countries had to sell their gold at a fixed price in terms of their currency. As a result, their gold reserves started to flow to the United States, which had broken free from the gold standard and was ready to stockpile gold

---

Economists: Friedrich A. Hayek, John Hicks, Nicholas Kaldor, Leonid V.Kantorovich, Joan Robinson, Paul A.Samuelson, Jan Tinbe 13 (2009).

[24] Franklin D. Roosevelt, Presidential Proclamation (No. 2039) – Declaring Bank Holiday, Mar. 6, 1933.

[25] Executive Order (No. 6102) – Requiring Gold Coin, Gold Bullion and Gold Certificates to be Delivered to the Government, Apr. 5, 1933.

[26] Franklin D. Roosevelt, Proclamation (No. 2072) – Fixing the Weight of the Gold Dollar, Jan. 31, 1934.

[27] Friedman and Schwartz, *supra* note 21, at 470.

[28] *Id.*

[29] This fund is still in existence. *See* Charles Proctor, *Mann on the Legal Aspect of Money* 70, n. 31 (2012).

as a commodity. Given their diminishing gold reserves, states were faced with the dilemma of whether to scale back the money available in their economy, through contraction, or abandon the gold standard.[30] Most of them abandoned it. Switzerland abandoned the gold standard together with France in September 1936 and Italy followed suit a month later.[31]

By 1936, the world was divided into blocks, each block with its own arrangement. The UK, its dependencies and some other Northern European countries continued to anchor their currencies to sterling despite the fact that the UK had left the gold standard. Central and South American countries pegged their currencies to the dollar.[32] Germany and Eastern European states abstained from international arrangements by abandoning the convertibility of their currencies into gold, and aimed for bilateral barter and self-sufficiency. 'It was on the basis of an exchange of [German] manufactured goods for crude foodstuffs and raw materials that Germany built up her bilateral clearing system'[33] with Eastern Europe.

The 1936 Tripartite Agreement was forged to stabilize the ERs of states through intervention in the gold and FX markets. It consisted of three almost identical communiqués issued by the major economic competitors – France, the UK and the United States.[34] These countries agreed to use their national stabilization funds to intervene in the gold and FX markets, as needed, to implement the agreement. They agreed, in principle, to refrain from competitive devaluations by maintaining currency values at existing levels as long as this did not interfere seriously with 'internal prosperity'.[35] This hard-to-quantify internal prosperity offered room to violate the spirit of the agreement by any of the parties if that was vital to them. The agreement was effective in stabilizing the ERs in the short term.[36] It helped rally around states when the French financial crisis, which erupted in June 1936, caused large outflows of capital destined for the United States.[37]

---

[30]   Friedman and Schwartz, *supra* note 21, at 467.

[31]   Barry Eichengreen and Douglas A. Irwin, *The Slide to Protectionism in the Great Depression: Who Succumbed and Why?*, 70 Journal of Economic History 871, at 893 (2010).

[32]   Nurske, *supra* note 8, at 198.

[33]   *Id.* at 199.

[34]   The Tripartite Monetary Agreement (consisting of Statements of French Government, British Treasury and the US Secretary of the Treasury), Sept. 25, 1936, *reprinted in* Annex VII, BIS Seventh Annual Report, Apr. 1936 to Mar. 1937.

[35]   Art. 2, *id.*

[36]   Michael D. Bordo et al., *Strained Relations: US Foreign-Exchange Operations and Monetary Policy in the Twentieth Century* 23 (2015).

[37]   Bordo et al., *supra* note 17, at 21.

Many have argued that the tit-for-tat devaluations that characterized the 1930s were the prequel to the war that followed them. Others have claimed that if competitive devaluations were endorsed 'more widely' and were 'coordinated internationally', they could have accelerated a reprieve from the Great Depression.[38] As international coordination remained piecemeal, financial crises moved from country to country. Each time a state's currency was attacked by speculators and the country had to devalue, 'a new country was elevated to the position of being the next one expected to fall'.[39] One of the calamities of global economic uncertainty was the decline in trade. The constant anxiety about the international economic conditions led market participants, including CBs, to keenly shed currencies they held in their FX reserves and replace them with gold.[40] Given the 'British inability and United States unwillingness to assume responsibility' for stabilizing the global economy, and the orientation of every country to the protection of its national private interest, the global public interest 'went down the drain, and with it the private interests of all'.[41] The disorganized approach to the '*international monetary reconstruction*' during the interwar years 'sowed the seeds of subsequent disintegration' through another war.[42]

---

[38] Barry Eichengreen and Jeffrey Sachs, *Exchange Rates and Economic Recovery in the 1930s*, 45 Journal of Economic History 925, at 928 (1985).

[39] *Id.* at 944.

[40] *Id.* at 945.

[41] Charles P. Kindleberger, *The World in Depression* 292 (1972, *reprinted in* 2013).

[42] Nurske, *supra* note 8, at 117. Emphasis added.

8. The Bretton Woods system

After World War II, it was time for peace, a peace anchored to new economic understandings. The Bretton Woods system[1] was the first monetary system put together at a global conference. The system established the gold-exchange standard anointing the dollar prime global reserve currency. Based on the gold-exchange standard, all currencies were pegged to the dollar. The dollar was the only currency pegged to the gold at the price $35 per ounce of gold. States were expected to intervene in the FX and gold markets to defend the value of their currencies with respect to the dollar, containing volatility within a band of 1% above/below the ER of their currency to the dollar.[2]

States had to adopt the gold-exchange standard because of the large amounts of money they had printed during the war. The supply of gold was simply not enough to underwrite the global money supply. Withdrawing money from circulation to re-establish the correspondence between money supply and gold reserves would have triggered recession and unemployment. At the same time, the floating ERs of the interwar period were deemed a poor solution because states had manipulated them to weaken their currencies and boost their exports. The Bretton Woods system was a compromise between fixed ERs and floating ERs. It provided for fixed, but somewhat adjustable ERs. States retained some control over their DEP by regulating the flows of capital.

The head of the US Treasury, Harry Dexter-White, and John Maynard Keynes, the head of the British delegation and a prominent economist, were the leading players at the Bretton Woods conference. Keynes proposed the creation of an international bank, an International Clearing Union (ICU). This ICU was to be the mechanism through which all states' BOP balances would be settled. A new currency, the bancor, was proposed to be the cornerstone of the union. Gold could be sold for bancors, but bancors could not buy gold, as the eventual goal was to replace gold with bancors.[3]

---

[1]   The conference that established the post-war monetary system was convened in Bretton Woods, New Hampshire, United States.
[2]   Art. IV, Sec. 3 (1), Articles of Agreement of the IMF, July 22, 1944 [hereinafter 1944 IMF Articles of Agreement].
[3]   Harold James, *The Multiple Contexts of Bretton Woods*, 28 Oxford Review of Economic Policy 411, at 417 (2012).

Deficit states, led by the UK, wanted to build a global economic system based on the symmetrical distribution of power between surplus states and deficit states. Much of the malaise in the interwar period had to do with the fact that the burden of 'adjusting', that is modifying their DEP priorities to address BOP imbalances, fell on deficit countries. The UK pointed to the enormous surplus accumulated by France between 1927 and 1930. The French surplus, which was a source of strain for a number of countries, demonstrated that many countries can experience deficits simultaneously just because of the large surplus of 'one important trading nation'.[4] The UK argued that both surplus countries and deficit countries should be required to adjust their economies to address global BOP imbalances. Deficit countries would have to devalue their currency and shrink domestic demand. Surplus countries would have to appreciate their currency and stimulate domestic demand.

The quotas for each country in the ICU were to be fixed as half of the average of their imports and exports over the past 5 years. These quotas would determine the limits up to which debtors could borrow from the ICU in bancors to address a BOP crisis. Debtors had to endure economic discipline to reduce their deficits. However, creditors were not off the hook. If the credit balance of a state exceeded half of its quota in the union, it would have to adopt expansionary policies by increasing domestic demand and wages and adopting tariff reductions and other measures, as necessary, to get rid of its surplus. In fact, creditor states were expected to pay interest to the Union if their surpluses (credits) rose above their assigned quota. The fundamental premise of the ICU was that creditors should strive to eliminate their surpluses as much as debtors should seek to get rid of their deficits. A fair ICU had to force debtors to reduce their deficits but also push creditors to expand their economies for the benefit of global economic peace.[5]

The United States, the big creditor state at the time, was not willing to succumb to international rules dictating US expansionary policies to correct global imbalances. Therefore, a palliative was adopted. The United States conceded that it would make it possible for deficit states to devalue their currencies, without IMF approval, when that was needed to eliminate a 'fundamental disequilibrium' in their BOP. The 'fundamental disequilibrium' provision[6] was inserted into the IMF Articles of Agreement at the insistence of the world's deficit countries led by the UK, despite initial US resistance. What constituted fundamental disequilibrium was not further defined. This gave

---

[4]   Ragnar Nurske, *The International Currency Experience: Lessons of the Inter-War Period* 223 (League of Nations, 1944).

[5]   James, *supra* note 3.

[6]   Art. IV, Sec. 5, 1944 IMF Articles of Agreement, *supra* note 2.

deficit states even more room to maneuver when they needed to devalue their currencies to address imbalances. The IMF had to evaluate whether a country really faced a 'fundamental disequilibrium' but it was not the final arbiter on the issue. A state could still alter its ER, even if the IMF disapproved of it, provided it was ready to forfeit IMF financial assistance.[7] As things developed in practice, the IMF refrained from second-guessing states' decisions to devalue their currencies.

Another issue extensively debated at Bretton Woods was the control of states over private capital. Many believed at the time that short-term capital flows undermined ER stability and were responsible for the Great Depression.[8] States were aware that they needed massive FX reserves and gold to correct abrupt BOP imbalances caused by 'the mass movements of nervous capital flight'.[9] States were further possessive of indigenous private wealth and resented seeing it flee to tax-lenient states. They stipulated, therefore, that 'fugitive capital' should not be sheltered in other states.[10]

Capital controls are, in essence, controls over access to FX. Restrictions on FX work like this: the CB of a state establishes a monopoly over the FX within that state's frontiers.[11] Any private actor seeking to exchange domestic currency for foreign currency or vice-versa must petition the state's CB, which may approve or disapprove the transaction.[12] The CB might, for example, deny provision of FX to a domestic resident who wants to buy a foreign company. Or the CB may refuse to provide domestic currency to a foreigner eager to buy real estate in the state.[13] By controlling the purchases and sales of FX, a government, through its CB, can restrict financial flows in and out of the state.[14] At Bretton Woods, the United States wanted to eliminate all FX restrictions in order to enable the free movement of capital. That was not acceptable to other states, which were fearful of both the invasion of foreign (US) capital and the exodus of their domestic capital holders.

Eventually the IMF Articles of Agreement prohibited capital controls for the settlement of current account transactions (e.g. imports and exports of goods) but allowed capital controls for the regulation of the financial/capital account[15] – the buying and selling of assets including stocks, bonds and real estate in

---

[7]   Art. IV, Sec. 6, *id.*
[8]   James, *supra* note 3, at 418.
[9]   Nurske, *supra* note 4, at 188.
[10] James, *supra* note 3, at 419.
[11] Thomas Oatley, *International Political Economy* 213 (2012).
[12] *Id.* at 214.
[13] *Id.*
[14] *Id.*
[15] Art. VI, Sec. 3, 1944 IMF Articles of Agreement, *supra* note 2.

other states. Most states just recovering from the war opted for strict capital controls as they were concerned about the destabilizing impact of haphazard capital movements on their economies. At the time, capital controls were viewed as a legitimate way to regulate national economies.[16]

The IMF Articles of Agreement allow states to restrict the convertibility of their currencies into other currencies for a 'transitional period'.[17] States that defer the convertibility of their currencies are subject to Article XIV. States ready to convert their currency into foreign currencies are referred to as the 'article VIII countries'. In the first years of the IMF, the only 'article VIII country' was the United States since it was the only country that had re-established the convertibility of the dollar into gold and into other currencies right after the war. All other states had such small FX reserves (dollars and gold) that they were reluctant to make their domestic currencies freely convertible into other currencies. The war had rendered states parsimonious. States preserved their FX for imports of food, capital goods and commodities that were vital for reconstruction. They knew that if they let their residents freely convert the domestic currency into dollars or gold, they would trigger a run on their currencies.

In 1947, the UK permitted the full convertibility of its currency. Under pressure from the United States, which supported the convertibility by providing the UK with a $3.75 billion loan, the UK let holders of sterling convert it into gold and dollars for CA transactions. That decision resulted in large capital outflows. The US loan and a large portion of the UK's FX reserves were wiped out in the effort to defend the sterling, forcing the UK to suspend convertibility. From this episode, it was surmised that market players would run on currencies if they suspected that countries did not have sufficient dollar reserves or gold.[18] The Bretton Woods system became fully operational only in 1958 when the majority of developed countries made their currencies fully convertible for CA transactions.

The IMF was established under the Bretton Woods system to provide resources to states 'under adequate safeguards' so that they can 'correct maladjustments in their balance of payments'.[19] The IMF was designed to be the primary multilateral defense mechanism against temporary disruptions in the international economic system. It was the means of affording temporary assistance to states in connection with seasonal, cyclical and emergency fluctuations in their BOP for current transactions.[20] Deficit states argued in vain

---

[16] Oatley, *supra* note 11, at 214.
[17] Article XIV(2), 1944 IMF Articles of Agreement, *supra* note 2.
[18] Oatley, *supra* note 11, at 216.
[19] Art. I(v), 1944 IMF Articles of Agreement, *supra* note 2.
[20] US Bretton Woods Agreements Act of 1945, 22 USC §286j.

that the IMF should be more than just a temporary liquidity provider. It made more sense to establish it instead as an unconditional lender of last resort, a sort of CB for all states. The United States, the only creditor at the time and the only issuer of reserve currency, was not keen on instituting the IMF, and thus implicitly itself, as the lender of last resort for other states.

The creation of the IMF limited the statehood of ordinary states.[21] A state could not change its ER without IMF approval, unless it was prepared to forfeit IMF assistance in times of crisis.[22] Another obligation that limited statehood was the inability of states to set the value of their currencies in terms of gold,[23] a sensible obligation given that Bretton Woods aimed to limit the monetary functionality of gold. States were prohibited from engaging in multiple currency practices[24] – such as establishing two different ERs, one for imports and another for exports, without IMF approval.

To become members of the IMF, countries were assigned quotas based on a formula intended to reflect the importance of each country in the world economy. Twenty-five percent of each member's quota had to be contributed in gold or a currency convertible into gold (at the time, the only currency convertible into gold was the dollar) – this was the so-called gold tranche. Seventy-five percent of each member's quota had to be contributed in the state's national currency.[25]

The amount a state could borrow from the IMF depended on its quota. As the world's largest economy, the United States contributed $2.75 billion to the IMF and held the largest quota. The UK contributed $1.3 billion and obtained the second largest quota. Other states had much smaller quotas. France, for example, had a quota of $450 million and Panama a quota of only $0.5 million. As of 1944, the IMF held $8.8 billion in contributions by states.[26]

When an IMF member state did not have enough FX reserves, it was allowed to purchase (i.e. borrow) amounts of foreign currency in return for an equivalent amount of its own currency. By borrowing from the IMF, a state could correct a temporary imbalance of payments without having to devalue its currency or restrict imports. Approval for the first withdrawals, equivalent to the gold tranche of a state, was automatic, since these withdrawals represented borrowings against the gold that the member state had contributed to the IMF. States could borrow another 25% without much conditionality. However, if

---

[21]   François Gianviti, *Current Legal Aspects of Monetary Sovereignty*, at 3, in 'Current Developments in Monetary and Financial Law' (Vol. 4, IMF, 2005).

[22]   Art.IV, Secs 5–6, 1944 IMF Articles of Agreement, *supra* note 2.

[23]   Art. IV, Sec. 2, *id.*

[24]   Art. VIII, Sec. 3, *id.*

[25]   Art. III, Sec. 3(b), *id.*

[26]   Schedule A, Quotas, *id.*

they wished to borrow additional amounts, they had to comply with the IMF conditions that assured the IMF that they would restore their BOP equilibrium. The conditions on the loans that the IMF provided made it clear that its resources were meant to address temporary BOP problems. States that borrowed had to pay an interest.[27] Countries were expected to repay their loans within 3–5 years. The loans had to be repaid in gold or convertible currencies. In most cases, the IMF was ready to provide credit only to states that entered into stand-by agreements with it. These agreements provided it with the opportunity to closely supervise debtor states to assess whether they implemented the economic reforms it prescribed for them.

The IMF was not established as a lender of last resort. In fact, after the first two years of its functioning, its lending operations diminished substantially. The United States, the new global sovereign, easily bypassed the IMF to shape international economic conditions to its liking. Two of the most important initiatives during this period, the Anglo-American Agreement and the Marshall Plan that aimed to revive European economies, were adopted without any IMF involvement.[28] The reconstruction of Germany was additionally facilitated by the 1953 German External Debts Agreement which settled all claims of private and official creditors against Germany.[29] It did so by reducing Germany's debt by about 50%[30] and extending the repayment of the remainder over 30 years.

In the 1950s the United States was in a position of strength because it had in its possession almost three-quarters of the world's gold. Since gold production was not expected to grow anytime soon, the rest of the states had no other option but to accumulate the currency of the financially strongest country in the world, the dollar. The dollar in this way assumed the role of global reserve currency – the currency for trade and investment and the currency that states held in their FX reserves.

However, the United States did not remain a surplus country for long. The world was a keen collector of dollars and the United States could print unlimited amounts of them. The temptation to run deficits was difficult to resist and the United States succumbed to it. It supplied the world with dollars by running deficits as it increased its imports from the war-battered states, helping them

---

[27]   Art. V, Sec. 8, *id.*

[28]   C. Randall Henning, *The Exchange Stabilization Fund: Slush Money or War Chest?*, at 15, Institute of International Economics (1999).

[29]   Agreement on German External Debts, Feb. 27, 1953, 33 UNTS 3.

[30]   Based on conservative debt reduction calculations. *See* Timothy W. Guinnane, *Financial Vergangenheitsbewältigung: The 1953 London Debt Agreement*, at 27, Discussion Paper Series No. 880, Economic Growth Center, Yale University, Jan. 2004. Some of the payments were to be made only after the reunification of the country. Germany made the last payment on its debt (EUR69.9 million) on October 3, 2010.

grow, and ramped up military spending to serve its foreign policy needs. As long as US deficits were settled in dollars, rather than gold, the United States could keep on printing the dollars necessary to power the global economy and pursue its foreign policy agenda. At that point, neither the United States nor other countries viewed these deficits as a problem.

By 1959, it became obvious that the US liabilities were much larger than its gold stock. Between 1958 and 1968, states and private dollar-holders started to convert their dollars into gold. As the United States was hemorrhaging gold, it insisted that surplus countries, Japan and Germany, had to do something to correct their trade surpluses by strengthening their currencies and importing goods from it. Surplus states insisted, though, that the United States should eliminate its large and persistent deficits by implementing the appropriate contractionary monetary and fiscal policies. Many envied the US' 'exorbitant privilege' – the privilege of financing CA deficits by printing dollars that the rest of the world was avidly collecting. However, by the same token, they could not master the collective will to squash that privilege. States knew that asking the United States to convert their dollars into gold would have badly shaken the US position as the world's sovereign. In like manner, such a request would have destabilized the global economic edifice and would have damaged all those, privileged and unprivileged, who had put their faith in it. If the dollar were to be eclipsed, it was unclear what the alternative could be.

At the time, the UK gold market was the largest market for gold in the world and its daily fixing price of dollar per ounce of gold was the barometer of markets' confidence in the Bretton Woods system. On October 20, 1960, the London price of gold temporarily reached the level of $40 per ounce of gold. As a result, foreign CBs rushed to convert their dollars into gold. They had no other option. Failure to exploit gold's appreciation would have exposed them to 'charges of imprudent management of the national reserves entrusted for their safekeeping'.[31] The gold pool was developed in the aftermath of this spike in the price of gold.[32] The pool was put together by the United States, France, the UK, Belgium, Italy, Netherlands, Switzerland and West Germany. Its goal was to intervene in the London market, as needed, to keep the price of gold in line with the official price of $35 per ounce of gold. The Bank of England acted as the pool's agent in London. It determined how much gold had to be sold to keep the ER of dollar/gold close to the official rate. Between 1961 and 1964, the gold pool was successful in taming speculation against the dollar.[33]

---

[31]   Michael D. Bordo et al., *Strained Relations: US Foreign-exchange Operations and Monetary Policy in the Twentieth Century* 178 (2015).
[32]   *Id.*
[33]   *Id.*

In 1965, things started to change as France was publicly criticizing Bretton Woods and accelerating the conversion of its dollar reserves into gold. This resulted in high demand for gold and the gold pool started to operate with a gold deficit, which the Bank of England financed by using its own gold reserves. Participants in the pool continued to sell gold and buy dollars in order to depress the price of gold. By June 1965, though, the pool developed a deficit of $170 million.[34] France withdrew from the pool and the United States agreed to pick up its share. Other countries expressed concerns about the pool's ability to shape the gold market and pushed for a more permanent solution to the problem. In 1967, the US Air Force was drafted to transfer gold from the US Fort Knox Repository of gold[35] to London to facilitate the operations of the pool. The demand for gold remained strong in 1968 causing consternation in the United States.[36] On March 17, 1968, the gold pool suspended operations. Between November 18, 1967 and its closing, it sold $3 billion worth of gold in order to depress its price. Out of these $3 billion, the US contribution was $2.2 billion.[37]

There was no doubt that the abundance of dollars was exerting downward pressure on the currency. The dollar, the new reserve currency, was the vehicle of liquidity in the world. Speculative capital flows from deficit countries (e.g. England) to surplus countries (e.g. Germany) were taking place through dollars. As a result, surplus countries accumulated large amounts of unwanted dollars. Speculators fearing the devaluation of the English pound, for example, would first sell pounds for dollars and then sell dollars for a strong currency like the Swiss franc or the German mark. Dollars, not pounds, therefore, flowed into the surplus countries. Many surplus countries' CBs had strict legal limits on the ratio they had to keep between their dollar and gold reserves. When that ratio was exceeded, they had to sell their unwanted dollars to the United States, expecting gold in return.[38]

After the gold pool disintegrated, a two-tier system made up of an official gold price and a market-driven price replaced it. The gold held by CBs was isolated from the markets. CBs continued to buy and sell gold among them-

---

[34] *Id.* at 179.

[35] *Id.* at 180. A large amount of US gold reserves is stored in a vault at the Fort Knox Bullion Depository. The vault is made from 16 500 cubic feet of granite, 4 200 cubic yards of concrete, 750 tons of reinforcing steel and 670 tons of structural steel. It is heavily guarded. US Department of the Treasury, Currency & Coins: Fort Knox Bullion Depository, https://www.treasury.gov/.

[36] Memorandum from the President's Special Assistance (Rostow) to President Johnson, Mar. 14, 1968 (stating: 'We can't go on as is, hoping that something will turn up').

[37] Bordo, *supra* note 31, at 181.

[38] *Id.* at 154.

selves, at the official price of $35 per ounce of gold, but agreed to refrain from intervening in the gold market. As a result, the market price of gold fluctuated between $37 and $40.

The gold pool was not the only mechanism marshaled to defend the dollar. The Treasury, starting in March 1961, was employing the ESF to intervene in the market to prop up the dollar. In order to keep up with that intervention it had to constantly replenish its reserves with deutschmarks, Swiss francs and pounds, as it had to keep on selling these currencies to buy back dollars. The Treasury and the FRS worked together to stabilize the dollar and safeguard the US gold stock. The FRS initiated swap agreements with other CBs. That swap network totaled $900 million by the end of 1962 and grew to $11.2 billion by 1971.[39] Through these swap agreements the FRS borrowed the currency of surplus countries from their CBs and used it to buy those countries' unwanted dollars. When it was time to reverse the swap, the Treasury borrowed foreign currencies from the IMF, issued foreign-currency denominated bonds or sold gold to obtain the needed foreign exchange. The interventions in the FX market made possible by the FRS' swap arrangements were successful, at least in the short term. The swap arrangements signaled cooperation among the world's leading CBs and averted excessive speculative behavior that could have damaged the Bretton Woods system even further.[40]

The General Arrangements to Borrow (GAB) were adopted on October 2, 1962 to provide the IMF with additional funds. The GAB were, in essence, a $6 billion line of credit to the IMF from the CBs of 11 states (the largest amounts were provided by Germany, Japan and the United States). The GAB were put together to address the FX needs of the United States, which needed foreign currency to sell in the market to support the dollar. The arrangements made it possible for the United States to borrow from the IMF foreign currencies above the amounts authorized by the IMF Articles of Agreement. It used these currencies to buy up the dollars sold in the market and to redeem the unwanted dollars held by foreign CBs. This way the United States was able to preserve most of its gold.[41] The creation of a new type of reserve currency, the Special Drawing Rights (SDR), served similar purposes.[42] The IMF Articles of Agreement explicitly established the SDRs as a 'principal reserve asset'.[43] SDRs were distributed to states based on their quota contributions to the IMF.

---

[39] *Id.* at 151.
[40] *Id.* at 149.
[41] *Id.* at 142.
[42] The SDR agreement was signed in 1968 and entered into force in 1969.
[43] Art. XXII, Articles of Agreement of the IMF, July 22, 1944, as amended effective January 26, 2016 by the Board of Governors Resolution No. 66-2, Dec. 15, 2010.

They have become, since then, part of states' FX reserves and can be used to borrow global reserve currencies.

The GAB, the SDRs and swap agreements with other states made it possible for the United States to resist external pressure to devalue the dollar. The dollar was the only currency linked to gold. The United States was aware that an official devaluation of the dollar would have eroded its reserve-currency status. However, at the same time, it was not ready to tame its deficits since that would have meant slower growth, higher unemployment and fewer military commitments abroad. From the US perspective, the surplus countries (Germany and Japan) had more room for maneuver. They could appreciate their currencies and stimulate domestic demand, including demand for US imports.[44] However, Germany and Japan did not want to let their currencies appreciate. Such appreciation would have hurt their exports and removed pressure from the United States to correct its deficits.[45]

By the late 1960s, widening US deficits made it obvious that the fixed ERs of the Bretton Woods system were no longer sustainable. The dollar had to depreciate against the gold, causing the appreciation of other currencies; or the other currencies had to appreciate against the dollar. In addition, a high inflation rate in the United States was diminishing the value of dollar reserves held by other states. The United States was not the only country having economic troubles. The devaluation of the French franc and British pound underlined the economic challenges faced by these states. Speculators attacked sterling because the UK was losing its competitive edge and its FX reserves were paltry given the size of its recurrent deficits.[46]

In the early 1960s, France was a surplus country. However, in 1968, protests and labor strikes, which led to capital outflows to Germany, generated speculation that the franc would depreciate. At the Bonn meeting of November 1968, the G-10 finance ministers persuaded France to devalue the franc. Eventually, because it was running out of reserves, France had to apply for a $985 million stand-by agreement with the IMF.[47] France paid back that debt in August 1971. Because it had to repay a portion of it in gold, it asked the US Treasury to exchange $191 million for gold,[48] intensifying US anxiety over the depletion of its gold stock.

All through this period, Germany conducted a tight economic policy and ran persistent trade surpluses that encouraged dollar inflows. Because of its large trade surpluses, Germany was more willing to make concessions to preserve

---

[44] Oatley, *supra* note 11, at 219–20.
[45] *Id.*
[46] Bordo, *supra* note 31, at 173.
[47] *Id.* at 187.
[48] *Id.*

the status of the dollar as the global reserve currency. One of these concessions involved the offset payments – arranging for a portion of US military expenditures in Germany to be offset by German purchases of US military equipment. These offsets reduced the extent to which military expenses in Europe contributed to the US deficit.[49] In addition, Germany agreed not to exchange the dollars it had accumulated for gold, unlike France which consistently demanded gold from the United States. Germany's readiness to support the dollar was limited, though, by that country's aversion to inflation. As faith in the dollar was collapsing, dollar holders began to sell their dollars for German marks, triggering the appreciation of the mark and hurting German exports. Germany intervened to stop the mark from appreciating by creating marks to buy dollars, fueling domestic inflation.[50]

The reluctance of states to make painful changes in their domestic economies to correct global imbalances doomed Bretton Woods. Everybody was nervous about the 'dollar glut' – that foreign holdings of dollars (nearly $50 billion) were much higher than the US gold reserves ($10 billion).[51] This put pressure on the dollar to depreciate. In the first 6 months of 1971, private holdings of dollars fell by $3 billion – a sign that market participants were anticipating the devaluation of that currency. European governments had to buy more than $5 billion in order to defend the dollar's fixed ER to the gold. In May 1971, Germany alone purchased $2 billion in 2 days, a record at the time.[52]

The Bretton Woods system stumbled and failed for a number of reasons. The official gold price, $35 per ounce of gold, was too low to encourage gold mining, which would have reduced the price of gold versus the dollar. At the same time, the United States ran higher and higher deficits. These deficits provided the world with ample liquidity and fueled global prosperity. However, by the 1960s, it was all too obvious that the US deficits far exceeded the US gold stock and this invited speculation against the dollar.

Bretton Woods could have survived if states were ready to make the compromises necessary to sustain it – the United States showing some motivation to reduce its deficits and other states demonstrating more readiness to cut down their surpluses. Instead of compromising, each state tried to solve the Trilemma on its own. Once the United States closed the gold window in 1971, Bretton Woods became moribund and eventually collapsed, ushering a period of uncertainty in international economic affairs that persists until today.

---

[49]   Oatley, *supra* note 11, at 220.

[50]   *Id.*

[51]   On the dollar glut and the resentment it created, *see* Jacques Ruef, *The Monetary Sin of the West* 184–7 (1972).

[52]   Oatley, *supra* note 11, at 220.

9.   The Bretton Woods collapse: the 1970s

The 1971 decision to free the dollar from the gold stemmed from the US disillusionment with the global arrangements and its desire to pursue a DEP unshackled from external commitments.[1] As gold was flowing out of the country, it was apparent that the growth rate sought by the government was incompatible with the gold standard.[2] If the United States wanted to keep its gold reserves, it would have to abandon that standard.

On August 15, 1971, the world abruptly discovered that they could no longer exchange their amassed dollars for gold. Not only that. The United States imposed a 10% tax on all imports.[3] The United States calculated that a uniform tax on imports would produce results equivalent to currency devaluation since it would make foreign products more expensive for US consumers and business. It claimed additionally that the surcharge was supported by the GATT,[4] which provides that countries can restrict imports to address BOP problems.[5] The United States expected that the import surcharge would trigger a 24% appreciation of the yen and 18% appreciation of the German mark.[6] Japan resisted the appreciation of its currency by intervening in the FX market.[7] It bought dollars and sold yen, increasing its dollar reserves by $2.7 billion, an increase of 30%. Even this large-scale intervention, though, did not stop the dollar's depreciation.[8] Japan eventually gave up and let the yen float and appreciate against the dollar. This was a 'dirty float', though, since the

---

[1]   Milton Friedman, *Money Mischief: Episodes in Monetary History* 42 (1994).

[2]   Douglas A. Irwin, *The Nixon Shock After Forty Years: The Import Surcharge Revisited*, 12 World Trade Review 29, at 30 (2013).

[3]   *Id.* at 37.

[4]   *Id.* at 5.

[5]   Article XII of GATT provides that a state party may restrict imports 'in order to safeguard its external financial position and its balance of payments' as long as these restrictions are necessary 'to forestall the imminent threat of, or to stop, a serious decline in its monetary reserves'. *See* General Agreement on Tariffs and Trade (GATT) 1994, Apr. 15, 1994, Marrakesh Agreement Establishing the World Trade Organization, Annex 1A, 1867 UNTS 187, 33 ILM 1153 (1994) [hereinafter GATT].

[6]   Irwin, *supra* note 2, at 38.

[7]   *Id.* at 39.

[8]   *Id.*

government was ready to intervene in the market to slow down the pace of appreciation.[9]

The 10% import tax on all goods from other states, which became effective starting on August 16, 1971,[10] was a blanket instrument. The United States wanted to penalize the big surplus countries, Japan and Germany, but the surcharge adversely affected all states. The IMF approved of the 10% surcharge as a legitimate way of improving the US BOP.[11] Under the GATT, though, the surcharge was proclaimed inappropriate given the nature of US imbalances and the 'undue burden of adjustment' it placed on third states.[12]

The closing of the gold window, on August 15, 1971, shocked the world. The European FX market remained closed for a week. When it reopened, European governments refrained from defending their Bretton Wood par values. On December 18, 1971, at the Smithsonian Institution in Washington, DC, the G-10 signed the Smithsonian Agreement. The United States pledged to peg the dollar at the price $38 per ounce of gold[13] – an 8% devaluation. Major European countries and Japan conceded to appreciate their currencies by 2% producing an overall dollar devaluation of 10%. In addition, the United States promised to drop the 10% import surcharge.[14] According to the agreement, currencies could fluctuate by 2.25% above/below their pegged rate to the dollar. The devaluation of the dollar achieved by the Smithsonian agreement was expected to increase US exports, decrease imports and create jobs. It was a victory for the United States, but the celebrations did not last long. Since no government was prepared to defend the realigned ERs, the system fell apart by 1973 when all industrialized countries abandoned their fixed ERs and floated their currencies.

After the demise of Bretton Woods, a market-driven system of ERs prevailed based on three core currencies – the dollar, the Japanese yen and the German mark. Market participants were expected to discipline states that carried large BOP imbalances by precipitating the depreciation of overvalued currencies and appreciation of undervalued currencies. Unfortunately, currency markets did not work as efficiently as expected. Countries with weak currencies and high inflation were punished by the markets and their currencies swiftly

---

[9]   *Id.* at 40.
[10]   Richard Nixon, Proclamation (No. 4074) – Imposition of Supplemental Duty for Balance of Payments Purposes, August 15, 1971.
[11]   The WHO Analytical Index: Guide to WHO Law and Practice, at 433, https://www.wto.org
[12]   *Id.*
[13]   Para. 5, Press Communiqué of the Ministerial Meeting of the Group of Ten, Dec. 18, 1971.
[14]   Para. 6, *id.*

depreciated at the mere inkling of economic trouble. The reserve currencies, though, withstood pressure to weaken even in periods of high inflation. In many cases, currencies remained trapped in an ER for prolonged periods even if that rate was clearly misaligned. The deviation of many ERs from their 'fundamental' value, the value that reflected the economic performance of states, invited rampant speculation that destabilized the FX market. As a result, states resolved to intervene in that market. Certain interventions were unilateral while others were coordinated among major states. In fact, some states became heavily involved in managing their ERs to achieve specific national economic objectives. At the periphery, small open economies opted to peg their currencies to a reserve currency: that currency was the German mark for European countries and the dollar for the rest of the world. Bretton Woods was the last link of currencies to the gold, a commodity whose scarcity controlled money growth. Countries no longer had to shed gold each time they ran CA deficits. The by-default acceptance of dollar as the prime reserve currency placed the United States at the driving seat of international economic developments.

In the chaotic economic conditions of the 1970s, states longed for the lost stability of fixed ERs. They attempted, therefore, to establish some rules for the administration of their floating ERs. On June 13, 1974, states adopted the 'Guidelines for the Management of Floating Exchange Rates'.[15] This was a way to legitimize their intervention in the FX market to control these rates. According to the guidelines, a state with a floating ER could intervene in the FX market 'as necessary to prevent or moderate sharp and disruptive fluctuations' in its ER.[16] A state had to refrain, though, from acting aggressively when managing its ER – that is, depressing it when it was falling, or boosting it when it was rising.[17] The assumption at the time was that, in a world of floating ERs, it probably made sense 'to offer a measure of resistance to market tendencies', especially if these tendencies were the culprit in the 'unduly rapid movements' of the ERs.[18]

States went further in 1976 by amending article IV of the IMF Articles of Agreement.[19] This was the second amendment[20] that codified the shift of the monetary system to floating ERs. The amended article IV states clearly that countries have the freedom to choose the ER arrangements that are suitable for

---

[15]   Decision No. 4232-(74/67), June 13, 1974, *reprinted in* IMF Annual Report of the Executive Directors for the Fiscal Year Ended Apr. 30, 1974, at 112.

[16]   *Id.* at 113.

[17]   *Id.*

[18]   *Id.* at 51.

[19]   Board of Governors, Resolution No. 31-4, Apr. 30, 1976.

[20]   The first amendment, adopted in 1969, revised the quotas of IMF member states.

them[21] as long as they notify the IMF promptly of these arrangements and sub-sequent changes they may make.[22] It further emphasizes that the ER adopted by a state is a matter of international concern. States are urged to collaborate to promote a 'stable system of exchange rates'. They must further 'avoid *manipulating exchange rates* or the international monetary system *in order to* prevent effective balance of payments adjustment or to gain an unfair com-petitive advantage over other members'.[23] Yet what type of behavior qualifies as ER manipulation or manipulation of 'the international monetary system' is left unspecified. The IMF has exhorted states to 'follow exchange policies compatible' with their obligations under article VI[24] and it is charged with overseeing these policies.[25] In fact, the fund has to exercise '*firm* surveillance' over states with regard to their ER policies and states must provide the IMF with the information necessary and consult with it when requested.[26]

The IMF adopted in 1977 the Decision on Surveillance over Exchange Rate Policies.[27] That decision included principles that guided the IMF in its surveil-lance of states. It also enumerated the 'developments' that the IMF had to con-sider before deciding whether to have a 'discussion' with a state regarding its ER policy.[28] These developments included: a protracted large-scale interven-tion in one direction in the FX market; and an economic policy that abnormally encouraged or discouraged capital flows.[29] The lack of quantification of these developments, though, made it difficult to operationalize IMF's surveillance.

An economic phenomenon that shook both states and markets during this period was stagflation, the peculiar combination of low growth, high unem-ployment and rising inflation. Stagflation pushed states to rethink how to achieve price stability. Up to the mid-1970s, governments believed that a dose of inflation could buy them more growth – what is known as the 'Philips

---

[21]   Art. IV, Sec. 2(b), Articles of Agreement of the IMF, July 22, 1944, as amended effective January 26, 2016 by the Board of Governors Resolution No. 66-2, Dec. 15, 2010 [hereinafter IMF Articles of Agreement].

[22]   Art. IV, Sec. 2(a), *id. See also* IMF, Article IV of the Fund's Articles of Agree-ment: An Overview of the Legal Framework, at 3, June 28, 2006.

[23]   Art. IV, Sec. 1(iii), IMF Articles of Agreement, *id.* Emphasis added.

[24]   Art. IV, Sec. 1(iv), *id.*

[25]   Art. IV, Sec. 3(a), *id.*

[26]   Art. IV, Sec. 3(b), *id.* Emphasis added.

[27]   Surveillance over Exchange Rate Policies No. 5392-(77/63), Apr. 29, 1977, *reprinted in* IMF Review of the 1977 Decision on Surveillance over Exchange Rate Policies: Further Considerations, and Summing Up of the Board Meeting, Feb. 14, 2007.

[28]   *Id.* at 34.

[29]   *Id.* at 34–5.

curve'.[30] As inflation was getting out of hand, without producing growth, core states delegated to their CBs the responsibility of keeping inflation in check.[31] The first signs of stagflation appeared after the first 'oil shock' – the skyrocketing of oil prices owing to the embargo put in place by the Organization of the Petroleum Exporting Countries (OPEC). High oil prices pushed up the prices of other goods while growth and employment remained stagnant. By 1974, the average inflation rate in the developed world reached 13.5%. The 1975 Rambouillet Summit[32] was the first global summit that grappled with stagflation. At the 1976 Puerto Rico Summit, states endorsed the view that sustained economic expansion was incompatible with a high inflation rate.[33]

Subsequent summits were characterized by a tug of war between Germany, the inflation vigilante, and the United States, whose priority was growth. The US motto, at the time, was: 'We would prefer that you expand your economies and thereby import more from us so that reduction of the US deficit can be achieved in a way consistent with growth for all parties. But if you are not willing to go along, then … we are just going to have to let the dollar depreciate more, in which case your exports to us will fall'.[34] At the Bonn Summit of 1978, the G-7 eventually agreed to reflate their economies so as to speed up the rate of recovery after the 1974–75 global recession.[35] They resolved to achieve this through coordinated fiscal expansion. Even Germany conceded to enact a tax cut to boost its economy.[36]

By the mid-1970s, many developing states had become members of the IMF.[37] It took two oil shocks, in 1973 and 1979, to realize the ramifications of this changed membership. The spike in the price of oil engineered by OPEC boosted the CA surpluses of oil-exporting countries. Saudi Arabia's CA surplus, for instance, increased from \$2.5 billion in 1973 to \$23 billion in 1974

---

[30] For an insightful analysis of the Phillips curve and why it does not always hold in practice, *see* Roberto Chang, *Is Low Unemployment Inflationary?*, 82 Federal Reserve Bank of Atlanta Economic Review 4 (1997).

[31] Rosa M. Lastra, *The Role of Central Banks in Monetary Affairs: A Comparative Perspective* 78, at 91, in 'The Rule of Law in Monetary Affairs' (Thomas Cottier et al., 2014).

[32] Declaration of Rambouillet, Nov. 17, 1975, http://www.g8.utoronto.ca.

[33] Joint Declaration of the International Conference, June 28, 1976, http://www.g8.utoronto.ca.

[34] Jeffrey A. Frankel et al., *Exchange Rate Policy* 293, at 305, in 'American Economic Policy in the 1980s' (Martin Feldstein, ed., 1994).

[35] Declaration, July 17, 1978, http://www.g8.utoronto.ca.

[36] Para. 3, *id.*

[37] Domenico Lombardi and Ngaire Woods, *The Political Economy of IMF Surveillance*, at 8–9, CIGI Working Paper No. 17, Feb. 2007.

and was about $14 billion for another 3 years.[38] These surpluses – the so-called petrodollars – were deposited with US and other global banks, making possible the infamous 'recycling of petrodollars'.[39] Global banks reveled in their new role of matching dollars deposited with them by oil exporting countries with various developing states that were eager borrowers.

Developing states borrowed to finance their CA deficits that were the result of high oil prices. Most of these loans were short-term loans with variable IRs[40] that made borrowing excessively risky. Loans granted under variable rates trigger mounting borrowing costs when the US IRs rise. Short-term loans are also riskier than long-term ones. If a state cannot pay back its short-term debt, and banks refuse to roll over that debt into new loans, default is the only option. In fact, defaults by peripheral states have been a permanent feature of the international economy. The financial system, as it evolved after Bretton Woods, has been pervaded by crises put in motion by the failure of states to continue making payments on their debt voluntarily.[41]

---

[38]   Thomas Oatley, *International Political Economy* 305 (2012).
[39]   *Id.*
[40]   A variable IR is the opposite of a fixed IR. A fixed IR makes interest payments on a loan predictable. A variable IR is based on a benchmark IR that may fluctuate over time owing to decisions of financial authorities or market conditions.
[41]   Anne O. Krueger et al., *IMF Stabilization Programs* 297, at 298, in 'Economic and Financial Crises in Emerging Market Economies' (Martin Feldstein, ed., 2003).

10. The 1980s

10.1 THE PLAZA AND LOUVRE ACCORDS

The high inflation of the 1970s was defeated in the 1980s at the cost of severe unemployment. On October 6, 1979, the FRS announced measures to put inflation under control, a policy at odds with the expansionary fiscal policy pursued by the Treasury. The divergent economic policies produced the infamous twin deficits: the tax cuts and increased spending led to a gaping budget deficit; the high IRs strengthened the dollar, causing a CA deficit. The sharp appreciation of the dollar did not seem to trouble the United States, at least initially. The government announced in 1981 that it would no longer intervene in the FX market except *in extremis*.[1] However, as the export sector started to feel the pain of the strong dollar, the US policy shifted from nonchalance to heavy-handed management of foreign economic affairs.

In the 1980s, the priority of most countries was to defeat inflation.[2] In the United States, the FRS raised the FFR to 20%. This increase brought the desired results and inflation was tamed. As the rest of states mimicked the United States, global contraction was much deeper than expected with unemployment reaching over 30 million in Organisation for Economic Co-operation and Development states.[3] Controlling inflation affected the US external position. The high IRs that had defeated inflation led to the appreciation of the dollar,[4] undermining US export competitiveness. The US deficits were offset by the large CA surpluses of Japan and Germany.[5] The loss of export competitiveness roused US protectionism. A bill introduced by Congress in 1985 threatened to impose a 20% tariff on Japanese imports.[6] The Yen/Dollar

---

[1]   James M. Boughton, *Silent Revolution: The International Monetary Fund 1979–1989*, at 34 (IMF, 2001).
[2]   Robert D. Putnam and Nicholas Bayne, *Hanging Together: Cooperation and Conflict in the Seven-Power Summits* 98 (1987).
[3]   *Id.* at 99.
[4]   Thomas Oatley, *International Political Economy* 229 (2012).
[5]   *Id.* at 227.
[6]   *Id.* at 231.

Agreement of May 1984 established the Yen/Dollar Committee, whose goal was to manage the ER between two currencies.[7]

To address the vexation of the United States with its ER, on September 22, 1985, the G-5[8] financial ministers and central bank governors met at the Plaza Hotel in New York. There they adopted the Plaza Agreement[9] that provided for direct intervention in the FX market with the goal of devaluing the dollar. The Plaza accord stated bluntly that the imbalances in the external positions of countries – the growing US CA deficit and large CA surpluses of Japan and Germany – were a source of concern. The ERs between these states' currencies had to 'play a role in adjusting' these imbalances through 'some further orderly appreciation of the main non-dollar currencies against the dollar'.[10] States were to cooperate to 'encourage' this appreciation.[11]

The Plaza accord was successful in the short term. Market participants interpreted it as a dramatic shift from the previous US support for a strong dollar. Because of the expected government intervention in the market, speculators knew that any attempt to bet on the dollar's appreciation would be futile. In fact, the dollar fell sharply even before any official intervention had taken place. The G-5 intervened in the FX market collectively in 'massive' amounts.[12] They had reportedly agreed that the dollar must depreciate against the Japanese yen and German mark by 10–12% and they contributed $18 billion to achieve that devaluation.[13]

The weakening of the dollar was, at that point, the focus of US FEP. Japan and Germany went along reluctantly. They knew that the appreciation of their currencies owing to the devaluation of the dollar would erode their export advantage. In March 1986, the Bank of Japan attempted to slow down the yen's appreciation. In September 1986, the German CB intervened to stabilize the mark.[14] However, the United States refused to relent. In fact, the FRS

---

[7]   Richard C. Koo, *The Escape from Balance Sheet Recession and the QE Trap: A Hazardous Road for the World Economy* 283 (2015). *See also* Jeffrey A. Frankel, *Exchange Rate Policy* 293, at 299, in 'American Economic Policy in the 1980s' (Martin Feldstein, ed., 1994).

[8]   France, Germany, Japan, the UK and the United States.

[9]   Announcement of Ministers of Finance and Central Bank Governors of France, Germany, Japan, the United Kingdom and the United States (Plaza accord), Sept. 22, 1985, http://www.g8.utoronto.ca.

[10]   Para. 18, *id.*

[11]   *Id.*

[12]   Michael D. Bordo et al., *Strained Relations: US Foreign-Exchange Operations and Monetary Policy in the Twentieth Century* 277–8 (2015).

[13]   Kathryn Mary Dominguez, *Market Responses to Coordinated Central Bank Intervention*, at 13, NBER Working Paper No. 3192, Dec. 1989.

[14]   *Id.* at 14.

reduced the discount rate, the rate at which it lends to banks, by 0.5% in 1986, to reinforce the view that the United States did not share other CBs' goals of stabilizing the dollar.[15] The United States did not buy foreign currency when the dollar was depreciating. Instead, it bought foreign currencies when the dollar was appreciating to resist the strengthening of its currency. At the same time, though, it did not wish to devalue the dollar to such an extent that its fall would be uncontrollable. The FRS was particularly worried over the possibility of a dollar freefall.[16] It was fearful that the aggressive depreciation tactics of the Treasury could damage the world's faith in the dollar.

After the Plaza accord, the United States continued to pressure Japan and Germany as the US deficit continued to widen and the Japanese and German surpluses kept on growing. The United States made it clear that, in the absence of coordinated action, it would not hesitate to unilaterally talk down the dollar. In 1986, the Treasury went as far as to advocate a coordinated reduction of the IRs of developed states to offset the effects of the slowing US economy and to address global BOP imbalances. The coordinated IRs declines, sought by the Treasury, took place eventually on March 6 and 7, 1986.[17] Since states were targeting a specific ER, in this case a certain amount of dollar depreciation, they could not afford to have an autonomous DEP.

Germany and Japan eventually sought a truce at the February 22, 1987 Louvre meeting of G-6 (G5 + Canada).[18] Both countries conceded to adopt domestic expansionary policies as long as the United States was ready to guarantee that the dollar would not fall any further. More specifically, Japan agreed to lower its IRs and stimulate domestic demand through fiscal measures.[19] Germany agreed to increase its already planned 1988 tax cuts.[20] The United States reiterated that it was willing to adopt targets to control its budget deficit.[21] The Louvre communiqué made it clear that further drastic shifts in the ERs of states were unwarranted and that a further substantial change in the ERs could damage growth.[22]

The Plaza and Louvre accords demonstrate that global economic cooperation is not that farfetched an idea, especially if aggressively pursued by the global sovereign. The implementation of these agreements was accomplished

---

[15]   *Id.*

[16]   Bordo, *supra* note 12, at 287.

[17]   *Id.* at 291.

[18]   Statement of the G-6 Finance Ministers and Central Bank Governors (Louvre accord), Feb. 22, 1987, http://www.g8.utoronto.ca.

[19]   Para. 7, *id.*

[20]   *Id.*

[21]   *Id.*

[22]   Para. 10, *id.*

by key interventions in the market and substantial modifications of monetary and fiscal policies. The agreements helped the sovereign avoid the Trilemma by keeping its economic policy focused on domestic objectives while using arm-twisting exercises to extract desirable commitments from others.[23] Japan viewed the accords as the beginning of the end of its economic prosperity. The strengthened yen, extracted through the agreements, had a recessionary effect on Japan's export-dependent economy. Japan attempted to offset the yen's appreciation by adopting an expansionary DEP. In fact, slowing down the yen's appreciation became a national priority pursued through monetary easing. In addition, it adopted an expansionary fiscal policy, mainly through an increase in public investment. These expansionary policies led to the Japanese asset bubble (1987 to 1991), which ended with a painful burst and the so-called 'Japan's Lost Decade'.

It is unclear whether the heavy-handed intervention in the currency market contributed to the crash of the stock market, the 'Black Monday' of October 19, 1987. After that crash, the CBs of developed states engaged in numerous large-scale interventions whose goal was to stem the further depreciation of the dollar. In their statement of December 22, 1987, the G-7 made it clear that they favored ER stability and were against the further devaluation of the dollar: 'excessive fluctuation of exchange rates, a further decline of the dollar, or a rise in the dollar to an extent that becomes destabilizing to the adjustment process, could be counter-productive by damaging growth prospects in the world economy'.[24] Despite this explicit statement, additional intervention in January 1988 was necessary to thwart the dollar's fall.[25]

A new dollar rally took place in 1989 as a G-7 meeting concluded that the strengthening of the dollar was inconsistent with long-term economic fundamentals,[26] signaling its commitment to keep intervening to correct the market when needed. Overall, though, the interventionist enthusiasm was cooling off. The FRS, never a fan of meddling in the FX market, started to actively push back against the Treasury's interventionist agenda. The changed attitude had to do with the realization that intervention produced only short-term results and that the United States would be served better if it signaled its stance on the ER via its DEP and not through interventions in the market.

---

[23]   Putnam and Bayne, *supra* note 2, at 239.

[24]   Para. 8, Statement of G7 Finance Ministers and Central Bank Governors, Dec. 22, 1987, http://www.g8.utoronto.ca.

[25]   Frankel, *supra* note 7, at 309.

[26]   Statement of the G-7 Finance Ministers and Central Bank Governors, Sept. 23, 1989, http://www.g7.utoronto.ca.

10.2   THE DEBT CRISIS

The petrodollars that inundated the financial system in the 1970s found aggressive lenders in banks and eager borrowers in many developing states. In the 1970s, the dollar-denominated debt of developing states amounted to $73 billion. By the 1980s, it had increased to $587 billion.[27] The 40 most heavily indebted countries owed $461 billion of this total.[28]

When a country piles up dollar-denominated debt, it needs dollar earnings to service it. A CA surplus based on increasing exports is certainly helpful in paying down debt. Unfortunately, for many developing states, exports did not keep up with the amount of debt they issued. The two oil shocks in fact produced CA deficits in many of these states, as the price of imports (oil) was greater than the prices commanded by their exports. In addition, most countries invested the amounts they borrowed in grand projects or subsidized consumption[29] instead of nurturing indigenous capital formation. The hike of the US IRs in the 1980s hurt, as a result, highly indebted developing states.

In August 1982, Mexico announced that it would no longer be able to service its debt.[30] Private banks immediately ceased lending to Mexico and, apprehensive that its problems were not unique, stopped lending to the rest of the developing states. The severe lack of credit caused economic contraction. Governments reduced their spending and cut social services as they could no longer borrow to finance deficits. The 1980s went down in history as a lost decade for developing states.[31]

Creditor states' approach to the crisis was that of 'divide and conquer'. Creditors distinguished between middle-income Latin America countries, which were heavily indebted to private banks, and low-income, mostly African states that owed most of their debt to other states.[32] With regard to low-income countries, creditor states acting through the Paris Club, a debt-restructuring institution, decided to reduce some of their debt burden under the terms agreed at the Toronto summit of 1988. It took more than a decade and many more summits, though – from the eruption of the debt crisis until 1996 – for creditor states to reconcile with the idea that the only solution to the debt overhang was substantial debt relief. The Heavily Indebted Poor Countries Initiative

---

[27]   Oatley, *supra* note 4, at 306.
[28]   *Id.*
[29]   *Id.* at 307–8.
[30]   *Id.* at 308.
[31]   Boughton, *supra* note 1, at 31.
[32]   *Id.*

provided, over time, $76 billion in debt relief for 36 countries, 30 of which were located in Africa.[33]

With regard to Latin America, creditors approached the crisis as a temporary liquidity problem rather than as a solvency issue. They therefore expected these states to continue servicing their debt to private banks by rescheduling payments, restructuring their economies and additional financing. Rescheduling involved the extension of debt maturities. There was a clear understanding among all concerned that all debt had to be repaid in the long term. Structural adjustment meant the reduction of imports and spending. To structurally adjust, furthermore, a country had to limit the role of government in the economy and to give more leeway to foreign private capital. The structural adjustment programs pioneered by the IMF at the instigation of creditor states focused on market and trade liberalization, privatization and deregulation.[34]

Creditor states were able to organize behind the IMF and, through it, articulate a coherent position on debt repayment. They decided to deal with each debtor separately, offering favorable treatment to states amenable to compromise. Debtor states, on the other hand, lacked the institutional cover and, thus, were unable to convincingly convey the threat of collective default.[35] Such a threat would have certainly rattled creditor states. The US Central Intelligence Agency (CIA), which was tasked with assessing the fallout from the potential establishment of a debtors' cartel, concluded that debtors were unlikely to collaborate.[36] Indeed, initial calls for solidarity among borrowers gradually vanished and each state fended for itself.

'Debt-for-equity swaps' were proposed in the mid-1980s as a way to address the crisis.[37] These types of swaps have been used in corporate finance when a company's creditors agree to cancel some or all of a company's debt in exchange for a piece of ownership in the company. Debt-for-equity deals usually take place when companies cannot repay their debt and, as a result, are taken over partly or wholly by their creditors. In mid-1980, the Latin American debt was sold at a *discount* in the secondary market. An investor could, thus, acquire that debt in that market and then, if a government was willing to do a debt-to-equity deal, redeem it for local currency at *face value*. Investors

---

[33] Debt Relief Under the Heavily Indebted Poor Countries (HIPC) Initiative, IMF Factsheet, Mar. 8, 2018.

[34] Oatley, *supra* note 4, at 312.

[35] *See* Cartagena Statement of Consensus, 23 ILM 1169 (1984), 11(26) EIR, July 3, 1984.

[36] CIA, *The Cartagena Group, Politicizing the Debt in Latin America: An Intelligence Assessment*, 1986, approved for release Apr. 2002.

[37] Mauro Megliani, *Sovereign Debt: Genesis – Restructuring – Litigation* 259–61 (2015).

gained from this deal because they bought the debt, at a discount, in the secondary market and then exchanged it, at full face value, for local currency, an ingenious way to acquire cheaply coveted assets in developing states.

From the perspective of developing states, debt-for-equity deals were far from lucrative. Selling off assets under financial duress produced paltry returns. Developing states resented the fire sales they were forced to complete under debt-for-equity swaps or other privatization deals. In many cases, debt-for-equity swaps were used to finance investments that would have taken place anyway.[38] Because developing states did not see much value in debt-for-equity, such deals never really took off.

The Latin American debt crisis was dragging on when US Treasury Secretary Brady introduced the Brady plan. Under that plan, debtor states were able to convert their debt, which was already selling at a discount, into bonds of lower face value, the so-called Brady bonds. The precise amount of debt reduction to be accomplished through this conversion was negotiated between the banks and each state. Various sticks and carrots were used to cajole banks into accepting the idea of debt reduction.[39] In the case of Mexico, for example, its debt was exchanged for bonds created under a new agreement. The agreement contained a clause making it clear that the debt conversion constituted a new contract through *novation*[40] – a process that substitutes an old contact with a new one extinguishing all rights and obligations under the old contract. Creditor states and the IMF advanced $30 billion to banks, an amount that guaranteed the principal payment of these Brady bonds.[41] This convinced them that it was better to accept the guaranteed repayment of a smaller amount of debt than go after full repayment.[42] In the case of Mexico, all banks signed onto the new debt-reduction agreement, which was adopted on February 4, 1990 during a public ceremony in Mexico City.[43] The debt reduction achieved through the Brady plan, in combination with lower global IRs that prevailed by the end of 1980s, helped states exit a crisis that had loomed over them for a whole decade.

---

[38]   Paul Krugman et al., *LDC Debt Policy* 691, at 720, in 'American Economic Policy in the 1980s' (Martin Feldstein, ed., 1990).

[39]   *Id.* at 702.

[40]   *Id.*

[41]   Oatley, *supra* note 4, at 319.

[42]   *Id.* at 320.

[43]   World Bank, *Mexico's External Debt Restructuring in 1989–90*, at 21, Working Paper 424, June 1990.

11. The 1990s

11.1 BACKGROUND

From the mid-1990s onwards, the United States has refrained from intervening in the currency market because of the ostensible incompatibility of such intervention with the independence of the FRS. The 1980s large-scale interventions to weaken the dollar conflicted with the contractionary policy pursued by the FRS to battle inflation. This confused the markets and created doubts about whether the FRS had the authority to devise an independent policy. The United States has decided to solve the Trilemma by opting for the free movement of capital, independence of DEP and a floating ER. Intervention in the FX market is viewed as a policy tool to be used sparingly, preferably in coordination with other states, to restore order in the event of market disorder. A shared understanding of what constitutes such disorder has however remained elusive among states.

Some of the notable interventions during this period included a collective intervention of the United States and European states to strengthen the dollar after the 1991 Gulf War. Another intervention to support the dollar took place between April 1994 and August 1995 in coordination with the BOJ and European CBs. The last collective intervention during this period happened in September 2000 to prop up the euro[1] when that currency lost 30% of its value soon after its launch in January 1999.

The adoption of the euro was preceded by the Exchange Rate Mechanism (ERM) of the European Monetary System, a system through which the peripheral states of Europe anchored their currencies to the German mark. That system came under speculative attack in 1992, forcing the Bank of England to abandon its pegged rate and triggering the severe depreciation of sterling. The ERM was a soft peg arrangement. The ERs of European states were *de facto* pegged to the mark, the strong currency in the region, and could float within certain margins. This semi-fixed ER system failed to convince the markets,

---

[1]   Para. 4, Statement of G-7 Finance Ministers and Central Bank Governors, Prague, Sept. 23, 2000, http://www.g8.utoronto.ca/.

which doubted that states would be willing to support the ERM at the expense of their DEP independence.

After the defeat of the ERM, the IMF endorsed the view that states had to choose between free floating ERs or irreversibly fixed ERs. Any intermediate regime would be challenged by the markets and was unlikely to survive.[2] The IMF sided with Argentina when that country decided to adopt a hard, fixed 1 peso/1 dollar ER. The IMF even supported dollarization by proposing that a new country, Timor Leste, would be better off adopting the US dollar instead of introducing a new national currency. When Ecuador made plans to make the US dollar its national currency the IMF went along with that decision.

After Argentina's economic crisis in the late 1990s, it was realized, though, that establishing an irrevocably fixed ER, a hard peg, does not necessarily bolster states' economic credibility. When an economy is in trouble, market players are always ready to test politicians' commitment to even irreversibly fixed ERs. Contractionary fiscal and monetary policies taken up during economic downturns to support fixed ERs produce too much social turmoil. As a rule, when their economies dip into recession, governments do not hesitate to abandon their fixed ER even at the cost of steep depreciation of their currency.

The G-7 meeting in Naples, Italy, in July 1994 marked the 50th anniversary of the IMF. Few were in the mood to celebrate. The general feeling was that 50 years of the IMF were more than enough.[3] Creditor states adopted the 'Naples Terms' under which they reduced the debt burden of low-income countries that had lingered from the past decade.[4] On September 26, 1999, a new group of countries emerged as a player in global economic affairs – the G-20. This group includes all of the G-7 members plus the world's major emerging market economies (Brazil, India, China, Argentina, Australia, Indonesia, Mexico, Saudi Arabia, South Africa, Russia, South Korea and Turkey) and the EU.

11.2   THE EAST ASIAN CRISIS

The spirit of the 1990s was encapsulated in the Washington consensus,[5] a list of economic policies that would have made 'British imperial administrators

---

[2]   James M. Boughton, *Tearing Down Walls: The International Monetary Fund 1990–1999*, at 23 (2012).

[3]   *Id.* at 21.

[4]   *Id.* at 39.

[5]   The Washington Consensus has been called the 'golden straightjacket'; once a country puts it on by committing to privatization, low inflation, balanced budget and openness to foreign investment, political maneuvering becomes much more difficult. In countries that wear the straightjacket, the differences between the left and the

a hundred years before' happy.[6] The consensus was endorsed by the IMF Interim Committee and was summarized by what the director of the IMF called the 'eleven commandments'.[7] The commandments specified what countries needed to do to thrive, which included the pursuit of low inflation, freedom of capital, fiscal discipline and structural reform. Structural reform included the liberalization of the labor market by dismantling restrictions on hiring and firing which governments had put in place in previous decades to enhance job security. Structural reform and the liberalization of capital were promoted as the recipe for growth. The director of the IMF clearly stated that article VII of the IMF's Articles of Agreement, which mandated the freedom of capital only for the settlement of the current account, was not ambitious enough. It must be expanded to cover the capital account as well.[8]

Most of the inflows of private capital into the developing world in the early 1990s took the form of lending. Banks provided short-term loans and investors bought bonds issued by developing states and their private sector. Most of the countries that borrowed from foreigners had pegged currencies to the dollar in various forms of hard or soft pegs. Many of these countries offered higher IRs on the debt they issued than those offered by the US because they wanted to attract foreign capital. Investors could, therefore, borrow cheaply in US dollars and then use these dollars to buy the higher-yielding debt of these countries. Some of this debt was issued by governments to finance fiscal deficits. Loans were also granted to commercial banks of developing states, which, in turn, lent the money to private local companies.

Mexico is a typical peripheral country that is sensitive to changes in US DEP. When the FRS increased IRs in February 1994, Mexico had to bump up its own IRs to prevent the outflow of capital to the United States. The liberalization of Mexico's capital markets in the early 1990s had generated large capital inflows into the country. Mexican banks used that capital to lend to businesses and consumers. The increase in the US IRs, which forced Mexico to increase its own IRs, hurt the banks that had already made loans at lower rates. In addition, those who had borrowed at variable rates started to have difficulties repaying their debt. The combination of bad loans and capital outflows produced a severe contraction. The contraction turned quickly into a currency

right are minimal. Thomas L. Friedman, *The Lexus and the Olive Tree: Understanding Globalization* 105–6 (2000).

[6]   Naill Ferguson, *The Ascent of Money* 309 (2008).

[7]   IMF, Partnership for Global Sustainable Growth, Interim Committee Declaration, Sept. 29, 1996.

[8]   IMF, Transcript of Press Conference by Interim Committee Chairman and IMF Managing Director, Apr. 28, 1997.

crisis as market players exited Mexico by selling their pesos and switching to dollar-denominated assets.

The fact that 60% of short-term bonds issued by Mexico were held by US investors compelled the US government to do something.[9] In January 1995, a $50 billion bailout of Mexico was announced consisting of US loans ($20 billion), an IMF stand-by facility ($17.8 billion), a BIS loan ($10 billion) and loans by commercial banks ($3 billion).[10] This rescue package was provided under the condition that Mexico would implement fiscal tightening and battle inflation along with pursuing more privatization.

At the G-7 summit of June 15, 1995, states noted their concern about 'the vast financial flows' that were 'commonplace in private markets'.[11] The summit underlined the need 'for changes to the architecture of the international financial institutions'[12] and urged the establishment of a new procedure for countries facing financial crises: the Emergency Financing Mechanism (EFM). The EFM was to provide faster access to the IMF with larger upfront conditional disbursements based on the exceptional circumstances clause.[13]

The Mexican crisis was followed by the 1997 East Asian financial crisis, the 1998 Brazilian and Russian crises and the default of Argentina. All the crisis-hit countries were bedeviled by similar economic conditions:

- some type of pegged ER to the dollar;
- dependence on short-term capital inflows – short-term capital inflows come to sudden stops and revert to core states when a peripheral state experiences an economic downturn;
- contagion – capital holders assume that dire economic circumstances in a peripheral country will affect similarly situated countries.

In the early 1990s, many East Asian countries had liberalized their financial markets, making it possible for their domestic banks to intermediate the flows of capital between foreign banks and domestic borrowers. It seemed at that

---

[9]   Mauro Megliani, *Sovereign Debt: Genesis – Restructuring – Litigation* 113 (2015).

[10]   IMF, IMF Approves US$17.8 Billion Stand-By Credit for Mexico, Press Release, Feb. 1, 1995.

[11]   Para. 5, The Halifax Summit Review of the International Financial Institutions: Background Document, June 16, 1995, http://www.g8.utoronto.ca/.

[12]   Para. 1, *id.*

[13]   Para. 5, *id.* The 'exceptional circumstances' clause was adopted in 1984. That year, the IMF board agreed that, in exceptional circumstances, the IMF could provide financing to states in amounts that exceeded their access limit. *See* Policy on Enlarged Access to the Fund's Resources: Criteria for Amount of Access in Individual Cases, *reprinted in* IMF Annual Report 1984, at 131.

point that everybody could benefit from such liberalization. The IRs offered in the United States were much lower than those prevailing in Asian states. Asian banks could, therefore, borrow money at relatively low IRs from US lenders, and then loan it out to domestic borrowers at higher IRs.[14] These loans were lucrative but also risky. Asian banks borrowed from foreign banks via short-term dollar-denominated loans. They used these loans to finance longer-term loans to domestic borrowers in local currency. In this way they exposed themselves to the ER risk emanating from a potential sharp devaluation of the domestic currency. If the domestic currency drastically weakened, the costs of servicing the dollar debt would be crippling. Another risk had to do with the difficulties of rolling over short-term loans into new loans in times of crisis. If foreign banks denied the possibility to roll over these loans, Asian banks would be forced to pay back the loan principal and accrued interest all at once. This could have triggered their default as the money they had borrowed was tied up in domestic long-term loans.[15]

All of these risks came into sharp focus in the spring of 1997 when Thailand's largest financial institution, Finance One, was declared insolvent. The outflow of capital depleted the Thai government's FX reserves and forced it to float the baht, the Thai currency. From Thailand, the crisis spread to the Philippines, Indonesia, Malaysia, Taiwan, Hong Kong and South Korea. A total of $60 billion of capital exited the region in the second half of 1997,[16] roughly two-thirds of the capital that had flowed in the year before. An additional $55 billion left in 1998.[17]

The South Korean crisis occurred in a period of high growth, low inflation and low public debt.[18] However, the private sector had amassed large amounts of dollar debt. Foreign banks chose not to renew credit lines to their Korean counterparts, not because they were concerned about their deteriorating financial health, but because this was the easiest way to minimize their exposure to East Asia, as country after country was expected to succumb to crisis.[19] Fears that South Korea was about to collapse triggered a speculative attack against the won. Korea's usable FX reserves were only $7 billion – a very small amount compared with its short-term debt.[20] Eventually, it had to relent, let the won depreciate and ask for the assistance of the IMF. Not all countries suc-

---

[14]   Thomas Oatley, *International Political Economy* 328 (2012).
[15]   *Id.*
[16]   *Id.* at 330.
[17]   *Id.* at 331.
[18]   IEO, *The IMF and Recent Capital Account Crises: Indonesia, Korea, Brazil*, at 16 (2013) [hereinafter IEO Capital Account Crises].
[19]   *Id.* at 17.
[20]   *Id.* at 18.

cumbed to the speculative attacks on their currencies. Hong Kong bought back its currency to prevent its devaluation. It also intervened in the stock market to avert its collapse,[21] delegating *laissez-fair* capitalism to the past.[22] China imposed capital controls and already had large FX reserves that made an attack on its currency prohibitive.[23] Singapore succeeded in fending off speculators because of its well-capitalized financial system.[24]

11.3 GLOBAL RESPONSE TO THE CRISIS

Most countries that were hit by the crisis turned to the IMF for assistance. This assistance was conditioned on reforms. Countries had to tighten their monetary and fiscal policies. They had to adopt structural reforms including trade liberalization, elimination of domestic monopolies and privatization of state-owned enterprises. The IMF pressed the Indonesian government to reduce the monopoly of state in the agricultural sector, privatize 13 state-owned enterprises and suspend its support for the development of indigenous automobile and aircraft industries.[25]

During the 1980s, the IMF required states to achieve certain economic objectives that were quantifiable, for instance, a specific reduction in their budget deficit. States were then usually given discretion on which policies they would pursue to achieve these objectives – for instance, what types of spending to reduce or which taxes to increase. In the 1990s, the fund adopted structural performance criteria, setting ceilings for *types* of public sector expenses or demanding certain *types* of spending cuts. Assessing a country's progress in achieving these objectives required an in-depth analysis of its economy. This analysis had to happen each time the IMF reviewed a country's performance and before it released the next tranche of financing to the government.

Asian states did not hesitate to challenge the authority of the IMF. In November 1997, 14 East Asian states adopted the Manila Framework through which they asked it 'to constructively examine the establishment of a new mechanism to provide short-term financing' because of 'the globalization

---

[21] Yu Syue-Ming, *The Role of the Central Bank in a Crisis Environment: The Experience of Hong Kong and Taiwan, 1997–9*, at 275, 281, in 'International Monetary Law: Issues for the New Millennium' (Mario Giovanoli, ed., 2000).

[22] *Id.* at 283.

[23] Galina Hale, *Could we Have Learned from the Asian Financial Crisis of 1997–98?*, at 2, Federal Reserve Bank of San Francisco Economic Letter, Feb. 28, 2011.

[24] Ramon Moreno, *What Caused East Asia's Financial Crisis?*, Federal Reserve Bank of San Francisco Economic Letter, Aug. 7, 1998.

[25] Oatley, *supra* note 14, at 331.

of financial markets and the increased scale of private capital flows'.[26] They emphasized that *preemptive* IMF lending was necessary to ward off contagious crises that had to do with the evaporation of investor confidence rather than the bad policies of states.

As soon as Russia defaulted on its debt in August 1998, the provision of precautionary financing to Brazil started to look like a sensible approach to a highly anticipated crisis. At the summit of October 30, 1998, the G-7 reiterated their commitment 'to ward off destabilizing market contagion' by establishing 'an enhanced IMF facility to provide a preemptive line of credit that could be drawn on if needed by countries pursuing strong IMF approved policies'.[27] The financial package for Brazil announced in November 1998 took the form of a regular IMF stand-by arrangement including loans from many institutions: $18.1 billion from the IMF; $4.5 billion from the World Bank; $4.5 billion from the Inter-American Development Bank; $13.3 billion from the BIS (guaranteed by 19 countries including the United States); and $1.25 billion provided by the Japanese government.[28]

11.4   ASSESSMENT OF GLOBAL RESPONSE

The IMF's own watchdog, the Independent Evaluation Office (IEO), criticized it for failing to foresee the 1990s financial crisis that rattled East Asian states. Foreseeing that crisis was not easy, though. The so-called Asian tigers were experiencing export growth, and low inflation and public debt. The IMF did not scrutinize the finances of banks and companies that were burdened by short-term foreign-currency debt. It failed to evaluate the impact of the short-term capital flows on developing economies.[29]

In hindsight, the IMF should have advised states against capital account liberalization when they lacked the institutions capable of overseeing that liberalization. Because of that premature liberalization, banking crises turned quickly into capital account crises (i.e. massive capital outflows).[30] Furthermore, the IMF allowed the crisis to fester for much too long and valuable time was wasted on negotiations and re-negotiations. The IMF's vexing ineptitude during the crisis led Japan to propose during the 1997 G-7 meeting in Hong

---

[26]   Para. 7, A New Framework for Enhanced Asian Regional Cooperation to Promote Financial Stability, Meeting of Asian Finance and Central Bank Deputies, Nov. 18–19, 1997.

[27]   Para. 4, G-7 Leaders Statement on the World Economy, Oct. 30, 1998, http://www.g8.utoronto.ca/.

[28]   IEO Capital Account Crises, *supra* note 18, at 136.

[29]   *Id.* at 62.

[30]   *Id.* at 11.

Kong the establishment of an Asian Monetary Fund. That proposal, which placed more emphasis on regional financing mechanisms in addressing crises, was rejected by the United States.

Many criticized the IMF for the unnecessary fiscal tightening it prescribed for Indonesia and South Korea given that the crises they were experiencing had nothing to do with the mishandling of public finances. It would have made more sense if these states had adopted fiscal loosening, instead of the IMF's prescribed tightening, and had pursued other expansionary strategies to boost growth.[31] This was especially true for South Korea. South Korea had the fiscal space to bear some of the costs of bailing out the banking sector without imposing additional taxes or shrinking spending.[32]

In all fairness, the IMF as an institution did not have much discretion on how to handle the crisis. Instead, it was executing the instructions of creditor states,[33] its major shareholders. Creditor states had already made up their mind that the deregulation of the economies of East Asian states was the *quid pro quo* for IMF's assistance. The interference of IMF's major shareholders in the work of the fund 'subjected the staff to micromanagement and political pressure' and generated suspicions about the real motives of IMF's involvement in East Asia.[34]

In the case of Indonesia, the creditor states at the IMF's Executive Board saw in the financial crisis the opportunity to lend a helping hand to those they considered 'reformers' in the Indonesian government, those who supported economic deregulation.[35] After Indonesia failed to implement the first IMF program, creditor states pushed the IMF to demand detailed structural reforms that had to be accomplished under a strict timetable.[36] The second IMF program for Indonesia was adopted on January 15, 1998, at an official ceremony, so as to improve its chances of being accepted by the populace. The heightened publicity ended up being harmful. A picture of the president of the country signing up for the IMF program with the managing director of the IMF looking over him went viral as the perfect depiction of loss of statehood that came with IMF meddling.[37] The president of Indonesia, who reluctantly endorsed the IMF

---

[31] *Id.* at 32.

[32] *Id.*

[33] The United States was particularly concerned that the crisis had not done much to weaken the 'nationalistic resistance to foreign ownership of assets'. *See* Richard P. Cronin, *Asian Financial Crisis and Recovery: Status and Implications for US Interests*, at 15–16, CRS, Apr. 6, 2000.

[34] IEO Capital Account Crises, *supra* note 18, at 5.

[35] *Id.* at 13.

[36] *Id.* at 15.

[37] *Id.* at 15, n. 9.

programs, viewed them as nothing more than a means to dethrone him.[38] The programs failed to even impress the markets because it was not clear how the conditionality imposed through them was to assist Indonesia in addressing the crisis. All in all, IMF's unnecessary conditionality diverted attention from the urgent reforms needed to resuscitate the country's banking sector.[39]

In the case of Korea and Indonesia, the IMF was confident in its analysis that these countries were unlikely to experience currency attacks because their ERs were not overvalued. The IMF discounted the 'animal spirits' of investors that are capable of setting off a spiraling depreciation of a currency without an initial overvaluation.[40] Those who believe in the efficiency of the markets tend to hold that a country's currency will be attacked only if that country's economic fundamentals are unsound. Market participants will sell off a state's currency if that state experiences low growth, high inflation or unsustainable debt. The 1990s financial crisis demonstrated that a country's fixed ER can be attacked despite that country's good fundamentals, simply because market participants perceive, justifiably or not, that the government does not have the will or the means to defend its currency.[41]

Self-fulfilling currency crises share similarities with bank runs. Rumors that a bank is in bad shape can trigger a bank run. This increases the chances that depositors will run on other banks. Bank runs are contagious. They can lead to insolvency of even financially sound banks simply because of the structure of the global banking system: banks do not have the cash in hand to pay all depositors at once. The same is true with runs on a country. A run on a country's currency can happen when the country faces a temporary cyclical downturn or does not have adequate FX reserves. This is likely to spur runs on countries that happen to be located in the same region or face similar economic circumstances. When markets are shaken up by panics, investors tend to divest massively from developing countries and to repatriate their money to their home markets, the safe havens for capital. When markets are panicking, a country can give in to a crisis even if it has good fundamentals (low inflation and high growth potential). Most countries are not stellar economic performers all of the time. They do not have enough reserves to defend themselves against massive currency attacks instigated by well-funded hedge funds. 'Destabilizing speculation' can be a 'problem in and of itself' for a country facing temporary economic problems.[42] If the efficiency of markets is taken as a given, those

---

[38]   *Id.* at 80.
[39]   *Id.* at 77.
[40]   *Id.* at 26.
[41]   Paul Krugman, *Are Currency Crises Self-Fulfilling?*, 345, at 346, in (11) NBER Macroeconomics Annual 1996 (Ben S. Bernanke and Julio J. Rotemberg, eds, 1996).
[42]   Maurice Obstfeld, *Comment, id.* at 402.

who speculate against a country's currency are just the ruthless communicators of bad news about that country's economy. They cannot be blamed for the collapse of currencies and countries. On the other hand, if speculators attack countries just because they can, it is easier to see them as destabilizing forces that sabotage countries to financially benefit themselves.[43]

After the East Asian crisis, the IMF reevaluated its staunch advocacy of liberalization of capital. In 2012, it started to urge states to implement the capital account liberalization most appropriate for their economies and to do so gradually. It cautioned against jumping into opening the capital account before establishing the institutional framework needed for monitoring that account.[44] This was a historic moment for the IMF.[45] All through the 1990s, it was fixated on the idea of establishing the freedom of capital as an international norm and was eagerly nudging states to endorse that norm. The IMF's conversion to a more cautious approach to the liberalization of capital flows is at odds with the OECD's endorsement of that liberalization and clauses in BITs that favor the freedom of movement of capital.[46]

---

[43] Krugman, *supra* note 41, at 346.

[44] IMF, *The Liberalization and Management of Capital Flows: An Institutional View*, Nov. 14, 2012.

[45] Claus D. Zimmermann, *A Contemporary Concept of Monetary Sovereignty* 44 (2013).

[46] *Id.* at 48–52.

12. The 2008 financial crisis

When the 2008 crisis erupted, the world was still split into deficit countries and surplus countries. The deficits of the United States were counterbalanced by the surpluses of Germany, China and East Asian states. Asian countries, which had decided to never again subject their economies to IMF control, made it a point to maintain large trade surpluses. These surpluses enabled them to stockpile FX reserves, the insurance they needed against unpredictable market events. Some called the monetary system that prevailed in the 2000s Bretton Woods II. It was obvious that the US trade deficits were driving growth in Asia, exactly the way they had fueled growth before in post-war Europe. Asian countries were the willing collectors of dollars that they used to buy safe assets, primarily US government bonds.

This system seemed to be working as long as the United States ran deficits and the Asian states kept on stockpiling US dollars and debt. In fact, before the 2008 crisis, the United States borrowed heavily at low IRs, via the T-bill market, from the surplus countries to finance its persistent deficits. Foreign governments' holdings of US government bonds rose from approximately $756 billion in 1999 to $3.3 trillion in 2008. Surplus countries and deficit countries used the IMF as a forum to argue about who had the duty to take action to correct the global imbalances.[1] Germany argued that because the eurozone as a whole had a deficit (Germany's surplus was offset by other states' deficits), global imbalances were not an EU issue.[2] China also deflected US pressure to appreciate the yuan.

Multilateral consultations through the IMF did not produce tangible results.[3] The IMF churned out a number of papers in which it re-iterated what it had been advocating for years: the United States should save more by shrinking its budget and BOP deficits. China and Japan should regurgitate domestic demand instead of relying on exports for growth. The euro area, and especially the country with the largest savings, Germany, could contribute to global growth

---

[1]   *See*, e.g. Jonathan D. Ostry and Atish R. Ghosh, *Obstacles to International Policy Coordination, and How to Overcome Them*, at 25, IMF Staff Discussion Note, SDN/13/11, Dec. 2013.

[2]   Thomas Oatley, *International Political Economy* 236 (2012).

[3]   *See*, e.g. IMF, Staff Report on the Multilateral Consultation on Global Imbalances with China, the Euro Area, Japan, Saudi Arabia, and the United States, June 29, 2007.

by investing its savings. Unfortunately, the IMF's chastisement of states was so mild that it was hardly heard. The IMF has admitted that its consultations with states yielded only 'modest policy commitments' from them.[4]

Another point of contention during this period was the IMF's 2007 revised surveillance decision.[5] That decision was not popular among emerging market states because it empowered the IMF to use its surveillance function to judge whether the ER of a state was 'fundamentally misaligned' or 'a threat to external stability'. China was not particularly keen on consenting to this type of surveillance because it knew it was conceived to discredit its FEP.[6] Calling an ER 'fundamentally misaligned' could also be used to bring action against a state at the WTO.[7] The GATT agreement provides that states 'shall not, by *exchange action, frustrate the intent* of the provisions' of GATT.[8] If a country considers that any '*benefit* accruing to it' under the GATT is being '*nullified or impaired*' because of the '*failure*' of another state to fulfill its obligations,[9] it can take action against that state. The open-ended nature of this provision makes it easy to allege that a country's ER policy is frustrating the intent of GATT, especially if the IMF is ready to support such allegations.

On September 15, 2008, the IMF was about to publish a report implying that the yuan was fundamentally misaligned. At about the same time, the Lehman Brothers collapsed, triggering an economic crisis in the United States. The ensuing global financial meltdown presented a great opportunity for emerging market states to criticize the IMF and, implicitly, the United States. They pointed out that it was the US economy that had eluded IMF surveillance.[10] The deputy governor of the Bank of China emphasized that the IMF needed to maintain a 'sharp focus on the risks in the major developed countries and their potential spillover effects' to the rest of the world.[11] He accused the IMF

---

[4]   IMF, *Initial Lessons of the Crisis*, para. 25, Feb. 6, 2009 [hereinafter IMF Initial Lessons].

[5]   Bilateral Surveillance over Members' Policies, Decision No. 13919-(07/51), June 15, 2007, *reprinted in* IMF Executive Board Adopts New Decision on Bilateral Surveillance over Members' Policies, Public Information Notice (PIN) No. 07/69, June 21, 2007.

[6]   Paul Blustein, *A Flop and a Debacle: Inside the IMF's Global Rebalancing Acts*, at 7, CIGI Paper No. 4, June 2012.

[7]   *Id.* at 20.

[8]   Art. XV(4), General Agreement on Tariffs and Trade (GATT) 1994, Apr. 15, 1994, Marrakesh Agreement Establishing the World Trade Organization, Annex 1A, 1867 UNTS 187, 33 ILM 1153 (1994). Emphasis added.

[9]   Art. XXIII(1)(a), *id.* Emphasis added.

[10]   Blustein, *supra* note 6, at 21.

[11]   Yi Gang, Statement at Eighteenth Meeting of the International Monetary and Financial Committee, at 3, Oct. 11, 2008.

of 'misfocused surveillance'[12] and asked it to 'consider an *ad hoc* consultation with the United States'.[13] Many at the time traced the root causes of the
financial crisis to the failures of the US financial system and deregulation of
US markets. However, targeting the United States was not fair either. The
readiness of the world to invest uncritically in US debt instruments, including
the unproven MBS, was also responsible for the crisis.

The 2008 G-20 meeting in Washington was the first global attempt to
address the crisis.[14] It was the first G-20 that met as a summit of heads of state
of the world's largest economies. Consensus was achieved at that meeting on
a number of principles, including strengthening market transparency, toughen-
ing the prudential oversight of financial firms and reforming the global financial institutions, such as the IMF. As the crisis continued to rage in 2009, more
concrete steps were adopted at the London Summit.[15] Governments decided
to put together a $1.1 trillion package dedicated to fixing the world economy.
They tripled the resources available to the IMF to $750 billion,[16] agreed to
a new SDR allocation of $250 billion,[17] supported at least $100 billion of additional lending by the multilateral development banks[18] and gave permission to
the IMF to sell some of its gold to finance credit to the poorest countries and
to stabilize its own finances.[19]

The G-20 endorsed bold measures to restore jobs and growth by undertaking
'an unprecedented and *concerted fiscal expansion*' targeted to create or save
millions of jobs which would have otherwise been destroyed.[20] This fiscal
stimulus was an add-on to the monetary stimulus since the CBs of states had
already 'cut aggressively' IRs and had 'pledged to maintain expansionary policies for as long as needed and to use the full range of monetary policy instruments, including unconventional instruments'.[21] States agreed to establish
'a new Financial Stability Board with a strengthened mandate', as a successor
to the existing Financial Stability Forum.[22] The Financial Stability Board was
to 'collaborate with the IMF to provide early warning of macroeconomic and

---

[12]   *Id.*
[13]   *Id.*
[14]   G-20 Declaration of the Summit on Financial Markets and the World Economy,
Nov. 15, 2008, http://www.g8.utoronto.ca/.
[15]   Global Plan for Recovery and Reform, Statement Issued by the G20 Leaders,
Apr. 2, 2009, http://www.g8.utoronto.ca/.
[16]   Para. 5, *id.*
[17]   *Id.*
[18]   *Id.*
[19]   *Id.*
[20]   Para. 6, *id.* Emphasis added.
[21]   Para. 7, *id.*
[22]   Para. 15, *id.*

financial risks and the actions needed to address' these risks.[23] At the 2009 Pittsburg summit, the focus was on achieving strong, sustainable and balanced growth by eliminating unsustainable global imbalances.[24] This was to be accomplished through a peer review process[25] that was eventually formalized as the Mutual Assessment Process under the IMF's auspices.[26] The IMF had already adopted the Flexible Credit Line (FCL)[27] as a tool for increasing its role in crisis prevention. The FCL was designed to provide substantial lending to states with very strong fundamentals and policies before the onset of a crisis. In the same vein, the Precautionary Credit Line was approved as a lending tool in August 2010.

On June 16, 2010, before the G-20 summit in Toronto, the US president sent a letter to the G-20 cautioning against a premature withdrawal of fiscal stimulus, which could result in renewed economic hardships and recession.[28] The letter was, in essence, a request by the world's sovereign to the rest of states not to abandon the fiscal stimulus that was enabling economic recovery. Germany, the leading state in Europe, rebuffed that request, asserting it was time to move from fiscal stimulus to fiscal consolidation.[29] The German finance minister stated bluntly: 'While US policymakers like to focus on short-term corrective measures, we take a longer view and are, therefore, more preoccupied with the implications of excessive deficits and the dangers of high inflation'.[30] Germany, therefore, instead of rooting for stimulus, began to cut its budget deficit and urged the shrinking of deficits of the rest of the eurozone states.[31] The divergence between the US approach to the crisis and the German-led EU approach could not be starker. While the United States addressed the crisis through fiscal stimulus (government spending, tax cuts) and monetary easing, the EU, under the leadership of Germany, adopted austerity (spending cuts and tax hikes). Even the ECB was initially reluctant to follow in the FRS' footsteps of monetary easing.

The divergent economic approaches of the United States and EU made it difficult to achieve consensus at the G-20 Toronto summit.[32] The primary

---

[23] *Id.*

[24] Para. 5, G-20 Leaders Statement: The Pittsburgh Summit, Sept. 24–25, 2009, http://www.g8.utoronto.ca/.

[25] Para. 15, *id.*

[26] IMF, The G-20 Mutual Assessment Process (MAP), Mar. 8, 2018, www.imf.org.

[27] Para. 20, *supra* note 24.

[28] Letter of US President Obama, June 16, 2010.

[29] Oatley, *supra* note 2, at 225.

[30] *Id.*

[31] *Id.*

[32] The G-20 Toronto Summit Declaration, June 27, 2010, http://www.g8.utoronto .ca/.

focus of that summit was recovery from the Great Recession that was grip-
ping the world, and the debt crisis that had splintered European states into
debtors and creditors. No agreement was reached at the summit, though, since
Germany insisted that it was time for austerity and fiscal retrenchment. The
commitment to fiscal consolidation was evident from the communiqué issued
at that summit, which clarified that the 'speed and timing of withdrawing fiscal
stimulus' would be differentiated for and tailored to national circumstances.[33]
Fiscal consolidation was expected to begin in advanced economies in 2011
or even earlier for countries experiencing significant fiscal deficits.[34] At the
conclusion of the summit, the United States remained concerned that its expansionary fiscal and monetary policies would probably spill over to Europe,
helping to increase German imports to the United States rather than propping
up US business and reducing domestic unemployment.[35] Eventually, for the
remainder of 2010, fiscal expansion was reversed in many countries, including
the United States, when a new leadership in Congress concluded that the US
budget deficit was a major problem.[36]

BRICS is the acronym for the emerging market economies of Brazil, Russia,
India, China and South Africa. The first meeting of the group was held in
January 16, 2009[37] at Yekaterinburg, Russia, to grapple with the fallout from
the financial crisis. The countries declared their support for the G-20 handling
of the crisis but at the same time demanded the reform of international financial institutions, a reform that would reflect changes that had taken place in the
world economy.[38] The BRICS claimed that 'emerging and developing economies must have greater voice and representation in international financial
institutions'[39] and that the leadership of those institutions should be appointed
through an 'open, transparent, and merit-based selection process'.[40] At the time
the declaration was issued, it had become an international practice for the head
of World Bank to be an American, and the head of IMF a European.

At the Gyeongju G-20 meeting of October 2010, the United States was
deluged with complaints about its QE policies. As the FRS was creating
dollars to buy assets and ease economic conditions, developing countries

---

[33]   Para. 10, *id.*

[34]   *Id.*

[35]   Oatley, *supra* note 2, at 240.

[36]   Jeffrey Frankel, *International Coordination*, at 8, 2015 Asian Economic Policy
Conference 'Policy Challenges in a Diverging Global Economy', Federal Reserve
Bank of San Francisco, Nov. 19–20, 2015.

[37]   Joint Statement of the BRIC Countries' Leaders, Jan. 16, 2009.

[38]   Para. 3, *id.*

[39]   *Id.*

[40]   *Id.*

were concerned that the increasing supply of dollars, in combination with the low US IRs, was to invade their economies through unsustainable credit and asset bubbles. The communiqué issued at that G-20 meeting reflected these concerns. It called for advanced countries to be vigilant about the disorderly movements of currencies, implying the excessive weakening of the dollar, which increased the volatility of capital flows.[41] The concerns of developing states did not really alter the policy of the United States. In fact, the country proceeded with its expansionary programs and unleashed a new round of QE in November.

At the Seoul G-20 summit, in November 2010,[42] the frustration of states was palpable.[43] The United States came to the summit ready to target surplus countries, and especially China.[44] The rest of the states, though, were more worried about the unconventional monetary expansion of the United States, which was weakening the dollar, rather than China's surplus. The United States and the UK were isolated at that G-20 meeting, because of their QE policies. Many states viewed the US QE as a stealth way to devalue the dollar. The abundance of newly created dollars, owing to monetary expansion, triggered the devaluation of the US currency and boosted US exports. At the conclusion of the summit, the IMF was tasked with developing guidelines to help identify large imbalances,[45] including CA deficits or surpluses, budget deficits, private debt and financial account imbalances. Countries with imbalances had to submit to a sustainability analysis of their imbalances. The IMF issued its first Sustainability Reports in 2011.[46] The reports flagged China, the United States, the UK, Germany, France, Japan and India for having large imbalances.

An act of solidarity during this period was states' joint intervention in the currency market to weaken the yen. The FRS, the Bank of England, the Bank of Canada and the ECB joined the BOJ on March 18, 2011 in a 'concerted intervention' in the FX market to devalue the yen. Japan was badly hit by an earthquake and a tsunami on March 11, 2011.[47] It was expected, therefore, that Japanese investors would try to repatriate their money to help rebuild

---

[41] Para. 2, Communiqué of the Meeting of Finance Ministers and Central Bank Governors, Gyeongju, Korea, Oct. 23, 2010, http://www.g8.utoronto.ca/.

[42] The G-20 Seoul Summit Leaders' Declaration, Nov. 12, 2010 [hereinafter 2010 Seoul Summit], http://www.g8.utoronto.ca/.

[43] Para. 7, *id.*

[44] Sewell Chan, *Nations Agree on Need to Shrink Trade Imbalances*, NY Times, Oct. 22, 2010.

[45] Para. 9, 2010 Seoul Summit, *supra* note 42.

[46] *See*, e.g. IMF, People's Republic of China Sustainability Report (2011); IMF, United States Sustainability Report (2011).

[47] Statement of G-7 Finance Ministers and Central Bank Governors, Mar. 18, 2011, http://www.g8.utoronto.ca/.

the country, boosting demand for the yen. Given the state of the Japanese economy, Japan could ill-afford the yen's appreciation.

After 2011, most global summits ended in bickering, as compromises that could be win–win for all remained elusive. In the meantime, capital holders, unhappy with the low IRs and sluggish economic growth in core states, continued to flock to emerging markets, hunting higher yields. In their 2012 Delhi Declaration, emerging market states yet again voiced their disagreement with the policies of the developed world. They decried the excessive liquidity pumped into the markets by the aggressive monetary policies of developed states that triggered financial instability.[48] Their pleas fell on deaf ears. Core states remained entrenched in their ways, urging others to put together appropriate policies, structural reforms and strong prudential controls so that they could deal with the volatile capital flows coming their way.[49] The IMF initially endorsed the expansionary policies of core states and discounted the negative externalities they inflicted on others. Finally, it started to take seriously the potential spillovers of policies of systemically important states.[50] By September 2013, when the IMF began to emphasize the negative externalities of QE, emerging market states were already dealing with them.[51]

The IMF failed to predict the 2008 crisis. This was not an easy prediction to make. The IMF was under the spell of rich states that at the time believed that financial markets were self-regulating and could function with minimal oversight.[52] The IMF admitted that its fragmented surveillance system made it difficult for it to apprehend the growing vulnerabilities and risks besetting the global economy.[53] It acknowledged that its warnings before the crisis were too 'scattered and unspecific' to attract the attention of states.[54] In addition, it underestimated the combined risks across sectors and the spillovers from the failure of the financial sector.[55] It finally realized that attaching labels to ERs, such as calling them 'fundamentally misaligned', risked damaging its credibility as an independent organization.[56]

---

[48]   Para. 5, Delhi Declaration, Fourth BRICS Summit, Mar. 29, 2012.

[49]   Para. 15, St Petersburg G-20 Leaders' Declaration, Sept. 6, 2013.

[50]   *See*, e.g., IMF, 2014 Triennial Surveillance Review – Report of the External Advisory Group, July 30, 2014.

[51]   IEO, *IMF Response to the Financial and Economic Crisis*, at 11 (2014).

[52]   *Id.* at 12.

[53]   Para. 2, IMF Initial Lessons, *supra* note 4.

[54]   Para. 23, *id.*

[55]   *Id.*

[56]   *See*, IMF, The 2007 Surveillance Decision: Revised Operational Guidance, at 1–2, June 22, 2009.

13. The International Monetary Fund and the world order

13.1 THE STRUCTURE OF THE IMF

Unlike other international institutions whose decision-making process is based on one state, one vote, at the IMF voting power is based on states' contributions (quotas). Upon joining the IMF, a state must deposit with the IMF its capital contribution, its 'quota subscription'. Large and rich states make bigger monetary contributions to the organization and, thus, have more quotas (shares) than smaller and poorer states. The IMF is supposed to function like a credit union. Its mandate has been to provide loans to states that are its members when they face BOP problems.

Twenty-five percent of a state's capital subscription to the IMF must be paid in SDRs or in a reserve currency (dollar, euro, yen, yuan, sterling), what the IMF calls 'freely usable currency'. This is the *reserve tranche* of the quota (*see* Box 13.1). The rest of the quota can be paid in the state's own currency.[1] States that encounter BOP difficulties can borrow their reserve tranche (such borrowing is called 'reserve tranche purchase')[2] from the IMF for free. To borrow more than their reserve tranche from the pooled contributions of all countries, states are charged an IR and are subjected to conditionality. A typical state, for instance Poland, has to contribute 25% of its quota in dollars (or other reserve currencies or SDRs) and the remaining 75% in Polish zloty. It can borrow the 25% reserve tranche without incurring interest charges. If it wishes to borrow more than its reserve tranche it has to pay interest since it will be borrowing, in effect, the reserve currencies contributed by other states. Core states that issue reserve currencies have the option to contribute 100% of their quota in their own currency. Since they can contribute their entire quota in their own currency, their reserve tranche, the amount they can borrow from the IMF without incurring interest charges, is 100% of their quota.

---

[1]   Art. III, Sec. 3(a), Articles of Agreement of the IMF, July 22, 1944, as amended effective January 26, 2016 by the Board of Governors Resolution No. 66-2, December 15, 2010 [hereinafter IMF Articles of Agreement].
[2]   Art. XXX (c), *id.*

BOX 13.1 FINANCIAL ENGINEERING AT THE IMF

What happens if a state does not have the SDRs or reserve currencies to pay the 25% reserve tranche of its quota?

*   the state borrows SDRs from a state that is willing to lend SDRs to it;
*   the state uses these 'borrowed SDRs' to pay the 25% of its quota;
*   the state then executes a 'reserve tranche purchase' – borrows from the IMF the 'borrowed SDRs' it has just used to pay for its quota in exchange for its domestic currency;
*   the state uses these SDRs to repay the SDR loan it received from the lending state.

This was the way the United States helped Zambia and Haiti to meet their quota obligations to the IMF. These types of transactions are usually completed within a day.

Source: IMF Financial Operations, at 100 (2016).

The quota of each state tends to reflect the size of its economy based on a formula developed by the IMF. Quota allocations are also influenced by political considerations. States care about their quotas because the quotas determine the amount of influence they have on the IMF decision-making and the amount of money they can borrow from it. States can borrow from the IMF an annual limit of 145% of their quota and a cumulative limit of 435% of their quota. In exceptional circumstances, though, the IMF can lend even more than those amounts.[3]

The quotas determine the voting power of a state at the IMF. States have *basic* votes and *quota-based* votes. The basic votes are 5.502% of the total voting power of all of the 189 member states. The basic votes are equally distributed among member states.[4] This equal distribution is supposed to benefit poor states that do not make large contributions to the IMF and their quota-based votes are rather small. The quota-based votes are allocated based on the contributions of states to the IMF and are calculated as 1 vote per 100 000 SDRs. The United States has the largest quota – a total 82 994 000 SDRs. This translates into 831 406 votes – 16.53% of the total votes at the IMF.

---

[3] *See* Access Policy and Limits in the Credit Tranches and under the Extended Fund Facility and on Overall Access to the Fund's General Resources, and Exceptional Access Policy: Review and Modification, Selected Decisions and Selected Documents of the IMF, 39th Issue, Mar. 31, 2017.

[4] This distribution provides each state with 1 464 basic votes.

China's 30 482 000 SDRs give it 306 293 votes – 6.09% of the total votes. China's quota is the third largest quota after those of the United States and Japan. Still, having 6.09% of total votes is quite small given that China is the second largest economy in the world. Towards the bottom of pyramid, Nauru, a small state, has only 2 800 00 SRDs giving it 1 492 votes, a mere 0.03% of total votes. Advanced developed states, the OECD states as a group, have overwhelming power at the IMF– 62% of voting power.

The decision-making organs at the IMF are the Board of Governors and the Executive Board. Each country that is a member of the IMF can appoint an official at the Board of Governors – usually that country's CB president or finance minister. The Board of Governors meets only once per year. It entrusts, therefore, many decisions to the Executive Board made up of civil servants. The Board of Governors retains power in crucial matters such as quota increases,[5] allocation and cancellation of SDRs,[6] admission of new members, requests for the compulsory withdrawal of a member[7] and amendment of IMF Articles of Agreement.[8] The Board of Governors is assisted by the International Monetary and Financial Committee. The Committe is made up of 24 members, usually finance ministers, and makes decisions by consensus.

The Executive Board is the primary legislative and executive organ of the IMF and manages its everyday operations. It usually makes decisions by consensus. It consists of 24 executive directors.[9] Five of those directors used to be appointed by the states with the largest quotas. These states were the United States, Japan, Germany, France and the UK. After the adoption of an amendment to the Articles of Agreement, on January 26, 2016, the IMF's Executive Board consists entirely of elected executive directors, ending the privileged category of states that could just appoint directors. Today, eight states, because of their large quotas, have enough voting power to vote for an executive director who represents their exclusive interests. These states are the United States, Japan, China, Germany, France, the UK, Russia and Saudi Arabia. The rest of the states form multicountry voting constituencies to elect the 19 remaining members of the Executive Board. For instance, Italy, with a voting power of 3%, teams up with Greece, Portugal, Albania, Malta and San Marino to knock together a constituency with a voting power of 4%. Other European states have followed similar strategies. European states, taking into account both single-state and multistate constituencies, appoint seven out of

---

5   Art. III, Sec. 2(c), IMF Articles of Agreement, *supra* note 1.
6   Art. XVIII, Sec. 4(d), *id.*
7   Art. XXVI, Sec. 2(c), *id.*
8   Art. XXVIII(a), *id.*
9   The Board of Governors may change the number of executive directors. *See* art. XII, Sec. 3(b)–(c), *id.*

24 executive directors at the IMF. On the contrary, African countries, because of their small quotas, have only two multistate constituencies, appointing only two executive directors.

The BRICS have complained that their voting power does not reflect the size of their economies. The 2016 IMF reforms were supposed to address the mismatch between countries' economic size and their quotas. Many states, however, have remained dissatisfied, especially because the United States is the only state that has retained a veto power at the IMF. Constitutive decisions at the IMF require an 85% majority of the Board of Governors. As a result, the United States, with about 17% voting power, is the only state that can veto these decisions. Germany, France and the UK, along with the voting constituency that includes Belgium and the Netherlands, master 19% of total votes. These states as a group can also become veto players.

On the other hand, the BRICS are unlikely to build alliances. If the BRICS were to cooperate, they could establish a veto-yielding alliance. China, Russia and the voting constituencies headed by Brazil, India and South Africa have enough voting power, all together, to block decisions that require an 85% majority. The rivalry between China and India, however, makes such a coalition doubtful. Furthermore, in order to form such an alliance, South Africa and Brazil must be able to carry along with them the other members of their voting constituencies – not an easy feat. Since developing states rarely form partnerships at the IMF, the interests of the core countries, the typical creditors, tend to prevail.

A way to change the power dynamics is to tweak the formula that the IMF uses to assign quotas to states. That formula was last changed in 2008 when rich states came under pressure to develop a simple and transparent formula that is feasible to implement based on high-quality and widely available data. The GDP, it was agreed, should be the most important variable in the formula because it helps classify states based on their economic strength.[10] Quotas are assigned, therefore, based on the GDP of states (50% weight in the formula), the openness of their economy measured by the extent of their participation in global trade and finance (30% weight), their economic variability (15% weight) and their international reserves (5% weight).[11] Economic variability, called the 'vulnerability variable' in the formula, is a measure of states' potential need for IMF resources. It is calculated based on the variability of capital flows – the higher the variability of capital flows the stronger the likelihood that a state may need financing from the IMF.[12] The formula includes a

---

[10]   IMF Financial Operations, at 14 (2016).
[11]   IMF Quotas, Factsheet, Apr. 19, 2018.
[12]   IMF, Quota Formula Review – Initial Considerations, at 23, Feb. 10, 2012.

'compression factor' whose practical purpose is to suppress the magnitude of quotas assigned to large states, and thus, to help increase the quotas of smaller states.[13] This compression factor has benefitted mostly upper-middle-income European states.[14]

13.2   SPECIAL DRAWING RIGHTS

The IMF creates SDRs and allocates them to states in proportion to their quotas. The SDRs are not used at this point as real money, a means of exchange in everyday transactions. They serve, though, as a unit of account and a store of value. Central banks hold SDRs in their reserves and an ER is calculated daily between the SDR and the world's reserve currencies. States can use their SDRs to obtain reserve currencies from other states to pay for their imports or pay back external debt. The SDRs, therefore, function more like a reserve asset rather than a reserve currency. They are a way to *mobilize* the currencies printed by the reserve-currency-issuing states.

The SDR is a basket currency. Its value is calculated daily based on the sum of weights of component currencies. These component currencies must be what the IMF calls, 'freely usable currencies' – the global reserve currencies.[15] For a currency to be considered freely usable, it must meet two conditions: it must be used widely in international transactions and traded in the global currency markets.[16] To assess whether a currency meets these two conditions, the IMF examines many factors, including the degree to which CBs of other states accumulate that currency in their FX reserves and the share of the currency in the FX turnover and global debt markets.[17] The SDR basket is made up as follows: the US dollar that has a 41.73% weight in the basket, the euro 30.93%, the yuan 10.92%, the yen 8.33% and the pound sterling 8.09%.[18]

A state can use the SDRs allocated to it to obtain reserve currencies. When they exchange their SDRs for reserve currencies, states become debtors. The country that receives these SDRs, because it supplied reserve currencies, is the creditor. The debtor pays interest on the amount of SDRs it exchanges for reserve currencies.[19] The SDRs' IR is determined weekly based on the weighted average of short-term bonds of states whose currencies make up the

[13]   IMF Financial Operations, *supra* note 10, at 15.

[14]   Edwin M. Truman, *Making Sense of the IMF Quota Formula*, Peterson Institute for International Economics, Aug. 30, 2012.

[15]   IMF Financial Operations, *supra* note 10, at 85–6.

[16]   Art. XXX(f), IMF Articles of Agreement, *supra* note 1.

[17]   IMF Financial Operations, *supra* note 10, at 97.

[18]   *Id.* at 86.

[19]   *Id.* at 8.

SDR basket.[20] The allocation of SDRs by the IMF is an unconditional form of lending. Unlike the rest of the IMF lending, states do not have to meet conditions to be allocated SDRs or to use the SDRs allocated to them by the IMF to borrow reserve currencies from other states.[21]

As we have seen in Chapter 8, SDRs were created in 1969 because the global supply of gold was not enough to back up the rapid creation of dollars. The dollar glut, created by the persistent US deficits, undermined the confidence of the world in the stability of the dollar as a reserve currency. As speculation against the dollar intensified, the United States convinced its allies to create the SDRs as a new reserve asset issued by the IMF. This made it possible for the United States to borrow other currencies from the IMF, such as German marks and Swiss francs, against its SDRs allocation to sell in the market to support the declining dollar. The creation of SDRs eliminated the need to have to sell gold to the IMF in order to get the currencies that the United States needed to intervene in the market to boost its currency. SDRs have been allocated three times. The first allocation happened between 1970 and 1972, totaling 9.3 billion SDRs. The second allocation was distributed between 1979 and 1981, amounting to 12.1 billion SDRs. The third allocation in August 2009 was the largest – 182.7 billion SDRs. The total SDRs amount to 204.1 billion.

The SDRs allocated to the United States are held at the ESF. Each year, the Treasury receives interest payments on the United States SDR reserves at the IMF because of the US creditor status at the fund. The SDRs at the Treasury's disposal increase its capacity to lend to foreign governments and conduct interventions in the currency market. The Treasury can even issue SDR certificates to the FRS in exchange for dollars. By issuing such certificates it obtains from the FRS the dollars it needs to intervene in the currency market or to provide credit facilities to other states. Issuing SDR certificates to obtain dollars *monetizes* the SDRs – it transforms them into dollars. Such monetization is permitted under the 1968 Special Drawing Rights Act.[22]

13.3   THE IMF AS LENDER OF LAST RESORT AND CONDITIONALITY

The IMF's mission is to ensure the stability of the international monetary system – the system of ERs and international payments that enables countries, and their people, to transact with one another. To achieve this global mission

---

[20]   *Id.* at 87.
[21]   *Id.* at 88.
[22]   C. Randall Henning, *The Exchange Stabilization Fund: Slush Money or War Chest?* 41, Institute for International Economics (1999).

the main responsibility of the IMF is to lend money to states that cannot find sufficient financing in the market on affordable terms to meet their international liabilities, for instance, to pay for imports or pay back their debt. Unlike other international institutions, such as the World Bank or regional development banks, the IMF is not technically a lending institution. Instead, it is a repository of states' currencies and a portion of their FX reserves that is contributed to it through their capital subscriptions in the form of quotas. The IMF uses the pool of reserve currencies it has at its disposal to extend credit to states when they face BOP difficulties.[23]

The IMF funds most of its lending programs through the capital contributions – the quotas – of states that amount to 477 billion SDRs ($653 billion). The IMF can supplement its capital by borrowing from states. The New Arrangements to Borrow (NAB) are credit arrangements between 38 member states and the IMF, based on which it can borrow from them temporarily. The NAB were originally set up in 1995 and were expanded to 370 billion SDRs in 2009. Because of the quota increase that took effect in 2016, the NAB were reduced to 182 billion SDRs. They are renewed periodically.[24]

The General Agreements to Borrow (GAB) are credit arrangements between 11 IMF members (plus Saudi Arabia, which has an associated agreement under the GAB) and the IMF. They were established in 1962 to augment the IMF's financial resources. In 1983, the GAB was expanded to 17 billion SDRs plus 1.5 billion SDRs provided by Saudi Arabia.[25] Both the NAB and GAB have been established to ensure that the IMF has sufficient financial ammunition in the case of a major crisis. However, the NAB is the IMF's first and principal recourse for funds after the quotas.[26] The IMF can tap into the GAB only when a proposal for the re-activation of the NAB, for an additional period, is rejected by the NAB participating states.

Another source of funding is the bilateral lending arrangements between the IMF and various states. Thirty-five bilateral agreements have provided the IMF with a 'second line of defense' of 281 billion SRDs ($379 billion).[27] Bilateral agreements constitute a second line of defense because they can be tapped only when the quotas and NAB are not sufficient and the IMF's available resources have fallen below 100 billion SDRs. The bilateral agreements plus the NAB (182 billion SDRs) plus the quotas (477 billion SDRs), after subtracting 20% that IMF keeps aside for prudential purposes, provide the IMF

---

[23] IMF Financial Operations, *supra* note 10, at 6.
[24] IMF, Consents and Adherences to the Proposed Expansion of the Fund's New Arrangements to Borrow (NAB), July 28, 2017.
[25] IMF Financial Operations, *supra* note 10, at 19.
[26] *Id.* at 19, n. 9.
[27] *Id.* at 22.

with a total lending capacity close to $1 trillion.[28] The IMF also holds gold because states used to pay a portion of their quota in gold. Its gold amounts to about 2 814 metric tons,[29] making the IMF one of the largest official holders of gold. The IMF can sell all or a portion of its gold after getting the approval of 85% of its members.[30] In December 2010, it sold 403.3 metric tons of gold[31] for 6.85 billion worth of SDRs.[32]

The IMF has made efforts to provide ex-ante precautionary lending to states that face economic difficulties but have not yet reached the crisis level. Not many states are eager to ask for precautionary lending though. They know that such requests publicize their economic troubles and trigger speculative attacks on their currencies. A typical debtor state that wants to improve its standing in the market knows that it would be stigmatized if it asked for precautionary assistance. Precautionary IMF lending includes the Flexible Credit Line (FCL) that is offered only to states that have strong macroeconomic fundamentals.[33]

Stand-by arrangements[34] are used for post-crisis lending. These are unilateral decisions of the Executive Board to provide assistance to a state.[35] They comprise a Letter of Intent, in which a state spells out its intention to borrow from the IMF and its decision to abide with IMF conditionality,[36] and two memoranda. The Memorandum of Economic and Financial Policy enumerates the policies that a state promises to adopt. The Technical Memorandum lists the performance criteria and targets that are used to determine whether a state abides with the IMF conditions. Quantitative Performance Criteria are measurable criteria based on which the IMF evaluates states in order to decide whether it is worth continuing engaging with them. Examples of Quantitative Performance Criteria include the achievement of a fiscal surplus of a certain percentage and limits on external borrowing. Structural benchmarks, non-quantifiable measures such as the reduction of the size of public sector, are also used to assess the economic performance of states.[37]

---

[28]   About 696 billion SDRs (approximately $954 billion).
[29]   In 2016, they were valued at 82.1 billion SDRs, about $110 billion, *id.* at 34.
[30]   Art. V, Sec. 12(c), IMF Articles of Agreement, *supra* note 1.
[31]   IMF Financial Operations, *supra* note 10, at 34–5.
[32]   *Id.* at 106, n. 4.
[33]   IMF Flexible Credit Line (FCL), Mar. 8, 2018, https://www.imf.org.
[34]   *See* arts V, Sec. 3(a), XXX(b), IMF Articles of Agreement, *supra* note 1.
[35]   *See* Claus D. Zimmermann, *A Contemporary Concept of Monetary Sovereignty* 67–8 (2013) (discussing whether stand-by arrangements are unilateral IMF decisions or agreements between the IMF and borrowing states).
[36]   On the legal nature of letter of intent, *see* Mauro Megliani, *Sovereign Debt: Genesis – Restructuring – Litigation* 133–4 (2015).
[37]   IMF Conditionality Fact Sheet, at 3, https://www.imf.org.

All loans provided by the IMF, except for the FCL, are subject to conditionality.[38] While the IMF has made efforts to streamline its conditionality, it is still imposes many conditions for providing loans to states. Most of these conditions touch on politically sensitive issues, such as freezes or reductions in wages, cutbacks in welfare programs and pensions, and tax hikes.[39] The purpose of conditionality is to ensure that states will be able to solve their BOP problems, within the timeframe of the IMF program, and that the IMF and other creditors will be paid back. Creditor states like to argue that doing away with conditionality will generate moral hazard. At the other extreme, imposing conditionality to the degree of pushing states to avoid the IMF at all costs is not the way to build a robust global economic system.

The IMF cannot qualify as lender of last resort because of its limited resources and the strict conditions it imposes on states that borrow from it. States that issue their own reserve currencies have lenders of last resort – their own CBs. Developing countries, especially those that borrow in foreign currency, cannot count on their CBs in time of need. Unless these CBs have substantial FX reserves, they cannot bail out their government, or private firms that have accumulated foreign debt. In fact, it is because the IMF is slow to act and imposes conditionality that developing countries have made it a priority to build up their reserves. The IMF resources are also much below the liquidity that many core countries with large liabilities might need in times of economic turmoil. The liabilities of the banking sectors of certain developed states, for instance Switzerland, are substantial multiples of their GDP.[40]

13.4   SURVEILLANCE AND COUNTRY CERTIFICATION

After the demise of Bretton Woods, the semi-orderly monetary system of fixed ERs ceased to exist. As states are now the makers of their FEP, the IMF has turned its focus on the surveillance of monetary and financial developments.[41] Surveillance implies control. Critics have noted that IMF surveillance has become the way for a small number of 'rule-making states' to dress up their

---

[38]   Art. V, Sec. 3, IMF Articles of Agreement, *supra* note 1.

[39]   *See generally* Jesse Griffiths and Konstantinos Todoulos, *Conditionally Yours: An Analysis of the Policy Conditions Attached to IMF Loans*, European Network on Debt and Development (EURODAC), Apr. 2014.

[40]   Maurice Obstfeld, *The International Monetary System: Living with Asymmetry* 301, at 314, in 'Globalization in an Age of Crisis: Multilateral Economic Cooperation in the Twenty-First Century' (Robert C. Feenstra and Alan M. Taylor, eds, 2013).

[41]   *See*, e.g. Decision No. 15203-(12/72) on Bilateral and Multilateral Surveillance, July 18, 2012.

preferences as universal standards that are best for all.[42] Many have criticized the ineffectiveness and lack of evenhandedness of IMF's surveillance[43] and the bias of its advice to states.[44]

The IMF conducts two types of surveillance: global and country-specific or bilateral surveillance. The results of global surveillance are reported in a number of publications, such as the World Economic Outlook, the Financial Sector Stability Assessment, regional economic outlooks and technical and policy studies. The IMF Spillover Reports analyze the externalities inflicted on others by the policies of four systemic countries and one region, what the IMF calls the S-5 – US, China, the eurozone, Japan and UK. The External Sector Report assesses states' FEP including their ERs, their BOP positions, the adequacy of their reserves and capital controls. The IMF claims to pay particular attention to the loose policies and lax financial regulations of core states that could trigger destabilizing capital flows to the periphery. The Financial Sector Stability Assessments are mandatory for states with important financial sectors. Twenty-nine states have been classified as such states.

Country-specific or bilateral surveillance is based on article IV of the IMF Articles of Agreement. The IMF has to conduct bilateral meetings with each and every state that is its member. These meetings are a way to evaluate the internal and external stability of states, especially states that finance themselves through the global bond market and are not dependent on the IMF. Bilateral surveillance can generate animosity between the IMF and the states surveyed.[45] The IMF has struggled to reconcile its two roles: that of advisor of states and that of relentless enforcer of fiscal discipline.[46]

The IMF issues standards and codes for international best practices in several areas, including economic and financial statistics, monetary and fiscal transparency, financial sector soundness and the promotion of good governance. Many states believe that their adoption of these standards may convince private investors that their policies enjoy the IMF's stamp of

---

[42]   Domenico Lombardi and Ngaire Woods, *The Politics of Influence: An Analysis of IMF Surveillance*, at 13, CIGI Working Paper No. 17, Feb. 2007.

[43]   *See*, e.g. IEO, *IMF Response to the Financial and Economic Crisis*, at 25 (2014).

[44]   *See*, e.g. IMF, 2014 Triennial Surveillance Review – Report of the External Advisory Group, at 7, July 30, 2014.

[45]   *See* Bessma Momani and Kevin A. English, *In Lieu of an Anchor: The Fund and its Surveillance Function* 429, in 'Handbook of International Political Economy of Monetary Relations' (Thomas Oatley and W. Kindred Winecoff, eds, 2014).

[46]   Nadia Rendak, *Monitoring and Surveillance of the International Monetary System: What Can be Learnt From the Trade Field?* 204, at 230, in 'The Rule of Law in Monetary Affairs' (Thomas Cottier et al., 2014).

approval.[47] The IMF's endorsement of standards enacted by the various global, standard-setting bodies,[48] like the FSB, elevates them into mandatory rules for states that covet the IMF's help.

---

[47] For a comprehensive discussion of these standards and states' compliance, *see* Lombardi and Woods, *supra* note 42, at 16–24.

[48] *See* Chapter 16.

PART IV

Global bodies, societies and guilds

14. The global law-making process

14.1 TRANSNATIONAL FINANCIAL REGULATION

Bankers frequently claim that financial markets need to be liberated from the tyranny of regulation to properly function. By this, they do not mean the abolishment of regulation. Calls for deregulation imply the delegation of regulation from state to non-state actors such as industry's associations, in other words, self-regulation. Because markets cannot function in an orderly fashion without the rule of law, including the sanctity of contracts, enforcement of property rights, legal personality and liability rules, they cannot be totally deregulated. However, the state can abstain from being directly involved in them. It can give license to market participants to self-regulate to some extent by entering into contractual agreements among themselves. When these contracts are violated, disputes can be decided in a court of law, because contracts – the bread and butter of financial self-regulation – are instruments enforced by courts and arbitral tribunals.[1]

Regulatory norms made by private bodies or through public–private partnerships (PPPs) have been acclaimed as the best way to codify the practices of private financial actors. *Lex mercatoria*, commercial law, is based on the practices of merchants worldwide and operates under states' blessing. Concomitantly *lex financeria* is the law based on the practices of financial firms. In fact, both commercial law and financial law are part of what some label *global administrative law*. Global administrative law,[2] or *transnational law*,[3] does not necessarily have to be made by international organizations established through treaties. Many other processes are available for making such law.

Transnational financial law has been made by *treaty-based organizations* such as the IMF. It has also been made informally by *government regulators*

---

[1]   Katharina Pistor, *A Legal Theory of Finance*, at 13, Columbia Law School, Public Law and Legal Theory Working Paper Group, Paper Number 13-348, May 9, 2013.
[2]   Benedict Kingsbury et al., *The Emergence of Global Administrative Law*, 68 Law & Contemporary Problems 15 (2005).
[3]   Philip Jessup, *Transnational Law* (1956).

from various states that get together to codify shared norms. Hybrid *PPPs* and even *private bodies* churn out standards, guidelines and codes of conduct. These private or quasi-private bodies often do not include participants from developing states. Most international bodies, the standard-makers and agenda-setters in international finance, have been structured to be exclusive and, thus, can place barriers on who may become a member. Others may have universal membership but their rule-making process is delegated to a minority of participants who usually come from core states.[4] For example, the International Organization of Securities Commissions is the international body that brings together the securities regulators of various states. However, not all states are represented or have the same voice in that body. Securities commissions that regulate the largest securities markets are basically the rule-making machinery at the International Organization of Securities Commissions. Despite this, or because of this, the organization considers itself 'the global standard setter for the securities sector'.[5]

The Society for Worldwide Interbank Financial Telecommunications (SWIFT), the nervous system of financial communications, is a Belgian private society tightly regulated by the EU that obeys US anti-terrorism laws. SWIFT has participated in a US surveillance program of financial transactions whose purpose is to stop the financing of terrorism. SWIFT also had to implement the EU financial sanctions against Iran by banning Iranian banks, including Iran's CB, from its network. Iran had no immediate recourse against a Belgian private company that had banned it from its network, even if that ban constituted, in essence, a financial blockade conducted by states it considered enemies.

The International Swaps and Derivatives Association (ISDA) is a non-profit industry association that manages the derivatives market. The ISDA has developed the so-called 'ISDA Master Agreement' and a number of other standards whose purpose is to ensure the enforceability of derivatives contracts. The ISDA standards are central to the functioning of the derivatives market even for the financial firms of states that do not belong to the ISDA.

Another exclusive NGO is the Group of Thirty (G-30), which calls itself 'a collection of leading minds'[6] on economic and financial issues. It was founded in 1978 in the United States as a non-profit organization with a grant from the Rockefeller Foundation. The group's members are drawn mainly from current or former central bankers, regulators, private sector bankers

---

   [4]   Chris Brummer, *Soft Law and the Global Financial System: Rule Making in the 21st Century* 188 (2012).

   [5]   About IOSCO, www.iosco.org.

   [6]   Group of 30, Frequently Asked Questions, www.group30.org.

and academic economists. Members participate in their individual capacity. Membership is limited to 30 individuals and is determined by the trustees of the group when a place becomes open.[7] In 2018, the European Ombudsman recommended that the president of the ECB suspend his membership in the G-30 because of the secrecy surrounding the group, especially regarding how its members are chosen and what is discussed at its meetings. Given that the G-30 includes representatives from a number of major banks, directly or indirectly supervised by the ECB, the participation of the ECB's president in the group created doubts about the ECB's independence.[8]

Chapter 16 examines the public, club-like bodies that consist of national official regulators from like-minded states that gather together to make global financial law that is *de facto* binding on all states. Chapter 15 examines the private, club-like bodies, including firms and industry associations, such as SWIFT and the ISDA mentioned above, which constitute the backbone of global financial infrastructure. The key position of these private bodies in the global financial system derives from the implicit understanding that they are capable of regulating themselves and policing their peers. The 2008 financial crisis put them under the spotlight, however, by revealing conflicts of interest that cast doubt on their effectiveness and independence. As a result, states started to supervise them and regulate them much more closely.

Some still claim that the privatization of economic lawmaking under public oversight is the best way to avoid the proliferation of global public bureaucracy. Nobody has the need or time for universal, sclerotic bodies incapable of action and inundated by states whose firms are irrelevant for the functioning of global markets. Having all states represented in international financial bodies based on one state, one vote, or population size can distend such bodies to the point of dysfunction that many universal public institutions display. Instead of relying on cumbersome inter-state bargaining, it is better to allow for the bottom-up production of law through private actors.

The problem with the private creation of law is the perpetuation of exclusiveness that pervades the world public order. The lack of inclusiveness of global financial bodies, their democratic deficit, makes global financial law look like a tool that safeguards the interests of a clan of states as they seek to expand and dominate others.[9] Yet private financial law enjoys the status of law since it is implemented and enforced by the majority of states. While many

---

[7] *Id.*

[8] Recommendations of the European Ombudsman on the Involvement of the President of the European Central Bank and Members of its Decision-Making Bodies in the 'Group of Thirty', Case 1697/2016/ANA, Jan. 15, 2018.

[9] B.S. Chimni, *International Institutions Today: An Imperial Global State in the Making*, 15 European Journal of International Law 1 (2004).

protest against the lawmaking privileges of rich dominant actors, they cannot really afford to rebel against the *status quo*. They know that such rebellion will be self-defeating, a self-inflicted ostracization from the global networks that facilitate transactions and trade and generate prosperity for states.

14.2 THE PRINCIPLES OF GLOBAL FINANCIAL ORDER

A private company backed by the political power of a state can be a frightening entity. An easy example is the East Indian Company, whose economic power was backed up by the political might of the British Empire. To ascertain the right of the company to sell opium to China, the empire waged two wars.[10] In 2013, it was revealed that the technology giants of the United States, including those beloved by the public, like Facebook and Apple, had allowed their networks to be used for surveillance by the US National Security Agency, throwing into question their independence from the state. The revelations prompted states, such as Brazil, to prevent US technology companies from operating in their territory unless they were ready to move some their data collection infrastructure to them.

Big powers tend to create corporate forms that enable them to spread their might to the world. The East Indian Company facilitated the expansion of the British Empire. The United States has invented the multinational corporation – the building block of US-type capitalism. US capitalism is based on the idea that a company established in a state can, while pursuing its private interest, become the most efficient instrument for broadening the dominance of that state over other states.[11] The state, based on the US model, is the underlying force of corporate power as it provides private firms with the legal infrastructure (e.g. legal personality,[12] limited liability)[13] that they need to thrive. In

---

[10]   Luigi Zingales, *A Capitalism for the People: Recapturing the Lost Genius of American Prosperity* 35 (2012).

[11]   After World War I, the United States could have structured its economy as state capitalism. Instead, it opted for the creation of multinational corporate monopolies, *see* Michael J. Hogan, *Informal Entente: The Private Structure of Cooperation in Aglo-American Economic Diplomacy, 1918–1928*, at 210–12 (1991).

[12]   Including the right to spend their money to influence elections and their right to enjoy religious freedom. *See Citizens United v. Federal Election Commission*, 558 U.S. 310 (2010); *Burwell v. Hobby Lobby Stores*, 573 U.S. 22 (2014). For an overview on how US corporations acquired rights equivalent to those of individuals, *see* Adam Winkler, *We the Corporations: How American Businesses Won their Civil Rights* (2018).

[13]   In *Jesner v. Arab Bank*, the US Supreme Court held that the *Alien Tort Statute*, which makes it possible for foreign nationals to initiate lawsuits in US courts for

contrast, in state capitalism, often associated with China, the state is upfront and present in the companies it builds and operates. State capitalism is based on a streamlined relationship between the central power of the state and its profit-generating units – its firms.

State capitalism, one could say, is more like a central processing unit while US capitalism is more like a distributed network – an internet. State capitalism is a primitive sort of economic order because the hand of the state is visible in every economic activity. US capitalism is much more advanced. The private companies that become the vehicles of hegemonic expansion conceal the aspiring hegemon through a diffusion of power that nurtures the incredible resilience of this capitalistic form.[14] US capitalism, we could say, functions like an octopus. The majority of the brain of an octopus resides in its arms. These arms do some of the octopus's thinking and remain responsive even when they are severed from its body.[15] This is exactly how US capitalism works: through a number of private companies or associations, non-governmental organizations (NGOs). These private entities, as they calculate how to advance their wealth and serve their interests, fulfill, wittingly or unwittingly, the purposes of the state that sponsors their global expansion.

China's state capitalism has started to emulate the US version.[16] China has many valuable privately held companies, including Baidu, Alibaba, Tencent and Xiaomi, collectively known as BATX, that are competing head-to-head with Facebook, Amazon, Netflix and Google, collectively known as FANG. It is hard to tell the difference between what is private and public in China because private corporations latch onto the state to ensure their predominance and longevity. The state, in turn, meddles in all industries that it considers strategic. 'Made in China by 2025', a Chinese government initiative, aimed to create national champions in robotics, biomedicine, electric vehicles and

---

breaches of international law, such as egregious human rights violations, could not be used to sue corporations. Justice Sotomayor in her dissent, however, argued that US corporations had political spending rights (*Citizens United*) and religious freedom rights (*Hobby Lobby*). It did not make sense, therefore, to have them enjoy the significant benefits of corporate form, and fundamental rights under that form, without requiring them to shoulder fundamental responsibilities. See *Jesner v. Arab Bank*, 138 S.Ct. 1386 (2018). *See also id.*

[14]   *See also* Daniel Immerwahr, *How to Hide an Empire: A History of the Greater United States* (2019).

[15]   Katherine Harmon, *Even Severed Octopus Arms Have Smart Moves*, Scientific American, Aug. 27, 2013.

[16]   We discuss here the economic systems of these two countries not their political systems. The democratic principles upon which the United States is based are very different from the one-party rule of the Chinese state. This is especially so after the 2018 elimination of term limits for China's presidency.

other technologies and demonstrates the large involvement of the state in the Chinese economy. The initiative was viewed as hostile in the United States, an effort to push US technology companies out of the Chinese markets.[17]

US capitalism is tinged with some of the protectionist streak of state capitalism. Tariffs have protected US home-grown industries since the nineteenth century. The government's military expenditures have helped create the internet, satellites and drones that have found commercial applications. The United States, through the FDIC, guarantees bank deposits up to quarter of a million for each depositor. As astutely observed, US capitalism is an 'endlessly calibrated balance between state subsidies, social programs, government contracts, regulation and free will, entrepreneurship and free markets'.[18] In the United States, companies are heavily involved in law-making by putting together NGOs and think-tanks staffed by experts. They lobby the legislature to enact laws that benefit them at the expense of their competitors, a classic form of rent seeking.[19] The United States intervenes in the markets when needed to prevent the acquisition of US firms by foreign companies. The Committee on Foreign Investment in the United States (CFIUS), an inter-ministerial body,[20] has been the fear and dread of many Chinese firms seeking to acquire US and European companies.

Despite their touted differences, in other words, the Chinese type and American way of capitalism are converging. In both cases, a sort of PPP between the state and private sector is at work. Similar partnerships rule the international financial world. The PPPs that are prevalent in finance today enjoy the benefits of two worlds: they are not subject to the transparency requirements of public bodies, while maintaining the prestige of power and benefits associated with being part of a national government or an international regulatory body.[21] For core states it makes sense to have semi-private entities make global financial law as this is an easy way to disguise the power exerted through that law. To give an example, the BIS, the first international financial institution, was created in the inter-war period to facilitate the interjection of

---

[17] US Chamber of Commerce, *Made in China 2015: Global Ambitions Built on Local Protections* (2017).

[18] Bhu Srinivasan, *Americana: A 400-Year History of American Capitalism* 485 (2017).

[19] Zingales, *supra* note 10, at 43.

[20] CFIUS includes the heads of the Department of the Treasury (chair), Department of Justice, Department of Homeland Security, Department of Commerce, Department of Defense, Department of State, Department of Energy, Office of the US Trade Representative and Office of Science & Technology Policy. The CFIUS was established by section 721 of the Defense Production Act of 1950 as amended by the Foreign Investment and National Security Act of 2007 (FINSA). *See* 50 USC §4565.

[21] Zingales, *supra* note 10, at 49.

the depoliticized bond market between the creditor state, the United States, and the debtor states, the European states. The primary purpose of the BIS, according to Young, the banker who sponsored it, was to turn Europe's anger away from their principal creditor, the United States. The BIS was useful because it could provide the '*color of commercialization*'[22] to the whole debt and reparations dispute that was damaging the relationship between the United States and its allies. Shifting the debt to the bond market was a means to shift the blame for its repayment, and the German reparations that had to be made to facilitate that repayment, away from the main creditor, the United States.

The seeming neutrality of global financial bodies, which dresses up their might, has worked relatively well in managing the global financial system. States that sponsor this neutrality have been tempted, though, to break up with it in order to sanction states they do not agree with. Using financial bodies, instead of bullets, as weapons is indeed an irresistible temptation. Global financial bodies are aware that their use as financial weapons of last resort, in violation of their neutrality mandates, would be a sure means to render them obsolete one day. If the global financial system as it stands today is to endure, by enjoying a modicum of legitimacy, its ostensible neutrality must be defended. Some have proposed even more radical objectives such as transparency, participation from a wider base of states,[23] and the possibility of review by non-participating states of the decisions made by the rule-making bodies[24] and their masters.

---

[22]   Beth A. Simmons, *Why Innovate? Founding the Bank for International Settlements*, 45 World Politics 361, at 394 (1993). Emphasis added.

[23]   Kingsbury, *supra* note 2, at 38–40.

[24]   *Id.*

15. Financial infrastructure

15.1 FINANCIAL MARKETS

15.1.1 Markets and Dark Pools

Stock exchanges are auctions, which today happen mostly electronically, where those who want to buy and those who wish sell stocks meet. The New York Stock Exchange (NYSE) has a market capitalization of $18.5 trillion based on the value of the stocks of companies traded there – a 27% share of the global equities market. Out of the 60 major stock exchanges only 16 make the '$1 Trillion Dollar Club', that is they have more than $1 trillion worth of listed shares. This exclusive group includes some of the most quoted names in finance, like NYSE, NASDAQ, LSE, Deutsche Borse and Tokyo Stock Exchange. The top 16 exchanges list 87% of the world's total value in equities. Overall, the stock exchanges of North America and Europe hold a vast share – 40.6 and 19.5%, respectively – of the world's stock market. In Asia, the stock market is dominated by exchanges located in Shenzhen, Hong Kong, Tokyo and Shanghai.

Stock exchanges are vital building blocks of the financial infrastructure of states. In 2018, the US Securities and Exchange Commission (SEC) rejected the sale of Chicago Stock Exchange to a group of private Chinese investors. Critics of the sale in Congress claimed that letting Chinese companies take a major stake in a US stock exchange would 'create a backdoor for the Chinese government to influence American financial infrastructure'.[1] The SEC rejected the deal because of concerns about the ownership structure of North America Casin Holdings, the prospective buyer, and potential difficulties involved in accessing financial records of owners based in China.[2]

Public exchanges provide transparency with respect to who is trading in them and at what price. This creates problems for many investors who prefer anonymity, especially when they buy or sell a large number of securities. Information on the participation in the markets of a large investor trying to

---

[1] Dave Michaels, *SEC Rejects Sale of Chicago Stock Exchange*, WSJ, Feb. 15, 2018.

[2] SEC, Release No. 34-82727, at 33–4, Feb. 15, 2018.

offload or acquire a large number of shares can move the price of those shares against her (*see* Box 15.1). This is why large investors prefer to use brokers that match buy/sell orders from their own, internal pool of customers – what is called *internalizing*. Other brokers send their clients' orders to firms that bypass public exchanges and execute orders in their privately owned '*dark pools*'. Dark pools are informal trading venues set up by banks designed to give those who trade in them anonymity. Using dark pools is cheaper for brokers because they do not have to pay the fees charged by the public exchanges. Dark pools also make it easier for large investors to camouflage their trading patterns. This reduces the chances of others detecting their activity and trading in a way that will disadvantage them (*see* Box 15.1).

BOX 15.1 HIGH-SPEED TRADERS

In 2010, *Hibernia*, a US company, started to build 'Project Express'– a fiber optic line beneath the Atlantic ocean to connect the financial markets of New York and London. A small group of high-frequency traders (HFTs) were keen on using the cable, despite the high fees they had to pay to access it. The cable was expected to reduce the speed of data transmission between New York and London from 64.8 to 59.6 milliseconds. For HFTs, even this tiny reduction in trading time could amount to increased revenue.

HFTs usually test the markets by placing small buy/sell orders at various exchanges. If these orders are quickly filled, it signals that a larger investor may be active in the market. Testing the markets through trial buy/sell orders is a way for HFTs to figure out how investors plan to trade. This enables them to front-run those investors, trade ahead of them and, thus, move the prices of securities against them. In 2017, it was estimated that high-frequency trading constituted 50% of all trades in the US stock market.

Source: Matthew Philips, *Stock Trading is About to Get 5.2 Milliseconds Faster*, Bloomberg, Mar. 29, 2012.

Some have argued that trading outside public exchanges is a step backwards from the progress that has been made by establishing public and transparent markets. Because of the abundance of dark pools, the publicly quoted prices of stocks today do not reflect the real market prices. About 45 dark pools and as many as 200 internalizers compete with 13 public exchanges in the United States. Furthermore, despite the fact that such dark pools are supposed to protect investors from the front-running of high-frequency traders (Box 15.1), some of them do not disclose the high-frequency trading that takes place in them. In January 2016, Credit Suisse and Barclays, two private banks, had to pay $154 million in fines for misleading their clients about the real organization of their dark pools. This and other similar incidents that showcase the advantages enjoyed by market insiders[3] have undermined public confidence in the functionality of free markets.

In addition to exchanges, securities can be bought and sold on the over-the-counter (OTC) market. The bond market and the FX market, the markets that have preoccupied us in this study, are OTC markets. Some derivatives contracts are still executed OTC. Regulators, however, have pushed for their clearance at central clearinghouses so as to increase the transparency of derivatives transactions. Other OTC markets include the money market, and its offshoot, the eurocurrency market.

The largest bond markets in the world are those of the United States ($41 trillion), China ($12.9 trillion), Japan ($12.5 trillion), the UK ($5.7 trillion) and France ($4.5 trillion).[4] States and companies can issue bonds in their domestic currency or in the currency of another state. As we have emphasized, many states issue dollar-dominated bonds to entice creditors to invest in their debt. Creditors know that the local currencies issued by developing states may lose their value, and prefer to invest in the dollar-denominated debt of these states. The currency that companies use to issue debt depends on the global IRs. For example, in 2014, when the real IRs in Europe were close to zero, many US companies ventured into the European bond market and issued euro-denominated bonds.

15.1.2 Currency Market

The currency market is a global, decentralized OTC market consisting of a number of interconnected national and regional markets. It involves all aspects of buying, selling and exchanging currencies at the current price (spot contracts) or at a future pre-determined price (futures and forward contracts). In terms of volume, it is the largest market in the world, followed by the bond market. Roughly $5 trillion are traded daily in it. Trade takes place in the top financial centers of the world (London, New York, Singapore, Tokyo and

---

[3]   *See*, e.g. Andrea Barbon et al., *Brokers and Order Flow Leakage: Evidence from Fire Sales*, Harvard Business School Working Paper 18-046, Dec. 2017; Marco Di Maggio et al., *The Relevance of Broker Networks for Information Diffusion in the Stock Market*, The Twelfth NYU Stern/New York Fed Conference on Financial Intermediation, May 5, 2017; Alan D. Jagolinzer et al., *Political Connections and the Informativeness of Insider Trades*, Rock Center for Corporate Governance at Stanford University, Working Paper 222, Sept. 2016.

[4]   BIS, Summary of Debt Securities Outstanding, June 4, 2019, https://www.bis.org/statistics.

Hong Kong). The largest volume of FX transactions consists of converting currencies into the US dollar, the world's prime reserve currency.

The currency market operates at several levels. At the inter-bank level, a small number of large financial firms execute large volumes of FX trading. These firms are known as the 'dealers'. Dealers facilitate international trade and investment by converting currencies. This so-called 'wholesale trading' is handled basically by two firms: Electronic Broking Services and Thompson Reuters Dealing. Electronic Broking Services was put together in 1990 by some of the worlds largest market-making banks, which sought to eliminate the monopoly power of Thompson Reuters. The inter-bank wholesale market accounts for 51% of all FX transactions. Other players in the currency market include smaller banks, multinational companies (that hedge their FX risk), individuals and well-funded hedge funds that place big bets on the direction of ERs. These rich hedge funds have the capability to move the FX market in the direction that benefits them and, under certain circumstances, their bets against currencies can even knock over powerful states.

In 1992, George Soros, a hedge fund manager and billionaire, bet against the English pound. The CB of England tried to defend its currency but eventually gave up and let it float and depreciate. This successful bet against the pound made Soros famous as the man who broke the Bank of England. The same fate awaited Malaysia in 1997, when speculators bet against its currency, the ringgit. For states, rich speculators who short their currency are profiteers who prey on economies that face temporary difficulties. Currency speculators, though, see themselves as 'vigilantes' who simply spot ahead of others the implosion of misguided government policies. They claim that there is nothing wrong with making money while disciplining governments that follow unsustainable policies. Speculators certainly speed up the impending economic collapse of a state and they do so guilt-free. Their rationale is that a snap collapse, which teaches a lesson to an incompetent government, is preferable to its continuing mishandling of an economy.[5]

Investment banks and asset management firms that manage the money of pension funds, endowments and wealthy families are also big players in the currency market. These firms need FX to purchase foreign stocks or foreign-currency denominated bonds for their clients. Investment firms know their customers and therefore can anticipate their needs. This entices them to take positions in the market to benefit their own bottom line at the expense of the people they are supposed to serve. The FOREX scandal that shook the markets in 2013 had to do with investment banks that took advantage of their

---

[5]   *See generally* Gregory Millman, *Around the World on a Trillion Dollars a Day: How Rebel Currency Traders Destroy Banks and Defy Governments* (1995).

knowledge of their clients' FX needs to front-run them, in this way stacking big profits at their expense. Traders used internet chat rooms to secretly exchange client information so as to rig the WM/Reuters, a benchmark rate in the FX market. Government investigations dug out transcripts of discussions among traders at competing firms that exchanged tips on the types and volume of trades they planned to place. The chat-rooms' names – 'Cartel', 'Bandits' Club', 'Mafia'– were perfect descriptions of traders' intentions.[6]

Central banks are big players in the currency market when they intervene in it to change the ER of their currency to achieve DEP goals. Most central bankers have in mind a target range for the ER of their currency. Sometimes they make it clear what that target ER is but often they like to keep markets guessing. Not all CBs have the ability to intervene in the FX market to change the direction of the ER of their currency. Many of them do not hold enough foreign currencies to sell in order to buy back their currency and stop its depreciation. Similarly the fear of inflation may inhibit CBs from printing large volumes of their currency to buy foreign currencies.

The FX market is dominated by the big private banks of the UK and the United States.[7] These banks are overseen by their respective CBs, but the supervision is largely informal as CBs have relied on market participants to self-regulate. In the United States, the FRBNY has facilitated the forging of an alliance among the major market makers in the FX market, the so-called Foreign Exchange Committee (FXC) that resides at the FRBNY. Similar CB-sponsored FXCs are active in other major financial centers. In the aftermath of the FOREX scandal, these FXCs decided to adopt a code of conduct so as to promote a 'robust, fair, liquid, open and transparent market'.[8] The code supplants the codes that existed before in various markets but were largely ignored by traders. Today the endorsement of the code by financial firms is a requirement for their membership in their country's FXC.

Work on the code began in May 2015, when the BIS commissioned a group of the Markets Committee, the Foreign Exchange Working Group (FXWG), to put together a single global code of conduct for the FX market. The development of the code was viewed as a PPP. The Markets Committee of the BIS, a public international body, worked closely with industry associations through

---

[6]   CFTC, CFTC Orders Five Banks to Pay over $1.4 Billion in Penalties for Attempted Manipulation of Foreign Exchange Benchmark Rates, Press Release Number 7056-14, Nov. 12, 2014.

[7]   These banks include Citibank (United States), Chase JP Morgan (United States), USB (Switzerland), Deutsche Bank (Germany), Bank of America (United States), Barclays (UK) and HSBC (UK).

[8]   Reserve Bank of Australia, Speech of Guy Debelle, Opening Remarks at the Launch of the FX Global Code, May 25, 2017.

each country's FXC. The code was touted as a global code because the 16 largest FX centers[9] in the world, in both developed and emerging markets, put it together.

The code consists of 55 principles that cover issues such as ethics, governance and execution of trades. The FXWG concluded that principles had a higher chance of being effective in regulating the conduct of traders than detailed rules. A principles-based code was expected to force market participants to scrutinize, through the legal departments of their firms, any potential behavior that might violate not only the letter but also the spirit of the code. The FXWG published a Statement of Commitment to the code and encouraged financial firms to explicitly endorse that statement as a way of communicating to the world their willingness to comply. By committing publicly to abide by the code, firms exert pressure on other firms to commit to the code as well. The Global Foreign Exchange Committee, which was established in May 2017, maintains and updates the code.

In summary, the FX market gives the impression of a decentralized and chaotic market in which speculators bet left and right on the value of currencies. After a number of scandals, major CBs have tried to organize the market by establishing committees of market participants, which, under government oversight, are closely scrutinizing trading in that market.

15.1.3 Money Market and Eurocurrency Market

15.1.3.1 Money market

The money market is not a formal market. The term is used to denote an informal network of banks and financial firms that deal in money market instruments – short-term debt obligations of firms and governments. A large portion of the money market consists of money market mutual funds. Investors invest in a *mutual fund* by buying the shares of that fund. Mutual funds can be stock funds, bond funds and *money market mutual funds* commonly known as money market funds (MMFs). Money market funds invest in high-quality, short-term debt including T-bills, high-quality municipal bonds, commercial paper and repos.[10] People invest in MMFs to manage their short-term cash needs. MMFs are divided into shares priced at $1 per share. Their goal is not to lose money by maintaining at all times the $1 per share valuation. If a fund's value falls below $1 per share, it 'breaks the buck'.

---

[9]   The largest FX centers were represented at the FXWG by their CBs – the CBs of Australia, Brazil, Canada, China, France, Hong Kong, India, Japan, Korea, Mexico, Singapore, Sweden, Switzerland and the UK as well as the ECB and the FRBNY.

[10]   On repos, *see* Chapter 3, Section 3.3.4.

In 2008, the Reserve Primary Fund, one of the oldest MMFs, 'broke the buck' by declaring that investors could no longer redeem their shares for the customary $1 per share. That declaration triggered a run on all MMFs. To stop the run, the Treasury used the ESF, for up to $50 billion, to guarantee payments when an MMF 'broke the buck', hoping to re-instate market confidence in these funds.[11] To prevent future government bailouts of non-government MMFs, the United States has adopted rules that distinguish between prime (non-government) and government MMFs. Others have proposed that, since MMFs offer bank-like services, they should be regulated like banks.[12]

15.1.3.2 Eurocurrency market

Eurocurrency is currency held in banks that are located outside the country where the currency is printed. Eurodollars are US dollars that circulate worldwide outside the United States. Eurodollars first circulated in Europe in the 1950s, owing to the US trade deficits and various regulatory measures that incentivized US capital holders to move their money abroad.[13] Since then, all dollars that circulate outside the United States have been called eurodollars. Other frequently used eurocurrencies include the eurosterling, the euroyen and the euroeuro.

The eurocurrency market channels money from lenders in one country to borrowers in another. More than 1 000 banks around the world deal in eurocurrency. The eurocurrency market increased from $2.3 trillion in 1988[14] to $5 trillion in the late 2000s[15] and is expected to reach $20–40 trillion by 2030.[16] Eurodollars are estimated to be more than 50% of the total eurocurrency market. Eurobonds are bonds denominated in a currency different from the currency of the country that issues them. They are usually issued by devel-

---

[11]   US Treasury, Treasury Announces Guaranty Program for Money Market Funds, Press Release, Sept. 19, 2008.

[12]   *See* Robert C. Hockett, *The Macroprudential Turn: From Institutional 'Safety and Soundness' to Systemic 'Financial Stability' in Financial Supervision*, 9 Virginia Law & Business Review 201, at 216 (2015). *See also* Morgan Ricks, *A Regulatory Design for Monetary Stability*, 65 Vanderbilt Law Review 1289, at 1293 (2012).

[13]   *See* Charles Proctor, *Mann on the Legal Aspect of Money* 59 (2012).

[14]   Anthony Saunders, *The Eurocurrency Interbank Market: Potential for International Crises?*, at 17, Business Review Federal Reserve Bank of Philadelphia, Jan./Feb. 1988.

[15]   Stephen A. Fowler, *The Monetary Fifth Column: The Eurodollar Threat to Financial Stability and Economic Sovereignty*, 47 Vanderbilt Journal of Transnational Law 825, at 828, n. 8 (2014).

[16]   *The Sticky Superpower*, Special Report World Economy, Economist, at 10, Oct. 3, 2015.

oping states. In an estimated $100 trillion global bond market,[17] the eurobond market is $28.5 trillion.[18]

Eurocurrencies are considered a sort of private transnational money because they are created by banks located outside the jurisdiction of the state that prints that money.[19] They are typically used to facilitate the movement of footloose capital. Large firms and rich individuals who wish to circumvent regulatory requirements, tax laws and IR ceilings in domestic jurisdictions can take their dollars or other currency overseas and deposit them with foreign banks. Interest rates on eurocurrency deposits tend to be higher than those on domestic currency deposits simply because eurocurrency deposits are not protected by governments' deposit guarantee schemes. Interest rates on loans obtained through the eurocurrency market are often lower than the rates offered in the domestic market because banks do not need to keep reserves for eurocurrency deposits. The lack of explicit reserve requirements for eurocurrencies is a serious concern for financial stability.

The eurocurrency market has been hailed as an efficient market that makes possible the swift transfer of money from capital holders in one country to capital seekers in others. Money transfers in the eurocurrency market take place electronically. The Clearing House Interbank Payments System (CHIPS), a clearing system based in United States, clears most eurocurrency transactions.

Countries can avoid the circulation of their currency as eurocurrency through capital controls. They can prohibit their residents from holding accounts in domestic currency at foreign banks and prevent foreigners from opening accounts in domestic currency within their jurisdiction. A state that wishes to limit the use of its currency as eurocurrency should restrict the use of that currency in the settling of international transactions.

15.1.4 Derivatives Market

As we have explored in Chapter 3, financial derivatives are hedging devices used to reduce the risks undertaken by investors. Companies hedge a number of risks including FX risk (the risk that a currency may appreciate/depreciate versus another currency), IR risk (the risk that IRs may go up/down), credit risk (the risk that a debtor may default) and commodity risk (the risk that commodity prices may increase/decrease).

---

[17] BIS, *International Banking and Financial Market Developments*, at 18, BIS Quarterly Review, Mar. 2014.
[18] *Id.* at 11.
[19] Proctor, *supra* note 13, at 61.

There are two parties to a derivatives contract: party A, who wishes to hedge a risk, and party B, who is willing to sell party A an instrument that will help it hedge that risk. For example, if a firm has bought bonds issued by a developing state, it can hedge the risk of potential default by that state by buying CDS, for a fee, from a firm that sells CDS. If the developing state defaults, the firm that sold these types of CDS must pay the bondholders who bought swaps from it. The bondholders who bought CDS will thus be able to recover the full amount they lent to the developing state minus the fee they already paid to purchase the CDS. If the state does not default, bondholders will get their money back from the state minus the fee they paid to buy the insurance provided by the CDS.

Derivatives have been called financial weapons of mass destruction. An example taken from the 2008 financial crisis is instructive about why this may be true. As we have seen in Chapter 3, a big US insurance company, the AIG, almost went bankrupt because it had issued a large number of CDS to holders of MBS. As these securities became worthless, the AIG did not have the resources to make the payouts to the holders of CDS. The US government, as a result, had to nationalize that company. Since 2009, efforts have been undertaken in the major financial centers where derivatives are traded to reduce the risks in the derivatives market. The majority of standardized derivatives contracts have to be settled now at centralized clearing houses, known as central counterparties (CCPs), rather than bilaterally in the OTC market. It is hoped that central clearing will increase transparency, making it easier to identify firms that take excessive risks.

The International Swaps and Derivatives Association (ISDA) is the organizing force of firms that are major players in the derivatives market. This is a private NGO of major issuers and brokers of derivatives that has played a critical role in the evolution of the derivatives market. The ISDA has standardized the derivatives contracts, adapted them to the legal systems around the world and hired attorneys in various jurisdictions to provide advice on their enforceability. The legal infrastructure that supports the derivatives market owes much to the lobbying efforts of the ISDA. Without that infrastructure, the derivatives market could never have become the multi-trillion dollar market that it is today.[20]

The *futures* market, a subset of the derivatives market, amounted to $34 trillion in 2017. In a futures contract, party A agrees to deliver to party B an underlying asset, usually a commodity, or its cash equivalent, at a future time at a pre-agreed price. Commodities are defined broadly to include 'all services,

---

[20] Katharina Pistor, *A Legal Theory of Finance*, at 10, Columbia Law School, Public Law and Legal Theory Working Paper Group, Paper Number 13-348, May 9, 2013.

rights and interests ... in which contracts for future delivery' can be made.[21] Farmers, manufacturers and financial institutions use the futures market to manage the risks to their business by betting on everything from wheat and cotton to oil and gold.

A *futures* contract must be distinguished from a *forward* contract. In a forward contract, like in a futures contract, the parties agree to trade an asset in the future at a pre-agreed price. The difference between them is that futures contracts are standardized contracts traded in centralized exchanges while forward contracts are tailored to the specific needs of trading parties in the OTC market. In the United States, futures contracts are regulated by the Commodity Futures Trading Commission (CFTC) while forward contracts are private contracts that are enforced in courts. Typically, futures contracts are used to *speculate* on the future value of a commodity. Forward contracts are entered into when parties agree to *physically deliver* the agreed commodity. A forward contract transfers the ownership of a commodity. A futures contract transfers the risk that the price of a commodity may change. One of the biggest players in the futures market is the Chicago Mercantile Exchange Group.

15.1.5 Commodities Market

Commodities can be traded for immediate delivery in the spot market. Forward contracts and futures are used to trade commodities to be delivered at a future date. Many developing states are large producers of commodities. Yet commodities are scarcely traded in their territory because they lack financial infrastructure and expertise.[22]

The commodities market can be easily rigged by those who have deep knowledge of how it functions. In 2014, the US Senate Permanent Subcommittee on Investigations concluded that financial firms had used their physical commodity business to manipulate commodity prices.[23] JP Morgan Chase, Morgan Stanley and Goldman Sacks, large US investment banks, had used their physical commodity business – they were owners of warehouses storing commodities – to manipulate the pricing of those commodities and increase their profits from commodities trading.

To be fair, it is difficult to make successful bets in the commodities market without information on the supply and demand dynamics in that market.

---

[21] 7 USC §1a(9).

[22] *See*, e.g. Ethiopia's *State-of-the-Art Commodity Exchange: High-Tech, Low Impact*, Economist, Feb. 2, 2017.

[23] US Senate, Permanent Subcommittee on Investigations, Wall Street Bank Involvement with Physical Commodities, Majority and Minority Staff Report, Nov. 20–21, 2014.

Unearthing information on the global supply of commodities has become a lucrative business. Some companies, for instance, track the number of excavator trucks and worker tents in mines in order to predict a metal's supply. Others use satellite images of oil production and storage facilities to estimate the global supply of oil.[24] The quantity of crude oil stored in US tanks is gauged by light aircraft that take photographs and infrared images of them.[25] Orbital Insight, a US company, has made a business out of measuring the shadows of Chinese floating-roof tanks to determine how much oil they contain.[26]

Obviously states have large stakes in the commodities market since they need the materials provided through it to run their economies. The United States is particularly aware that commodity shortages can cripple its economy. The US Strategic Petroleum Reserve was created after the mid-1970s oil shock to address potential disruptions in the flow of imported oil. In 2017, despite the fact that the United States was the world's largest producer of shale oil, the strategic reserve held 688 million oil barrels, making it the biggest global oil reserve.[27]

Oil is not the only commodity the lack of which can devastate an economy. In 2019, when the United States was in the throes of a trade war with China, a war that some called the new Cold War, there were concerns that China could retaliate by banning the exports of rare earths to the United States. Rare earths are essential for the production of a number of devices from dishwashers to military equipment. The excavation and processing of rare earths, a highly polluting industry, was at that point a near Chinese monopoly.[28]

15.2 PLAYERS

15.2.1 Banking Industry

Commercial banks are what most people regard as the 'real banks'. They are depository institutions. They open and maintain deposit accounts for businesses and individuals. They use the money deposited with them to provide

---

[24] *Satellites are Being Used to Expose Tightly Held Secrets in the Commodity Trading World*, Fortune, Dec. 16, 2017.
[25] *Why Too Much Oil in Storage is Weighing on Prices: Full Tank*, Economist, Mar. 16, 2017.
[26] Benoit Faucon and Sarah McFarlan, *OPEC Faces New Concern over Global Oil Stocks: China*, WSJ, June 5, 2018.
[27] Alison Sider and Erin Ailworth, *Trump Budget Prompts Question: Does the US Still Need to Hoard Oil in Reserve?*, WSJ, May 25, 2017.
[28] *US Risks 'Devastating' Blow from China's Rare Earth's Monopoly*, Bloomberg, May 29, 2019.

loans to those in need of financing. *Investment* banks intermediate, as dealers or brokers, in the purchase and sale of bonds, stocks and other investments. They additionally act as market makers and assist firms with their inital public offerings.

The banking system of a country is central to its financial stability. The world's largest banking system is that of China, whose assets amount to $33 trillion. The eurozone follows with $31 trillion, the United States with $16 trillion and Japan with $7 trillion.[29] Despite the large size of the Chinese banking sector, it is US investment banks that dominate finance in terms of trading revenue. US investment banks have a 58% market share. The largest European firms are far behind (36% market share).[30] No Chinese bank is among the top 10 investment banks, including the big banks sponsored by the Chinese state, such as the Industrial and Commercial Bank of China, the Agricultural Bank of China and the China Construction Bank.

European banks tend to lag behind their US counterparts because of the fragmentation of European banking.[31] Such fragmentation is prevalent not only among European countries, which are keen on preserving their national banks and domestic banking regulations, but also within some European states that tend to have too many banks. The German and the French banking systems are of similar size (EUR8 trillion each). France, however, has a rather centralized banking system that relies on national champions, some of which cultivate their global presence zealously. Germany's banking sector boasts a large number of small banks. Even large German banks, with the exception of Commerzbank and Deutsch bank, have a local focus.

Today, the global banking system is run by a strict hierarchy:

- At the top are the five US giants (Goldman Sachs, Morgan Stanley, JP Morgan, Citigroup and Bank of America) – the really global network banks. The global network bank does everything. It lends to and shifts money for multinationals in many countries, does securities trading, maintains deposit accounts and provides auto loans and mortgages.
- Second are strong regional players, such as Deutsche Bank, Barclays and HSBC.[32]

---

[29] Ben Chapman, *China's Banking System Overtakes Eurozone to Become the Biggest in the World*, Independent, Mar. 6, 2017.

[30] Yalman Onaran, *Wall Street Banks Trampled All Over their European Rivals in 2018*, Bloomberg, Feb. 25, 2019

[31] Charles Goodhart and Dirk Schoenmaker, *The United States Dominates Global Investment Banking: Does it Matter for Europe?*, Bruegel Policy Contribution, Issue 2016/06, Mar. 2016.

[32] Many of these banks were hobbled by the heavy fines they had to pay for violating US sanctions against Iran and North Korea. *See* Nate Raymond, *BNP Paribas*

- Third are some national banks serving the banking needs of their home countries, such as the Australian and Canadian banks.
- Finally, small, specialist wealth management boutiques provide specialized advice. Some of these boutiques cater to marginalized states and companies often neglected by the big banks.[33]

15.2.2 Shadow Banks

The Financial Stability Board (FSB), an international regulatory body, divides firms, which act as financial intermediaries, into three categories:

- banks, that is deposit-taking corporations (DTCs);
- non-DTCs, such as insurance companies, that do some financial intermediation but are not subjected to the strict regulations affecting DTCs;
- shadow banks, firms that are not DTCs but provide loans while they are themselves dependent on short-term credit – shadow banking activities also encompass securitization and the buying/selling of derivatives.

In 2015, the assets managed by shadow banks ($92 trillion)[34] were approaching those managed by traditional banks, the DTCs ($133 trillion).[35] Furthermore, despite the FSB's attempt to separate shadow banks from traditional banking, firms that do traditional banking are frequently involved in shadow banking activities, such as securitization.[36] The term 'shadow banking' does suggest a gray operation aimed to circumvent government regulations on the provision of credit. The infamous 2008 crash of MBS, that were put together by some of the best investment banks and enjoyed some of the highest credit ratings, did not help to elevate the reputation of shadow banking. Shadow banking is an ancient profession, though, as many payday lenders would proudly confess. It happens every time the regulated DTCs are restricted with regard to the quantity and quality of credit they are permitted to provide. The tighter the restrictions on traditional banking, the higher the growth of shadow banking. The emergence of shadow banking may, in fact, suggest that traditional banking should benefit from less regulation.[37]

Sentenced in $8.9 Billion Accord over Sanctions Violations, Reuters, May 1, 2015; Jill Treanor, *Deutsche Bank Fined $630m over Russia Money Laundering Claims*, Guardian, Jan. 31, 2017.

[33] *A World of Pain: Global Banks*, Economist, Mar. 5, 2015.

[34] FSB, *Global Shadow Banking Monitoring Report 2016*, at 16, May 10, 2017.

[35] *Id.* at 10.

[36] *Id.* at 29.

[37] Steven L. Schwartz, *Shadow Banking and Regulation in China and Other Developing Countries*, at 10, Duke Law Scholarship Repository, Nov. 16, 2016.

In China shadow banking increased from 40% of GDP in 2014 to 78% in 2016.[38] In many emerging markets, shadow banking is usually lightly regulated, even though it is well known that it presents a threat to financial stability. Many developing economies struggle to establish a balance between restricting shadow banking and accepting it as a type of alternative financing. In China, for instance, shadow banking is very important for small and medium-sized enterprises, including entrepreneurial start-ups, because the banks owned by the Chinese state typically do not provide credit to such companies.[39] Property development trusts, credit associations, rural cooperative foundations and even pawnshops are, therefore, large sources of credit provision in China.[40]

15.2.3 Asset Management Companies

Asset management companies are financial firms that manage assets (stocks, bonds, mutual funds) on behalf of others. Their customers can be individuals or institutional investors, like pension funds and insurance companies. Seven out of the top 10 asset management firms are based in the United States, including the behemoths of Blackrock, which manages $6.2 trillion in assets, and Vanguard, which manages $4.9 trillion. Many asset management firms are multinational corporations. Blackrock, for example, is the main shareholder of UniCredit, Italy's biggest bank. This and its other Italian holdings make it Italy's biggest shareholder after the government.[41]

Asset management firms are not generally viewed as threats to financial stability. Unlike banks, which hold deposits and loans on their balance sheet, asset management firms manage other people's money. Banks can quickly go bankrupt if their assets lose value and are vulnerable to runs. Asset managers, because of the discretion they enjoy about when and how to invest, are considered a stabilizing force in the markets. Asset managers can go bargain hunting during a financial crisis, picking up distressed securities and preventing further price declines.

At the same time, nobody really knows what exactly may happen if investors lose confidence in one of these gigantic asset management firms. If, for instance, Blackrock suffered reputational damage, a large number of its clients would shed their holdings in its funds. In that case, Blackrock would have to liquidate the huge long positions it holds in many markets. Such liquidation

---

[38] *Id.* at 1–2.
[39] *Id.* at 3–4.
[40] *Id.* at 4–5.
[41] Sonia Sirletti, *BlackRock Becomes UniCredit's Biggest Investor with 5.2% Stake*, Bloomberg, Mar. 14, 2014.

would trigger an enormous market sell-off.[42] Furthermore, it is hard to contend that competitive markets are alive and well when some big firms manage such large sums of wealth and consequently have enormous influence on them.

15.2.4 Pension Funds and the Insurance Industry

The insurance industry holds close to $5 trillion in insurance premiums world-wide.[43] The industry makes money by investing these premiums in the market in relatively safe assets, such as Treasuries and high-quality corporate bonds. Insurance companies do not seem to be the type of companies that would be vulnerable during a financial crisis. Most insurance companies strive to perfect the job of segregating the persons they insure based on their risk profile, from too risky to low risk, so as to minimize the chances of a payout under an insurance contract. Unfortunately, they are not always successful in understanding the full extent of risks they undertake. As we explored in Chapter 3, during the 2008 financial crisis, AIG, the biggest US insurance provider, defaulted and was nationalized by the US government.

Pension funds are some of the largest institutional players in the financial markets.[44] The assets managed by pension funds across 22 major countries amount to $41.3 trillion.[45] In most countries, public pension funds are required to invest a portion of their money in the debt issued by their government. Public pension funds include the US Social Security System established in 1935, in the aftermath of the Great Depression. US social security funds, about $2.9 trillion,[46] are invested in US Treasuries. Another big pension fund is Japan's Government Pension Investment Fund. With $1.4 trillion in assets, it is the world's second biggest public investor after the US Social Security System.[47] The Government Pension Investment Fund keeps about two-thirds of its assets in bonds, mostly Japanese government bonds. It follows various benchmarks passively and hardly invests abroad. On the contrary, the public sector funds of Australia and Canada have opted for a more risky investment style. These funds behave like the big asset managers we examined above. They are active investors in the stock market and do not hesitate to challenge the management of firms whose shares they own.

---

[42] Massimo Massa et al., *Who is Afraid of BlackRock?*, INSEAD Knowledge, 2018.

[43] *World Insurance in 2016: The China Growth Engine Steams Ahead*, at 48, Swiss Re Institute sigma No. 3/2017.

[44] *See generally* Gordon L. Clark, *Pension Fund Capitalism* (2000).

[45] Chris Flood, *Value of Global Pension Assets Surges to $41.3tn*, FT, Feb. 4, 2018.

[46] David Pattison, *Social Security Trust Fund Cash Flows and Reserves*, 75(1) Social Security Bulletin (2015).

[47] GPIF, Overview of Fiscal Year 2017, July 6, 2018.

Pension funding is marred by problems of intergenerational transfer. A pension scheme that is not fully funded depends on future workers to make up for its funding shortfalls. Many European public sector funds are based on 'pay as you go' (PAYG) schemes. People contribute to these schemes throughout their working lives in order to receive payments after they retire. Most believe that the money they contribute during their lifetime is saved in a high-yielding account to ensure future payments when they reach the retirement age. However, this is not the case with most PAYG plans. Instead, the contributions of current workers are used to pay current retirees. This is why PAYG schemes look like intergenerational Ponzi schemes; they remain viable only because new generations are willing to provide for the elderly under the assumption that their children will do the same for them. However, if future generations are not as populous or wealthy as the current ones, the PAYG schemes will fall apart. According to an estimate, the world's largest pension systems, those of the United States, UK, Japan, Netherlands, Canada and Australia, will have a joint shortfall of $224 trillion by 2050. By that year there will be only four workers for each retiree compared with eight as of 2017. Adding China and India to this calculation, the countries with the world's largest populations, the combined shortfall reaches $428 trillion by 2050, five times the size of the 2017 global GDP.[48]

15.2.5 Hedge Funds

The mission of hedge funds, as their name indicates, is to hedge against the market – that is to provide returns uncorrelated with the overall market performance. This is often accomplished by betting against various securities (i.e. shorting them) and using derivatives. Hedge funds are active investors – they monitor and may try to change the strategies of firms in which they invest. Some hedge funds do not even hesitate to bet against states.

In 1994, Argentina started to issue bonds based on the Fiscal Agency Agreement ('FAA bonds'). The coupon rates on these bonds ranged from 9.75 to 15.5% with maturity dates from April 2005 to September 2031. Argentina defaulted on its $80 billion debt in 2001, including the FAA bonds, amid high unemployment and inflation while its currency was under attack. As its bonds were sold off in the markets, at fire sale prices, many hedge funds with expertise in distressed debt bought some of these bonds at the heavy discount of 10

---

[48] *We'll Live to 100 – How Can We Afford It?*, at 22, World Economic Forum, May 2017.

cents on the dollar. One of these hedge funds was NML Capital, a subsidiary of Elliott Management.[49]

Argentina stopped making principal and interest payments on its bonds from the day of its default in 2001 until 2005. In 2005, it offered to exchange the bonds on which it had defaulted for new bonds at a rate of 29–25 cents on the dollar – a 71–75% discount on par value. To induce bondholders to accept the offer, Argentina warned that those who did not exchange their bonds for the new, heavily discounted ones would not receive any payment. Seventy-six percent of Argentina's bondholders accepted the exchange offer. Argentina repeated that offer in 2010, inviting even greater participation. Overall, by exchanging the existing FAA bonds for the new discounted ones, Argentina succeeded in restructuring over 91% of the foreign debt on which it had defaulted in 2001.

NML Capital, and other hedge funds that specialize in distressed debt, refused to participate in the bond exchange and sued Argentina in New York. The FAA was governed by New York law and provided for jurisdiction in any state or federal court in the City of New York. The creditors argued that the *pari passu* clause (equal treatment of bondholders clause) included in the FAA meant that all Argentina's bondholders had to be treated equally with regard to the repayment of Argentina's debt.

The district court of the Southern District of New York sided with the holdout bondholders. It concluded that Argentina could not continue making payments on the new, discounted bonds held by the *exchange bondholders* unless it made *pro rata* payments to the *holdout bondholders* under the old bonds.[50] The court made it clear that *pro rata* payments meant that Argentina's payment of interest to the exchange bondholders triggered its obligation to pay the accelerated principal plus accrued interest to the holdouts. As a result, the exchange bondholders would receive 25–29 cents on the dollar while the holdouts would get full repayment. The court argued that this differential treatment made complete sense because the exchange bondholders had opted, by exchanging their bonds, for the safety of diminished returns. The holdouts, on the other hand, had taken on the burden of litigating; therefore, they had to be paid in full. All in all, the New York court treated Argentina as a 'uniquely recalcitrant debtor'.[51] For the court, the maintenance of the integrity of US capital markets meant that borrowers like Argentina had to be held strictly to

---

[49] NML Capital paid no more than 28 cents on the dollar on average for all Argentina's bonds it bought before and after the 2001 default.

[50] *NML Capital, Ltd. v. Republic of Argentina*, No. 08 Civ. 6978, 2012 WL 5895786 (SDNY, Nov. 21, 2012).

[51] *NML Capital, Ltd. v. Republic of Argentina*, 727 F.3d 230, at 247 (2d Cir. 2013).

the terms of their debt contracts. This was also important for preserving the status of New York as a global commercial center.

The New York court further ordered the banks of New York, which were acting as agents of Argentina and processing payments to the exchange bondholders, to stop making such payments unless they were instructed by the country to make simultaneous payments to the holdouts. Having to obey the court order, and given that Argentina had ruled out any negotiation with the holdouts, the Bank of New York Mellon refused to process Argentina's payments.[52] Since no bank was prepared to facilitate its payments, the country defaulted anew on its debt in 2012.

NML Capital tried to execute the New York ruling by attaching Argentina's assets both in the United States and around the world, including the seizure of an Argentine naval vessel, Argentina's presidential plane and funds that Argentina's CB kept in custody with the FRS.[53] It took a change in government to find a compromise. On February 29, 2016, the newly elected government of Argentina reached an agreement with the holdouts. It paid those who had sued it a total of $4.7 billion.[54] The settlement with all of the 220 holdout bondholders amounted to $9.3 billion. These payments were facilitated by issuing new government debt, a total amount $16.5 billion. Elliott Management, the hedge fund that had led the fight against Argentina,[55] made a 392% return on the principal it had invested in the FAA bonds.[56] Bracebridge Capital got the best returns, achieving a 952% gain on its principal of $120 million – a total of $1.1 billion. Other hedge funds fared a little worse. Blue Angel Capital received 186% return on its principal, and Aurelius Capital a 254% return.[57]

Santiago Bausili, the Undersecretary of Finance for Argentina, explained why the returns of Elliott Management and Bracebridge were so high. These

---

[52] Anna Gelpern, *Sovereign Debt: Now What?*, 41 Yale Journal of International Law 45, at 71 (2016).

[53] *Foreign Sovereign Immunities Act of 1976 – Postjudgment Discovery – Republic of Argentina v. NML Capital Ltd*, 128 Harvard Law Review 381, at 382 (2014).

[54] Daniel A. Pollack, *Special Master Announces Settlement of 15-Year Battle Between Argentina and 'Holdout' Hedge Funds*, PR Newswire, Feb. 29, 2016.

[55] Elliott Management had experience in dealing with states in default. It had already tested in Peru the tactics it used against Argentina. *See*, e.g., *Elliott Associates L.P. v. Banco de la Nacion*, 194 F.3d 363 (2d. Cir. 1999). For more details on that litigation, *see* Mauro Megliani, *Sovereign Debt: Genesis – Restructuring – Litigation* 512–16 (2015).

[56] On an initial investment of $617 million, the final payout was $2.4 billion.

[57] Case NML Capital against the Republic of Argentina, Second Supplemental Declaration of Undersecretary of Finance Santiago Bausili in Further Support of the Republic of Argentina's Motion, by Order to Show Cause, to Vacate the Injunctions Issued on November 21, 2012, and October 30, 2015, Exhibit (SDNY, Feb. 29, 2016).

firms had acquired a large number of bonds that were issued in 1998 which, unlike most of the other FFA bonds, were floating rate accrual notes – they were paying a floating coupon rate that was periodically reset to match market rates. In 2001, when Argentina was facing economic difficulties, the yields on its bonds started to climb rapidly. When the bonds came due, in 2005, their yield froze at 101.5% per year. This was the rate that accrued on these bonds from 2005 until the day of the final settlement of the amount owed. It was obviously Argentina's problem that it had issued this type of bonds. The hedge funds were merely doing their job of taking advantage of this opportunity to deliver returns that, as they promise, must be much superior to those offered by the regular market. One cannot help but feel a certain sort of queasiness, however, when lenders receive a 186–952% return on the credit they provide. It comes as no surprise that Argentina and those sympathetic to its situation have called hedge funds that specialize in distressed debt 'vulture funds'.[58]

15.2.6   Private Equity Companies

The goal of private equity companies is to invest capital in ways that produce better returns than those offered by the markets. Some private equity firms – the so-called 'venture capitalists' – invest in new companies that may need funds to commercialize their inventions. Other firms invest in troubled companies. Often they acquire these companies through a leveraged buyout – they buy them by borrowing money. After the acquisition they focus on cost cutting – such as closing down facilities and firing employees – so as to restructure these companies, pay off the debt and return them to profitability. This aggressive cost-cutting, which may entail large layoffs, does not endear these firms to the public. Bain Capital, KKR, Blackstone, Carlyle and Apollo, all based in the United States, are the largest private equity players worldwide. Their clout in the market stems from the sheer number of companies they have bought through various leveraged buyouts and other deals. Carlyle owns approximately 275 companies and KKR 115.[59] Pension funds and sovereign wealth funds invest in private equity firms hoping that the superior returns of private equity investments will overcompensate for the mediocre returns they receive from conventional investing.

---

[58]   Martin Guzman and Joseph E. Stiglitz, *How Hedge Funds Held Argentina for Ransom*, NYT, Apr. 1, 2016.

[59]   *The Barbarian Establishment: Private Equity*, Economist, Oct. 22, 2016.

15.2.7   Sovereign Wealth Funds

A sovereign wealth fund (SWF) is a fund established by a state with the goal of augmenting that state's wealth by investing at home and abroad for the benefit of present and future generations. States with abundant FX reserves, which they accumulate owing to large CA surpluses, have built large SWFs that are very active in the financial markets. The first SWF was established in 1953 by Kuwait, the Kuwait Investment Authority, with the mandate to invest the country's surplus from oil revenues in ways that will diversify its economy. Some of the world's largest SWFs include Norway's Government Pension Fund-Global with assets above $1 trillion, China Investment Corporation ($900 billion), the Abu Dhabi Investment Authority ($828 billion), the Kuwait Investment Authority ($524 billion) and the SAMA Foreign Holdings of Saudi Arabia ($494 billion). South Korea, Singapore and Qatar also have sizable SWFs.

Norway's SWF saves for future generations. When the oil runs out, the returns on the fund are expected to continue to benefit the Norwegian population. The fund is worth more than double the country's GDP. It owns 2.4% of all shares listed in Europe and 1.4% of shares listed globally. Some of its largest holdings are the big US technology companies among 9 146 companies in 72 countries. When the price of oil fell in 2016, the annual revenues of the fund exceeded the income the state received from exporting oil. The fund is an independent entity within Norway's CB. It is overseen by the finance minister and monitored by the parliament. It is run transparently: every investment it makes is reported online. It has grown rapidly because of a social consensus that it makes sense to save as much as possible now for the future. A budgetary rule stops the government from borrowing from the fund more than 3% of its expected annual returns.

Rich SWFs have geopolitical clout. In 2016, Glencore, a Swiss commodities company, and its biggest shareholder, the Qatar Investment Authority (QIA), the SWF of Qatar, agreed to buy an $11.3 billion stake in Rosneft, a Russian state-owned company, amounting to 19.5% of that company.[60] At the time, Rosneft was isolated owing to the European and US sanctions imposed on Russia for its 2014 war with Ukraine. The partial privatization of Rosneft through its sale to Qatar was helpful to Russia. It provided the country with some breathing space from the US–EU sanctions and made it possible for it to shrink its deficit. It is unclear whether the Russian government intended to privatize Rosneft, though. The deal seemed to include an unusual clause based

---

[60]   Katya Golubkova, *Russia Signs Rosneft Deal with Qatar, Glencore*, Reuters, Dec. 10, 2016.

on which Russia could buy back a portion of the stake of Glencore/Qatar at a future time. This buyback arrangement was allegedly negotiated directly between the Russian President and the Emir of Qatar.[61] If such a buyback agreement was indeed part of the deal, the temporary privatization was in essence a sanctions-busting loan. The complex structure of the deal made it difficult to follow the money trail. Glencore and Qatar did not directly own the shares of Rosneft. Instead, the shares were owned by a UK limited liability partnership.[62]

The impact of SWFs on the global economy is also evident in the role they played in stabilizing European banks after the 2008 financial crisis and in their overall sizable holdings of Western technology companies. As of 2017, some of the largest investors in Credit Suisse, a Swiss bank, were the QIA and a Saudi conglomerate – the Olayan Group. Qatar Holding (which is owned 100% by the QIA) was the biggest shareholder of Barclays, a UK bank. In May 2017, Japan's Softbank Group and Saudi Arabia's Public Investment Fund, one of Saudi Arabia's SWFs, contributed $28 and $45 billion respectively to create a $93 billion private equity fund to invest in new technologies such as robotics and artificial intelligence. Other big investors in this so-called Vision Fund included Abu Dhabi's Mubadala Investment, an SWF of Abu Dhabi. Saudi Arabia hoped that its investment in the fund would help it obtain access to foreign technology and diversify its oil-dependent economy.[63] In 2017, the SWFs of oil-producing states had enough capital to take over many Western companies. If the price of oil were to reach $200 per barrel, fueling a buying spree of Western firms by the oil-rich states,[64] many US and EU companies could end up being acquired by these states. Whether such foreign ownership was to be tolerated by the West remained unclear. Some expected a severe backlash if the majority of Western assets were taken over by Middle East states.[65] In matters of ownership of one country by another, certain psychological and political barriers cannot be crossed if states wish to avoid war.[66]

The sovereign wealth funds of less-developed states have tried to mimic the strategies of rich states. Botswana has a $6.6 billion SWF that, like the Norwegian SWF, invests mainly abroad. The Nigerian Sovereign Investment Authority, on the contrary, allocates 40% of its assets to an infrastructure fund

---

[61] Sarah McFarlane and Summer Said, *Russia Could Buy Back Stake it Sold in Rosneft*, WSJ, June 7, 2017.

[62] *Id.*

[63] Andrew Torchia, *Softbank Saudi Tech Fund Becomes World's Biggest with $93 Billion of Capital*, Reuters, May 20, 2017.

[64] Thomas Piketty, *Capital in the Twenty-First Century* 459 (2014).

[65] *Id.* at 460.

[66] *Id.*

for investment in domestic projects, such as power generation, highways and farming, a more reasonable investment strategy given the country's needs.

The International Forum of Sovereign Wealth Funds (IFSWF) is a global network of SWFs established in 2009 to enhance collaboration among them and propose best practices for their governance. About 30 SWFs, holding together $5.5 trillion under management and representing 80% of assets managed by SWFs globally, are members of the IFSWF. The IFSWF has endorsed the 'Generally Accepted Principles and Practices' for SWFs. These principles, known as the 'Santiago Principles',[67] emphasize transparency, the independent auditing of SWFs' finances and ethical responsibility. Ethical responsibility may entail refraining from investing in companies that produce weapons or sell tobacco. Ethical investment may mean investing in green companies and avoiding companies that produce an excessive amount of greenhouse gases.[68]

15.2.8   Credit Rating Agencies

Moody's and S&P (based in United States) and Fitch (based in the UK) are 'The Big Three' – the largest credit rating companies in the world, generally known as credit rating agencies (CRAs). As of 2017, they held close to a 90% market share of credit ratings issued worldwide.[69] This was so despite the fact that the US SEC had recognized 10 CRAs (including 'The Big Three') as NRSROs and the fact that the European Securities and Markets Authority (ESMA) had approved 31 CRAs as registered[70] and certified in accordance with the European regulations.[71]

In January 2017, Moody's, one of 'The Big Three', paid close to $864 million[72] to settle charges that it failed to objectively rate the MBS that proved toxic during the 2008 crisis. That failure was due to a conflict of interest that

---

[67] IFSWF, Sovereign Wealth Funds: Generally Accepted Principles and Practices, 'Santiago Principles', Oct. 2008.

[68] Norges Bank Investment Management, *Responsible Investment: Government Pension Fund Global*, at 4.2 (2016) (reporting disinvestments from mining, pulp and paper, and the seafood industry).

[69] SEC, Annual Report on Nationally Recognized Statistical Rating Organizations, at 11, Dec. 2017; ESMA, Competition and Choice in the Credit Rating Industry, at 6, ESMA/2016/1662, Dec. 16, 2016.

[70] ESMA, *id.*

[71] Regulation (EC) No. 1060/2009 of the European Parliament and of the Council of 16 September 2009 on credit rating agencies, OJ L 302/11, 17.11.2009.

[72] US Justice Department, Justice Department and State Partners Secure Nearly $864 Million Settlement with Moody's Arising from Conduct in the Lead Up to the Financial Crisis, Press Release, Jan. 13, 2017.

Moody's did not address adequately. Moody's was paid by the banks which issued MBS to rate these securities, something that was common practice in the industry. In theory, these payments should not have affected Moody's ratings since, as a CRA, it is supposed to appraise companies and securities objectively. At the same time, an unfavorable rating of MBS would have affected Moody's ability to attract future business from banks. It appears that Moody's tweaked its credit ratings model to avoid giving these securities poor ratings. In its settlement with the US Justice Department, Moody's acknowledged that it had violated its own code of professional conduct that touted the importance of the 'integrity, objectivity, and transparency of the credit ratings process'.[73] However, the settlement contained no findings that Moody's had violated the law in any way. The settlement received very little publicity and hardly affected Moody's status in the market.

The EU has taken a number of initiatives to increase competition in the credit rating business and bust the oligopoly of 'The Big Three'. It has established a European rating agency and increased the opportunities for small CRAs to compete with them. The Credit Rating Agencies Regulation (CRAR),[74] adopted in 2013, assigned to the ESMA the job of overseeing the CRAs. On June 1, 2017, the ESMA fined Moody's EUR1.24 million for 'negligent breaches' of the CRAR regarding ratings it had issued between 2011 and 2013. The ratings had to do with the creditworthiness of nine supranational EU entities, including the European Investment Bank, the ESM and the EU.[75] The ESMA berated Moody's for appraising the securities issued by these entities without providing any comprehensive description of the methodology it had used. In 2016, the ESMA fined Fitch EUR1.38 million for failing to give Slovenia 12 hours to respond to a downgrade of its credit rating in 2012, as required under the CRAR.[76] Because of repeated instances of professional misconduct by the CRAs, the FSB[77] issued recommendations in 2012 that encouraged national authorities to reduce the role that CRAs' ratings play in national laws and regulations.[78]

---

[73] Settlement Agreement between Department of Justice and Moody's, Annex 1, Jan. 13, 2017.

[74] Regulation (EU) No. 462/2013 of the European Parliament and of the Council of 21 May 2013 amending Regulation (EC) No. 1060/2009 on credit rating agencies, OJ L 146/1, 31.5.2013.

[75] ESMA, ESMA Fines Moody's €1.24 Million for Credit Rating Breaches, Press Release, June 1, 2017.

[76] ESMA, ESMA Fines Fitch Ratings Limited €1.38 Million, Press Release, July 21, 2016.

[77] *See* Chapter 16, Section 16.3.2.

[78] *See* Thematic Review on FSB Principles for Reducing Reliance on CRA Ratings: Peer Review Report, at 5, May 12, 2014.

India has been eager to create a CRA that could, one day, rival 'The Big Three'. At the 2017 BRICS summit, in Xiamen China, India reiterated its support for the creation of a BRICS' CRA to counter 'The Big Three' and cater to the needs of developing nations. China was not very keen on the idea, however, as it feared that a BRICS-sponsored CRA may not enjoy much credibility. China has encouraged, instead, its domestic firms to form partnerships with 'The Big Three'.[79]

Developing countries are right to be concerned about potential biases of CRAs. They tend to downgrade developing countries speedily at any inkling of financial trouble. These downgrades create panic and contagion, turning financial crises in the developing world into self-fulfilling prophecies. The big CRAs, for example, aggravated the 1990s East Asian crisis through constant downgrades that failed to reflect the solid economic fundamentals of some of the Asian countries. This increased these countries' costs of borrowing and precipitated the fleeing of foreign capital.[80] The ratings of rich countries, on the other hand, rarely suffer because of financial crises or geopolitical surprises. In times of crisis, instead, the debt of core countries becomes the safe asset coveted by all.

15.2.9 Payment Systems and Economic Sanctions

It is the job of the CB of a state to safeguard the smooth functioning of the national payment system. It does so by supervising and regulating the payment services market – the banks and firms that compete with each other to provide payment services to consumers and corporations. Users of payment systems vary from individuals, who make small purchases, to large corporations that engage in large money transfers. Users look for low-cost payment systems that are protected by laws safeguarding the security and privacy of their transactions. On the supply side, companies that provide payment services seek to make profits by charging fees for the transactions they intermediate.

Companies which intermediate payments communicate with each other through messaging and routing systems. For instance, in the United States, money is moved from one checking account to another through the American

---

[79] Jin Sheng, *China's Emerging Credit Rating Industry: Regulatory Issues and Practices*, at 6, Working Paper CBFL-WP-SJ-03, Center of Banking & Finance Law, National University of Singapore, Apr. 15, 2016.

[80] *See* G. Ferri et al., *The Procyclical Role of Rating Agencies: Evidence from the East Asian Crisis*, 28(3) Economic Notes 335, Nov. 1999; Marek Hanusch et al., *The Ghost of a Rating Downgrade: What Happens to Borrowing Costs when a Government Loses its Investment Grade Credit Rating?*, MFM Discussion Paper No. 13, World Bank, June 2016.

Bankers' Association routing transit number, which is used to identify the bank that initiates a payment. The Clearing House Association was founded in 1853 and it is the oldest bank association and payment processor in the United States. It operates CHIPS that facilitates payments for large dollar transactions. SWIFT, a cooperative society based in Belgium, links financial institutions in more than 200 countries. The SWIFT code for payment transfers among banks that are located in different countries is similar to the American Bankers' Association routing transit number that identifies the bank that initiates a money transfer to the bank that receives that transfer.

Clearing and settlement are important for the smooth functioning of payments. Clearing is the process of determining the obligations of the parties to a transaction – who owes what to whom. Settlement is the process of actually fulfilling these obligations, by transferring money as needed from one account to another. Most clearing and settlement systems work as PPPs. They are set up privately by a bank or an association of banks and are closely supervised and regulated by the CB that has jurisdiction over them.

In 2001, the BIS Committee on Payment and Settlement Systems (CPSS), which was later renamed the Committee on Payments and Market Infrastructures, introduced a set of guidelines called the Core Principles for Systemically Important Payment Systems (SIPS).[81] SIPS are systems that have the potential to trigger or transmit systemic disruptions. This includes systems that are the sole payment system in a state or the principal system in terms of the aggregate value of payments.[82] SIPS include systems that handle time-critical, high-value payments or affect the settlement of payments in other markets.[83] In the United States, the Dodd–Frank Act gives the FSOC the authority to designate as systemically important private companies that play the role of financial utilities. A *financial market utility* is defined 'as any person that manages or operates a multilateral system for the purpose of transferring, clearing, or settling payments, securities, or other financial transactions'.[84] A financial utility will be designated as systemically important if its failure creates or increases the risk of significant liquidity or credit problems spreading through the market and undermining the financial stability of the

---

[81]   BIS CPSS, *Core Principles for Systemically Important Payment Systems*, Jan. 2001. These principles were updated in 2012. *See* BIS CPSS, *Principles for Financial Markets Infrastructures*, Apr. 2012 [hereinafter Principles 2012].

[82]   *Id.* at 12.

[83]   *Id.*

[84]   12 USC §5462(6). Securities exchanges, registered futures associations and swap data repositories are not considered financial market utilities.

United States.[85] The FSOC has designated eight companies as systemically important financial market utilities.[86]

The fact that many clearing and settlement systems are US-based has been exploited to facilitate the imposition of US economic sanctions on other states. On January 8, 1986, the US president froze all dollar-denominated assets of the Libyan government, including assets held in foreign branches of US banks. Following the freeze, the Libyan Arab Foreign Bank (LAFB) decided to withdraw all of the funds it held in its Bankers Trust account in London. The Bankers Trust claimed that the asset freeze prevented it from making the payment and blocked the withdrawal. On May 13, 1986, the LAFB sued the Bankers Trust in the UK courts asking the Trust to give back all the funds it held for the LAFB in London.[87] The Bankers Trust argued that practice in the eurodollar market dictated that such payment had to be processed through CHIPS. The use of CHIPS would have violated the US order to freeze Libyan assets.[88] The UK court ruled against Bankers Trust by concluding that CHIPS was not the exclusive means through which that bank could satisfy the LAFB's demands.[89] Furthermore, the place of performance of the deposit agreement, between the Bankers Trust and the LAFB, was London. The fact that the funds had to be cleared through New York did not make New York the place of payment. In short, the payment was not illegal under English law, and this was the law that governed this specific eurodollar deposit contract.

In *Jesner v. Arab Bank*,[90] 6 000 foreign plaintiffs sued the Jordanian Arab Bank (JAB) in the United States for injuries perpetrated by terrorist groups in Israel. They claimed that the JAB cleared automatic electronic wire transfers through the US-based CHIPS for foreign groups designated by the United States as terrorist organizations. The main reason for suing the bank in US courts had to do with the CHIPS transactions executed by JAB's New York branch. Plaintiffs invoked the 1789 Alien Tort Statute, which had been used in the past to sue foreign nationals before US courts for violation of international

---

[85] 12 USC §5464.

[86] CHIPS; CLS Bank International; Chicago Mercantile Exchange; Depository Trust Company; Fixed Income Clearing Corporation; ICE Clear Credit; National Securities Clearing Corporation; and Options Clearing Corporation.

[87] *Libyan Arab Foreign Bank v. Bankers Trust Co.* [1989] QB 728.

[88] *See also* Corinne R. Rutzke, *The Libyan Asset Freeze and its Application to Foreign Government Deposits in Overseas Branches of United States Banks: Libyan Arab Foreign Bank v. Bankers Trust Co.*, 3 American University International Law Review 241, at 260 (1988).

[89] *Id.* at 260–61.

[90] *Jesner v. Arab Bank*, 138 S.Ct. 1386 (2018).

norms.[91] The US Supreme Court ruled, in this case, though, that the Alien Tort Statute did not grant jurisdiction to US courts to hear lawsuits against non-US defendants brought by foreign plaintiffs with regard to alleged violations of international law perpetrated outside the United States. Foreign companies, like the JAB, therefore, could not be defendants in lawsuits[92] brought under the Alien Tort Statute unless Congress adopted legislation that specified otherwise. The court was clearly reluctant to get mired in foreign policy matters that are under the purview of the political branches of government.

15.2.9.1 Credit cards and internet payments

Visa and MasterCard are multinational corporations headquartered in the United States. The credit cards issued under their name are used by individuals and small businesses to make payments worldwide. We must clarify here that Visa and MasterCard do not issue cards, extend credit or set the fees for the usage of their cards by consumers. Instead they provide banks with their branded products, which banks use to provide credit to their customers. Credit card companies have attempted to argue, albeit unsuccessfully, that because they work with banks rather than the end-users, they are not really payment systems.[93]

Visa is the world's second largest card payment company, after being surpassed by China UnionPay, based on the annual value of card payments transacted and number of issued cards. UnionPay's predominance has to do with the large size of its domestic market. Visa is dominant in the rest of the world as it has captured a 50% market share in global card payments.

With regard to e-payments, China's internet payments market is the world's biggest with $11.4 trillion in transactions – twice the size of the US credit card industry.[94] Ant Financial and Tencent, two Chinese private companies, control most of that market. Ant Financial is, in fact, 16 times larger than Paypal, its US counterpart.[95] In 2017, Ant Financial was in the process of buying

---

91   The statute was used successfully, in the 1980s, to win cases against non-US citizens for acts they had committed *outside* the United States that were in violation of public international law, such as the prohibition against torture, *see Filártiga v. Peña-Irala*, 630 F.2d 876 (2d Cir. 1980).

92   *See also Sosa v. Alvarez-Machain*, 542 U.S. 692 (2004); *Kiobel v. Royal Dutch Petroleum Co.*, 133 S.Ct. 1659 (2013).

93   An Australian court has ruled that all systems supportive of the payment infrastructure are payment systems. *See Visa International v. Reserve Bank of Australia* (2003) FCA 977. For an analysis of the case, *see* Proctor, *supra* note 13, at 49.

94   Mancy Sun et al., *The Rise of China Fintec: Payment, the Ecosystem Gateway*, at 3, Goldman Sachs Equity Research, Aug. 7, 2017.

95   *China's Digital-Payments Giant Keeps Bank Chiefs Up at Night: Ants in Your Pants*, Economist, Aug. 19, 2017.

MoneyGram, a US-based money transfer system active in 200 countries. The deal, which was scrutinized by the US government on national security grounds, eventually did not take place.[96]

In 2010, Visa, MasterCard and Paypal suspended the use of their cards and services for making donations to Wikileaks, an NGO financed by private online donations.[97] Wikileaks owns a website that publishes, among other things, classified information on US military operations. Free speech advocates around the world condemned the payment companies for their decision to disconnect Wikileaks. They accused them of using financial blockade to silence that organization. Visa and MasterCard claimed, on the other hand, that their rules prohibited their customers from engaging in or facilitating illegal actions – in this case the publication of top secret information on US military operations. The blockade was temporarily successful. Wikileaks announced that it would stop publishing secret information and focus on raising money through alternative means.

15.2.9.2 SWIFT

The Society for Worldwide Interbank Financial Telecommunications (SWIFT) is an *industry-owned limited liability cooperative society* established under Belgian law. It is controlled by its member banks, which include the CBs of core states and many private banks. The mission of SWIFT is to provide secure messaging services to its members. SWIFT was founded in 1973 by 239 banks from 15 countries that aspired to strengthen the security of their communications so as to enable cross-border payments. Because of the role it plays in securing global transactions, SWIFT is considered the backbone of the global banking system. As of 2009, it connected 9 000 banks from more than 200 countries and territories and carried 3.76 billion messages per year. SWIFT is owned by its member-banks. Not all banks qualify to become members since SWIFT has standards that banks must comply with before they become part of the society. Members benefit from all the services offered by SWIFT while participant banks have access to limited services that pertain to their business.

A series of articles published on June 23, 2006 in a number of newspapers, brought to the fore the Terrorist Finance Tracking Program, a secret program conducted by the US Treasury Department and the CIA after the September 11, 2001 terrorist attacks on the United States. The goal of the program was to secretly track terrorist financing activity through SWIFT. The revelation of the

---

[96] Greg Roumeliotis, *US Blocks MoneyGram Sale to China's Ant Financial on National Security Concerns*, Reuters, Jan. 2, 2018.

[97] Andy Greenberg, *Visa, MasterCard Move to Choke WikiLeaks*, Forbes, Dec. 7, 2010.

program generated doubts about the privacy of communications facilitated by SWIFT. In September 2006, the Belgian government announced that SWIFT's dealings with the US authorities constituted a breach of Belgian and European privacy laws.

The EU and the United States eventually reached an understanding about how to track terrorist financing activities through SWIFT. The Terrorist Finance Tracking Program Agreement was adopted in 2010.[98] Based on that agreement, Europol's Joint Supervisory Body has the responsibility to assess whether the implementation of the agreement violates the data protection rights of individuals. On March 2, 2011, the joint body pointed out that the United States' requests for information were 'too general and too abstract', making it difficult for Europol to evaluate the necessity of providing the data requested.[99] The joint body was more positive in its subsequent appraisal of the Terrorist Finance Tracking Program, but the conflict between the expected privacy of transactions and transparency required for tracking the financing of terrorism remained largely unresolved.[100]

SWIFT's nature as a private company and its establishment within the European Union, a close ally to the United States, make it a convenient means for imposing financial sanctions on states. In January 2012, an advocacy group called United Against Nuclear Iran launched a campaign asking SWIFT to terminate all of its relationships with Iran's banking system, including the CB of Iran. United Against Nuclear Iran asserted that Iran's membership in SWIFT violated the US and the EU financial sanctions against that country. In February 2012, the US Senate Banking Committee unanimously approved sanctions against SWIFT pressuring the private Belgian financial telecommunications society to terminate its ties with the Iranian banks. On March 17, 2012, following an agreement two days earlier between all 27 states of the EU Council,[101] SWIFT disconnected all Iranian banks, including the CB of

---

[98] Agreement between the European Union and the United States of America on the processing and transfer of Financial Messaging Data from the European Union to the United States for purposes of the Terrorist Finance Tracking Program, OJ L 8/11, 13.1.2010.

[99] Europol Joint Supervisory Body, US and EU Agreement on Exchanging Personal Data for the Purposes of the Terrorist Finance Tracking Program (the TFTP Agreement) – First Inspection Performed by the Europol Joint Supervisory Body (JSB) Raises Serious Concerns about Compliance with Data Protection Principles, Press Release, Mar. 2, 2011.

[100] Europol JSB Inspection of the Implementation of the TFTP Agreement, Report 15/28, Sept. 8, 2015.

[101] *See* Council Regulation (EU) No. 267/2012 of 23 March 2012 concerning restrictive measures against Iran and repealing Regulation (EU) No. 961/2010, OJ L 88/1, 24.3.12.

Iran,[102] from its network.[103] Banning Iranian banks from using the backbone of the global banking system, disabling their communications with other banks, inflicted a huge blow on Iran's financial system.

Since this Iranian precedent, SWIFT has been pressured by a variety of NGOs and states that seek to punish certain governments. SWIFT has been pressured to ban Russian banks from using its network because of Russia's conflict with Ukraine. It has also been pressured to ban Israeli banks by pro-Palestinian states. In general, SWIFT has tried to maintain its neutrality and has resisted being used as the financial weapon of last resort. In the case of Iran, SWIFT defended its actions by claiming that as 'a private cooperative and a utility with a systemic global character' it had no authority to punish states. Because it is incorporated under Belgian law, though, it had to comply with the EU regulations that Belgium implements as a member of the EU.

The bottom line is that SWIFT is a Belgian private company, not an international organization. States whose banks are disconnected from SWIFT owing to Belgian law do not have a readily available course of action against it. SWIFT may claim to be neutral, but given the way it is legally structured there is no guarantee that it has the capacity to remain open to all states in case of a global upheaval that upsets relationships among them. Because of threats that it could be disconnected from SWIFT, Russia has developed an alternative system. Since January 2016, 330 Russian banks have been connected to the financial messaging system of the Bank of Russia, the SPFS, the Russian response to SWIFT. At this point, this system cannot rival SWIFT in terms of the volume of transactions it carries. It does, however, ensure that, in case SWIFT is not available owing to geopolitical conflict, Russia has an alternative to help it conduct transactions with other states. The Cross-Border Interbank Payment System established by China constitutes another more serious source of competition to SWIFT.

15.2.9.3 Clearing houses

Clearing houses or CCPs are firms that clear and settle securities transactions. After the 2008 financial crisis, the G-20 made it mandatory to settle non-customized derivatives contracts through clearing houses. By 2016, about 62% of the $544 trillion global derivatives market, previously settled

---

[102] The CB of Iran contested the sanctions unsuccessfully. *See Central Bank of Iran v. Council*, Case C-266/15 P, Apr. 7, 2016.

[103] SWIFT, SWIFT Instructed to Disconnect Sanctioned Iranian Banks Following EU Council Decision, Press Release, Mar. 15, 2012.

OTC, was cleared through CCPs.[104] This rendered some clearing houses too-big-to-fail, making further regulatory vigilance necessary.

The Depository Trust & Clearing Corporation (DTCC) clears and settles most securities transactions in the United States, amounting to $1.6 quadrillion in 2014.[105] Because of its dominant role, the DTCC is an systemically important financial market utility that can be used by the United States to lock countries out of its financial markets. On August 29, 2017, the DTCC announced that it would no longer settle certain Venezuela bond trades because of the US sanctions imposed on that country. According to the US Executive Order issued on August 17, 2017, all transactions related to the provision of financing to Venezuela involving a US person or person located within the United States (including branches of foreign banks) were prohibited.[106] The DTCC's refusal to settle claims on Venezuelan bonds was not expected to be that detrimental to the country given that Venezuela's debt is cleared mostly through Europe-based clearing houses. The US Treasury, however, warned that even indirect bond transactions involving Venezuela, for example those executed in European markets but conducted by a US person or person located in the United States, would violate the sanctions.

15.3   THE LIBOR FINANCIAL SCANDAL

A benchmark is an index that helps evaluate the performance of an investment. As we have explained in Chapter 4,[107] benchmark developers can shape the global financial markets because they are the *de facto* arbiters of how investors allocate their money in those markets. In 2016, 11.7 trillion in assets tracked the benchmarks developed by the S&P Global, the company that manages the S&P 500 and DJIA.[108] The MSCI indexes were tracked by $11 trillion in assets including hedge funds and pension funds.[109] The fact that benchmarks are followed by so much money gives index providers significant leverage in the market. If the S&P Global decides, for various reasons, to drop a company from its indexes, funds that follow those indexes would have to sell all the

---

[104]   BIS, Statistical Release: OTC Derivatives Statistics at End-June 2016, at 4, Nov. 2016.

[105]   DTCC, New DTCC Data Products Service to Provide Dynamic Data Provisioning and Easier Access to DTCC Data, Press Release, June 30, 2015.

[106]   White House, Presidential Executive Order on Imposing Sanctions with Respect to the Situation in Venezuela, Aug. 25, 2017.

[107]   Chapter 4, Section 4.1.5.

[108]   S&P Dow Jones Indices Annual Survey of Assets, Dec. 31, 2016.

[109]   Global Indexes: Delivering the Modern Index Strategy, at 2, MSCI Brochure, May 2017.

stocks of that company. This huge divestment could trigger an abrupt drop in that company's stock. The market power of index companies is even more problematic because of the opaque methodologies they use to develop indexes.

Index companies not only index companies; they index countries. Because of this, they can be pressured by their home country to eject from their indexes states it considers its enemies. JP Morgan, an investment bank, develops indexes that track the performance of emerging market government bonds. Because of that role, it was under pressure in 2017 to exclude Venezuela's dollar-denominated debt from its Emerging Market Bond Index so as to help implement the US sanctions against that state.[110]

LIBOR (London InterBank Offered Rate) is a benchmark IR that is anchored to the rates banks expect to be charged in the interbank market. The calculation of LIBOR is not based on actual transactions but on a survey of large banks that make up the LIBOR panel. The banks are asked the following hypothetical question: 'At what rate *could* you borrow funds, were you to do so by asking for and then accepting inter-bank offers in a *reasonable* market size just prior to 11 am London Time' (emphasis added). In 2007, 16 banks made up the panel that helped determine LIBOR for the US dollar by submitting their notional borrowing rate for 15 maturities in that currency. Because LIBOR was not based on actual transactions, but on responses to an open-ended question submitted by banks, it could be easily manipulated. Banks provided the rates they claimed they could borrow at, but the methodologies they used for determining these borrowing rates were not disclosed to the public.

On May 29, 2008, the *Wall Street Journal* reported that several banks were submitting very low borrowing costs for the calculation of the daily LIBOR. The *Wall Street Journal* suggested that these banks were 'low-balling their borrowing rates to avoid looking desperate for cash'.[111] At the peak of the 2008 financial crisis, LIBOR rates seemed at times to be below what was expected based on other related benchmark IRs. Eventually, the UK and US authorities concluded that a number of private banks were involved in an elaborate scheme to manipulate LIBOR. Seven financial institutions had to settle charges with the CFTC and the US Department of Justice. The cumulative penalties and fines paid in the United States were more than $3 billion. Penalties paid in other jurisdictions exceeded $6 billion. The heavy fines were imposed

---

[110] Emily Glazer, *US Sanctions Could Prompt JP Morgan to Push Venezuela from Bond Index*, WSJ, Aug. 24, 2017.

[111] Carrick Mollenkamp and Mark Whitehouse, *Study Casts Doubt on Key Rate*, WSJ, May 29, 2008.

after it was determined that the banks had colluded to benefit themselves at the expense of their clients.[112]

At the time of the eruption of the scandal, the British Bankers Association, a private, non-profit body, was responsible for administering LIBOR. This tainted the standing of all private banking associations that were administrating IRs critical for the functioning of the markets. Today LIBOR is administered by ICE, a company based in the United States that is considered a financial utility. Moreover, the UK Financial Conduct Authority, a government body, has assumed responsibility for supervising the administration of LIBOR.

Because of its fall from grace, some have proposed getting rid of LIBOR and developing alternative benchmarks to take its place. However, 'ending LIBOR' is not that simple. As of 2017, contracts worth $150 trillion were still tied to US dollar LIBOR. Untangling these contracts from LIBOR was expected to be a laborious and expensive exercise necessitating renegotiation and redrafting.[113] Moreover, alternative rates had to be established before ending the use of LIBOR. In 2014, the Board of Governors and the FRBNY put together the Alternative Reference Rates Committee, a group of large banks, and tasked it with identifying alternatives to LIBOR. The Alternative Reference Rates Committee proposed the Secured Overnight Financing Rate (SOFR). The SOFR is based on the cost of borrowing cash overnight among banks using Treasury securities as collateral – the Treasury repo market. Unlike LIBOR, the SOFR is transactions based. The SOFR was first published in April 3, 2018. It is now published every business day by the FRBNY.[114]

15.4 ALTERNATIVE PAYMENT SYSTEMS

15.4.1 Digital Cash

In many rich countries, notes and coins make up only a small portion of the money in circulation. Most money moves around electronically, rarely taking physical form. In fact, new technologies, including electronic payments and mobile cash, should have made physical cash completely obsolete. However, cash endures. Cash has an advantage that no other method of payment possesses. It enables anonymous transactions. This is why it is used to purchase illegal drugs and to compensate unlawfully hired employees or to avoid taxa-

---

[112] Several private actors brought lawsuits against the banks, *see*, e.g. *In re: LIBOR -Based Financial Instruments Antitrust Litigation*, 935 F.Supp.2d 666 (2013).

[113] Jerome H. Powell, *Reforming U.S. Dollar LIBOR: The Path Forward*, at 6, Remarks at the Money Marketeers of New York University, Sept. 4, 2014.

[114] FRBNY, Statement Introducing the Treasury Repo Reference Rates, Press Release, Apr. 3, 2018.

tion. The cost of cash to a government is the tax revenue it forgoes from cash transactions. Because these transactions do not have to be recorded anywhere, people can easily avoid paying the taxes associated with them. A conservative estimate of this forgone tax revenue in the United States is $100 billion annually.[115] Large denomination notes like the EUR500 are especially useful for unlawful cash transfers. It is estimated that EUR295 billion circulates globally in EUR500 notes. Yet most Europeans rarely see these notes as they are hoarded by those who move large amounts of cash around illegally. Discontinuing the printing of large denomination notes should help governments track criminals.[116]

India was one of the first countries that decided to eliminate large notes. On November 8, 2016, it announced that the 500 rupee (a functional equivalent of $50) and the 1 000 rupee (a functional equivalent of $100) notes would no longer be legal tender.[117] This amounted to a huge demonetization given that 86% worth of cash in circulation became suddenly worthless. People holding the disbanded notes were given until December 31, 2016 to deposit them with banks. Large deposits that seemed unusual were investigated and subjected to taxes and penalties. The government planned the demonetization secretly and announced it suddenly, placing India at the forefront of the crusade against cash. The prime minister of the country declared that his aim was to create a cashless society. Getting rid of India's massive informal cash economy, estimated at $2 trillion, by demonetizing the large notes that are used to store wealth, was the first step in that direction. The demonetization created a severe cash crunch, though, and shrank the revenues of street vendors who only dealt in cash. The well-off remained unperturbed and resorted to money laundering to hide their wealth. To avoid depositing large amounts of cash, business owners started to pay employees months in advance. Others claimed higher sales to justify their large cash holdings. Some even bought gold, which was easy to take out of the country and exchange for global reserve currencies. Critics argued that the government's aggressive drive to uproot the informal economy would eventually shake people's faith in the currency as a store of value.

The United States is much less keen on demonetization. As the US Treasury has stated, the chances of discontinuing the $100 bill are quite slim simply

---

[115] Bhaskar Chakravort, *The Hidden Costs of Cash*, Harvard Business Review, June 26, 2014.

[116] Kenneth Rogoff, *Costs and Benefits to Phasing out Paper Currency*, Paper Presented at NBER Macroeconomics Annual Conference, Apr. 11, 2014.

[117] Geeta Anand and Hari Kumar, *Narendra Modi Bans India's Largest Currency Bills in Bid to Cut Corruption*, NYT, Nov. 8, 2016.

because it is the world's reserve asset.[118] CBs around the world keep stacks of $100 bills in their vaults in addition to gold. Converting the whole US economy into digital cash is also difficult simply because 8% of the population is unbanked. Loss of faith in banks and zero IRs, which were prevalent after the 2008 panic, are other reasons that motivate people to hold on to physical cash. The number of $100 bills in circulation as of December 2016 was estimated to be $1.5 trillion – a 76% increase since 2009.[119]

When the Swiss CB introduced negative IRs in 2014, the 1 000 Swiss franc note enabled people to avoid the banks altogether by keeping their stash of cash at home. Economists, therefore, urged the Swiss CB to abolish the 1 000 franc note. At the other extreme, members of Zurich's parliament put forward a proposal to create a 5 000 franc note. According to them, keeping wealth stockpiled in cash, and out of the reach of banks, digital payment systems or governments, is a fundamental human right that guarantees privacy and freedom.[120]

15.4.2   Bitcoin

The 2008 financial crisis motivated many people to seek alternatives to traditional banking. The bitcoin system, which started to capture public's attention in 2010, looked like an attractive, open payment system: a peer-to-peer way of running a currency that promised to make money transfers as easy as sending emails. Bitcoin was allegedly developed by someone called Satoshi Nakamoto, who published his ideas online and then disappeared without anybody knowing his real identity. This mythic founding of the bitcoin technology, the blockchain, contributed to the hype surrounding the currency.

The blockchain can be visualized as a gigantic ledger that keeps track of who owns how much bitcoin. The coins themselves are not physical objects or digital files but entries on the blockchain ledger. Owning bitcoin means possessing a piece of information written on the blockchain. Defining the blockchain as a big version of a regular bank's ledger makes it sound like a dull technology. What renders it revolutionary is the way it is organized. While a bank's ledger is centralized and private, the blockchain is public and distributed widely. Theoretically anyone can download a copy of it. Unlike a bank ledger, which can be changed by the bank on its own will or at the request of a government, the blockchain cannot be changed without simultaneously

---

[118] Statement of Jacob Lew, US Treasury Secretary quoted in Adam Creighton, *Cash is Dead. Long Live Cash*, WSJ, Apr. 9, 2017.

[119] *Id.*

[120] *See*, e.g. Bruno J. Schneller and Miranda Ademaj, *Put into Respective: Ahead of the Mainstream*, at 14, Skënderbeg Alternative Investments, Mar. 2016.

modifying all of the copies downloaded on the thousands of computers located worldwide. What the blockchain looks like is determined by the majority vote of the computers that manage it.

In the traditional banking system, a bank stands between two parties as a neutral intermediary for the transfer of money between them. For bitcoin, the blockchain is this trusted third-party intermediary. It is a database that contains the history of every bitcoin in circulation. The identities of the owners of bitcoin are protected by public key cryptography, but the rest of the system is entirely transparent to those with the technological means to access it. It is this transparency that acts as a shield against fraud. The public key cryptography used to protect the anonymity of bitcoin owners requires that each person who wishes to transfer bitcoins holds two 'keys'. One key is the private key. This key is the secret of the owner, very much like a computer password. The other key is the public key – the key that makes it possible for the rest of the bitcoin world to identify the owner. The private and public keys are connected through an algorithm embedded in the bitcoin software that makes it possible for users to authenticate bitcoin ownership by simply seeing only the public key.

Person A, who wants to transfer bitcoins to person B, creates a message to the bitcoin network, a 'transaction', asking for the transfer of bitcoins from her public address to B's public address. She signs her request with her private key. A's public key enables everybody who uses the network to authenticate that the transaction was indeed signed with A's private key, and that B is the owner of bitcoins transferred to him by A. The transaction is recorded and time-stamped. It is there on the blockchain for anybody to see it as one of the transactions that make a block of the blockchain.[121] Every transaction that occurs in the bitcoin network is registered on the blockchain, the bitcoin's distributed public ledger. The blockchain is designed in such a way as to guarantee that each bitcoin is unique so that the sender does not spend the same bitcoin more than once.

Like any technology, the blockchain has to be maintained by people who have the incentive to keep it functioning. The incentive here is the award of newly minted bitcoins.[122] Every 10 minutes a number of computers belonging to different owners called miners take a block of pending transactions and use it as the input for a mathematical puzzle. The first computer to find the solution to the puzzle announces it to the rest, which check whether it is right. If the majority (51%) concur, the block of transactions is authenticated

---

[121] Jerry Britto et al., *Bitcoin Financial Regulation: Securities, Derivatives, Prediction Markets, and Gambling*, 16 Columbia Science and Technology Law Review 144, at 149–50 (2014).

[122] *The Magic of Mining: Bitcoin*, Economist, Jan. 10, 2015.

and becomes part of the blockchain, which chains the blocks of transactions together sequentially. The owner of the computer that solves the puzzle gets new bitcoins as a reward, and the computers move on to authenticate a new block of transactions.[123] Committing fraud in the bitcoin world, spending for example the same bitcoins twice, can be accomplished by tampering with the consensus mechanism of authenticating transactions – that is, controlling more than 51% of the capacity of computers that make the bitcoin network. Such hacking attack would be very expensive. It is estimated that it could cost at least $425 million in equipment and electricity.[124]

During bitcoin's infancy, most miners were individuals who created bitcoins using their home computers. As the value of the currency increased, miners started to combine their computing power and share the rewards. Most of bitcoin mining today is done by pools of miners.[125] Miners use specialized hardware powered by customized chips known as Application Specific Integrated Circuits. Some mining has moved to the cloud as cloud companies have started to sell online mining capacity in gigahashes per second, that is enough computing power to enable one billion attempts per second to solve a 'hash function' – the puzzle that must be solved to authenticate a block of bitcoin transactions.[126] Like any other energy-intensive industry, mining bitcoins can be done on a large scale in places where electricity is inexpensive and reliable. Countries with cold climates have an advantage because of their lower costs of cooling down the computers used to solve hash functions.[127] Miners in Inner Mongolia, where electricity is cheap, have built large-scale bitcoin operations.

A big myth about bitcoin is that it operates without institutional intermediaries. In fact, a number of intermediaries make possible the functioning of bitcoin. Bitcoin wallets, offered by various companies, provide the software that makes it possible for people to carry bitcoin balances and to pay with bitcoins. Bitcoin exchanges make it possible to convert real-world currency, such as dollars and euros, into bitcoin.

Mt. Gox was a private bitcoin exchange established in 2010 in Tokyo, Japan. By 2014, it was the biggest bitcoin exchange in the world, handling more than 70% of all bitcoin transactions. In February 2014, it suspended its operations and turned off its website while simultaneously announcing that about 850 000 bitcoins were missing from its wallet and probably stolen, an amount valued at more than $450 million at the time. In the beginning it was unclear whether

---

[123] *Id.*
[124] *Id.*
[125] *Id.*
[126] *Id.*
[127] *Id.*

the reason for the disappearance was theft or fraud. In 2015, investigations revealed that Mt. Gox had been hacked and that the missing bitcoins had been stolen gradually from its wallet starting in 2011. In January 2015, Bitstamp, another bitcoin exchange, suspended operations after reporting that 19 000 bitcoins had disappeared owing to a hacking attack.[128]

The US regulatory agencies started to investigate the bitcoin world as early as 2013. The Financial Crimes Enforcement Network of the Treasury (FinCEN) issued guidance in March 2013 clarifying that bitcoin exchanges qualified as money transmitters under the Bank Secrecy Act.[129] Because of that, they had to register with the FinCEN as money services business in every state in which they operated. The Bank Secrecy Act makes it clear that money transmitters must comply with 'know your customer' rules, have in place anti-money-laundering programs and file 'Suspicious Activity Reports' on the transactions of their clients.[130] In May 2013, federal agents siezed $5 million from Mt. Gox because the company had failed to register with the FinCEN.[131] The US tax authority, the Internal Revenue Service, issued a guidance in 2014 on the tax treatment of bitcoins to quell the tax avoidance opportunities provided by the currency.[132]

The volatility of bitcoin alienates many users and makes it look like a speculative investment. Small miners have tried to keep bitcoin small and outside the purview of government. The big mining companies hope to bring bitcoin to the mainstream and are willing to accept more government oversight. These two groups tend to disagree over the 'block' – the number of transactions processed together at once through the bitcoin network. On August 1, 2017, bitcoin experienced a breakup, a 'fork', that led to the creation of a new digital currency called Bitcoin Cash. Bitcoin's block size limit remained 1 megabyte, but Bitcoin Cash increased the limit to 8 megabytes, making it possible for 2 million transactions to be processed daily.

Despite its reputation as an anonymous currency, bitcoin's anonymity is good as long as nobody is interested in finding the identities of those who use bitcoins. The public nature of the blockchain means that unless users channel their transactions through software that encrypts them, they can ultimately be traced. New technologies have been developed, therefore, to place additional layers of anonymity on bitcoin transactions.

---

[128] *Id.*
[129] Bank Secrecy Act of 1970, 31 USC §§ 5311–32.
[130] 12 CFR 21.11.
[131] Jose Pagliery, *How Mt.Gox Went Down*, CNN, Feb. 26, 2014.
[132] IRS, Virtual Currency Guidance: Virtual Currency is Treated as Property for US Federal Tax Purposes, Press Release, Mar. 25, 2014.

A big irony about bitcoin is that it is digital currency that needs safekeeping in the real world. People keep their bitcoins secure by protecting their private keys. They make copies of those keys on hard drives which they then store in safety deposit boxes all over the world.[133] Even those who have faith in the technology, like doubting Thomases, feel the need to fiddle with the intangible to convince themselves it is real.

15.4.3   Gold

The existing above-the-ground stock of gold is 184 000 metric tonnes. Seventeen percent of this stock is held by CBs worldwide in their reserves; 20% is privately held as investment; 47% is privately owned as jewelry; and 14% is used in other fabricated products. The remaining 2% is unaccounted for.[134]

The total official gold reserves are 33 249 tonnes; out of this amount, the United States holds 8134 tonnes and the eurozone 10 786 tonnes. The United States and the eurozone, in other words, hold together 57% of all official gold reserves.[135] The rest of officially held gold is dispersed among 86 states and the IMF. Gold constitutes 74% of US FX reserves, 68% of Germany's reserves and 54% of the reserves of the eurozone as a whole. In contrast, gold is only 2% of China's FX reserves.[136] In terms of private holders of gold, one of the world's largest is an exchange-traded fund, the SPDR Gold Trust launched in 2004, whose gold is stored in vaults in London. The fund holds 26 798 117 ounces of gold[137] (833 metric tonnes). This is more than the gold held by the CB of Japan.

Gold has been demonetized, which means that it cannot be used formally as a means of exchange. The question, then, is why CBs and individuals continue to hold gold. Some amass gold because they believe it can provide a hedge against inflation. Others stockpile it because they do not have much faith in the value of the currency their government prints. Still others believe that the world's economic system founded on the dollar may someday collapse. At that point, gold would be the only thing that could be used as a means of exchange. Some of these intuitions are correct. Gold may not provide a good hedge against day-to-day inflation but it does provide a decent protection against hyperinflation and currency debasement.

---

[133]   Britto et al., *supra* note 121, at 173.
[134]   US Geological Survey (USGS), 2014 Minerals Yearbook: Gold [Advance Release], at 31.1.
[135]   IMF International Financial Statistics (IFS), Jan. 2017.
[136]   *Id.*
[137]   Prospectus SPDR Gold Trust, at 2, May 8, 2017.

Because of its monetary utility gold is a unique commodity. The market price of gold is not very attached to the supply and demand of gold, as happens with other commodities, but reflects how people feel about economic growth and the potential threats that emanate from the geopolitical environment. High unemployment, terrorist bombings or the testing of nuclear devices by a rogue state can all affect the price of gold. Because people view gold as a store of wealth, some have argued that it should assume an official role in the international monetary system.[138] The United States goes to extraordinary lengths to keep its gold safe. The US Bullion Depository, Fort Knox, is a fortified building next to the US Army post of Fort Knox, Kentucky. It holds 4176 metric tonnes of gold, making it second to the FRBNY's underground vault in Manhattan, which holds about 6350 metric tonnes, some of it in trust for other countries and international organizations.

Other places that are famous for their secure gold vaults are London, Switzerland and Dubai. In 2016, the Industrial and Commercial Standard Bank of China bought Barclays' London precious metals vault, giving the Chinese bank the capacity to store gold worth more than $80 billion. The vault, one of the largest in Europe, was expected to facilitate the entry of the bank into the London precious metals market. The Dubai Multi Commodities Center competes with the USB and Credit Suisse, the leaders in gold storage in Switzerland. The gold vaults beneath the Dubai Multi Commodities Center, at Jumeirah Lakes Towers, are five stories underground and one story below sea level.

Switzerland is a country that people naturally associate with gold. The Swiss franc was the only currency that was explicitly backed by gold until 2000, long after many countries had switched to fiat currencies. Switzerland imports the equivalent of 81% of the world's gold production.[139] States and organizations that contest the world order are also obsessed with hoarding gold. When the Islamic State in Iraq and Syria (ISIS), a terrorist organization, was trying to stabilize its rule in the Middle East in 2016, it tried to disentangle itself from the dollar and establish a new currency based on gold. Russia, which was bombarded by US financial sanctions after it annexed Crimea to its territory, quadrupled its gold stock between 2004 and 2017, to 1615 metric tonnes. It was also actively investing in mining projects in southern Siberia to unearth

---

[138] Ettore Durrucci and Julie McKay, *The International Monetary System After the Financial Crisis*, at 34, ECB Occasional Paper Series No. 123, Feb. 2011.

[139] John Letzing, *Switzerland's Niche in Global Gold Trade Draws Scrutiny*, WSJ, Dec. 25, 2016.

more gold. The Russian CB viewed the stockpiling of gold reserves as a '100% guarantee against legal and political risks'.[140]

A powerful industry association plays a vital role in setting the market price of gold – the London Bullion Market Association (LBMA). Members of the LBMA are banks that deal with gold or silver bullion in the London market. These banks pay between £5 000 and £12 000 annually to become members of the LBMA, depending on the membership type they are entitled to. Becoming a member of the LBMA is not for the uninitiated. When applying for membership, a company must list three LBMA members as sponsors. Each sponsor must provide a letter of recommendation that confirms the candidate's suitability for membership in the association.

An important benchmark for gold transactions is the London Gold Fixing (or Gold Fix). It is used to fix the gold price for the settlement of contracts in the London bullion market. It is employed also, more broadly, as a benchmark for pricing the majority of gold futures products and derivatives exchanged throughout the world's markets. The banks that do the fixing are the market makers of the LBMA. The monopoly of the LBMA in determining the price of gold has been challenged by China. China has ambitions to become one of the world's leading gold trading centers. China's position as one of the world's largest producers and buyers of gold has been used to leverage the Shanghai market as a gold trading hub. The fraudulent manipulation of the London Gold Fix by Western banks[141] provided an opportunity for the Shanghai Gold Exchange (SGE) to grab some of London's market share. The SGE Gold Fix is determined by the board of the SGE, which consists of some 67 mostly Chinese firms and some foreign banks. It is calculated based on the contracts for physical gold that are trading at the SGE. The London Gold Fix, on the other hand, is much more opaque. It is put together by a much smaller club of Western banks on the basis of undisclosed OTC trades.

The lack of transparency of the London Gold Fix has not served it well. In 2014, UK regulators fined Barclays $34 million for manipulating the fix. The rigging of the London Gold Fix and the establishment of the SGE forced the LBMA to alter its governance. While the LBMA still owns the intellectual property rights associated with the fix, it has assigned its administration to a US corporation, the ICE.

---

[140] Thomas Grove, *Siberian Gold Find Brightens Ruble's Future*, WSJ, Feb. 7, 2019.

[141] *See*, e.g. Jonathan Stempel, *Deutsche Bank to Pay $60 Million to Settle US Gold Price-fixing Case*, Reuters, Dec. 2, 2016.

15.4.4 Informal Payment Networks

Informal payment networks are those that operate outside the conventional banking system.[142] The hawala is the informal network in the Middle East through which people pay cash at one location to a money changer and the recipient draws the equivalent amount of money at another place without money actually moving. Informal payment networks are used largely for remittances, payments from people who work abroad to their families in their home countries. Informal payment networks are also employed by companies and government agencies that need to conduct business in countries with underdeveloped banking systems. Because informal payment systems can offer both security and anonymity, they are also used to conduct illegal activities. After the September 11, 2001 terrorist attacks, informal payment systems are scrutinized constantly to prevent money laundering and the financing of terrorism. In 2016, for instance, some of the 1600 money changers in Iraq facilitated wittingly or unwittingly ISIS's transactions. The Iraqi CB banned about 140 of them from receiving dollars in the hope of crippling ISIS operations, but it could not disband them all. Closing them down was a sure way to choke the economy since half of Iraqi trade took place through them.

The design of the hawala system was copied by France, Germany and the UK when they developed a payment system, the Instrument in Support of Trade Exchanges (INSTEX),[143] the purpose of which was to bypass payment systems associated with the dollar, such as SWIFT. The system was to be used to make possible transactions with Iran after the new sanctions imposed on that country in 2019 by the United States. INSTEX would initially facilitate trade in goods that were not covered by the US sanctions, such as medicines and consumer goods. After the initial trial period, it was expected to be expanded to cover all European trade with Iran. This is how INSTEX was to process the sale of medicines by a German company to an Iranian buyer. The German exporter would not be paid by the Iranian buyer but by a German company that imports Iranian goods to Germany. Similarly, the Iranian buyer of the medicine would pay the Iranian exporter of goods to Germany.[144] No dollars would

---

[142] *See generally* Nikos Passas, *Informal Value Transfer Systems, Terrorism and Money Laundering: A Report to the National Institute of Justice* (2003).

[143] Joint statement of foreign ministers of France, Germany and the UK on the creation of INSTEX, the special purpose vehicle aimed at facilitating legitimate trade with Iran in the framework of the efforts to preserve the Joint Comprehensive Plan of Action (JCPOA), January 31, 2019, https://www.diplomatie.gouv.fr.

[144] Justin Scheck and Bradley Hope, *The Dollar Underpins American Power: Rivals are Building Workarounds*, WSJ, May 29, 2019.

be involved in the transaction, which meant that the United States would have no jurisdiction over it.

The extensive use of the dollar to punish foes and intimidate allies has pushed many countries to question the merits of their dependence on it[145] and to invent roundabouts to free themselves from it.[146]

---

[145] Statement of Bruno Le Maire, Foreign Minister of France: 'Do we want to be vassals blindly following the decisions made by the US?' *cited in France Urges Europe to Push Back Against 'Unacceptable' US Sanctions on Iran*, www.france24.com, May 11, 2018.

[146] Sahil Mahtani, *The Dollar may be Knocked off its Pedestal*, WSJ, May 22, 2019.

16. Global financial regulation

16.1 REGULATING THE FINANCIAL INDUSTRY

16.1.1 Sources of Financial Instability

A sound financial system is a public good; it brings stability that is essential for the everyday transactions and maintenance of economic peace. Financial stability means the absence of volatile swings in asset prices (stocks, bonds, housing). Excessive financial instability has the potential to ruin an economy. *Consumer price instability* that is accelerating inflation or deflation and *financial asset instability* expressed by booms and busts in the markets are collective action problems. Only an institution that serves the public interest can address them effectively. For most states, that institution is the CB. CBs can decrease the MB to squash *consumer price inflation* or increase it to address *consumer price deflation*. CBs can tighten the supply of credit to tackle *asset price inflation* (booms) or ease credit to deal with *asset price deflation* (busts).[1]

Central Banks do not have a good track record in taming financial instability, as witnessed by the booms and busts that characterize many economies. Being a central banker is a thankless job. CBs are charged with controlling instability in a financial system set up to be unstable owing to the creation of money through credit. Borrowing money is always risky but the risk increases depending on the type of borrowing. When companies borrow, and rely on their future cash flow to repay their debt, borrowing looks safe as long as they keep growing. When firms rely on their cash flow to make interest payments, but keep rolling over the principal amount of their debt, they engage in speculative financing that can backfire when future growth does not materialize. Some firms are even confident enough to engage in Ponzi financing. This happens when the cash flow they generate covers neither the interest nor principal amount of their debt. Firms speculate, instead, that an asset they possess, for instance, a new technology, will appreciate to an extent that it will help

---

[1] Robert C. Hockett, *The Macroprudential Turn: From Institutional 'Safety and Soundness' to Systemic 'Financial Stability' in Financial Supervision*, 9 Virginia Law and Business Review 201, at 230 (2015).

them pay back all of their debt and produce profits at a future date. Because this does not typically happen, Ponzi schemes tend to fail.[2]

Rational optimism during an economic boom can look like a Ponzi scheme during a bust. When the economy is doing well companies are willing to take on more debt to take advantage of every opportunity to grow. Banks, which share the same mentality, do not hesitate to lower credit standards. Amid the exuberance, it is difficult to tell whether the expectations of future growth are rational. Everybody knows booms do not last forever, but nobody can predict the bust. At some point, though, the bust occurs. This usually happens when debt levels reach breaking point and asset prices start to collapse. Then people are as eager to exit the markets as they were keen to enter them before.

This herd behavior of market participants brings us to the second dynamic that makes the financial system unstable: contagion. Contagion can lead to the failure of the banking system when the run on a bank triggers runs on all banks. In market economies, peoples' savings are borrowed by others who want to invest in new ventures. This transformation of savings into debt is the engine of growth in these economies. Savers are aware, though, that the banking system is based on fractional banking (Fig. 1.3). It is not surprising, therefore, that they seek to be the first in line when they hear rumors that their bank may be in trouble. They know that opting out of the line will not stop the run and that they risk losing everything by not queuing along with others.[3] Given that all depositors react this way, the collapse of a bank becomes a self-fulfilling prophecy. The collapse of a bank brings to light potential vulnerabilities of other banks. As a result, the whole banking system of a state may eventually fail.

The run on a market starts with a run from a security offered in that market that is deemed to be losing value. The run is the result of the herd mentality of investors. The run may start when an investor who holds a large number of securities of a company sells a significant chunk of these securities, betting that the company's stock will fall. The bet succeeds and the company's stock dips. As a result, other investors jump on the bandwagon and sell their stocks. At some point, the selloff takes on a dynamic of its own until the company's shares lose all value. Some investors will continue selling, even at a significant loss, to avoid losing everything. Because of contagion, the stocks of companies that do business with that company will also be shorted, eventually causing a market collapse.[4] In fact, as markets are becoming more interconnected,

---

[2]   Hyman P. Minsky, *The Financial Instability Hypothesis*, Working Paper No. 74, Jerome Levy Economics Institute of Bard College, May 1992.

[3]   Hockett, *supra* note 1, at 208.

[4]   *Id.* at 213.

the chances of contagion have multiplied. When firm A owes firm B, A's insolvency increases the chances of B's insolvency. If B, in turn, owes C, A's failure threatens the survival of C also. And so on. This chain reaction can lead to the simultaneous demise of many companies.

The integration and globalization of the markets have contributed to the instability of the financial system. Some have argued that the 2008 crisis was amplified by the homogeneity of the financial markets caused by globalization. Banks, insurers, hedge funds and many others bought the same debt securities, the MBS, to diversify their individual portfolios. From the viewpoint of each firm that bought these securities, this made sense. From a systemic standpoint, however, it seemed that everybody was betting on the appreciation of the same assets. The fact that banks were following similar risk models by assigning less risk to mortgage debt, in compliance with the Basel II standards, did not help either.

16.1.2   The Role of Regulation

The purpose of financial regulation is to correct market failure, the negative externalities of economic activities. Financial regulation aims to undercut firms' ability to inflict externalities on the whole financial system, and the population that depends on that system, because of their own risk-taking activities.[5] The tendency of firms to collude and create monopolies and oligopolies is another reason to closely regulate them. Competition among firms on the price and quality of products and services they offer does not happen spontaneously. It is made possible by the enactment of pro-competition laws and anti-trust regulations. While companies are born to accumulate market power by eradicating or colluding with their competitors,[6] the state's job is to break up monopolies and oligopolies for the benefit of the average consumer. Related to their oligopolistic tendencies are the conflicts of interests that many firms face, one of which is whether to serve their own interests at the expense of those of their clients. Today, global financial firms possess economies of scale that enable them to intermediate the transactions between capital owners and capital seekers. At the same time, these economies of scale fuel their oligopolistic tendencies and make them prone to conflicts of interest.[7]

---

[5]   Thomas Oatley and Kindred W. Winecoff, *The Domestic Rooting of Financial Regulation in an Era of Global Capital Markets* 474, at 483, in 'Research Handbook on Hedge Funds, Private Equity and Alternative Investments' (Phoebus Athanassiou, ed., 2012).

[6]   *See* Peter Thiel, *Competition is for Losers*, WSJ, Sept. 12, 2014.

[7]   *See* Chapter 15.

After the panic of 2008, macro-prudential regulation, enacted by CBs and other regulatory agencies, has been considered necessary to protect the financial system from the negative externalities of financial activities. The drive to protect and regulate, however, has to be counterbalanced by the pursuit of growth – the need to move capital to the most productive uses.[8] Tradeoffs have to be made because the stricter the financial regulation, the higher the cost of capital. Too much regulation decreases the quantity of money available through credit and curtails economic activity.

16.1.3   National Regulators: Cooperation, Coercion, Exclusion

States are not the most skillful regulators as they have to grapple with their own conflict of interests. States are aware that they need to adopt and enforce regulation for the benefit of their people. At the same time, they are reluctant to over-regulate domestic firms, especially the national champions.[9] States tend to regulate their banks lightly and help them establish themselves as quasi-monopolies. They are apprehensive that, if their banks are strictly regulated, they will lose market share to banks of states with looser standards. Guaranteeing monopoly privileges, and thus profits, also blunts incentives to engage in aggressive lending and makes banks safer. In the United States, the 1933 Glass–Steagall Act, which separated investment banking from commercial banking, did so partly to guarantee that commercial banks would not to have to face competition from investment banks. Guaranteeing the profitability of domestic industry is precisely the reason why states prevent foreign financial firms from entering their domestic markets or limit the types of services that such firms provide. Despite the freedom-of-capital rhetoric, states believe that having an indigenous financial industry will help them grow. The suggestion that opening the door to foreign competitors would boost rather than replace home-grown companies, by forcing them to sink or swim, to many states sounds quite treacherous.

All states have an interest in regulating their banking sector to achieve financial stability and manage the tumultuous boom and bust cycles that hit their economies. Not all states have the same priorities, though. The United States, a country with a strong financial pedigree, can afford to regulate its financial sector more strictly and consistently by requiring its financial firms to apply more rigorous credit standards and to hold more capital to address future

---

    [8]   Daniel K. Tarullo, *Banking on Basel: The Future of International Financial Regulation* 8 (2008).

    [9]   Philip G. Cerny, *Rethinking Financial Regulation: Risk, Club Goods and Regulatory Fatigue* 343, in 'Handbook of International Political Economy of Monetary Relations' (Thomas Oatley and W. Kindred Winecoff, eds, 2014).

losses. Developing states, which have a much less developed financial sector and whose economies are in a more embryonic stage, may, on the other hand, wish to give their banks more latitude to grant credit to small or medium-sized companies whose credit is untested.

When banking started to globalize in the 1970s, many US banks felt constrained by US laws and regulations, especially those regarding the amount of capital they needed to put aside in order to provide credit. US firms claimed that the lower capital requirements adopted by other states gave foreign banks an unfair competitive advantage in the global marketplace. Banks asked the US authorities to level the global playing field.[10] This could be accomplished by:

- laxer US requirements;
- cooperation with other countries that could be convinced or coerced to adopt standards similar to those of the United States – the extra-territorial application of US regulations;
- closure of the US financial market to other states' firms – a coercive measure given the central role of the United States in the global financial system.

Cooperation with other states that worked with the United States to develop global rules was the way the United States chose to protect its banks. In the 1970s, at the time of the adoption of Basel I, the first set of global banking standards, the US financial industry was facing increasing competition from the banking sectors of Japan and Germany. Japanese banks, which were subject to lower capital requirements than their US counterparts, were gaining market share both in the United States and internationally. By 1988, the three largest US banks, Citigroup, Chase and Bank of America, had fallen to the 11th, 39th and 41st place, respectively, in the list of largest global banks.[11]

In 1986, the United States worked together with the UK to adopt a common agreement on the capital requirements for banks. After the conclusion of that agreement, the United States asked Japan, Germany and France to endorse the standards established in that agreement. Otherwise, the United States would require their banks, which had subsidiaries in the United States, to comply with the capital adequacy requirements prescribed in the US–UK agreement or to exit its financial markets. Eventually, all G-10 countries acquiesced to the adoption of Basel I, which incorporated the principles included in the US–UK

---

[10] Oatley and Winecoff, *supra* note 5, at 486.
[11] Tarullo, *supra* note 8, at 47.

agreement.[12] The large financial markets of the United States and the UK made it possible for these two countries to dictate the global banking standards. The other states were aware that it would be painfully costly if their firms were to be excluded from the largest financial markets of the world.[13] States that participated in the Basel I negotiations made it clear that their priority was the impact of regulations 'on *their* banks'.[14] The harmonization of banking standards was the first onslaught on the financial autonomy of states. It was followed by demands for the harmonization of accounting standards and tax laws.

16.2   THE TORTUROUS ROAD FROM BASEL I TO BASEL III

After the 2008 financial crisis, regulators focused on making banks less susceptible to bank runs. One way to achieve that was to alter how banks finance their business. Banks can finance the loans they make using shareholders' equity (capital raised in the market) or money borrowed from depositors and other creditors. Regulators wanted banks to rely more on their equity to make loans rather than on borrowed money. Asking banks to maintain a certain amount of equity decreases the chances that their creditors will suffer losses if banks fail. When a bank becomes insolvent, the first to suffer losses are its shareholders, the owners of the bank. Next in line are its bondholders. Depositors are usually protected, up to a certain amount, by the various deposit guarantee schemes enacted by states.

States usually intervene after a bank's equity is exhausted to restructure that bank's debt to minimize bondholders' losses. Because the banking system is central to the health of the economy, most states would even nationalize private banks to ensure that depositors would not have to face losses. States, through their CBs, are lenders of last resort. The bailout of private banks when they are in trouble helps minimize economic disruption. Bailing-in bondholders and depositors, that is, telling them to bear losses if a bank fails, undermines faith in the banking system and can lead to social chaos. States ruled by responsible governments are risk-adverse. They will not risk destroying the financial system that they have painstakingly put in place by damaging people's trust in it. If bail-in is not an option and bailout is undesirable, the only other way to safeguard the banking system is to ask banks to hold more equity.

---

[12]   Narissa Lyngen, *Basel III: Dynamics of State Implementation*, 53 Harvard International Law Journal 519, at 524 (2012).

[13]   Oatley and Winecoff, *supra* note 5, at 493–4.

[14]   Tarullo, *supra* note 8, at 51. Emphasis in the original.

Regulators have used many methods to try to figure out how healthy banks are. *The capital to deposit ratio* provides a rough idea of how many resources a bank has at its disposal to protect its depositors in case it fails. The capital to deposit ratio differs from the RRR, which we analyzed in Chapter 1. The RRR measures the cash, the most liquid type of capital a bank holds, versus the money deposited with it. The *solvency ratio* measures the assets of a bank weighted based on how risky they are versus the bank's equity. This is usually expressed as capital divided by risk weighted assets (RWAs). For the ratio to be calculated a certain risk weight must be assigned to the various assets (loans) of a bank – something that can be highly subjective. Banks, in order to get around regulatory scrutiny, try to lower their RWAs. They can achieve that by making less risky loans or by using risk models that make their borrowers appear less risky than similar borrowers of other banks. It seems that banks calculate differently the probabilities of default of similar borrowers and losses they may sustain if these defaults materialize.[15]

The Basel framework is built around the idea that banks must hold a certain amount of *qualified regulatory capital to total risk-weighted assets*. The Basel I rules that were adopted in 1988[16] divided capital held by banks into two classes:

1. Tier 1 capital that included mostly shareholder equity; and
2. Tier 2 capital that included hybrid (debt/equity) instruments and subordinated debt.[17]

The weights that were assigned to calculate the riskiness of banks' assets were kept as simple as possible. Banks' assets could be assigned five risk weights: 0, 10, 20, 50 and 100%.[18] A 0% weight was attached to claims of banks on OECD governments. On the other hand, a 100% weight was assigned to private debt with the exception of loans secured by mortgages on residential property, which were assigned only a 50% risk weight.[19] This standardized method oversimplified the risk calculations for various assets. Banks complained that assets entailing different economic risk were lumped together under the same weight. The standardized risk weights that ranged from 100% for corporate loans to 0% for the debt of developed states were not always accurate.

---

[15] BCBS, Report to G-20 Finance Ministers and Central Bank Governors on Monitoring Implementation of Basel III Regulatory Reform, at 11–12, Apr. 2013.

[16] BCBS, International Convergence of Capital Measurement and Capital Standards, July 1988 (updated April 1998).

[17] *Id.* at 14.

[18] *Id.* at 8.

[19] *Id.* at 11.

The big difference between Basel I and Basel II was that the latter prescribed that banks could use their *internal risk* management models, their own proprietary methods, for measuring the risks they took by holding various assets. Based on the internal ratings-based approach, banks could rely on their own estimates of risk components for determining the capital requirements for each of their assets.[20] Banks lobbied aggressively for the official endorsement of internal risk calculation models. Skeptics, on the other hand, pointed out that there is no better way for a bank to game its capital requirements than developing its own internal models to dictate what those requirements should be.[21] After the adoption of Basel II, the RWAs to total assets, what is called RWA density, started to fall for many banks, making them look much less risky. This decline had nothing to do with a reduction in the real risks banks undertook. It had to do with how banks calculated those risks. Banks developed many complicated models for evaluating the risks entailed in the loans they were making.

The Basel III rules attempt to correct the shortcomings of Basel II. They do so by strengthening the capital requirements – the quality, consistency and transparency of capital that banks must keep.[22] To simplify here, banks' capital is divided into 'first class' capital, which is the capital banks raise in the market and their retained earnings. We call this first class capital because it is the capital that can readily absorb the losses of a bank in trouble. Owners of a bank's stocks make money when their bank does well, but they risk losing everything if their bank starts making losses. 'Second class' capital is the sort of capital that cannot always absorb the losses of a bank (e.g. debt). Creditors of a bank who hold collateral will have to be paid in full even if a bank fails. Other creditors, who are 'subordinated' to these senior creditors, may not be paid back when a bank is on the brink of insolvency. The goal of regulators when they adopted Basel III was to first, ensure that banks held enough first class capital that could be used to absorb their losses, and second, set clear expectations about which creditors would have to be bailed in – i.e. lose the money they had lent to a bank – in case that bank became insolvent. Establishing *ex-ante* bail-in rules was essential to avoid bailouts – states' intervention to save private banks using taxpayers' money.

To use the terminology of Basel III:

*   Banks need to keep *minimum total Tier 1 capital*, which includes common equity Tier 1 capital and additional Tier 1 capital (AT1). This Tier 1 capital

---

[20]   BCBS, International Convergence of Capital Measurement and Capital Standards: A Revised Framework, at 52, June 2006.

[21]   Tarullo, *supra* note 8, at 168–70.

[22]   BCBS, Basel III: A Global Regulatory Framework for More Resilient Banks and Banking Systems, Dec. 2010 [hereinafter Basel III].

must be 6% of RWAs.[23] One component of Tier I, the common equity Tier 1, includes all common shares issued by a bank and its retained earnings and must always be 4.5% of the RWAs.[24] The other component of Tier 1, the AT1, consists of preferred shares and other instruments with no fixed maturity date that are subordinated to depositors' and other creditors' claims. Holders of AT1 instruments are likely to suffer losses immediately after the ordinary shareholders. Contingent convertible securities (often referred to as CoCos) could be a major component of AT1 and serve as an available source of capital for banks in times of crisis. CoCos can absorb losses either by being converted into common equity or by suffering a principal write-down when a bank is in trouble.

- Banks also need to keep *Tier 2 capital*, consisting of lower quality or less reliable capital when compared with the capital included in Tier 1 – that is capital less effective at absorbing the losses of a bank.
- The *minimum total capital of a bank* – Tier 1 capital plus Tier 2 capital – must be at least 8% of RWAs at all times.[25]
- The *minimum total capital plus capital conservation buffer* cannot be less than 10.5% of RWAs.[26] Basel III adds a new capital requirement for banks – the *capital conservation buffer*. Banks need to limit the distribution of dividends to their shareholders if they do not meet the minimum capital plus conservation buffer requirement.
- SIFIs bear an additional *SIFI surcharge*, which means they must hold more capital than other financial firms. The United States imposes an even higher surcharge on global systemically important banks than what is required by the Basel III rules. In the United States, these banks are subject to surcharges ranging from 1 to 4.5%,[27] as opposed to the surcharge proposed by Basel of 1–2.5%.[28]

For calculating their RWAs, banks have to take into account, in addition to the riskiness of their assets, their operational risk.[29] The BIS defines opera-

---

[23] *Id.* at 28.

[24] *Id.*

[25] *Id.*

[26] *Id.* at 64.

[27] FRS, Federal Reserve Board Approves Final Rule Requiring the Largest, Most Systemically Important US Bank Holding Companies to Further Strengthen their Capital Positions, Press Release, July 20, 2015.

[28] BCBS, Global Systemically Important Banks: Updated Assessment Methodology and the Higher Loss Absorbency Requirement, at 12, July 2013.

[29] BCBS, Operational Risk – Revisions to the Simpler Approaches, Oct. 2014. *See also* BCBS, Consultative Document Standardised Measurement Approach for Operational Risk, Mar. 2016.

tional risk as 'the risk of loss resulting from inadequate or failed internal processes, people and systems or from external events'. Operational risk includes
legal risk, but excludes strategic and reputational risk.[30] It is a way to assess
how a bank's own actions, rather than unfavorable economic or market conditions, may be responsible for its failure. A large number of legal settlements,
for instance, is an indicator that a bank is more risky than other banks; thus, it
must hold more capital than others. Accounting for operational risk means that
past transgressions may continue to haunt banks. In 2017, it was estimated that
$236 billion in capital had to be retained, owing to operational risk, at the four
largest US banks because of their past lapses related to the 2008 crisis and its
aftermath. Banks claimed that having to hold so much capital, instead of using
it to make loans, contributed to the slow growth of the economy.[31] Banks view
operational risk as a form of punishment[32] for their past misconduct. Others
argue that past misdeeds are indicative of future risks given the high rate of
recidivism in corporate misconduct.[33]

Basel III requires banks to meet a minimum *universal leverage ratio* above
and beyond their capital adequacy requirements. This leverage ratio is calculated the same way across banks by simply dividing the capital of a bank
(assets minus liabilities) by its total assets. More specifically, the leverage
ratio divides the *capital measure* (equity) by the *exposure measure* (debt).[34]
The leverage ratio was adopted because, after the financial crisis, the idea that
banks could accurately assess the capital they needed based on the riskiness of
their lending was totally discredited.

Banks lobbied against the adoption of the leverage ratio. They complained
that it was a crude measure that failed to take into account the various shades
of risk presented in their operations. It is a well known fact, for instance, that
the chances of a bank losing money on a T-bill are significantly lower than
those of losing money on a car loan. However, the simplistic leverage ratio
has no way of distinguishing between the two. Because of such complaints,

---

[30]   BCBS, Principles for the Sound Management of Operational Risk, at 3, n. 5, June
2011.
[31]   Telis Demos, *The 93 Words that Could Unlock $200 Billion in Bank Capital*,
WSJ, Apr. 30, 2017.
[32]   Punishing banks and publicizing their malfeasance dents peoples' faith in the stability of the banking system. *See* Marcelo Medureira Prates, *Why Prudential Regulation
Will Fail to Prevent Financial Crises: A Legal Approach*, at 13, Working Paper 335,
Banco Central do Brasil, Nov. 2013.
[33]   *See supra* note 31.
[34]   The exposure measure is the sum of on-balance sheet debt, derivatives exposures, securities financing transaction exposures; and off-balance sheet items. *See*
BCBS, Basel III Leverage Ratio Framework and Disclosure Requirements, at 2, Jan.
2014.

the Basel Committee watered down the rules it published in January 2014 on the leverage ratio.

Basel I and Basel II did not include rules to address shortages of liquidity in the banking system. Even well-capitalized banks may face a liquidity crisis – not having enough cash to meet their needs – when credit markets freeze. Many well-capitalized banks that accept eurodollar deposits can easily succumb to runs because they do not have access to the FRS. Basel III takes the first step towards establishing liquidity requirements for banks. It does so by asking them to calculate the liquidity they need to have to avoid short- and long-term liquidity crises. Runs on banks by their depositors or other banks that refuse to lend to them in the inter-bank lending market can create highly contagious crises. The short-term liquidity ratio, the liquidity coverage ratio, assesses a bank's short-term liquidity needs by determining whether the bank has sufficient high-quality liquid assets (HQLAs) to withstand a 30-day freeze in the credit markets. The long-term liquidity ratio, the 'net stable funding ratio', dictates how much in assets a bank must have in order to survive a year-long liquidity crisis. Both of these ratios go beyond the capital adequacy requirements as they determine how much *liquid* capital a bank must have relative to the outflows it may experience during a crisis.[35]

Banks are expected to report the liquidity coverage ratio only in their country's currency. However, this does not mean that they must maintain adequate liquidity only in that currency. They are expected to maintain HQLA 'consistent with the distribution of their liquidity needs by currency'.[36] This forces banks to hold a higher proportion of HQLA in foreign currencies to account for foreign exchange risk.[37] Forcing banks to maintain liquidity for all of their currency exposures amounts to a 'global reserve requirement regime' for banks.[38] Regulators have made it clear that they prefer banks to hold cash-like assets in their reserves for all of their currency exposures instead of other less liquid assets.

Basel III has not satiated the desire to regulate banks. Further rules have been adopted under a Basel IV regime.[39] Not everybody agrees, though, that harmonizing banking standards through global rule-making boosts financial stability. Too much standardization creates a homogenous banking culture, prompting

---

[35] BCBS, Basel III: The Liquidity Coverage Ratio and Liquidity Risk Monitoring Tools, para. 4, Jan. 2013.

[36] Para. 42, *id.*

[37] Para. 60, *id.*

[38] Zoltan Pozsar, *What Excess Reserves?*, Global Money Notes #5, at 1, Credit Suisse Economic Research, Apr. 2016.

[39] BCBS, Basel III: Finalising Post-Crisis Reform, Dec. 2017. These revised rules, which have been informally labeled Basel IV, will come into full effect in 2027.

banks to make loans to similar types of borrowers and this increases system vulnerability. Harmonization can cause a backlash if the rules one seeks to harmonize all over the world are not the right rules for all states.[40] The United States, a highly financialized state that often seeks to export its own financial regulations, has had conflicts with other countries with different priorities. For some states, complying with the Basel rules could actually do more harm than good. In certain countries, for instance, improving regulatory supervision may increase corruption. In nations where holding government positions is the way to exercise arbitrary power, strengthening the hand of a bank supervisor may increase lending to firms from which he solicits kickbacks.[41]

Since the majority of countries are not members of the Basel Committee, they tend to view the Basel regime as a non-representative system, a system, through which rich countries promote rules appropriate for their developed markets but ill-advised for states suffering from underdevelopment.[42] Nations that are not Basel Committee members do not have to comply with the Basel rules. Despite that, over 100 of them have voluntarily espoused the rules. They know that doing otherwise is a way to ostracize themselves from the global financial system, and the mechanism that powers that system: the US markets.

16.3 GLOBAL REGULATORY BODIES

The political system of capitalist democracies is organized based on the equality principle of 'one person, one vote'. This is so despite the fact that some persons have more wealth and thus wield more power than others. What is important for the legitimacy of the political system is that people trust that the 'one person, one vote' principle will be upheld at all costs. When the informal power of the wealthy elite becomes tyrannical, the 'one person, one vote' retains the capacity to rally disaffected majorities to overthrow a government that lends support to the rich and overbearing minority.

At the other extreme, the economic system of free-market democracies is premised on inequality. In capitalist societies, all strive to amass more riches than others. As people compete to create and stockpile more wealth than their

---

[40] Chris Brummer, *Soft Law and the Global Financial System: Rule Making in the 21st Century* 131 (2012).

[41] Roberta Romano, *For Diversity in the International Regulation of Financial Institutions: Critiquing and Recalibrating the Basel Architecture*, 31 Yale Journal on Regulation 1, at 29 (2014).

[42] *See generally* Robert P. Delonis, *International Financial Standards and Codes: Mandatory Regulation without Representation*, 36 NYU Journal of International Law and Policy 563 (2004).

peers, they unleash their creative spirit into new enterprises and ventures and grow the economy for the benefit of all.

The economic system and political system often co-exist in peace. This is a contentious peace, though, as the egalitarian principle of democracy is hard to reconcile with the 'winner takes all' spirit of capitalism. The same tension exists in our world order. The global economic bodies that administer this order are a reflection of the principles of the economic system. They are club-like organizations with selective membership. They comprise mostly rich states and their clan-based foundations clash with the premises of the global constitutive charter, which is based on the sovereign equality of all states.[43] The majority of states, which remain disenfranchised in the global economic order, therefore often complain about the 'democratic deficit' of that order.

International financial institutions are obeyed by the majority of states despite their democratic deficit, though. Financial expertise, their hallmark, gives them an air of objectivity. Many states bow to the dictates of the IMF because they need its stamp of approval on their economic policies. And they do so despite the fact that this stigmatizes them as less than equal to other states. Many states vie to join various financial bodies because it is considered a privilege to be a member. Submission and conformity generate legitimacy but also discontent. It is natural for outsiders to experience discontent when insiders draft the rules they comply with.

International politics are a push and pull between the power of the elite and the resentment it provokes in other states. Aware of this resentment, many global bodies maintain a low profile. Treaties that attract international publicity and protracted negotiations are rarely used to establish them. Instead, in most the cases, they are incorporated under the laws of core states. Their charters and bylaws are rough organizational plans that do not provide much insight into the operations.[44] Some global regulatory institutions have attempted to become more open and democratic, though, by sporadically displaying inclusionary tendencies.[45]

16.3.1 Basel Committee on Banking Supervision

The Basel Committee on Banking Supervision (BCBS) has become the *de facto* standard-setter in the banking sector. The BCBS does not possess supranational authority.[46] As a result, the standards it promulgates for the regulation

---

[43] *See* Chapter 3, note 1.
[44] Brummer, *supra* note 40, at 66.
[45] *Id.* at 202.
[46] Art. 3, Basel Committee Charter, June 5, 2018 [hereinafter Basel Charter].

of the banking industry are not legally binding on any state.[47] Despite that, many states have adopted them out of fear that non-compliance will ensure their lack of access to global financial markets.

The Basel Committee members consist of the senior members of CBs (i.e. deputy governors) and members of government agencies[48] that supervise banks in their countries. Membership is not open to all CBs and supervisory agencies, though. Instead, the Basel Committee makes recommendations to the Group of Governors and Heads of Supervision on the acceptance of new members after taking into account the importance of a state's banking sector for global financial stability.[49] Thus, the decision of whether to accept new members is taken at the highest level. The BCBS refrained from expanding its membership for many years. After its establishment in 1974, the Committee expanded its membership only in 2009 and in 2014. Today, it consists of 45 members from 28 states, making it a very exclusive international body (Box 16.1). To compensate for its exclusionary culture, the Basel Committee has established the Basel Consultative Group, the purpose of which is to maintain a dialogue with non-members. It has also put into place a public consultation process[50] through which it seeks input from all relevant stakeholders on its policy proposals. Decisions at the Basel Committee are adopted by the consensus of its members.

BOX 16.1 MEMBERS OF BASEL COMMITTEE OF BANKING SUPERVISION AS OF 2019

United States: Board of Governors of FRS, FRBNY, Office of the Comptroller of the Currency, FDIC

Europe: EU (2); France (2); Germany (2); Italy (1); Belgium (1); Luxembourg (1); Netherlands (1); Spain (1); Sweden (2); Switzerland (2); UK (2)

BRICS: China (2); India (1); Russia (1); Brazil (1); South Africa (1)

Others: Australia (2); Canada (2); Japan (2); Mexico (2); Indonesia (2); Korea (2); Argentina (1); Saudi Arabia (1); Hong Kong (1); Singapore (1); Turkey (2)

---

[47] *Id.*
[48] Art. 8.3, *id.*
[49] Art. 4, *id.*
[50] Art. 17, *id.*

16.3.2 Financial Stability Board

The Financial Stability Board (FSB) is an international body that monitors the global financial system. It was established in 2009 at the G-20 London summit to succeed the Financial Stability Forum. The FSB prepares reports on issues identified by the G-20 as important and coordinates the work of global regulatory bodies[51] in a way that does not undermine their independence.[52] Member states of the FSB are the United States and its close allies, two financial centers,[53] the BRICS, Argentina, Indonesia and Turkey. All states that are FSB members must undergo periodic peer reviews to determine the effectiveness of their implementation of global standards and the FSB's policies. Submitting to reviews is a condition of FSB membership and is supposed to spur 'a race to the top' by states that are FSB members.

The global impact of the FSB emanates from the authority it has over states that are not its members. Some of these non-members are states that do not stand a realistic chance of ever becoming part of the FSB because of the size of their economy and underdeveloped financial sector. At the G-20 London summit that took place in 2009, the FSB was charged with the task of examining the adherence of all countries to international financial standards and of identifying non-cooperative states or jurisdictions.[54] This complemented initiatives spearheaded by the OECD to promote adherence to international tax standards, and by the Financial Action Task Force (FATF) to propagate the adoption of standards on anti-money laundering and combating the financing of terrorism.

In order to determine whether a country is a non-cooperative state, the FSB has to examine the Reports on the Observance of Standards and Codes prepared by the IMF and World Bank. These reports contain information on whether states implement many of the standards issued by the international regulatory bodies including the International Organization of Securities Commissions' (IOSCO) Principles of Securities Regulation, the Basel Core Principles and the Insurance Core Principles issued by the International Association of Insurance Supervisors. The FSB does not venture into assessing a state's compliance if the IMF and the World Bank certify a state as 'compliant' or 'largely compliant'[55] with the international standards.

---

[51] Art. 2, Charter of the Financial Stability Board, June 2012.
[52] Art. 6(3), *id.*
[53] Hong Kong and Singapore.
[54] *See* FSB, Promoting Global Adherence to International Cooperation and Information Exchange Standards, at 1, Mar. 10, 2010.
[55] *Id.* at 4.

The FSB's authority to determine which states constitute the 'black sheep' of global financial order is even more problematic because the board is not an international organization. In 2012, at the G-20 Los Cabos summit, the FSB was established as a non-profit association under Swiss law. Today it is hosted by the BIS under a five-year renewable service agreement.[56] The Plenary of the FSB comprises all of its members. Not every state has the same voting power, though. The number of seats assigned to a state reflects the size of its economy, financial market activity and 'national financial stability arrangements'. This has been interpreted to mean that countries like the United States and China are allocated three seats each at the plenary; Australia and Mexico occupy two seats each; and countries like Argentina and Saudi Arabia have one seat. The FSB's decisions are made by consensus. About 170 countries, representing 20% of the world's GDP and one-third of the world's population, are not members of the FSB. The lack of representation is aggravated by the fact that the FSB is not the most transparent of global bodies.

16.3.3   International Organization of Securities Commissions

The IOSCO, which identifies itself as 'the global standard setter' for securities markets regulation,[57] brings together the securities regulators of various states to develop standards for the sound functioning of securities markets. The IOSCO was created in 1983, when 11 securities regulators from North and South America decided to transform an inter-American regional association into an international body. The IOSCO was established as a private non-profit association in Quebec, Canada, in 1987.[58] When, in 1999, the IOSCO's headquarters moved from Quebec to Madrid, it was incorporated under Spanish law as a public utility association. The bylaws of the IOSCO do not clarify the legal nature of the organization. They simply mention that national securities regulators have decided to 'assemble together in the International Organization of Securities Commissions, governed by the present By-Laws'.

A national securities commission or a similar body can become an ordinary member of the IOSCO provided it is willing to sign the IOSCO Multilateral Memorandum of Understanding (MMoU) Concerning Consultation and Cooperation and the Exchange of Information. National securities regulators that aspire to become members must commit to the cooperation and exchange

---

[56]   Art. 1, Articles of Association of the Financial Stability Board, Jan. 28, 2013.

[57]   About IOSCO, https://www.iosco.org.

[58]   Antonio Marcacci, *IOSCO: The World Standard Setter for Globalized Financial Markets*, 12 Richmond Journal of Global Law & Business 23, at 25 (2012).

of information detailed in that MMoU.[59] Each ordinary member of the IOSCO is a member of the Presidents' Committee, which is the decision-making organ of the IOSCO. The Presidents' Committee makes decisions by majority vote.[60] Other organs of the IOSCO include the Growth and Emerging Markets (GEM) Committee,[61] four Regional committees (Africa/Middle East, Asia Pacific, Europe and Inter-American)[62] and the Board. The GEM is the largest committee within the IOSCO, representing over 75% of IOSCO's ordinary membership. It consists of 88 members including 10 emerging market states belonging to the G-20.

The Board is the executive, standard-setting body of the IOSCO.[63] It drafts the resolutions that go through the Presidents' Committee for examination and final approval. The composition of the Board is determined by the Presidents' Committee through a formal resolution.[64] As of 2017, the Board consisted of 34 members out of which 18 were permanent members, the so-called 'nominated members'. These included the United States and some of its closest allies, and Brazil, China, India and Hong Kong.[65] These 18 members are nominated by the states with the largest securities markets in the world. The rest of the Board members are appointed or elected by the GEM and the four regional committees.[66]

The MMoU establishes the parameters for the cross-border cooperation of securities regulators so as to enable them to fight cross-border securities fraud. States non-signatories of the MMoU are stigmatized as likely to be welcoming dubious financial practices. At the 2012 IOSCO Annual Conference, the Presidents' Committee created a watch list of states that had applied to become MMoU signatories, but had failed to do so by January 1, 2013. This watch list, which has been dubbed since then the '2013 list', works like a blacklist and it is regularly updated. As of 2018, the states that were blacklisted included Algeria, Barbados, Bolivia, Chile, Costa Rica, Ghana, Kazakhstan, Kyrgyz Republic, Papua New Guinea, Philippines, Ukraine and Uzbekistan.[67]

The IOSCO has issued many regulations and guidelines. 'The IOSCO Objectives and Principles of Securities Regulation' includes 38 principles of

---

[59] Multilateral Memorandum of Understanding Concerning Consultation and Cooperation and the Exchange of Information, Appendix B, www.iosco.org.

[60] Para. 36.4, IOSCO By-Laws, www.isco.org.

[61] Para. 15, *id.*

[62] Para. 59, *id.*

[63] Para. 40.1, *id.*

[64] Para. 17, *id.*

[65] Art. 2 and Annex A, Resolution of the Presidents' Committee on the Composition of the IOSCO Board, Res. 5/2013, as amended by Res. 2/2015.

[66] Art. 2, *id.*

[67] IOSCO, 2013 List of Non-signatories to the MMoU, www.isco.org.

securities regulation based on three objectives: protecting investors; ensuring that markets are fair, efficient and transparent; and reducing system risk.[68] After the LIBOR Scandal, the IOSCO published principles for the establishment of financial benchmarks.[69] In 2015, to address lapses in the professional conduct of CRAs, it published a code of conduct specifically for them.[70] The IOSCO's 'Principles on Dark Liquidity' specify that, in states where dark trading is allowed, regulators should encourage the use of transparent orders and promote market openness.[71]

16.3.4 Financial Action Task Force

The FATF is an inter-governmental body established by the 1989 G-7 summit in Paris to coordinate the fight against money laundering and the financing of terrorism. The FATF consists mostly of developed states, the BRICS, Malaysia, Turkey, Mexico and two financial centers, Hong Kong and Singapore. These 37 FATF members make up the FATF's Plenary, the FATF's primary decision-making organ. The FATF's purpose is the promulgation of standards for anti-money laundering (AML)/combating the financing of terrorism (CFT). These standards are encapsulated in a number of recommendations it has issued over time.[72] Certain recommendations constitute the basic standards. States that observe these standards must prohibit their banks from opening anonymous accounts. They must additionally require that they employ due diligence in identifying the beneficial owners of accounts, keep records of transactions for at least five years and report suspicious transactions to the appropriate government authorities.

The FATF polices whether states implement the standards it issues. Members of the FATF must submit to mutual evaluations. The purpose of evaluations is to assess countries' technical implementation of FATF standards, their formal incorporation into domestic legislation and the effectiveness of implementation.[73] A typical team that judges countries' compliance consists of four experts – a legal expert, two financial experts and a law enforcement

---

68   IOSCO, Objectives and Principles of Securities Regulation, June 2010.
69   IOSCO, Principles for Financial Benchmarks: Final Report, July 2013.
70   IOSCO, Code of Conduct Fundamentals for Credit Rating Agencies, Mar. 2015.
71   IOSCO Finalizes Principles to Address Dark Liquidity, Press Release, IOSCO/ MS/07/2011, May 20, 2011.
72   FATF, International Standards on Combating Money Laundering and the Financing of Terrorism & Proliferation: The FATF Recommendations, Feb. 2012 (updated Feb. 2018).
73   FATF, Methodology for Assessing Technical Compliance with the FATF Recommendations and the Effectiveness of the AML/CFT, at 5, Feb. 2013 (updated Feb. 2018).

expert – who come from different countries.[74] In addition to examining the documents that a country provides to prove its compliance, the assessment team conducts on-site visits to the country.

The FATF is run by its President, who is appointed by the FATF plenary from among its members for a term of one year, and is funded by contributions of its members based on a formula that takes into account the size of their economies.[75] To achieve the global implementation of its recommendations, the FATF relies on a global network of FATF-style regional bodies (FSRBs).[76] These FSRBs are independent bodies. However, both the FATF and the FSRBs follow the same principles and have the same objectives.[77] Over 150 states worldwide have committed to the FATF recommendations through this global network of FSRBs.

To become a member of the FATF a country must first of all demonstrate substantial compliance with the AML/CFT standards detailed in the FATF recommendations. Additionally, it should be strategically important in terms of the size of its GDP, banking, insurance and securities sectors, and its population. Other factors taken into account include: the country's impact on the global financial system, including the degree of openness of its financial sector; its active participation in one of the FATF's regional bodies; and the level of AML/CFT risks it faces, and efforts it has undertaken to combat those risks. A final consideration has to do with whether, if the country were to become a member, the FATF's geographic balance would improve.

The FATF has been successful in naming and shaming countries by putting together lists of non-cooperative states. As of 2018, the FATF had reviewed over 80 countries and publicly identified 65 as having weak AML/CFT regimes. Out of these, 61 addressed their AML/CFT weaknesses and are no longer on the list. The FATF identifies jurisdictions with weak AML/CFT regimes in two public documents it issues three times a year. One of these, the FATF's Public Statement, known as the blacklist, identifies countries with serious strategic deficiencies in AML/CFT. The FATF calls on states to take counter-measures against these countries. North Korea and Iran have

---

[74] FATF, AML/CFT Evaluations and Assessments Handbook for Countries and Assessors, at 6, April 2009.

[75] FATF Annual Report 2015–2016, at 55.

[76] These FSRBs are spread all over the world and include the Asia/Pacific group, Caribbean group, Eurasian group, Eastern & Southern Africa group, Central Africa group, Latin America group, West Africa group and Middle East and North Africa group.

[77] FATF, High-Level Principles and Objectives for FATF and FATF-Style Regional Bodies, at 1, Oct. 2012 (updated Feb. 2018).

consistently been on the FATF's blacklist.[78] Other countries with weak AML/CFT regimes, but not on the blacklist, are Pakistan, Serbia, Sri Lanka, Syria, Trinidad and Tobago, Tunisia and Yemen.

Compliance with the FATF standards and similar sweeping US legislation[79] have cut off some developing states from the global economic system. Many global US banks, the pillars of global financial infrastructure, have severed their links with banks of states blacklisted or likely to be blacklisted by the FATF by closing those banks' correspondent accounts. As of 2017, US banks had shed some 19 000 high-risk clients, that is, banks and financial firms located in a variety of fragile states including the Central African Republic, Nicaragua, Latvia, Belize and Liberia.[80] As a result, money transfers switched to informal, much less regulated and transparent channels.[81]

[78]   FATF, Public Statement, June 23, 2017.

[79]   *See* 31 CFR 1010.610 *et seq*.

[80]   *A Crackdown on Financial Crime Means Global Banks are Derisking: Rolling up the Welcome Mat*, Economist, July 8, 2017.

[81]   World Bank, *Withdrawal from Correspondent Banking: Where, Why, and What to Do About It*, at 40, Nov. 2015.

17. Foundations of a minimum economic order

17.1 BANK OF INTERNATIONAL SETTLEMENTS

The BIS was established in 1930 by an international treaty[1] as an international organization and a bank[2] that lends and takes deposits from its members who are the CBs of various states. As explained in Chapter 7, the motivation behind the foundation of the BIS was to help Germany make the reparation payments it owed the UK and France after World War I. These payments were badly needed by these two countries to pay back their debt to the United States. The Young Plan,[3] named after the banker who put in motion the idea of a global bank, envisioned the BIS as a financial body removed from political interference.[4] A neutral, technocratic body became the vehicle for depoliticizing the debt and reparation payments that were poisoning the relationships among states.

The CBs, the members and shareholders of the BIS, use the bank as their own CB to facilitate their transactions. Despite the fact that the BIS is the CB of central banks, not all CBs are granted membership in it. In fact, in the beginnings of the BIS, only European CBs, and the United States, through a unique arrangement,[5] were BIS members. The initial capital of BIS, consisting of 500 000 million Swiss francs, was divided into 200 000 shares. The UK, France,

---

[1]   Convention Respecting the Bank of International Settlements, Jan. 20, 1930, 104 LNTS 441.
[2]   Constituent Charter of the Bank of International Settlements, Jan. 20, 1930. The Charter incorporates the bank under Swiss law and specifies that it is founded by the CBs of the signatory states plus a US banking group (consisting of JP Morgan, the First National Bank of New York and the First National Bank of Chicago). The FRS was not formally a member of the Board of Directors until 1994.
[3]   Report of the Committee of Experts on Reparations, 1929 Cmd.334 [hereinafter Young Plan].
[4]   'The operations of the institution will be assimilated to ordinary commercial and financial practice. Its organization will be outside the field of political influences ...'. *Id.* at 10; *see also* A. Beth Simmons, *Why Innovate? Founding the Bank for International Settlements*, 45 World Politics 361, at 394 (1993).
[5]   *See supra* note 2.

Germany, Belgium, Italy, the United States and Japan,[6] the founding members of BIS, subscribed to 16 000 shares each and some small European states purchased 4 000 shares each.[7] Out of these initial shares, some 165 100 were purchased by 23 countries while the rest were sold in the market.[8]

The BIS is a *sui generis* international organization protected under Swiss law that owes 'no single fiscal allegiance' to any nation.[9] Under the convention that established the BIS, Switzerland undertook the responsibility to grant it a charter under Swiss law. However, Switzerland cannot repeal or change that charter without the agreement of the rest of the founding states.[10] This hybrid legal genesis of the first global financial institution has guided the development of other such institutions, as we examined in Chapter 16. Establishing financial bodies that function globally but are incorporated under domestic law can equip them with resilience. When deciding the first case brought against the BIS, the Swiss courts shielded it from both the bondholders and the politicians by holding the bank to the limited standard of trusteeship under Swiss law.[11]

All 60 CBs participate in the General Meeting, the governing body of the BIS. Voting rights at the meeting are based on the number of shares that each CB holds.[12] The founding banks have more votes because of the large numbers of shares they hold. The Board of Directors consists of 21 members including six *ex officio*, not elected, directors – the governors of CBs of Belgium, France, Germany, Italy, the UK and the United States.[13] Each *ex officio* member

---

[6]   In 1952, Japan renounced its rights as a founding member of the BIS.

[7]   *See* Kazuhiko Yago, *The Financial History of the Bank of International Settlements* 205, n. 67 (2012).

[8]   On September 11, 2000, the BIS decided to compulsorily withdraw all shares held by private shareholders. That decision was challenged by them and the case was decided by the PCA. *See Bank for International Settlements* (Reineccius et al. v. BIS), PCA Case 2000-04, Partial Award, Nov. 22, 2002; *Bank for International Settlements* (Reineccius et al. v. BIS), PCA Case 2000-04, Final Award, Sept. 19, 2003.

[9]   Young Plan, *supra* note 3, at 12.

[10] Art. 1, BIS Convention, *supra* note 1.

[11] Anna Gelpern, *Courts and Sovereigns in the Pari Passu Goldmines*, at 20, Scholarship at Georgetown Law Center, Feb. 2016 (referring to *Aktiebolaget Obligationsinteressenter v. BIS*, Swiss Federal Supreme Court, Judgment of May 26, 1936). *See also* David J. Bederman, *The Bank of International Settlements and the Debt Crisis: A New Role for the Central Bankers' Bank*, 6 Berkeley Journal of International Law 92, at 100, n. 52 (1988).

[12] Art. 44, Statutes of the Bank of International Settlements, Jan. 20, 1930, as amended Nov. 7, 2016.

[13] Art. 27(1), *id.*

appoints another member of the same nationality on the board.[14] The remaining nine governors are elected to the board by a two-thirds majority vote.[15]

Becoming a member of the BIS is a privilege not a right. To become a member, a CB must receive an invitation from the BIS Board of Directors to subscribe to the bank's capital. To grant such an invitation, the board takes into account the importance of associating the BIS with the largest possible number of CBs that make a substantial contribution to international cooperation.[16] The BIS board can increase the BIS capital 'on one or more occasions' by issuing a third tranche of 200 000 shares.[17] The distribution of these shares is decided by a two-thirds majority of the board.[18] The founding members of BIS are always entitled to subscribe to at least 5% of any new tranche of shares.[19] The BIS has issued the shares of the third tranche gradually as it has invited various CBs to become shareholding members. By 2017, the total BIS shares issued were 559 125 valued at 5 000 SDRs each.[20]

The BIS has contributed to the stabilization of states' currencies during periods of financial turmoil. The first such scheme took place in June 1966 when BIS provided the UK, which was unwilling to seek IMF assistance, with a $400 million line of credit.[21] In 1976, the BIS granted Portugal a loan by accepting as collateral Portugal's gold reserves.[22] In 1982, it extended a loan to Hungary. Hungary had no recourse to the IMF, at that point, because it was not one of its members. It was one of the original members of the BIS, though, making it possible for it to secure a $300 million line of credit from the bank.[23]

The BIS played a constructive role during the 1980s Latin America crisis. In the summer of 1982, Mexico experienced a BOP crisis. In the first weeks of the crisis, the BIS in coordination with the FRBNY arranged for a $700 million line of credit to Mexico. On August 30, 1982, the BIS and the FRBNY provided an additional $1.85 billion line of credit. Mexico paid back the BIS loan with the IMF funding it eventually received.[24] Overall between 1982 and 1983, the BIS lent nearly $4 billion to Hungary, Mexico, Brazil, Argentina and Yugoslavia.[25] These were six- to nine-month loans but they were rolled

---

[14] Art. 27(2), *id.*
[15] Art. 27(3), *id.*
[16] Art. 8(3), *id.*
[17] Arts 5 and 6, *id.*
[18] Art. 8(2), *id.*
[19] *Id.*
[20] BIS, Statement of Account, June 30, 2018, www.bis.org.
[21] Bederman, *supra* note 11, at 104.
[22] *Id.* at 105
[23] *Id.*
[24] *Id.* at 107.
[25] *Id.* at 108.

over when a country was unable to make payments.[26] Most of these loans were arranged in collaboration with the CBs of core states. In some cases, the BIS lent money on its own account, only after securing as collateral gold reserves of borrowing states.[27]

17.2 CURRENCY SWAPS

Currency swaps (*see* Table 3.3) between CBs are increasingly used because, in a globalized economy, private banks tend to have mismatched assets and liabilities. Banks provide loans in their country's currency but can accept deposits or borrow money in another currency because of the lower IRs offered in that currency. Currency swaps between CBs enable them to provide liquidity to their banking sector in foreign currencies. A CB that is notified by the private banks it supervises that they face shortage in a foreign currency can arrange with a foreign CB to swap the local currency for the currency it lacks. This way it can supply its banks with the foreign currency liquidity they need. CBs may also swap their currencies to facilitate their intervention in the FX market.

In a swap agreement, the liquidity provider CB takes on the credit risk of the borrowing CB. In the event that the borrowing CB is unable to reverse the swap at the mutually agreed future date, the lending CB is left holding the borrowing bank's currency and bearing the ER risk associated with that holding. In Chapter 3, Section 3.3, we discussed the swap agreement between the FRS and the ECB in the midst of the 2008 global financial crisis. If the ECB had failed to reverse the swap at the mutually agreed date, the FRS would have been free to sell in the market the collateral, the euros it had received for the dollars it had provided. Such a sale could have generated losses for it in case the euro had depreciated. A similar swap agreement with the CB of Poland would have entailed even more risk because the FX market for the Polish zloty is much less liquid than that for the euro. It is far easier to sell large quantities of euros in the market than large quantities of Polish zloty. CBs evaluate the creditworthiness of borrowing CBs before they decide to enter into a swap agreement with them. This is why during the 2008 financial crisis the ECB agreed to provide Poland and Hungary with euros but only against high-quality collateral denominated in euros. Certain European countries, including the Czech Republic, Lithuania and Bulgaria, that were facing euro shortages did not receive any swap lines from the ECB.[28]

---

[26] *Id.*

[27] *Id.*

[28] William A. Allen and Richhild Moessner, *Central Bank Co-operation and International Liquidity in the Financial Crisis of 2008–09*, at 13, BIS Working Paper No. 310, May 2010.

During the 2008 panic, there were several currency shortages. The largest liquidity shortage was of US dollars in the euro area – around $400 billion.[29] The economies with the largest US dollar shortages, namely the eurozone, the UK, Canada and Brazil, all received swap lines from the FRS. However, Russia, Turkey, India, Indonesia, Chile, Hungary and Iceland, which also experienced dollar shortages, did not receive such swap lines. Russia withstood the crisis because of its substantial FX reserves. India obtained a dollar swap line from the Bank of Japan that acted as an agent for Japan's Ministry of Finance.[30] On October 31, 2013, six major CBs announced that they were making permanent their previously *ad hoc* swap lines. The Bank of Canada, the Bank of England, the Bank of Japan, the ECB, the FRS and the Swiss National Bank announced that their temporary bilateral liquidity swap arrangements were converted into standing arrangements, that is, were to remain in place until further notice. These standing arrangements were to serve 'as a prudent liquidity backstop' to the financial system.[31] The United States usually makes available currency swaps to foreign states when US investors, who have assets in these states, risk large losses if such swap lines are not provided. Granting a swap line to a state whose currency is under attack is an endorsement by the sovereign of the soundness of that currency. Such an endorsement can stop a currency attack in its tracks and limit the losses of those who hold assets in that currency.

China has more than 30 bilateral currency swap agreements with other states valued at 2.9 trillion yuans ($468 billion).[32] China's currency swap lines have been activated in times of emergency. In 2015, Pakistan drew the equivalent of $600 million out of a swap line of 10 billion yuans ($1.6 billion) based on its 2013 swap agreement with China.[33] This made it possible for it to beef up its FX reserves and avert a currency crisis. In a similar move, Argentina drew upon its swap line with China to address a dollar scarcity in 2014.[34] Both Pakistan and Argentina were able to convert yuans into dollars in the offshore yuan market.[35] The People's Bank of China does not have a swap agreement with the FRS. It has entered into swap agreements with the Bank of England

---

[29]   *Id.* at 13.

[30]   *Id.* at 29.

[31]   FRS, Federal Reserve and Other Central Banks Convert Temporary Bilateral Liquidity Swap Arrangements to Standing Arrangements, Press Release, Oct. 31, 2013.

[32]   Cindy Li, *Banking on China through Currency Swap Agreements*, Federal Reserve Bank of San Francisco Pacific Exchange Blog, Oct. 3, 2015.

[33]   *Id.*

[34]   *See* Chapter 4, Section 4.2.3.1.

[35]   Li, *supra* note 32.

($53 billion equivalent) and the ECB ($49 billion equivalent).[36] It also holds some of the largest FX reserves in the world.

Most swap agreements are freely agreed and revocable contracts between the CBs of states. The swap lines provided through these agreements can never be guaranteed to be available on demand. This is because the liquidity-providing CB is the one that decides how much liquidity it is ready to make available in its currency.[37] Making swap agreements semi-permanent, through an international treaty, has not been politically feasible. Reserve-currency-issuing states do not have the incentives to enter into an agreement that would compel them to supply liquidity to the rest of the world. Instead, they use swap lines as a bargaining chip for obtaining geopolitical concessions from peripheral countries. Securing swap lines from the sovereign or other reserve-currency-issuing states signals international support for peripheral countries and their currencies.[38] A prudent state that does not have sufficient FX reserves, and knows it is unlikely to be offered swap lines by other states, must adopt *ex ante* regulatory measures to force its banks to limit their foreign currency exposure.

17.3   REGIONAL ECONOMIC ARRANGEMENTS

17.3.1   Chiang Mai Initiative Multilateralization

The Chiang Mai Initiative (CMI), the evolution of the 1977 ASEAN Swap Arrangement, was adopted in 2000, after the Asian financial crisis, by the Association of Southeast Asian Nations (ASEAN)[39] plus three other states – China, South Korea and Japan. The CMI matured into the Chiang Mai Initiative Multilateralization (CMIM) in 2010 as it became obvious that the CMI, a network of bilateral swap arrangements, was too primitive to address the 2008 financial crisis and its aftermath.[40] The 2010 CMIM is a multilateral currency agreement.[41] The 2014 amendment to that agreement doubled the size of the CMIM from $120 to $240 billion[42] and introduced the CMIM pre-

---

[36]   Edd Denbee et al., *Stitching Together the Global Financial Safety Net*, Annex A1, Financial Stability Paper No. 36, Bank of England, Feb. 2016.

[37]   *Id.* at 11.

[38]   Allen and Moessner, *supra* note 28, at 43.

[39]   The ASEAN includes Brunei, Cambodia, Indonesia, Laos, Malaysia, Myanmar, Philippines, Singapore, Thailand and Vietnam.

[40]   *See generally* Chalongphob Sussangkarn, *The Chian Mai Initiative Multilateralization: Origin, Development and Outlook*, ADBI Working Paper No. 230, July 2010.

[41]   Bank of Japan, The Amended Chiang Mai Initiative Multilateralization (CMIM) Comes into Effect on July 17, 2014, Press Release, July 17, 2014.

[42]   *Id.* at 1.

cautionary line of credit.[43] China and Japan pledged to contribute $77 billion each to the CMIM and South Korea contributed $38 billion. All in all, China's, Japan's and Korea's contributions make up 80% of the resources of CMIM. The remaining 20% ($48 billion) is contributed by the ASEAN countries.[44]

States are entitled to borrow from the CMIM a 'purchasing multiple' of their contributions.[45] Indonesia, for instance, which contributes $9.1 billion, can borrow 2.5 times its contribution, up to $22.76 billion. Out of this $22.76 billion, though, only 30% ($6.8 billion) can be quickly and unconditionally disbursed. The remaining 70% becomes available only if the country agrees to be bound by an IMF conditionality program.[46] Given that 70% of the CMIM financing is based on IMF conditionality, an anathema for many states, the CMIM is useful for addressing short-term liquidity difficulties and supplementing, rather than replacing, IMF funding. The resources of the CMIM are also inadequate to address a panic that simultaneously affects multiple countries, like the 1990s East Asian crisis.[47] Another weakness of the CMIM is that it is only as good as the pledges of its members. The CMIM's members do not have to contribute paid-in capital. Substantial paid-in capital contributions would have strengthened market confidence in the efficacy of the CMIM during crises.

17.3.2 Latin American Reserve Fund

The Latin American Reserve Fund, *Fondo Latinoamericano de Reservas* (FLAR), is an initiative of the Andean countries (Colombia, Venezuela, Ecuador, Peru and Bolivia) to expand the Andean Reserve Fund, established in 1978, to the rest of Latin America. Today Costa Rica, Uruguay and Paraguay are also members of the FLAR, whose ambition is to convince Argentina, Brazil, Chile and Mexico to join the fund.[48] Both Brazil and Argentina are large enough to become anchors of a reserve fund like the FLAR but they have economic and political problems of their own that preclude their spearheading of regional economic coordination. Mexico has been more attached to the North since its collaboration, through the North American Free Trade Agreement, with the United States. As a result, FLAR has been mostly an

---

[43] *Id.*
[44] Attachment 2, *id.*
[45] *Id.*
[46] Central Bank of Philippines, Chiang Mai Initiative Multilateralization, at 2, Sept. 2018.
[47] *Id.*
[48] *See*, e.g. Daniel Titelman et al., *A Regional Reserve Fund for Latin America*, CEPAL Review 112, Apr. 2014.

initiative of small countries.[49] It has retained its ambition, though, to one day become the Latin American Monetary Fund by expanding its presence to all states in the region.

The subscribed capital of the FLAR is approximately $3.9 billion, of which $2.9 billion is paid-in capital. Out of this $3.9 billion, the larger countries, Colombia, Costa Rica, Peru and Venezuela, contribute about $656 million each and the rest of states about $328 million.[50] The fund is an international organization established by a treaty[51] with its headquarters in Bogota, Colombia.[52] It is administered by the Assembly of Representatives (finance ministers or their deputies)[53] and the Board of Directors (governors of the CBs of states), which is the primary decision-making body.[54] The FLAR is unique among international financial institutions because of its democratic governance. Voting in both the Assembly and Board is based on one vote per state as long as states have paid their required minimum paid-in capital contribution.[55]

During the 1980s Latin American debt crisis, the FLAR offered financial support to Peru, Ecuador and Bolivia. In July 1991, the FLAR helped Peru make a $367 million delayed payment to the Inter-American Development Bank. Between 1978 and 2003, the FLAR contributed resources equivalent to 60% of the financing provided by the IMF to the Andean Community countries. During the 2008 financial crisis, it granted assistance to Ecuador and Venezuela.[56] The FLAR considers itself a short-term lender whose job is to provide bridge financing to its members until they receive IMF funding.[57] In addition, the FLAR provides deposit, asset management and custody services for states. The fund can receive deposits from any CB in the region (member or non-member).[58] As of May 2014, it had $6.4 billion assets under management.

Another regional arrangement that could deepen economic integration in Latin America is the reciprocal payments and credits agreement (RCA) of the

---

[49]   Ghangyong Rhee et al., *Regional Financial Safety Nets: Lessons from Europe and Asia*, n. 1, Bruegel Working Paper 2013/6, Nov. 2013.

[50]   Art. 5, FLAR, Constitutive Agreement, Apr. 2016 (including the Agreement for the Establishment of the Latin American Reserve Fund and its Bylaws) [hereinafter FLAR, Constitutive Agreement].

[51]   Art. 1, *id.*

[52]   Art 2, *id.*

[53]   Art. 14, *id.*

[54]   Art. 21, *id.*

[55]   Arts 14 and 21 ($250 million for large states, $125 million for the rest of states).

[56]   Carlos Giraldo, *Experiences in South-South Collaboration from Africa, Asia and Latin America*, Presentation at the University of Witwatersrand, Johannesburg, May 11, 2017.

[57]   *Id.*

[58]   Art. 8 (a), FLAR, Constitutive Agreement, *supra* note 50.

Latin American Integration Association, which is also known by its Spanish acronym ALADI. In 1982, the CBs of Argentina, Bolivia, Brazil, Colombia, Dominican Republic, Ecuador, Mexico, Paraguay and Uruguay signed the Latin American Integration Association RCA, whose purpose is to facilitate the flow of funds and trade among them. The RCA, by guaranteeing the convertibility of local currencies into reserve currencies, promotes the use of local currencies in intra-regional trade. This can be very useful during recessions and financial crises, when reserve currencies become scarce.[59]

17.3.3 BRICS Contingent Reserve Arrangement

The purpose of the $100 billion BRICS contingent reserve arrangement is to provide a regional safety net for the BRICS – help them address 'actual or potential short-term balance of payments pressures'.[60] Only 30% of financing provided under the contingent reserve arrangement is not subject to IMF conditionality, and even that amount is not disbursed automatically.[61]

17.4 DEVELOPMENT BANKS

The World Bank and regional development banks have been a source of countercyclical financing for developing states that face economic downturns. During the 2008 crisis, the World Bank increased the loans it provided to Latin America from $4.6 billion in 2008 to $14 billion in 2009. Regional banks, whose resources have been tapped during crises, include the Inter-American Development Bank, the Development Bank of Latin America[62] and the Central American Bank for Economic Integration.[63]

Since 2002, the Asian Development Bank has been working to develop local currency bond markets in Asia in order to minimize foreign-currency-denominated borrowing. This Asian Bond Markets Initiative gave birth to the ASEAN+3 Bond Market Forum, whose goal is to integrate

---

[59]   Eugenia López-Jacoiste Díaz, *The Latin American Integration Association* 23, at 31, in 'Latin American and Caribbean International Institutional Law' (Marco Odello and Francesco Seatzu, eds, 2015).

[60]   Art. 1, Treaty for the Establishment of a BRICS Contingent Reserve Arrangement, July 15, 2014.

[61]   Arts 5(c)–(d), 14, *id.*

[62]   The Latin American Development Bank was established in 1968 as the Andean Development Corporation, Corporacion Andina de Fomento (CAF), and it has kept the acronym CAF.

[63]   *See* José Antonio Ocampo and Daniel Titelman, *Regional Monetary Cooperation in Latin America*, at 12, ADBI Working Paper No. 373, Aug. 2012.

the Asian bond markets and to standardize the national banking messaging systems by 2020.

The Asian Infrastructure Investment Bank (AIIB) was established on June 29, 2015[64] with an initial callable capital of $100 billion, out of which about $30 billion was provided by China, $8.4 billion by India and $6.5 billion by Russia. The rest was provided by 37 regional members and 21 non-regional member states.[65] Twenty percent of all capital contributed to the AIIB is paid-in capital.[66] By 2017, the bank had already amassed close to $20 billion paid-in capital ready to be invested in infrastructure projects. The fact that China supplied the bulk of capital for the AIIB gave it the majority of voting rights – about 28.9% voting power. China is the only shareholder of the AIIB that can veto its decisions. India, the second largest shareholder, has only 8% voting power. The number of shares allocated to each AIIB member state is based on a formula that takes into account the size of that state's economy and whether it is a regional or non-regional member. Non-regional members can hold only 25% of the voting shares.[67] Unlike other global development banks, the AIIB allows entities that are 'not sovereign' to become members.[68] State-owned enterprises and SWFs of member countries could potentially become members of the bank.[69]

The development of the AIIB was somewhat contentious. China, whose idea was to establish the bank, argued that the AIIB was necessary since the World Bank, led by the United States, and the Asian Development Bank, led by Japan, were focused mostly on poverty reduction rather than infrastructure development. The United States, which saw the AIIB as 'China's World Bank', a vehicle for the expansion of Chinese influence, objected when the UK, France, Italy and Germany applied to join the bank in 2015. Some even suspected that US firms might not be able to bid for infrastructure projects funded by the AIIB.[70]

The New Development Bank was established by the BRICS on July 15, 2014.[71] The bank is headquartered in Shanghai and aims to become a source of infrastructure financing for emerging market economies and other developing

---

[64]   AIIB Articles of Agreement, June 29, 2015.

[65]   *See* Art. 4(1) and Schedule A, *id.*

[66]   Art. 4(2), *id.*

[67]   Art. 5(3), *id.*

[68]   Art. 3(3), *id.*

[69]   Martin A. Weiss, *Asian Infrastructure Investment Bank (AIIB)*, at 7, CRS Report, Feb. 3, 2017.

[70]   *Id.* at 18–19.

[71]   Fortaleza Agreement on the New Development Bank (including Articles of Agreement), July 15, 2014.

countries. The initial contributions of its members were made in US dollars. The subscribed capital was $50 billion, out of $100 billion authorized capital, and was equally distributed among its members.[72]

17.5   DEBT RE-ORGANIZATION

The need for a global safety net is most manifest when states cannot pay back the debt they owe to other states or private creditors and need to re-negotiate, '*re-organize*', that debt. Debt re-organization can consist of debt rescheduling – the deferral of some of the principal and interest payments. *Debt rescheduling*, called also *debt reprofiling*, is costly. This is because interest accumulates as interest in arrears, interest charged on interest in arrears and penalty charges for missing payments. *Debt restructuring*, on the other hand, is a more drastic re-organization of the whole debt with the goal of easing some of the debt burden.[73] Debt restructuring can, in fact, amount to debt relief if the repayment of the debt is deferred so much into the future that inflation and expected growth make future payments appear inconsequential.

In the past, governments that defaulted on their debt risked economic sanctions, the imposition of foreign control over their finances and even military intervention. Between 1870 and 1913, a country that defaulted ran the risk of gunboats blockading its ports and creditor nations seizing fiscal control.[74] Only countries that surrendered their fiscal autonomy for an extended period of time were able to issue new debt in the London capital market. Britain, France and Germany, the creditor nations, did not hesitate to pursue aggressively the interests of private bondholders. Bondholders were also organized and lobbied governments to protect them when states that owed them money defaulted. The Corporation of Foreign Bondholders was formed by the British creditors in 1868 to forge unity among them. Its purpose was to ensure that creditors kept a common stance against debtors.[75]

In 1898, soon after its independence, Greece came under creditors' control because it defaulted on the debt it had issued. In that case, Germany was the major player that protected the interests of foreign bondholders. By all appearances that protection was guaranteed by a Greek law but, in fact, Germany

---

[72]   Art. 7(a)–(c), *id.*

[73]   Alexis Rieffel, *The Role of the Paris Club in Managing Debt Problems*, at 19, n. 4, Essays in International Finance, No. 161, Department of Economics, Princeton University, Dec. 1985.

[74]   *See* Stephen D. Krasner, *Sovereignty: Organized Hypocrisy* 127–51 (1999).

[75]   Paolo Mauro and Yishay Yafeh, *The Corporation of Foreign Bondholders*, at 5, IMF Working Paper WP/03/107, May 2003.

dictated the terms of debt restructuring.[76] Committees of foreign bondholders, backed by the military power of leading creditor nations, administered customs collection and controlled the finances of Serbia, Egypt, Turkey, Latvia, Morocco, Santo Domingo and Tunis after their default.[77] Things seemed to change after World War II. After that war, West Germany agreed with the Allied states to defer some of the payment of its war debt until it was reunified with East Germany. This pushed its debt repayment back to the future. Germany made the last payment on its war debt (EUR69.9 million) on October 3, 2010. Most states are unable to extract from their creditors such generous treatment.

17.5.1   The Paris and London Clubs

The Paris Club is an international body put together by creditor states that work together to make sure that they collect the debt owed to them by debtor states. Club membership was initially restricted to developed countries, the typical creditors. Today emerging market economies have joined the club – Russia in 1997 and Brazil and South Korea in 2016. The club consists of 22 members. China, a big bilateral creditor,[78] is not a member of the club.

The club was established in 1956 and between 1956 and 2016 it entered into 433 deals that restructured or rescheduled $583 billion in debt.[79] The club assumed a prominent role in the 1980s when the debt of many developing countries jumped to more than 100% of their GDP. In the mid-1990s, it was evident that most of these countries would be unable to pay back their debt. The club endorsed, therefore, along with the G-7, the Heavily Indebted Poor Countries Initiative, through which it forgave about $126 billion in debt of 36 poor countries.[80] Paris Club members may concede to reschedule the debt of a developing state for political reasons,[81] for instance, to support a government ready to massively privatize public assets by inviting foreign bidders. The

---

[76]   Kris James Mitchener and Marc D. Weidenmier, *Supersanctions and Sovereign Debt Repayment*, at 17, NBER Working Paper 11472, June 2005.

[77]   Krasner, *supra* note 74.

[78]   *See* Ann Gelpern, *Sovereign Debt: Now What?*, 41 Yale Journal of International Law 45, at 60 (2016).

[79]   Paris Club, Annual Report 2016, at 22 [hereinafter PC 2016 Report].

[80]   *Id.* at 6.

[81]   Thomas M. Callaghy, *Innovation in the Sovereign Debt Regime: From the Paris Club to Enhanced HIPC and Beyond*, at 53–54, Working Paper No. 98, World Bank, July 9, 2002.

United States granted some debt relief to Iraq after it invaded it in 2003 in order to support the newly installed political regime of the country.[82]

The club attributes its longevity to the lack of formal legal personality and the fact that it operates as a 'non-institution',[83] an informal forum for renegotiating states' bilateral debt. The chairman of the club is the head of the French Treasury. A 10-person permanent secretariat staffed by French Treasury officials was set up in the 1970s to facilitate the work of the club. The club holds negotiations with debtor countries on an *ad hoc* basis. It holds monthly discussions among its members to evaluate the overall external debt owed to them. These 'Tour d'Horizon' meetings are held in private.[84]

A state's debt is reorganized at its own request. The debtor state asks the club for a debt renegotiation after it concludes an agreement with the IMF. Its agreement with the IMF serves as evidence that it is in imminent default and needs debt restructuring. The debtor country and the club endorse the 'Agreed Minutes' after the conclusion of their negotiations.[85] These minutes establish the terms under which the debtor country can sign binding debt restructuring agreements with each of its creditors.[86] The club has endorsed a number of principles that it applies to all its negotiations with debtors:

- Solidarity among creditors – the creditors agree to act as a group in dealing with debtors. This prevents debtors from applying 'divide and conquer' tactics by treating some creditors better than others.
- Consensus for making decisions.
- Information sharing among members of the club and confidential discussions.
- Case-by-case treatment of debtors – the club refuses to treat debtors as a group. It uses 'divide and conquer' strategies to thwart the formation of 'debtor cartels' likely to have more negotiating power than each individual debtor.
- Conditionality – the club negotiates debt restructurings with countries that have a good track record of implementing IMF conditionality programs. It reschedules debt for short periods even if it is clear that a more generous debt restructuring is necessary. Short-term debt rescheduling contracts are

---

[82] Martin A. Weiss, *The Paris Club and International Debt Relief,* at 3, CRS Report for Congress, Dec. 11, 2013.

[83] PC 2016 Report, *supra* note 79, at 4.

[84] *Id.* at 50.

[85] *See* Mauro Megliani, *Sovereign Debt: Genesis – Restructuring – Litigation* 292 (2015).

[86] PC 2016 Report, *supra* note 79, at 50.

preferred because they keep debtors on a 'short leash'.[87] They force them to ask for repeated debt reschedulings and, thus, keep up their compliance with IMF conditionality.

- Comparability of treatment. A debtor who enters into bilateral agreements with Paris Club creditors cannot enter into an agreement with a non-Paris Club creditor offering that creditor more generous treatment than that offered to the Paris Club.[88] The comparable treatment of creditors is controversial[89] and can be costly. It goes against the flexibility that the IMF advocates for successful debt renegotiations.[90]

To use the Paris Club terminology, the club provides appropriate *debt treatments* for states. These treatments can consist of: (i) debt rescheduling; (ii) the reduction of debt for a defined period – a *flow treatment*; and (iii) the reduction of debt, *debt stock*, by applying a *haircut* on the whole debt – a *stock treatment*.

The London Club is the sister institution of the Paris Club and deals with the debt owed to banks. The first meeting of the London Club took place in 1976 in response to Zaire's debt problems. The London Club is an even more *ad hoc* arrangement than the Paris Club. It does not have a regular meeting location. Each London Club is dissolved after the conclusion of a debt restructuring. A London Club meeting is convened when a state contacts its major private creditors asking to renegotiate its debt. All banks that have lent money to the debtor can participate in the London Club negotiations. Smaller banks, though, are typically represented by the leading big banks that have larger exposures to the debtor. These banks make up the Bank Advisory Committee (BAC) or creditors' committee, which handles the debtor. The BAC may offer a number of options to the borrowing state: extension of debt maturities; new lending; or even the reduction of debt. Once an agreement is reached between the BAC and the debtor state, the BAC presents it to the rest of the banks. All banks must consent for this agreement to become binding. The London Club process is generally streamlined but disagreements and holdouts still spoil some negotiations.

The London Club played a central role in the 1980s Latin America debt crisis. The crisis was resolved a decade after its ignition and engendered much animosity among the major players: the Latin American states, the banks that lent money to them and the IMF. Today most states issue debt in the bond

---

[87]   Rieffel, *supra* note 73, at 26.

[88]   PC 2016 Report, *supra* note 79, at 57.

[89]   IMF, *Sovereign Debt Restructuring – Recent Developments and Implications for the Fund's Legal and Policy Framework*, at 40–41, Apr. 26, 2013 [hereinafter IMF Sovereign Debt Restructuring].

[90]   *Id.*

market. Therefore, the Paris and London clubs play a marginal role in debt restructuring. Disputes between a state and its bondholders are usually handled by a committee convened by the debtor or a self-appointed committee put together by creditors. The Institute of International Finance, a private association of banks, has played a central role in mediating creditor–debtor disputes. If a dispute cannot be resolved through negotiations, it is adjudicated at the London Commercial Court or Southern District of New York. These are the two jurisdictions predominantly used to resolve creditor–debtor disagreements.

17.5.2   Collective Action Clauses in Debt Contracts

In Chapter 15, we discussed how some hedge funds vetoed the restructuring of Argentina's debt. Argentina's experience has underscored the utility of adding collective action clauses (CACs) in debt contracts, especially if these contracts are governed by foreign law. A CAC is a provision that makes it possible for a qualified majority of bondholders to restructure the debt of a state even if a minority objects to the restructuring. When CACs are included in debt agreements, the decision of the majority of bondholders to restructure the debt of a state binds the minority. If Argentina had included such clauses in the bonds it had issued, the decision of the majority of bondholders to exchange their existing bonds for new, discounted bonds would have bound the minority. Argentina would have avoided in this way the disruptive litigation that led to its repeated defaults.

CACs have been touted as market-friendly clauses that make possible the orderly default of states. CACs are better, it is argued, than establishing a global body dedicated to restructuring states' debt – a Sovereign Debt Restructuring Mechanism (SDRM). Brazil and Mexico were against the development of such a mechanism when it was put on the negotiating table in 2003 by the IMF. They argued that an SDRM could increase their cost of borrowing. Markets tend to treat core states' debt as information-insensitive.[91] However, they are hypersensitive to information about the potential insolvency of peripheral states. An SDRM, likely to be used mostly by default-prone states, was expected to boost that hypersensitivity of creditors.

In the early 2000s, Brazil and Mexico endorsed CACs as the solution to the collective action problems stemming from default. At the time, both states had ample access to the bond markets. They were ready to exploit their newfound autonomy and cultivate their indigenous debt markets rather than to root for

---

[91]   *See also* Bengt Holmstrom, *Understanding the Role of Debt in the Financial System*, BIS Working Paper No. 479, Jan. 2015.

a global restructuring mechanism.[92] In 2003 Mexico issued bonds governed by New York law that included CACs, signaling its preference for those clauses. By the end of 2003, approximately 80% of new debt issued by emerging market states under New York law included CACs.[93]

States that issue bonds under their domestic law do not need to include CACs in those bonds because they can unilaterally enact legislation to restructure their debt. Greece had to restructure its debt in 2012. Out of the total EUR205 billion debt, EUR184 billion was covered by Greek law and did not contain CACs. Greece was able to enact legislation that retroactively included CACs in the bonds it had issued. It did so despite the fact that its creditors obviously disliked the retroactive application of that legislation.[94] The legislation enabled a qualified majority of bondholders to bind all holders of Greece's debt to the terms of the restructuring deal. For Greece, domestic legislation worked better than CACs because it made possible the aggregation of all creditor claims across all bonds that the Greek state had issued through the years under Greek law.[95]

On the other hand, 7.3% of the Greek debt was governed by English law. These bonds included CACs. The inclusion of CACs was not helpful to Greece because the holdouts prevailed by obtaining a blocking majority that prevented the restructuring of some of that debt. CACs bind bondholders on an *issue-by-issue basis*. Therefore, it is possible for bondholders to block the restructuring of a bond issue if they obtain a majority in that issue. In the case of Greece, about EUR6.5 billion or 30% of the Greek bonds issued under foreign law was not restructured, despite the fact that these bonds included CACs. This happened simply because the majority of bondholders decided to hold out and blocked the restructuring. From a debtor's perspective, therefore, CACs are not really *the* answer to the collective action problems presented by debt restructuring. A majority of bondholders can block debt restructuring even if CACs are included in bonds. Bondholders will not always prefer to 'get something rather than nothing' by consenting to a restructuring deal.

To avoid being chased around the globe by holdouts, some states have opted to employ CACs that allow for the aggregation of creditors' claims *across issues*. This is a contractual way of stopping creditor holdouts in an individual

---

[92]   Anna Gelpern and Mitu Gulati, *The Wonder-clause*, at 20–21, Duke Law Scholarship Repository, Feb. 2, 2013.

[93]   *Id.* at 20.

[94]   *Id.* at 32–3.

[95]   IMF Sovereign Debt Restructuring, *supra* note 89, at 29.

bond issue from rattling a debt restructuring deal. Typically for the activation of such *aggregated CACs*, two majorities are needed:

- holders of 75% (or 85%) of *aggregated debt principal* of *all bond issues* to be affected by the restructuring must consent to it; and
- holders of 66.66% of the debt principal of *each individual bond issue* affected by the restructuring must consent to it.[96]

These are definitely not easy majorities to achieve. Aggregated CACs that require supermajorities for each individual bond issue will not necessarily facilitate restructurings.[97] Some have proposed, therefore, getting rid of the issue-by-issue supermajorities and opt for *single-limb aggregation*. Single-limb aggregation makes it possible to restructure debt based on a single supermajority *across all bond issues* without requiring *bond-by-bond issue* supermajorities.[98]

In addition to CACs, another means to weaken the leverage of potential holdouts during debt restructurings is to use the qualified majority clauses included in some bond issues to amend the *non-payment terms* of those issues – what is called 'exit consent'. Certain clauses in bonds make it possible for a qualified majority of bondholders, when they exchange their existing bonds, to alter the non-payment terms of these bonds for the sole purpose of making them unattractive to potential holdouts. Such non-payment terms include the waiver of sovereign immunity, submission to jurisdiction and acceleration in the event of default.[99] The amendment of non-payment terms in order to make bonds less appealing saddles holdouts with bonds of reduced market value. This may motivate them to accept the offer of the debtor to exchange their bonds for new, discounted ones.[100]

---

[96]   *Id.* at 29.

[97]   *Id.* at 29–30.

[98]   Agnès Bénassy Quéré et al., *Reconciling Risk Sharing with Market Discipline: A Constructive Approach to Euro Area Reform*, at 13, Center for Economic Policy Research, Policy Insight No. 91, Jan. 2018. *See also* Technical Study Group Report, *Sovereign Debt Restructuring: Further Improvements in the Market Based Approach*, at 5, UN Department of Economic and Social Affairs, Aug. 30, 2017.

[99]   Many bond contracts contain acceleration clauses so that if a debtor misses an interest payment, creditors can ask for immediate payment of all principal and accrued interest. Cross-default clauses usually specify that defaulting on one creditor triggers acceleration on all debt issued.

[100]   Megliani, *supra* note 85, at 371–2.

17.5.3   A Sovereign Debt Restructuring Mechanism

The IMF has proposed the establishment of an SDRM as a permanent institution devoted to the management of states' debt. This is not the first time that a debt restructuring mechanism has been proposed. During the UNCTAD V meeting in 1979, the G-77, a group of developing nations, proposed the establishment of a permanent International Debt Commission to replace both the Paris and London clubs. Rich states, though, were not ready to abandon their clubs.[101]

The SDRM proposal was put forward to address the collective action problems presented in debt restructurings because of the variety of interests of numerous bondholders and other private and public actors who hold states' debt. It is difficult for states with unsustainable debt burdens to get their diversified pool of creditors to agree on the necessity of debt restructuring. As we saw in the case of Argentina, certain creditors prefer to hold out from collective settlements and take their chances with various courts to fully recover the debt owed to them. Creditors that hold CDS may be reluctant to restructure a state's debt, hoping to trigger that state's default and collect full payment from the issuer of the CDS.[102] The fact that some creditors opt out from debt restructuring discourages other creditors from participating in debt renegotiations. This is especially so if they believe that the holdouts will receive full payment.[103] The SDRM is based on the premise that the majority of *all* of a state's creditors should be able to bind the minority to a restructured debt agreement no matter the type of debt (e.g. bank loans or bonds). If the majority of creditors sign on for debt restructuring, even those who disagree with it will be bound by it.[104]

The debt restructuring mechanism proposed by the IMF incorporates principles from the bankruptcy laws of various states. These principles include: the protection of creditors from each other; the protection of creditors from dishonest debtors; and the protection of an honest debtor from rapacious creditors, including the restoration of her business, if possible, and the prevention of forced sale of assets.

Bankruptcy procedures in domestic laws that can be incorporated into international law include:

- A stay on enforcement of creditors' rights during negotiations. Without a stay, creditors will fiercely compete to attach debtor's assets.

---

[101]   *See,* e.g. Rieffel, *supra* note 73, at 24–5.

[102]   Anne O. Krueger, *A New Approach to Sovereign Debt Restructuring,* at 8 (IMF, Apr. 2002).

[103]   *Id.*

[104]   *Id.* at 15.

- Measures to protect the interests of creditors during the period of stay, such as preventing the debtor from transferring assets to insiders or making payments to favored creditors.
- Mechanisms to supply new financing to the debtor.
- The requirement that all creditors will be bound by the renegotiated debt agreement from the moment that agreement has been accepted by a qualified majority of creditors.[105]

Obviously, dealing with an insolvent company and dealing with a state are not the same. Creditors can always liquidate a firm but cannot liquidate a state to force debt repayment. Bankruptcy laws typically provide that creditors cannot be forced to accept a debt restructuring if that restructuring provides them with less than what they would have received if they had liquidated the debtor. This provision cannot be applied when the debtor is a state. Furthermore, some laws make it possible for the creditors of an insolvent firm to acquire it by transforming their debt claims into equity, after wiping out the existing shareholders. This is something not possible when the debtor is a state,[106] although efforts have been made to arrange debt-for-equity swaps with states.[107] Finally, it is unclear how private creditors can force a debtor state not to engage in actions that harm their interests. Creditors, for instance, cannot order a state to use the taxes it collects to pay off its debt[108] instead of paying social security to the elderly.

The SDRM[109] has the potential of streamlining the restructuring of a state's debt, but has yet to be established. This is because the pro-debtor approach of domestic bankruptcy laws is not supposed to apply to foreign states. States try to protect their insolvent private debtors, but they are rarely interested in helping foreign states. In 1981, Costa Rica suspended debt payments to a syndicate of 31 banks. An agreement for the restructuring of Costa Rica's debt was eventually reached, but one of the creditors, Fidelity Union Trust, decided to sue Costa Rica in the United States through its agent, Allied Bank. In a 1984 ruling, the US Court of Appeals upheld a lower court's ruling that was favorable to Costa Rica. The court held that the actions of Costa Rica – stopping payments on its external debt – were consistent with the law and policy of the United States.

---

[105] *Id.* at 11.

[106] *Id.*

[107] *See* Chapter 10, Section 10.2.

[108] Krueger, *supra* note 102, at 12.

[109] For other similar proposals, *see*, e.g. Jürgen Kaiser, *Resolving Sovereign Debt Crises: Towards a Fair and Transparent International Insolvency Framework*, Friedrich Ebert Stiftung, Oct. 2013.

The court argued that, based on Chapter 11 of the US Bankruptcy Code,[110] when a company files for bankruptcy all claims against it are automatically stayed. This happens in order to make it possible for the company to prepare an acceptable plan for the reorganization of its debt and to prevent a disorderly scramble for its assets. Costa Rica's stay on the payment of its external debt was 'analogous' to Chapter 11. It did not constitute a repudiation of its debt but rather a 'deferral of payments while Costa Rica attempted in good faith to renegotiate its obligations'.[111] The court ruled for Costa Rica under the assumption that the US government was on board with the ongoing restructuring of that country's debt. It reversed itself in 1985[112] after a rehearing of the case during which the US government argued that it was opposed to Costa Rica's unilateral debt restructuring.

This case, in combination with the most recent cases brought and won against Argentina, demonstrates that the pro-debtor bias of many domestic bankruptcy laws is not the norm in international law with certain exceptions, such as the latitude granted to Germany after World War II and Nicaragua in 1982.[113] Furthermore, it is not in the interest of US and UK courts, which typically adjudicate such issues, to espouse a pro-debtor bias. Such bias would probably prompt bondholders to flee to other jurisdictions willing to accommodate their interests. This would erode the oligopoly of the United States and the UK and the revenues of multiple firms that depend on this oligopoly.

17.6   ENFORCEMENT AGAINST STATES' ASSETS

Suing a state in the courts of another state is not the easiest thing. The doctrine of sovereign immunity[114] prevents the submission of state to the jurisdiction of the courts of another state. Not all acts of state enjoy immunity, though. In the jurisdictions where most debt disputes are litigated – the US and UK – it is generally accepted that immunity is not granted to acts a state executes in its commercial capacity (*acta jure gestionis*). Immunity is granted only to the acts a state performs as public entity (*acta jure imperii*). In 1992, the US Supreme Court concluded that issuing bonds is a commercial transaction and, therefore,

---

[110] 11 USC §103(a).

[111] *Allied Bank v. Banco Credito Agricola de Cartago et al.*, 23 ILM 742, 746 (1984).

[112] *Allied Bank v. Banco Credito Agricola de Cartago et al.*, 757 F.2d 516 (2nd Cir., 1985).

[113] *See* Megliani, *supra* note 85, at 255.

[114] *See*, e.g. UN Convention on Jurisdictional Immunities of States and their Property, G.A. Res. 59/38, Annex, UN Doc. A/RES/59/3, Dec. 2, 2004 [hereinafter UN Immunity Convention].

Argentina did not enjoy sovereign immunity and could be sued in US courts.[115] In 2005, on the other hand, an Italian court stated that Argentina's moratorium on debt repayment was a sovereign act.[116] In 2003, a German court clarified that the doctrine of sovereign immunity bars the execution of a judgment against a state in the courts of a third state because this hurts international relations.[117] The rationale behind the sovereign immunity doctrine is, after all, to avert the aggravation of relationships among states.

Courts are reluctant to rule that a state does not enjoy immunity especially with regard to an execution of a judgment against that state's assets. The outcome of litigation initiated by NML Capital when it attempted to attach assets of Argentina located in other states, based on a judgment it obtained in a NY court, is very instructive. The UK Supreme Court ruled that Argentina could not invoke sovereign immunity to prevent the execution of the NY judgment against its assets in the UK.[118] The court clarified that sovereign immunity is not absolute. The UK had already adopted legislation that favored the restrictive version of sovereign immunity. This version made it clear that in matters relating to commercial transactions, including 'any loan or other transaction for the provision of finance',[119] a state does not enjoy immunity. The court added that Argentina's bonds included a waiver of sovereign immunity and provided for the submission of Argentina to the jurisdiction of foreign courts.

On the other hand, France's Supreme Court, on March 28, 2013, issued three judgments stopping execution against assets owned by Argentina and located in France. The court concurred with NML Capital that Argentina had waived sovereign immunity with regard to the bonds it had issued. However, it had not *specifically* waived its immunity from enforcement with respect to the categories of assets NML Capital was trying to attach in France. NML was using the French court system to enforce the judgment it obtained in NY against fiscal and social security debts owed to Argentina by local branches of French companies, namely BNP Paribas, Total Austral and Air France.[120] The French court relied on Article 19(a) of the 2004 UN Immunity Convention.[121] This

---

[115] *Republic of Argentina v. Weltover Inc.*, 504 US 607 (1992). *See also* art. 2(1)(c)(ii), UN Immunity Convention, *id.*

[116] Corte di Cassazione, Ordinanza, May 27, 2005, *cited in* Meglioni, *supra* note 85, at 395.

[117] Landgericht of Frankfurt am Main, Judgment, Mar. 14, 2003, No. 294/02, *cited in id.* at 396.

[118] *NML Capital Limited v. Republic of Argentina* [2011] UKSC 31, July 6, 2011.

[119] Para. 20, *id.*

[120] *Enforcement Against State Assets: France's Latest Contribution to the Argentinean Saga*, Clifford Chance Briefing Note, Apr. 25, 2013.

[121] *See supra* note 114.

article states that post-judgment measures, including attachment or execution against the property of a state, can be taken by courts of other countries only if that state has *expressly* waived immunity with respect to these measures.

In 2007, NML Capital brought an action to attach assets of Argentina held in the custody of the FRBNY. The FRBNY intervened in the proceedings to support Argentina. NML Capital argued that Argentina's use of the funds it maintained at the FRBNY constituted 'a commercial activity in the United States', under 28 USC §1610(a), because the funds were to be used by Argentina to pay the IMF. The court disagreed, stating that Argentina's relationship with the IMF is not commercial in nature. Therefore, the use of funds it kept at the FRBNY to pay the IMF could not constitute commercial activity.[122] In this way the court stopped the attachment of Argentina's assets held in the custody of the FRBNY.

In 2015, NML Capital brought an action against Argentina's CB by claiming that the CB was the *alter ego* of Argentinean government. Its assets, therefore, could be attached to execute the judgment it had obtained against that government. The court disagreed, stating that the fact that Argentina's government worked closely with its CB to resolve the debt crisis 'did not establish extensive control over the day-to-day operations' of that CB so as to transform it into Argentina's *alter ego*.[123] The court, citing the *amicus curiae* filed by the US government, stated that weakening the immunity enjoyed by CBs of foreign states in the United States could prompt those states to withdraw their reserves kept in US custody and place them in other countries. Such a withdrawal could have immediate, adverse impacts on the US economy and global financial system.

NML tried to further execute the NY judgment against the assets that Argentina's CB kept at the BIS.[124] The Swiss Federal Supreme Court, taking into account the headquarters agreement of the BIS with Switzerland, stated that the BIS enjoyed immunity for all of its acts.[125] The fact that the BIS was a recipient of assets coming from the CB of Argentina had to do with the purpose of the BIS, which acts as a CB of CBs, in accordance with the

---

[122] *EM Ltd. v. Republic of Argentina*, 473 F.3d 463 (2d Cir. 2007). *See also LNC Invs., Inc. v. Banco Central De Nicaragua*, 228 F.3d 423 (2d Cir. 2000).

[123] *EM Ltd. v. Banco Central de la República Argentina*, 800 F.3d 78 (2d Cir. 2015).

[124] *NML Capital Ltd. and EM Limited v. Bank for International Settlements and Debt Enforcement Office Basel-Stadt*, Final Appeal Judgment, No. 5A 360/2010, BGE 136 III 379 (partial), ILDC 1547 (CH 2010), July 12, 2010.

[125] Para. 4.3.1, *id.*

provisions of the Swiss law that recognizes the immunity of international organizations.[126]

NML Capital even tried to attach an Argentinean warship, the *ARA Libertad*, which had arrived at a port of Ghana on October 1, 2012, an action that Argentina contested.[127] The High Court of Ghana accepted jurisdiction over the matter and subsequently issued an order for 'interlocutory injunction and interim preservation' that led to the detaining of the *ARA Libertad*. To implement the court's injunction, the Ghanaian authorities stopped the warship from leaving the port. On October 30, 2012, Argentina initiated arbitration proceedings against Ghana regarding the detention of its warship at the International Tribunal for the Law of the Sea. The Tribunal ruled in favor of Argentina, stating that, 'in accordance with general international law, a warship enjoys immunity'.[128] As a result, 'any act which prevents by force a warship from discharging its mission and duties is a source of conflict that may endanger friendly relations among States'.[129] The Tribunal concluded that the urgency of the situation required the prescription of provisional measures as requested by Argentina. It ordered Ghana to 'unconditionally release' the warship and its crew.[130]

Another action was brought before the Belgian courts to attach assets located in the bank accounts of Argentina's diplomatic mission in Brussels. The Supreme Court of Belgium ruled against NML Capital.[131] The court based its decision on: (i) Article 22(3) of the Vienna Convention on Diplomatic Relations[132] that specifies that the premises of a diplomatic mission are immune from search, attachment or execution; (ii) Article 25 of same convention that provides that the host state of a diplomatic mission must accord full facilities for the performance of the functions of that mission; and (iii) the rule of customary international law, namely the principle *ne impediatur legatio*. According to the court, this principle implied that all assets dedicated to the functioning of a diplomatic mission enjoy an autonomous immunity from execution, distinct from that of the sending state. As a result, no seizure

---

[126] *See* Thore Neumann and Ann Peters, *Switzerland* 221, at 246, in 'The Privileges and Immunities of International Organizations in Domestic Courts' (August Reinisch, ed., 2013).

[127] *See 'ARA Libertad' (Argentina v. Ghana)*, Provisional Measures, Order, 2012 ITLOS Reports 332, Dec. 15, 2012.

[128] Para. 95, *id.*

[129] Para. 97, *id.*

[130] Para. 100, *id.*

[131] November 22, 2012.

[132] Vienna Convention on Diplomatic Relations, Apr. 18, 1961, 23 UST 3227, TIAS No. 7502.

or enforcement measure could be taken against these assets unless the sending state conceded explicitly to such measures.[133]

In addition to the sovereign immunity defense, debtor states have tried to raise various substantive defenses against creditors.[134] Most of these defenses have not been tested recently in courts. Argentina, for instance, claimed that creditors were abusing their rights since they were suing it at a time when the country was facing an acute economic crisis. That defense was not successful in court.[135] The abuse of rights or odious debt doctrines may become more successful in the future. Odious debt is debt amassed by the government of a state that is not in the best interests of that state. Because of the odious nature of the debt, the obligation to pay it back does not bind future governments.[136] The UNCTAD Principles on Promoting Responsible Sovereign Lending and Borrowing adopted in 2012[137] specify that a creditor that buys the bonds of a state at a time that the state is in financial distress, with the intent of forcing a preferential settlement of his claim outside of a consensual restructuring process agreed by the other creditors, is acting abusively.[138] In the same vein, the *Champetry defense*[139] prohibits litigating on a claim purchased exclusively for the purposes of filing a lawsuit. That defense has not been successful in courts because of the difficulty of establishing intent. Debt holders can always

---

[133] Further action was brought in the Supreme Court of Belgium. Creditors claimed that the refusal to attach assets located in the bank accounts of Argentina's mission in Belgium violated art. 6 of the European Convention on Human Rights for a fair trial. The court rejected the argument. *See* Cour de Cassation de Belgique, Arrêt, No. C.13.0537.F, Dec. 11, 2014.

[134] Megliani, *supra* note 85, at 430–60.

[135] *Lightwater Corp. v. Republic of Argentina*, No. 02 Civ. 3804, 2003 WL 1878420 (SDNY, Apr. 14, 2003).

[136] *See* Robert Howse, The *Concept of Odious Debt in Public International Law*, No. 185 (UNCTAD, July 2007). *See also Tinoco Claims Arbitration* (Great Britain v. Costa Rica), Opinion and Award of William H. Taft, 1 RIAA 375, Oct. 18, 1923. Before leaving office and the country, Frederico Tinoco, the President of Costa Rica, took out a loan from the Royal Bank of Canada for his personal use. The question, before the arbitration panel, was whether Costa Rica had to repay the loan. The panel ruled that it did not have to, but added that, in general, government succession does not affect a state's debt obligations. Costa Rica won the case because the lender knew that the debt was for Tinoco's personal use.

[137] UNCTAD, Consolidated Principles on Promoting Responsible Sovereign Lending and Borrowing, Jan. 10. 2012 [hereinafter UNCTAD Principles].

[138] *Id.* at 8.

[139] New York law prohibits the purchase of any 'bond, promissory note, bill of exchange, book debt, or other thing in action, or any claim or demand, with the intent and for the purpose of bringing an action or proceeding thereon'. N.Y. JUD. LAW 489 (McKinney 1983).

claim that they bought the debt of a state with the intention to get paid, not to litigate.[140]

One could argue that those who provide credit to *debt intolerant* states should suffer losses when those states default. Debt intolerant countries are countries with weak institutions that use external borrowing to avoid making tough decisions on taxing and spending.[141] Creditors' complicity in the corruption of government officials during the borrowing process should also, in principle, bar debt repayment.[142]

17.7 THE FOUNDATIONS OF A MINIMUM ECONOMIC ORDER

The minimum economic order that prevails today is inadequate. This order consists of national lines of defense, states' FX reserves, bilateral swap lines, regional financing arrangements and the IMF. Most states do not have enough FX reserves to withstand a currency attack or pay back their creditors during a crisis. Regional financial arrangements can be tapped during a crisis, especially because they carry less stigma than the IMF. The problem is that their lending capacity remains minimal and conditional.[143]

Developing states have lamented the lack of a global safety net.[144] This has prompted the IMF to propose the establishment of a Global Stabilization Mechanism. This mechanism would be available to countries with sound economic fundamentals (e.g. low inflation) that suffer from financial market disruptions, such as sudden stops in capital inflows caused by contagion via external shocks that are outside their control. For this mechanism to work, the CBs of reserve-currency-issuing states would have to cooperate and be willing to assist with the liquidity problems of other states.

Unfortunately, reserve-currency-issuing states are not ready to make the commitment to provide lender of last resort facilities to all states that may need such facilities. The CBs of core states keep swap lines with one another, but rarely do they extend such lines to other states. Reserve-currency-issuing states like to maintain a latent ambiguity regarding the countries they may

---

[140] Federico Sturzenegger and Jeromin Zettelmeyer, *Debt Defaults and Lessons from a Decade of Crises* 67 (2006).

[141] Carmen M. Reinhart et al., *Debt Intolerance*, Brookings Papers on Economic Activity, No. 1, 2003.

[142] Sturzenegger and Zettelmeyer, *supra* note 140, at 67.

[143] CGFS, *Global Liquidity – Concept, Measurement and Policy Implications*, Paper No. 45, at 26, Nov. 2011.

[144] *See*, e.g. Javier Guzmán Calafell, Remarks at the 7th Annual Conference of the Banco Central De Reserva del Perú, at 9, July 6, 2016.

assist in times of crisis. This 'constructive ambiguity approach' to the provision of lender of last resort facilities has many proponents who believe that any *ex ante* promise of liquidity provision to the periphery would create moral hazard. Given that the CBs of reserve-currency-issuing states are reluctant to be lenders of last resort to others, the only international institution that could play that role is the IMF. As we have seen, however, the IMF imposes strict conditionality on states for the limited assistance it provides. Furthermore, the IMF has at its disposal approximately $1 trillion – far below the $6 trillion that emerging market states believe they may need in times of financial calamity.[145]

As a result, our world is divided. Reserve-currency-issuing states have access to liquidity any time. They simply 'print their way out of a crisis'.[146] The rest of the world cannot do this. In addition, the unpredictability of swap lines, the financial costs and risks of reserve accumulation and the reputational costs of IMF borrowing make the economic conditions of many states quite precarious. Most states have paltry FX reserves and are not members of regional financial arrangements. These states have to rely on the generosity of regional development banks when they are faced with the spillovers of crises that start somewhere else.

Countries that cannot print their way out of a crisis will always be vulnerable. Countries able to print their way out of a crisis, the issuers of the safe haven assets that are in high demand during panics, do not have the motivation to change this *status quo*.[147] The lack of incentives of core states to establish a robust economic order that benefits the majority is the reason for the absence of such an order. There is no indication that these incentives may be changing. Economic sovereignty has remained concentrated. The United States is the global economic superpower, despite the efforts of some states to grab some of that power. Most cross-border capital movements still take place in dollars. Most cross-border debt is denominated in dollars. Two major reserve currencies – the dollar and, much behind it, the euro – are dominant. The global banking and financial infrastructure is located in two core states – the United States and the UK.

If the United States, the sovereign, wished to establish a maximum economic order, it could do so easily. It could triple the capital of the IMF to $3 trillion. It could make it possible for the FRS to extend liquidity to foreign CBs without limits. The FRS could establish swap lines with states that do not have permanent swap lines with it, including China and India.[148] The United

---

[145] *The Sticky Superpower*, at 6, Special Report the World Economy, Economist, Oct. 3, 2015.

[146] IMF, *Adequacy of the Global Financial Safety Net*, at 37, Mar. 10, 2016.

[147] *Id.*

[148] *The Sticky Superpower*, *supra* note 145, at 14.

States could also take steps to guarantee the impartiality of the global payment system and could refrain from using that system for settling geopolitical claims. Limitations on the extra-territorial application of US financial law and the establishment of a new impartial body that would objectively assess whether states manipulate their currency to obtain commercial advantages over others could also improve the global economic order. Moreover, states whose debt is unsustainable, could be given more time to pay back that debt and granted debt relief when necessary, instead of their temporary weakness being used to deplete them of assets at fire sales.

Obviously, this is an ideal state of affairs. In reality, it is more likely that the United States' benign neglect of the global economic order will continue, begetting fear and resentment. Today, the dollar rules; so does the firm desire to circumvent its reign by establishing competing monetary and financial arrangements.

18. Case study: the Greek debt crisis (2009–2018)

18.1   EUROCRISIS

18.1.1   Eruption

The eurocrisis erupted in 2009 when the world was still reeling from the 2008 global panic. Ireland was the first to succumb to the crisis. Soon after that, in October 2009, the Greek government announced that its deficit would be 12.5% of its GDP – a figure much higher than the 3.7% reported before.[1] Greece declared that it was ready to bring the deficit within the limits prescribed in the EU treaties by adopting the necessary austerity measures. However, as the yields on its debt soared, it lost access to the credit markets and had to ask the EU and IMF for a loan. They agreed in May 2010 to give Greece a EUR110 billion loan provided it achieved budget cuts of EUR30 billion.

On October 18, 2010, the German chancellor and the French president issued a joint declaration in Deauville, France[2] making it clear that the solution to the crisis would entail losses for private creditors.[3] That announcement shattered creditors' expectations that eurozone states were ready to bail each other out in order to safeguard the survival of their common currency,[4] and caused panic and widespread loss of confidence in all of the European periphery.[5] Before their entry into the eurozone, markets tended to view European peripheral states as a 'convergence play'. Creditors bought Greek bonds, for instance, because of the high yields they offered compared with the low risk assigned to

---

[1]   *See* European Commission, Report on Greek Government Deficit and Debt Statistics, at 3, COM(2010) 1 final.

[2]   Franco-German Declaration, Statement for the France–Germany–Russia Summit, Deauville, Oct. 18, 2010.

[3]   Referring to an 'adequate participation of private creditors' for 'orderly crisis management', *id.*

[4]   Jean Tirole, *The Euro Crisis: Some Reflexions on Institutional Reform* 225, at 228, Banque de France Financial Stability Review, No. 16, Apr. 2012.

[5]   IMF, Greece: 2013 Article IV Consultation, IMF Country Report No. 13/154, at 6, June 2013 [hereinafter IMF Report 13/154].

a country that was 'converging' to adopt the euro. After Deauville, creditors realized that their turn was coming to contribute to the bailouts of Greece and other peripheral states and suffer large losses.[6]

The Achilles' heel of many peripheral states was the unhealthy feed-back loop between their government and the banking sector: when a state was in trouble, its private banks, which held its bonds, suffered because of the declining trust in the creditworthiness and the deposit guarantee schemes provided by their now economically crippled state. Conversely, when banks were in trouble, states' ability to shore up their banking sector came under question simply because of the large sums of money they needed to dedicate to bail out that sector.[7] Eventually, on July 26, 2012, the ECB declared that it was ready to do whatever it took to preserve the euro.[8] The Bank announced soon thereafter the unlimited purchases of government bonds of troubled eurozone states, the open market transactions.[9] This discouraged speculation against the euro and prevented further contagion.

18.1.2   The 2010 Loans

Eurozone states tried to initially address the crisis by assuaging private creditors. They 'repeatedly and relentlessly' declared that 'as a matter both of policy and of sacred honor' no default or debt restructuring would ever happen in the eurozone.[10] Eventually, on March 25, 2010, the European Council conceded that Greece needed a bailout.[11] Under strict conditionality, a EUR110 billion loan was granted to Greece. The loan was not granted by the EU, but by eurozone states on a bilateral basis, giving them substantial flexibility in handling their debtor. The bulk of the loan was financed by Germany (27.9%), France (21%) and Italy (18.4%). The total amount granted to Greece by eurozone states, through the so-called Greek Loan Facility, was EUR80 billion. The IMF contributed EUR30 billion under a stand-by arrangement. Greece was placed under close supervision to ensure that the emergency loan would be paid

---

[6]   Arturo C. Porzecanski, *Borrowing and Debt: How do Sovereigns Get into Trouble?* 309, at 320–31, in 'Sovereign Debt Management' (Lee C. Buchheit and Rosa M. Lastra, eds, 2014).

[7]   Jean Pisani-Ferry, *The Euro Crisis and its Aftermath* 13 (2011).

[8]   ECB, Mario Draghi Speech at the Global Investment Conference in London, Press Release, July 26, 2012.

[9]   *See* Chapter 4, Section 4.2.

[10]   Lee C. Buchheit and G. Mitu Gulati, *Talking One's Way Out of a Debt Crisis* 37, at 38, in 'Filling the Gap in Governance: The Case of Europe' (Franklin Allen et al., eds, 2016).

[11]   Council of the European Union, Statement by the Heads of State and Government of the Euro Area, Press Release, Mar. 25, 2010.

back. A team of inspectors from the European Commission, the IMF and the ECB – the so-called 'troika'– visited Greece regularly to ensure that it would abide by the conditions of its bailout. It was the first time that the EU had been so closely involved in monitoring a state.[12] Germany insisted on the involvement of the IMF in the Greek emergency loan as a counterweight against the European Commission, which Germany believed could not be objective enough to monitor Greece's implementation of conditionality.

The official refinancing of the Greek debt changed the ownership of that debt. Before the official loans were granted to it, Greece owed money to French and German banks.[13] Greece used the 2010 loan facility to pay back creditor states' banks. In this way the bulk of the Greek debt was transferred from the private sector to the public sector. The official EUR110 billion loan that helped Greece pay back its private debt spared the banking system of creditor states the repercussions of a Greek default estimated at EUR200 billion.[14] In 2010, the IMF declared that it had faith that the 2010 deal would be sufficient to stave off any further problems. Secret documents that were leaked in 2013 revealed, though, that there was disagreement among the IMF members about the soundness of the Greek bailout.[15] Many countries argued that the Greek loan facility could not possibly alleviate the debt burden of Greece since it included no debt restructuring, such as forgiving debt principal, reducing IRs or extending the payment schedule to make debt service bearable.[16] In Germany, the 2010 loan to Greece was viewed as a French victory and a German defeat. In much of the German press, the eurozone was disparaged as a mutual bailout association, a transfer union.[17]

The IMF was severely criticized for the role it played in the 2010 bailout of Greece. The IMF's watchdog, the Independent Evaluation Office (IEO), concluded that the IMF's involvement in the troika undermined its agility as 'a crisis manager'.[18] The IMF was the 'junior' partner in the troika. Political pressure by creditor states that held a disproportionate amount of power on

---

[12] Kevin Featherstone, *The Greek Sovereign Debt Crisis and EMU: A Failing State in a Skewed Regime*, 49 Journal of Common Market Studies 193, at 205 (2011).

[13] BIS, BIS Quarterly Review: International Banking and Financial Market Developments, at 19, 21, June 2010.

[14] Ronald Janssen, *Greece and the IMF: Who Exactly is Being Saved?*, at 6, Center for Economic and Policy Research, July 2010.

[15] Thomas Catan and Ian Talley, *Past Rifts over Greece Cloud Talks on Rescue*, WSJ, Oct. 7, 2013.

[16] *Id.*

[17] Wolfgang Proissl, *Why Germany Fell out of Love with Europe*, at 32, Bruegel Essay and Lecture Series, July 1, 2010.

[18] IEO, *The IMF and the Crises in Greece, Ireland, and Portugal*, at 33, 2016 [hereinafter IEO 2016].

the IMF's Executive Board weakened its technical judgment. Some even characterized the IMF's reluctance to confront creditor states 'a public policy scandal of the first order'.[19] The IMF's mistake was that it agreed to give a loan to Greece despite the fact it had claimed that the country's debt was non-sustainable with a high probability of default.[20] Typically, when a country's debt is unsustainable the IMF refuses to refinance it unless creditors are ready to agree to preemptive debt restructuring.[21] Instead of sticking to its policy, the IMF amended its internal procedures to accommodate the creditor European states that wanted it to participate in the Greek bailout. Creditor states were steadfast in their refusal to condone the preemptive restructuring of the Greek debt. They viewed such restructuring as a slippery slope that could trigger an avalanche of debt restructurings in all peripheral states.

For the sole purpose of accommodating creditor states, the IMF created the '*systemic exemption*'. The exemption made it possible for it to participate in the Greek bailout, *without* insisting on prior debt reduction, despite uncertainty about debt sustainability, simply because of the high risk of contagion.[22] This amendment of an internal IMF procedure was adopted by the IMF management without consulting with all of the members of the Executive Board, and was buried in a staff report regarding the Greek request for a stand-by arrangement.[23] The IMF press communiqué released at the time made no mention of this change in policy.[24] The IMF bending over backwards to please eurozone's creditors smacked of European exceptionalism[25] and sullied the reputation of the fund as a neutral, technocratic institution. The fund, which has blamed itself for not having the courage of its convictions, has since emphasized the importance of rigorous Debt Sustainability Analysis.[26]

The IMF failed to predict the deep recession caused by the conditionality it imposed on Greece.[27] It put too much emphasis on labor reforms (elimination of collective bargaining and trade unions) at the expense of product reforms

---

[19] Quote attributed to economist Ambrose Evans-Pritchard, *id.* at 5.

[20] *Id.* at 18, n. 39.

[21] *Id.* at 15.

[22] After the fiasco of the 2010 Greek bailout, the systemic exemption has been eliminated, *see* IMF Survey: IMF Reforms Policy for Exceptional Access Lending, Jan. 29, 2016.

[23] IEO 2016, *supra* note 18, at 18.

[24] IEO, *The IMF Executive Board and the Euro-Area Crisis – Accountability, Legitimacy and Governance*, at 17, 2016 [hereinafter IEO 2016a].

[25] *Id.* at 25.

[26] IMF, *Sovereign Debt Restructuring – Recent Developments and Implications for the Fund's Legal and Policy Framework*, at 9–10, Apr. 26, 2013.

[27] IEO 2016, *supra* note 18, at 5.

(e.g. deregulation of industries to improve competition).[28] As a result, salaries and wages fell, but products and services remained expensive, increasing social misery and failing to restore competitiveness. At the time, the German model of increasing 'competitiveness-through-the-wage-restraint' was used to judge all eurozone states.[29] In the early 2000s, Germany had introduced the decentralized bargaining of wages. This accelerated de-unionization and increased employment at the expense of job security and higher incomes.

18.1.3   The 2012 Debt Restructuring

By 2011, it was evident that Greece needed additional loans to pay back its existing debt.[30] By that time, though, markets were expecting something worse than a Greek default. European leaders seemed to relish cultivating anxiety by hemming and hawing that the single currency might break up and that countries under pressure would have to return to their national currency.[31] In 2011, the Greek prime minister decided to put to a referendum the fiscal austerity demanded by creditor states. That referendum never took place after an implicit Franco-German blackmail that a referendum of this nature would jeopardize the chances of Greece getting fresh loans, and even its EU membership. The Greek prime minister came under intense pressure from his European partners and eventually resigned. This rough-handling of the prime minister of a small eurozone state[32] served as a warning to other debtor states. After the ousting of the elected prime minister, a caretaker government was installed at the urging of the creditors, undermining democratic legitimacy at the moment that it was most needed.[33]

In 2012, the EU Council of Ministers officially concluded that private sector involvement (PSI) was necessary for the write-off of more than 50% of Greek debt. The PSI was touted as a voluntary deal proposed by private bondholders. In essence, it was imposed on them as a *fait accompli* by the eurozone states. Since Greece's official creditors (the IMF, the ECB, eurozone states) were excluded from the debt restructuring, private creditors had to incur even larger losses. Obtaining an agreement among the various private creditors

---

[28]   *Id.* at 26.

[29]   Martin Sandbu, *Europe's Orphan: The Future of Euro and the Politics of Debt* 240 (2015).

[30]   William Boston and Andreas Kissler, *Troika Says Greek Debt not Sustainable*, WSJ, Oct. 20, 2011. *See also* IMF, EU, ECB, 'Troika', *Greece Debt Sustainability Analysis*, Oct. 21, 2011.

[31]   Sandbu, *supra* note 29, at 128.

[32]   *Id.* at 74.

[33]   *Id.* at 75.

and between those creditors and the eurozone governments was a torturous exercise, which became even more onerous owing to the lack of transparency and disclosure among creditors.[34] With regard to Greece, 'the tree had fallen and it lay helpless on the ground, being snapped and snarled at by the other two players'[35] – the creditor states and the bondholders. The advantage that Greece held was that it had issued the majority of its debt under Greek law. As a result, the government could pass a law to restructure these bonds unilaterally.[36]

The bondholders knew that they would have difficulty impounding Greece's assets. However, they could freeze further lending to Greece. They could sue Greece in other states in order to obtain judgments against it. The bondholders could threaten the eurozone by claiming that their losses on the Greek debt would drive them to sell off all the periphery debt, worsening the crisis. Most bondholders, though, eventually concluded that it was not worth fighting the eurozone, especially because it was the only institution that could guarantee repayment of the Greek debt. The eurozone could force Greece to cut spending and hike taxes. The new discounted bonds, which were to be exchanged for the old ones, were European Financial Stability Facility (EFSF) bonds.[37] These bonds were backed by guarantees from all eurozone states.

The new loans granted to Greece under the restructuring deal amounted to EUR164.5 billion until the end of 2014. Out of this amount, the eurozone contributed EUR144.7 billion through the EFSF, the facility put in place to deal with the eurocrisis. The IMF contributed EUR19.8 billion out of a EUR29 billion extended fund facility it put in place for Greece for four years. The official sector loans were supplemented by the PSI. On February 24, 2012, Greece invited bondholders to exchange the Greek bonds they held for new rescheduled bonds. The total eligible amount of bonds was EUR205.6 billion. The day before the offer, on February 23, 2012, Greece adopted a law[38] that made it possible for it to insert a CAC in the existing bonds governed by Greek law. Eventually, out of 205.6 billion in bonds eligible for the exchange offer, approximately 197 billion, or 95.7%, were exchanged, including bonds of small bondholders, individuals who had believed in the safety of debt issued

---

[34] *How the Greek Debt Reorganisation of 2012 Changed the Rules of Sovereign Insolvency*, Allen & Overy – Global Law Intelligence Unit, at 20, Sept. 2012.

[35] *Id.* at 11.

[36] *See* Chapter 17, Section 17.5.2.

[37] For more details on the EFSF, *see* Chapter 4, Section 4.4.3.1.

[38] Greek Law 4050/2012, Rules of Amendment of Titles Issued or Guaranteed by the Hellenic Republic with the Bondholders' Agreement, Government Gazette of the Hellenic Republic A' 36/23.02.2012.

by their state.[39] The terms of the bond exchange were spelled out in a memorandum[40] that included commitment letters of the two major Greek political parties. The parties committed to be bound by the memorandum if they were elected to government.

Bondholders exchanged their bonds for new bonds with a face value of 31.5% of the existing bonds.[41] In addition, 15% of the existing bonds was paid back through cash-like, short-term notes issued by the EFSF (amounting to an overall discount on the original value of bonds of 53.5%). Accrued interest on the existing bonds was paid to the bondholders in the form of six-month EFSF notes. Greece could borrow EUR23 billion from the EFSF to compensate the Greek banks for their losses owing to the PSI, if the funds available to the Hellenic Financial Stability Fund[42] were not sufficient to preserve financial stability.[43] The Greek banks that held a large amount of Greek bonds and suffered large losses because they were bailed in under the PSI were eventually bailed out by the government.

The specifics of the PSI were crystallized in a number of multilateral agreements between the EFSF, on the one hand, and Greece and the Bank of Greece on the other. The Private Sector Involvement Liability Management Facility provided a EUR30 billion loan to Greece – the value of the EFSF cash-like notes that the EFSF issued for Greece.[44] A loan of EUR35 billion was provided to Greece, through the ECB Credit Enhancement Facility, to enable it to buy back the existing bonds at the discounted value.[45] A Bond Interest Facility of EUR5.5 billion was put in place to make possible the payment of interest on

---

[39]   These bondholders sued Greece at the European Court of Human Rights, *see Mamatas and Others v. Greece* (application Nos 63066/14, 64297/14 and 66106/14), European Court of Human Rights, Judgment, July 21, 2016. The Court ruled that the debt restructuring did not constitute a violation of property rights of bondholders.

[40]   Memorandum of Understanding between the European Commission Acting on Behalf of the Euro Area Member States, and the Hellenic Republic, Mar. 1, 2012 [hereinafter Memorandum on Greek Bond Exchange].

[41]   *Id.* at 4.

[42]   The Hellenic Financial Stability Fund is a bank rescue fund. It was founded in July 2010 as a private entity. *See* Greek Law 3864/2010 (Government Gazette A' 119/21.7.2010) amended by Greek Law 4051/2012 (Government Gazette A' 40/29.2.2012) amended by Greek Law 4456/2017 (Government Gazette A' 24/1.3.2017).

[43]   Memorandum on Greek Bond Exchange, *supra* note 40, at 5.

[44]   Financial Assistance Facility Agreement between EFSF, the Hellenic Republic and the Bank of Greece – Private Sector Involvement Liability Management (PSI LM) Facility Agreement, Mar. 1, 2012 [hereinafter PSI LM].

[45]   Financial Assistance Facility Agreement between the EFSF, the Hellenic Republic and the Bank of Greece, ECB Credit Enhancement Facility Agreement, Mar. 1, 2012 [hereinafter ECB Credit Enhancement Facility Agreement].

the existing debt.[46] Furthermore, a co-financing agreement was signed between Greece, Wilmington Trust, the EFSF and the Bank of Greece. Based on this agreement, Wilmington Trust, a private company based in London, was to act as the trustee for the bondholders and the Bank of Greece was to function as the government's paying agent.[47] The bank had to hold the amounts paid by Greece for servicing its debt in trust for the creditors.[48] In the event of a shortfall in payments, the bank had to distribute the amount it received from the government *pro rata* between the EFSF and the bondholders.[49] In this way Greece could not default on its bondholders without defaulting on the EFSF at the same time.

All of these agreements had a common clause according to which the law that governed the agreements was English law and the courts of Luxembourg had exclusive jurisdiction over any issues that could arise from the agreements. Furthermore, Greece and the Bank of Greece 'irrevocably and unconditionally' waived all immunity from legal proceedings and from execution and enforcement against their assets 'to the extent not prohibited by mandatory law'.[50] According to the opinion of the legal advisor to the Greek Ministry of Finance attached to the agreements, neither Greece nor the Bank of Greece nor 'any of their respective property' was immune, based on sovereignty or other grounds, from 'jurisdiction, attachment ... or execution' with regard to any action having to do with the debt agreements.[51] For the Greek CB, the waiver of immunity[52] meant that its foreign reserves and gold could be attached, especially if held abroad, making it more difficult for Greece to revert to the drachma, the original Greek currency, in case the country decided to leave the euro.

Three Memoranda[53] between Greece and the EU/ECB/IMF troika spelled out the specific reforms that Greece had to adopt – including extensive pri-

---

[46] Financial Assistance Facility Agreement between the EFSF, the Hellenic Republic and the Bank of Greece (Bond Interest Facility), Mar. 1, 2012.

[47] *See* Co-financing Agreement between the Hellenic Republic, the Bank of Greece (acting as Bond Paying Agent), the EFSF, the Wilmington Trust London Limited (acting as Bond Trustee) and the Bank of Greece (acting as Common Paying Agent), Mar. 1, 2012.

[48] Art. 6, *id.*

[49] *Id.*

[50] *See*, e.g., art. 13(4), PSI LM, *supra* note 44.

[51] *See*, e.g., Annex 4, ECB Credit Enhancement Facility Agreement, *supra* note 45.

[52] For the importance of preserving the immunity of CBs, *see* Note, *Too Sovereign to Be Sued: Immunity of Central Banks in Times of Financial Crisis*, 124 Harvard Law Review 550, at 567 (2010).

[53] These Memoranda were: the Memorandum of Economic and Financial Policies, the Memorandum of Understanding on Specific Economic Policy Conditionality

vatization, increased tax collection and cuts in social spending – for receiving the installments of loans granted to it. If Greece failed to adopt creditors' prescribed reforms, the emergency financing would be suspended. Greece could not propose or implement measures that might infringe on the free movement of capital. It could not introduce any voting or acquisition caps in the assets that were to be privatized. It could not establish 'any disproportionate and non-justifiable veto rights or any other form of special rights in privatized companies'.[54] In order to comply with the privatization demands, the government had to repeal the special rights granted to the state in the process of privatization.[55] Greece had to repeal the Law on Strategic Companies (art. 11, law 3631/2008)[56] and to transfer to the Hellenic Republic Asset Development Fund, which was structured as a private company and monitored by the troika, a number of state assets including motorways, ports and public utilities. This is the privatization under duress[57] that many insolvent states experience.

By 2010, the scramble for Greek assets that had become available at fire sale prices was in full swing. For China, Greece was a strategic point of entry into Central and Eastern Europe and it was looking into purchasing Greek ports to facilitate its trade with the Balkans. China COSCO Shipping made an investment in the Greek port of Piraeus in June 2010, leasing two container terminals for 35 years at the price of $5 billion. By 2012, the privatization of the DEPA, the Greek gas utility, and the DEFSA, the Greek gas pipeline, were dragging. Two Russian companies, Gazprom and Sintez, came up with the highest offers to acquire these companies. The United States and the EU, though, voiced disapproval and the Hellenic Republic Asset Development Fund urged all bidders to seek Western firms as collaborators.[58] Deutsch Telecom succeeded in acquiring 45% of the Hellenic Telecommunications company between 2008 and 2018. In 2017, a German-led consortium obtained a 67% stake in the Thessaloniki port, the second largest port in Greece.[59]

---

and the Technical Memorandum of Understanding. The Memoranda are reprinted in European Commission, The Second Economic Adjustment Programme for Greece, First Review, Annex 3, Occasional Paper 94, Mar. 2012 [hereinafter Economic Adjustment Programme for Greece].

[54]   *Id.* at 126.
[55]   *Id.* at 127.
[56]   Greek Law 3631, Official Gazette A' 6/29.1.2008.
[57]   Jared A. Blacker, *Privatization under Duress: The Privatization of the Greek Economy* 30, in 'Perspectives on Business and Economics – Greece: The Epic Battle for Economic Recovery' (2012).
[58]   *Darkness at Midnight: Renewed Greek Troubles*, Economist, June 15, 2013.
[59]   THPA, Sale of THPA: Agreement Signing Between HRADF and South Europe Gateway Thessaloniki Limited, Press Release, Dec. 22, 2017.

The Greek debt restructuring was facilitated by a creditors' committee, which acted as the representative of bondholders. This committee was put together by a private association, the Institute of International Finance.[60] The committee was a self-appointed body that derived its legitimacy from the fact that it was accepted by the creditor states, Greece and the bondholders. After the 2012 restructuring, the economic surveillance of Greece by the troika became draconian.[61] The European Commission strengthened the task force for Greece, which had a 'permanent presence' on the ground in Greece.[62] The head of the task force was a German national whom the media called the 'German Governor of Greece'. Greece had to isolate its debt service payments in a segregated account and ensure that a legal framework was in place so that the debt servicing payments had priority over any other payments. A provision to this effect was to be incorporated in the Greek Constitution.[63]

In May 2013, the IMF released an assessment of its own and the EU's handling of the Greek crisis. In it, it conceded that the restructuring of the Greek debt encountered 'notable failures', including the loss of market confidence, a 30% reduction in bank deposits and a severe recession.[64] The IMF criticized the eurozone leaders for not tackling the Greek debt decisively at the outset of the crisis, and for sending inconsistent signals to the markets. The delayed debt restructuring, according to the IMF, 'provided a window' for private creditors to reduce their exposure and shift debt into official hands.[65] The Greek debt crisis, according to the IMF, shed light on the shortcomings of the euro area architecture. The ER inflexibility and restrictions on fiscal autonomy made eurozone states vulnerable to crises that undermined their economies.[66]

In 2013, the Greek CA deficit was shrinking, but this was happening mainly because of the severe recession and the contraction of the economy.[67] The

---

[60] The Steering Committee, put together by the Institute of International Finance, to negotiate the Greek debt restructuring was made up of 30 banks.

[61] *See also* Mauro Megliani, *Sovereign Debt: Genesis – Restructuring – Litigation* 21, 24 (2015).

[62] European Commission, Q&A on the Task Force for Greece and its Second Quarterly Report, Press Release, MEMO/12/184, Mar. 15, 2012.

[63] Council of the European Union, Eurogroup Statement, Press Release, Feb. 21, 2012.

[64] IMF, Greece: Ex Post Evaluation of Exceptional Access under the 2010 Stand-by Arrangement, at 1, IMF Country Report No. 13/156, June 2013.

[65] *Id.* at 33.

[66] *Id.* at 34.

[67] IMF, Greece: Third Review under the Extended Arrangement under the Extended Fund Facility, at 5, Country Report No. 13/153, June 2013 [hereinafter IMF Third Review]. The economy contracted 22% between 2008 and 2012 and unemployment reached 27%. Youth unemployment was at 64%.

political situation seemed stable, albeit fragile, because of social tensions having to do with high unemployment, especially among young people.[68] While Greece and the periphery states were struggling, many core states were benefitting from the crisis. Germany, as a big stakeholder in the euro, would have been harmed if that currency had collapsed. As long as the euro remained the currency of the eurozone, however, Germany reaped many benefits. The German debt, much like US Treasuries, is considered a safe-haven asset. The more the peripheral states deteriorated, the safer the German debt looked. In fact, as the overall economy of the eurozone weakened, German bond yields became negative in real terms (*see* Box 4.1). Investors were willing to lose money to keep their capital safe in Germany. In a continent that was experiencing deflation, with millions of people out of work, capital holders were content to keep their capital idle in Germany and to tolerate negative real returns instead of funding projects that could have spawned growth opportunities in peripheral states.[69]

18.1.4   The 2015 Conflict

The final collision between Greece and its creditors took place in 2015. The Greek–German standoff during that summer sharply showcased the lack of eurozone unity. At that point, the Greek public had become weary of the various elected and unelected governments that looked completely hapless and creditors' relentless drive to control the economy as the *quid pro quo* for fresh lending. Out of the EUR215.9 billion new loans that were granted to Greece between 2010 and 2012, only EUR9.7 billion, or less than 5%, was not used for debt-related payments and bank recapitalizations and, therefore, contributed to the Greek budget.[70]

In Greece and other debtor states, the austerity imposed by the creditors was viewed as unjust and illegitimate, a violation of their statehood.[71] These feelings of injustice that had been boiling up since 2010 led to the unprecedented rise to power in the 2015 elections of the Coalition of the Radical Left (Synaspismós Rizospastiks Aristerás), mostly known by the abbreviation Syriza, a marginal leftist party never thought of as capable of winning an election. Syriza was elected on a platform to keep Greece in the euro while, at the same time, lessening the austerity demanded by the creditors and securing

---

[68]   *Id.* at 21.

[69]   Sandbu, *supra* note 29, at 199.

[70]   Jörg Rocholl and Axel Stahmer, *Where did the Greek Bailout Money Go?*, at 4, ESMT White Paper No. WP-16-02, 2016.

[71]   Rebecca M. Nelson, *The Greek Debt Crisis: Overview and the Implications for the United States*, at 1, CRS Report, Apr. 24, 2017.

some debt relief. The negotiations between the new government and the creditors reached an impasse in the summer of 2015 when the government decided to call a referendum asking the people to decide whether the conditionality proposed by the creditors in exchange for fresh loans should be accepted.

The decision to hold a referendum was announced on June 25, 2015. Between that day and the day of the referendum (July 5, 2015), the IMF, the European Commission and the German finance minister urged Greek voters to vote yes to conditionality and threatened that a 'No vote' would mean the exit of Greece not only from the euro but also from the EU. Eventually a majority of over 61% of Greek citizens rejected the austerity measures proposed by the creditors. Voters were willing to disregard the dire consequences of 'Grexit' as they concluded that, given the widespread economic malaise, they had nothing more to lose. The resounding rejection of austerity came as a surprise because creditors had backed their threats with deeds. The government had to close the banks on June 28, 2015, and impose capital controls as capital was fleeing with frenzy and the ECB had frozen the emergency liquidity assistance.

Resorting to capital controls made it clear that the euro was no longer a single currency; it had split into the 'southern' euro and the 'northern' euro. While the two currencies looked exactly the same, the southern euro was much more limited because it could get ensnared in the banking system of a peripheral state.[72]

The dismal financial situation of the country forced the prime minister to restructure its cabinet and start new negotiations with the creditors, effectively annulling the 'No vote' of the referendum. On the eve of these negotiations, the German financial minister tabled a new proposal: if Greece refused to accept creditors' conditions, it would have to exit the eurozone unilaterally or though a mutually negotiated temporary suspension. With this Damoclean sword over its head, the government conceded to the conditionality of a third bailout package of EUR86 billion, a large chunk of which was used to pay back existing debt.[73]

The defeat of Greece at the hands of its creditors helped contain anti-austerity, left-leaning movements in Spain and Portugal. The handling of Greece as a disposable state forced other states to fall back into line with the policies of

---

[72]   As one commentator put it: 'If confidence in national banking systems diverges, such that a deposit in one jurisdiction is seen to be worth less than a deposit in another, then money within the euro area is no longer unquestionably single'. *See* Yves Mersch, *Law, Money and Market: The Legal Dimension of Monetary Policy*, Speech at the Information Club Meeting, Luxembourg, May 31, 2014. *See also* Willem Buiter, *The Euro Area: Monetary Union or System of Currency Boards?* Global Economics View, Citi Research, Mar. 19, 2015.

[73]   Rocholl and Stahmer, *supra* note 70.

austerity. Since then, Europe has remained politically fragmented. In France, Germany, Italy, and Spain new euro-skeptic parties have openly challenged the alleged benefits of European integration. The crisis drove home the point that, in a union of economically weak and strong states, the weak did not stand a chance of directing their political fate.[74]

Greece eventually exited its last bailout program in August 2018 after going through four governments, receiving EUR274 billion in loans, implementing 450 reforms and enduring a depression far beyond anything seen after World War II.

18.2   CAUSES

Much of the blame for the eurocrisis was placed on Greece and its acknowledgment in 2009 that it had a much higher deficit-to-GDP ratio than it had declared before. Markets were warned about the accounting failings of Greece, though, well before 2009. Both the IMF and Eurostat, the EU statistical agency, had issued warnings in the mid-2000s about the shortcomings of Greece's official statistics.[75] Damaging publicity in the midst of a global financial crisis certainly has a magnified impact in comparison with bad news that comes out in calm times. Yet while it is true that Greek mischief helped launch the eurocrisis, the causes of that crisis run much deeper.

From its beginnings the euro was 'threatened not only by the persistence of high budgetary imbalances' of eurozone states, but also by 'the lack of transparency with which the process of reduction in these imbalances' was taking place.[76] The use of derivatives to obfuscate debt obligations became notorious in the case of Greece,[77] but was not isolated to it. Italy,[78] Poland, Belgium and Germany used derivatives to fudge their debt figures.[79] Eurostat tolerated the

---

[74]   Sandbu, *supra* note 29, at 10.

[75]   Eurostat, *Report on the Revision of the Greek Government Deficit and Debt Figures*, Nov. 22, 2004; IMF, Greece: Report on Observance of Standards and Codes – Fiscal Transparency Module, IMF Country Report No. 06/49, Feb. 2006.

[76]   Gustavo Piga, *Derivatives and Public Debt Management*, at 143 (ISMA and Council of Foreign Relations, 2001); Jürgen von Hagen and Guntram B. Wolff, *What do Deficits Tell us About Debt? Empirical Evidence on Creative Accounting with Fiscal Rules in the EU*, 30(12) Journal of Banking & Finance 3259 (2006).

[77]   Nicholas Dunbar and Elisa Martinuzzi, *Goldman Secret Greece Loan Shows Two Sinners as Client Unravels*, Bloomberg, Mar. 5, 2012; Nick Dunbar, *Revealed: Goldman Sachs' Mega Deal for Greece*, Risk Magazine, July 1, 2003.

[78]   Sarfraz Thind, *Italy's Use of Derivatives for EMU Access under Scrutiny*, Risk Magazine, Jan. 2002.

[79]   European Parliament, MEPs Hear Views of Leading Figures on the Greek Fiscal Crisis, Press Release, Apr. 14, 2010.

non-disclosure of derivatives activity carried out by EU member states. There was no legal or accounting framework to record derivatives transactions in the national accounts. Furthermore, some governments, including Greece and Germany, securitized their future revenues (e.g. taxes) and sold these securities to investors in order to exhibit higher current revenues.[80] It has been argued convincingly that the Maastricht Treaty, by putting pressure on states to reduce debt and deficits, indirectly pushed them to use derivatives, creative accounting and misreporting to obfuscate their real deficit and debt numbers.[81]

Some EU states did not even hesitate to openly flout the EU's budget deficit ceilings they had urged others to adopt. Germany and France, the two most powerful states in the EU, were among the first states to disrespect these ceilings. In November 2003, Germany and France violated the deficit ceiling (3% deficit-to-GDP ratio). The European Commission sued France and Germany at the ECJ[82] and the Court sided with the Commission.[83] However, eventually France and Germany prevailed. Political interference to exempt large EU countries from the rules strengthened beliefs that the rules could be easily bent.[84] The Stability Pact was watered down officially in 2005,[85] reinforcing convictions that it was never meant to be enforced.

In the case of Greece, the poster child for the eurocrisis, none of the fundamentals of the Greek economy (inflation, GDP, growth potential) changed much from the moment Greece entered the eurozone until the time of the crisis. On the other hand, short-term capital flows to Greece skyrocketed to EUR35 billion in 2008, from EUR9 billion in 2002. Greece was compelled to liberalize the flows of capital as a prerequisite for its entry into the eurozone. In May 1994, the Greek government adopted a law that made it possible for short-term capital to move freely in and out of the country.[86]

---

[80] Timothy C. Irwin, *Accounting Devices and Fiscal Illusions*, at 8, IMF Staff Discussion Note SDN/12/02, Mar. 28, 2012.

[81] Piga, *supra* note 76, at 95.

[82] *Commission of the European Communities v. Council of the European Union*, Case C-27/04, July 13, 2004.

[83] Paras 95–7, *id.*

[84] Céline Allard et al., *Toward a Fiscal Union for the Euro Area*, at 9, IMF Staff Discussion Note, SDN/13/09, Sept. 2013.

[85] It was amended to give states latitude in addressing 'economic bad times'. *See* art. 5, Council Regulation No. 1055/2005 of 27 June 2005 amending Regulation (EC) No. 1466/97 on the strengthening of the surveillance of budgetary positions and the surveillance and coordination of economic policies, OJ L 174/1, 7.7.2005.

[86] Anastasios P. Pappas, *The Short-Term Determinants of Capital Flows for a Small Open Economy: The Case of Greece*, 15 Review of Development Economics 699 (2011).

The idea that capital should be free to cross borders became prevalent in the EU in the late 1980s. Before that, the predominant view was that short-term capital movements could have destabilizing effects on a state's economy and infringe on the exercise of an independent DEP. Therefore, the decision of how much capital should move, and when, was left to the discretion of national governments. In fact, what is labeled 'financial repression'[87] today, in those days was commonsense economic discipline.[88] The United States and the UK were the trailblazers in the liberalization of capital flows, followed by Germany. France eventually converted to the ideology of freedom of capital as a *quid pro quo* for Germany's concession to a monetary union.[89] Germany and the UK had to persuade other states, such as Italy and Greece, to liberalize capital flows.[90]

With the adoption of the Maastricht Treaty, which established the Economic and Monetary Union (EMU), capital has been free to cross national frontiers in the EU along with goods, services and people whose freedom of movement had been guaranteed in previous treaties. Free capital movements have been inserted, in other words, in the constitutional structure of the EU.[91] Embedding this economic ideology in the EU constitutional structure became a sort of sclerosis. The EU drew no lessons from the Asian financial crisis of the late 1990s. That crisis forced international institutions such as the IMF to reconsider their position on free capital movements and propose cautious restrictions on the freedom of capital.[92]

Capital imports can damage the economic and political stability of states when they stop and revert back to their country of origin. The EU debtor states suffered from such a stop and reversal, starting in 2009, when the bond market began to reconsider the economic fundamentals of these states. The reversal of capital flows was dramatic in 2012 when there was intense speculation that Greece and then other peripheral countries would default and possibly exit the euro. Before 2009, markets were happy to ignore flaws in the fundamentals of the Greek economy or the bloated banking sectors of Ireland and

---

[87]   *See*, e.g. Carmen M. Reinhart et al., *Financial Repression Redux*, 48 Finance & Development 22, June 2011.

[88]   Rawi Abdelal, *Capital Rules: The Construction of Global Finance* 48–9 (2007).

[89]   *Id.* at 9–10.

[90]   *Id.* at 71–2.

[91]   Art. 63, TFEU, *see* Consolidated Versions of the Treaty on European Union and the Treaty on the Functioning of the European Union (TFEU), OJ C 326/1, 26.10.2012. The European Court of Justice has championed the freedom of capital in a number of rulings, *see*, e.g. *Commission v. France*, Case C-483/99, [2002] ECR I-4785, June 4, 2002; *Commission v. Portugal*, Case C-367/98, [2002] ECR I-4756, June 4, 2002.

[92]   IMF, *The Liberalization and Management of Capital Flows: An Institutional View*, Nov. 14, 2012.

Spain. Capital flocked to Greece as the country was eager to borrow at the low IRs that became available to it after its accession to the euro. The abundance of capital fueled a private sector borrowing spree and fiscal largesse.[93] 'Channeled through transfers, subsidies, and investments, fiscal expansion lifted private income and consumption which in turn boosted tax revenues and masked the true size of the underlying fiscal gap'.[94] The global financial crisis led to a 'retrenchment of cross-border flows and unmasked Greece's underlying fiscal and structural imbalances'.[95]

The design of the euro was meant to cause the flows of capital from the core to the periphery. One of the reasons states adopted the euro was to facilitate the integration of their economies. It was hoped that a common currency would make it simpler for capital holders to find good investment opportunities in the eurozone because they would no longer have to worry about the ER risk. The euro made it easier for capital to flow from countries with abundant capital, and relatively low returns on investment, to capital-poor countries that offered higher returns. The freedom of movement of capital was supposed to make possible the economic convergence of the eurozone, the economic catching up of the South with the North of the EU.

Before the introduction of the euro, peripheral countries used devaluation as a tool for maintaining their competitiveness. As a result, German goods were expensive and hard to sell to the periphery. The euro, from the perspective of Germany, facilitated trade with the peripheral economies of Europe through the abolition of those countries' currencies so that they became incapable of using devaluation to stem the tide of German goods coming their way. As a *quid pro quo*, the periphery was supposed to gain from a strong currency and low IRs. The scheme worked to some extent: German goods became cheaper. Owing to low IRs, consumers could afford to borrow to buy German goods. As a commentator succinctly put it, in the years before 2009, it was the PIIGS' economic bubbles that fueled German growth. The low IRs maintained by the ECB during the pre-crisis period fueled cheap credit in the south of Europe and strengthened German exports, allowing the newly re-united German economy to grow.[96] By 2007, Germany had the world's largest trade surplus thanks to the PIIGS.[97] However, in 2009, when the whole world was in panic mode, the excessive borrowing of the periphery triggered banking and debt crises. In countries where the banks financed the standard of living of people, like

---

[93]   IMF Report 13/154, *supra* note 5, at 4.
[94]   *Id.*
[95]   *Id.*
[96]   Richard C. Koo, *Learning Wrong Lessons from the Crisis in Greece*, at 8, Nomura Research Institute, May 20, 2011.
[97]   *Id.*

Ireland and Spain, a banking crisis erupted. In Greece, where the government borrowed to act as the employer of last resort, the crisis was triggered by budget deficits and government debt.

Given the fact that, after the adoption of the euro, the periphery had lost DEP autonomy (*see* Box 4.1), the ECB should have scrutinized the large capital flows from the core to the periphery and the nature of these flows – short-term portfolio investments, the hot money. As a rule, during good times, the benefits of the free flows of capital are shared by both the core and the periphery. In bad times, though, the risk from the retrenchment of capital flows is borne exclusively by the periphery.[98] The country that receives capital flows risks serious financial disruption when these flows freeze. The country that is the source of capital bears no such risk. In short, the periphery of the eurozone took on the systemic risk and swallowed the costs that came with the establishment of the common currency area.[99]

In 2013, the ECB published a report on the financial integration of Europe[100] which, from its content, could easily have been titled 'Financial Disintegration in Europe'.[101] In that report, the ECB stated the obvious – that the eurozone was divided into distressed and non-distressed countries.[102] Because of this division, capital flew to non-distressed countries, the safe havens. The borrowing costs of safe-haven countries, consequently, plummeted, while those of troubled countries skyrocketed.[103] As we have explained before, bond markets know which states are sovereign.[104] When the peripheral countries were facing financial collapse, their euros flew to Germany to find a safe haven there. Germany's bonds were yielding negative returns but still investors were ogling them as safe assets (*see* Box 4.1). This is how the bond market understood who in Europe was sovereign.

---

[98] *See also* Kash Mansori, *Why Greece, Spain and Ireland Aren't to Blame for Europe's Woes*, The New Republic, Oct. 11, 2011.

[99] *Id.*

[100] ECB, *Financial Integration in Europe* (2013) [hereinafter Financial Integration].

[101] For further insights on this, *see* Ashoka Mody, *EuroTragedy: A Drama in Nine Acts* (2018).

[102] Financial Integration, *supra* note 100, at 19.

[103] *Id.* at 27–28.

[104] *See also* Hans Kundani, *Germany as a Geo-economic Power*, 34(3) Washington Quarterly 31 (2011).

18.3   DEMOCRATIC STATES IN MONETARY UNIONS

Controlling economic depressions is the acid test of global economic cooperation.[105] Instead of cooperating to control the eurocrisis, European states focused on grand-standing and skirmishing. This 'turned a manageable debt problem into a decade of economic stagnation, social upheaval, and political protest'.[106] The mismanagement of the eurozone debt crisis was one of the biggest failures in the history of European integration.[107]

By 2018, Greece's GDP per person had fallen by about 45% and unemployment remained around 21% (45% among the young) – the worst performance ever by a developed state.[108] The whole eurozone ran a surplus that caused trade squabbles with the United States and the UK, which had deficits. The convergence between the European North and South, the promise implied by euro's adoption, had stalled and, in some cases, unraveled. The euro worked fine for all members of the eurozone except for three: Greece, Portugal and Italy. Italy, the third largest economy in the eurozone, had seen no net growth in its GDP per person since euro's inception in 1999. This was the reason why two of its main political parties favored a referendum on euro membership. Other states had problems as well. Except for Germany, the aggregate unemployment rate across 18 eurozone countries was still 4% higher than before the crisis.

The motto of the eurozone during the crisis was that:

- debt and deficits are ill-advised;
- the ECB must be restricted in the support it provides to governments;
- the solution to too much borrowing is a combination of default and forced repayment rather than the mutualization of debt burden.[109]

Conflicts between creditors and debtors are not atypical. In terms of morality, most debt crises are the outcome of reckless borrowing and irresponsible lending. Creditors and debtors usually clash when debt becomes unsustainable. Creditors insist on being paid in full and debtors are bent on debt restructuring.

---

[105] Alvin H. Hansen, *Fiscal Policy and Business Cycles* 450 (1941, reprinted in 2013).

[106] Jeffry Frieden, *A Plan to Save the Euro*, VOX CEPR Policy Portal, May 23, 2018.

[107] Athanasios Orphanides, *The Euro Area Crisis Five Years After the Original Sin*, 48(4) Credit and Capital Markets–Kredit und Kapital 535 (2015).

[108] *See also* Nikos Konstandaras, *Greece's Great Hemorrhaging*, NYT, Jan. 10, 2019.

[109] Matthew C. Klein, *The Euro Area's Fiscal Position Makes No Sense*, FT, Mar. 14, 2018.

Both sides have bargaining chips: creditors threaten to block future access to credit and debtors threaten to stop paying. This battle has clear winners and losers unless someone intercedes and succeeds in commanding allegiance to a unifying political ideal or principle.

In the eurocrisis, the creditors won. Because of the disproportionate influence of creditor states on the IMF's board, they managed to convince it to change its own rules. Based on its pre-2010 rules, the IMF should have asked for a substantial restructuring of the Greek debt in 2010. With the IMF's acquiescence, creditor states temporarily refinanced Greek debt using their taxpayers' money so as to shelter their banks from the costs of a Greek default.[110] Then they demanded that Greece fully repaid its debt by increasing taxes and cutting down spending.[111]

Creditors managed to frame the crisis as a problem caused by the debtors who, as a consequence, had the burden of resolving it.[112] In Germany, more specifically, the dominant narrative was that of 'northern saints and southern sinners', not only in the media but also in the more serious national dialogue.[113] The blame game that characterized the eurocrisis shocked those who had bought into the idea that the euro was a political project aiming to unite Europe. States cannot really claim that they are freely united to pursue their mutual interest when they are so much divided by debt. States cannot be European 'partners' when it is clear that creditors have the upper hand over debtors.

The lack of democratic underpinnings of the EU, the infamous 'democratic deficit', is an old complaint. None of the organs of the EU, except for the Parliament, are democratically elected. The dispute over debt threw into question anew the legitimacy of the EU. There are three types of legitimacy. *Source* legitimacy has to do with how an institution is elected. Democratic institutions are considered legitimate because they are elected by the people. Unelected institutions enjoy much less legitimacy because their source of authority is much less clear. *Process* legitimacy involves the processes institutions use to achieve their objectives. Transparent institutions tend to enjoy more legitimacy than secretive institutions. *Results* legitimacy has to do with how effective institutions are in fulfilling their mission. Effective institutions are more legitimate than wasteful and inefficient ones.[114]

---

[110] Jeffry Friedman and Stefanie Walter, *Understanding the Political Economy of the Eurozone Crisis*, 20(1) Annual Review of Political Science 371, 388–9 (2017).

[111] *Id.*

[112] *Id.*

[113] *Id.*

[114] *See generally* Odette Lienau, *The Challenge of Legitimacy in Sovereign Debt Restructuring*, 57 Harvard International Law Journal 151, 162–71(2016).

To simplify matters here we condense these three types of legitimacy into two variables: 'control' and 'like'. We view institutions as legitimate if one of two conditions are satisfied: 'control' and 'like'. We consider an institution legitimate if we have some control over it because we participate directly in the decision-making or elect the people who make the decisions for us. We like an institution and thus confer legitimacy to it when we trust it, have faith in it, have confidence that it applies the right processes. We also like an institution when it has demonstrated competence in managing the matters assigned to it and has produced results. Control has to do with how much say[115] we have on how the institution is run. If we do not control an institution, we consider it legitimate only if we like the impact it has on our lives.

Figure 18.1 depicts the legitimacy of institutions based on the two variables of 'control' and 'like' and gives examples of such institutions. When we control and like an institution, that institution enjoys a high degree of legitimacy. The institution is more like a club where we socialize with like-minded equals. In terms of political regimes, direct democracy is the closest we have come to a political institution that we both control and like. Direct democracy is legitimate because the people who make the decisions are those affected by the outcomes.

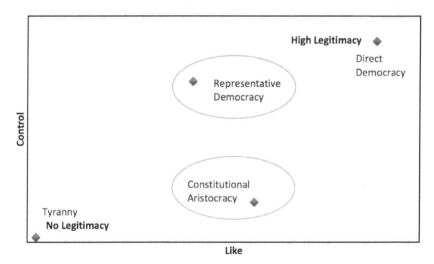

Figure 18.1   Map of institutional legitimacy

---

[115] *See* Albert O. Hirschman, *Exit, Voice, and Loyalty: Responses to Decline in Firms, Organizations and States* 4–5 (1970).

When we control an institution, but we do not always like it, that institution can enjoy various degrees of legitimacy (from high to medium to low) (Fig. 18.1). A good example is representative democracy. In a representative democracy regime, people are in control because they elect presidents, prime ministers and members of parliament (source legitimacy). Some are not happy with representative democracy and prefer more direct democratic models that make active citizen participation in the political affairs possible.[116] At the same time, there is a consensus that, owing to increasing populations and unenviable alternatives, representative democracy is the best political regime because at least the people decide who to elect in office. Many, though, often disagree with the decisions made by the elected officials (results legitimacy). Citizens are usually unhappy when major decisions that affect their lives are made behind closed doors (process legitimacy). The beauty of democracy has to do with the fact that, when people are unhappy with those they have put in power, they can throw them out of office at the next election. Citizens can also protest, strike and form new political parties.[117] In democratic states, when citizens dislike their governments, they are not afraid to vocalize and act on their dissatisfaction.

When we do not control an institution and dislike it, an obvious case being that of a tyranny, the institution is illegitimate (Fig. 18.1). We cannot afford to leave without risking serious repercussions[118] and it is impossible to voice our dissatisfaction. Revolution, and the ensuing social chaos, is the unpalatable alternative. Finally, there are institutions that we like but cannot control. An example is that of constitutional aristocracy (Fig. 18.1). A constitutional aristocracy is not elected. However, it differs from other oligarchies because it operates based on due process and the rule of law. This non-elected aristocracy strives to bring peace and prosperity to those it governs. Therefore, people appreciate the benefits it brings despite the fact that they do not elect it.

The legitimacy of the EU, like that of a constitutional aristocracy, has never been based on its democratic credentials. Europeans like the EU because it has been effective at bringing peace and prosperity to a divided continent afflicted by many conflicts (results legitimacy). Greece joined the EU shortly after it restored democracy, because EU membership was supposed to act as bulwark against foreign-engineered dictatorship. Eastern European countries joined the Union to shield themselves against Russian imperialism. Most Europeans

---

[116] *See* Elli Louka, *Water Law and Policy: Governance without Frontiers* 205–43 (2008) (analyzing models of participatory democracy).

[117] *See*, e.g. Hirschman, *supra* note 115, at 66.

[118] *See*, e.g. John Haltiwanger, *Killed Journalist Jamal Khashoggi's Children, Some of Whom are Dual US Citizens, are Reportedly Barred from Leaving Saudi Arabia*, Business Insider, Oct. 24, 2018.

endorsed the euro because it was expected to bring benefits to all economies. Once things started to go wrong Europeans protested. Only their protests had the wrong audience. They could throw out their governments (and they did so multiple times) based on the democratic principles of the nation state, but they could not disband the European institutions or sack the governments of other eurozone countries. Yet it was creditor states, under the cover of European institutions, that dictated the economic conditions in the periphery. Vis-à-vis these core eurozone governments, the citizens of the periphery were disenfranchised.

Creditors decided to address the crisis by imposing fiscal austerity and reducing wages in the European South. Such an inequitable program, which privileged the North and demanded sacrifices from the South, never had a chance of being voluntarily endorsed. Therefore it had to be imposed using 'technocratic intergovernmental processes that masked the political nature' of the brewing distributional fight.[119] Implicit in these processes was a simple blackmail: money from the creditors in return for control over debtors.[120] Creditors staunchly believed that the remedy for Greece, which could not devalue its currency, was what is euphemistically called *internal devaluation* – the reduction of wages and prices that was supposed to make Greece more competitive. According to this view, high unemployment, no matter how grisly, was the key for internal devaluation to succeed. High unemployment reduces wages, and lower wages must lead to lower prices, depressing the whole economy. Internal devaluation was expected, at some point, to restore the BOP by reducing spending and to bring the economy to full employment.[121] The rationale behind the economic measures imposed on Greece by its creditors, in other words, was that economic depression was a desirable and necessary prerequisite for eliminating the inefficiencies and weaknesses of the Greek economy. The appropriate cure for Greece's past deficits was severe belt-tightening for both individuals and the government.[122]

The only way to instill discipline in a regime that demands such a quick and drastic reduction in the standard of living of a population is to make credible

---

[119] Fritz W. Scharpf, *The Southern Euro*, International Politics and Society Journal, Dec. 26, 2017.

[120] Sandbu, *supra* note 29, at 8.

[121] Joseph Stiglitz, *The Euro: How a Common Currency Threatens the Future of Europe* 220–21 (2016).

[122] A similar economic rationale was prevalent during the Great Depression in the United States, *see* Milton Friedman and Anna Jacobson Schwartz, *A Monetary History of the United States, 1867–1960*, at 409 (1963).

the threat of expulsion or exit.[123] The constant threat of expulsion, Grexit, that hung over the Greek state for almost a decade, created uncertainty. This uncertainty became the instrument of control that kept Greece and other peripheral states on their toes and guaranteed the continuity of the *status quo*. The *quid-for-quo* dynamic, debt refinancing in exchange for economic control, led some to question the idea of a united Europe because: 'If Europe is nothing but a bad version of the IMF, what is left of the European integration project?'[124] The debtor states had invested their financial and political future in the euro membership and the costs of exiting the euro were tremendous. When entry in an organization is expensive or requires severe initiation, threats to leave it sound hollow.[125] If exit is accompanied by implied sanctions, such as economic isolation, the very idea of exit is unthinkable. Organizations that deprive their members of both exit and voice are tyrannies. Exit from such organizations, if ever attempted, is equivalent to suicide-bombing.

It has been said that, if someone strikes us on the right cheek, we must turn to offer her the left. Today the name of the game is to stop the first strike preemptively by blowing off the hand that is about to inflict it – 'precautionary self-defense'.[126] If this is not feasible, one must be able to administer a second strike effectively – self-defense. Not many states are capable of defending themselves, and this is true especially of debtor states. Most states, however, can clearly distinguish between their allies and enemies.[127] This does not necessarily mean that they have to go to war with the latter. It means that they can exercise caution not to enter voluntarily into unions with states that will wrong-foot them when they face trouble. It means that, no matter their fragility, they must strive to achieve some elemental autonomy by improving their terms of trade and FX reserves.

For Greece it was unrealistic to believe that, with a GDP of $195 billion and at a largely de-industrialized stage,[128] it could ever become a truly equal partner to Germany, an industrial behemoth. Elites tend to be captivated by

---

[123] Yanis Varoufakis, *Schäuble Leaves but Schäuble-ism Lives on*, www.yanisvar oufakis.eu, Sept. 28, 2017.

[124] Luigi Zingales, *The Euro Lives for Another Day, This European Project is Dead Forever*, www.europaono.com, July 14, 2015.

[125] Hirschman, *supra* note 115, at 96.

[126] Elli Louka, *Precautionary Self-Defense and the Future of Preemption in International Law* 951, in 'Looking to the Future: Essays on International Law in Honor of W. Michael Reisman' (M. H. Arsanjani et al., eds, 2011).

[127] *See* Carl Schmitt, *The Concept of the Political* 26 (foreword by Tracy B. Strong, 2007).

[128] For the deindustrialization of southern Europe, *see* Pisani-Ferry, *supra* note 7, at 139.

myth systems,[129] such as that of sovereign equality of states.[130] After a civil war and a foreign-imposed dictatorship, Greek political elites were sincere, albeit in retrospect naïve, in believing that Greece's participation in the EU was the *sine qua non* for its prosperity and security. Greek leaders genuinely endorsed the idea that surrounding Greece with a number of democratic and forward-looking states would guarantee democracy and help their country grow. The crisis severely tested these beliefs.

The EU could have done better. It could have taken measures to scrutinize the finances of the Greek state, at least, in terms of examining more closely the concerns of Eurostat about the Greek budget numbers. It could have adopted the appropriate macro-prudential measures or could have hiked IRs to curb incontinent lending. Instead of acting preventively, the EU decided to act *ex-post facto* by punishing, through taxation and widespread unemployment, all those who had gained nothing from the previous largesse. Not only that: it undermined a young democracy by telling a frustrated public that no matter who they elected their fate would be the same.

European identity is a pretend identity. Europeans fully endorsed this manu-factured identity, believing that it would grant them powers they had never had before. The idea of the EU emanated from the equality among its member states that had emerged similarly scarred from many wars. As these states diverged in policies and growth paths, their European identity kept them together, despite the fact that some of them achieved more growth and prosperity than others. When the eurocrisis turned into economic conflict, the European identity crumbled. The trumpeted equality of member states, the force behind their integration, was unmasked as a fairy tale. The EU can still punish the weak, peripheral states,[131] but it is powerless against the dominant states that define the rules and the exceptions to the rules – the real sovereigns.[132]

---

[129] *See* W. Michael Reisman, *The Quest for World Order and Human Dignity in the Twenty-first Century: Constitutive Process and Individual Commitment* 92 (2012).

[130] Chapter 3, note 1.

[131] *See,* e.g. Yanis Varoufakis, *And the Weak Suffer What They Must? Europe's Crisis and America's Economic Future* (2016).

[132] *See* Carl Schmitt, *Political Theology: Four Chapters on the Concept of Sovereignty* 5–6 (translation George Schwab, 1985).

Index